Studies in the Transformation of U.S. Agriculture

Other Titles in This Series

†Available in hardcover and paperback.

About the Book and Editors

In recent years, the consensual view of rural society has been challenged by theorists identifying the conflict, exploitation, and power relations in rural society. Beyond this theoretical challenge, empirical studies of the sociology of agriculture have provided a fresh understanding of the dynamics of U.S. agriculture. This book contributes to the growing literature by providing a historical perspective. The contributors explore historical developments in U.S. agriculture within the context of the larger political economy.

The book opens with a review of the similarities and differences between the critical rural sociology of today with that of the 1930s and moves on to a study of the accumulation process in U.S. agriculture. Other issues covered include the erosion of the southern class structure during and after the 1930s, the landed aristocracy's reassertion in the post-bellum south, changes in the class structure and locus of agriculture in the midwest, and historical developments in the labor process and in capitalist agriculture in California. The concluding chapter provides a framework for studying both the origins and the consequences of state agriculture policies.

Until his death on June 28, 1984, **A. Eugene Havens** was professor and chairman of the Department of Rural Sociology at the University of Wisconsin in Madison. He served as director of the Center for Developing Nations Program from 1968 to 1970 and was a consultant to the Ford Foundation on agriculture and rural development in Latin America from 1975 to 1979. He also consulted with CIERA in Nicaragua on many aspects of post-revolutionary agricultural adjustment and planning. **Gregory Hooks** is assistant professor of sociology at the University of Indiana, **Patrick H. Mooney** is assistant professor of sociology at the University of Kentucky, and **Max J. Pfeffer** is a graduate student in the Department of Sociology/Rural Sociology at the University of Wisconsin.

Studies in the Transformation of U.S. Agriculture

edited by A. Eugene Havens,
with Gregory Hooks,
Patrick H. Mooney,
and Max J. Pfeffer

Westview Press / Boulder and London

Rural Studies Series, Sponsored by the Rural Sociological Society

Published in 1986 in the United States of America by Westview Press, Inc.; Frederick A. Praeger, Publisher; 5500 Central Avenue, Boulder, Colorado 80301

Library of Congress Cataloging-in-Publication Data
Main entry under title:
Studies in the transformation of U.S. agriculture.
  (Rural studies series)
  Bibliography: p.
  Includes index.
  1. Agriculture—Social aspects—United States—
Addresses, essays, lectures. 2. United States—Rural
conditions—Addresses, essays, lectures. I. Havens,
A. Eugene. II. Series: Rural studies series of the
Rural Sociological Society.
HD1765.S78 1986   307.7′2′0973   85-3308
ISBN 0-8133-7058-2

Composition for this book was provided by the editors
This book was produced without formal editing by the publisher
Printed and bound in the United States of America

10   9   8   7   6   5   4   3   2   1

Contents

Foreword

It is fitting that Gene Havens, the youngest of eight children, grew up on a small farm near Corning, Iowa, the site of much agrarian unrest, including the founding of the National Farmers Organization. In many ways, Gene's life was a struggle to reconcile poverty, exploitation, and injustice with the belief structure of his origins. He began life immersed in the "American Gothic" ideal—that rugged individualism and hard work would provide equal opportunity for all, that rural society was "classless" in nature, that authority deserved unquestionable respect, that the freehold family farmer was a keystone of democratic capitalist society.

Early in his career, Gene used the agrarian rules to succeed within the system. He earned a bachelor of science degree from Iowa State University, where he was a student leader, and later a master of science and a doctorate of philosophy from The Ohio State University in 1960 and 1962, respectively. Enrico L. Quarantelli (social psychology), Everett M. Rogers (adoption-diffusion), Raymond F. Sletto (statistics) and A. Raymond Mangus (social interaction theory) were influential in his early intellectual development. Gene was a key collaborator in Everett Rogers' early works on innovativeness and was greatly influenced by the social behaviorists and social psychologists, as were nearly all graduate students of this era. In reality, 1960s rural sociology was synonymous with adoption-diffusion of innovations. The McCarthy era still weighed heavily on the field of sociology and even the writings of C. Wright Mills, mild by today's standards, were considered too extreme, value-laden, and non-quantitative for most graduate programs in the land grant system. Gene and his fellow graduate students from OSU and other universities began, however, to question inquiries that started by considering individuals before the social totality was understood. This generation of rural sociologists was recruited mostly from small farms and small towns and often from families who did not prosper under the rapidly changing technological and social conditions of rural life at mid-century. These individuals did not share the ministerial backgrounds of the earliest rural sociologists nor, more important, did they share the notion that cultural and personal defects of rural people were responsible for the farm problem. Instead they believed that the farm problem was connected to the rural non-farm problem and to the small town problem. They did not seek to adapt the individual to "inevitable" changes in the agricultural and social system. They traded the "social problems" orientation for a social structural bent; they wondered about the basic worth and designs of programs instead of the organizational details that might make ordained programs perform more smoothly. Gene's dissertation, however, was in the tradition of adoption-diffusion and social psychology models, and its published version received the Cornell University Rural Social Award for best article in the field of change and development.

In an effort to incorporate structural effects in their analysis, the new generation examined community norms and values but found that these, too, were insufficient to explain the barriers and structural blockages their parents had faced. Gene, a leader in this dissent, wondered aloud why the discipline was studying achievement motivation, status aspirations, and adoption-diffusion instead of rural poverty, minorities, small farmers, and the consequences of agricultural mechanization.

Gene was still, at this time, an "organization man"—an Army reserve officer and assistant dean of men as well as a very young and brilliant assistant professor at The Ohio State University. In 1962, he received the Outstanding Young Administrator award from the Ohio Staters Inc. Throughout his career, however, Gene was Gene—an individual who worked hard and played hard, a charismatic teacher and stimulating colleague—unchangeable qualities.

In 1962 the award of a Fulbright Lectureship to the faculty of Sociology at the National University of Colombia began a new phase early in Gene's career. The social realities of Latin America and Roscoe C. Hinkle's theory courses led him to more questions about the social psychological models of modernity. He focused instead on the need for structural changes. Subsequent work with the University of Wisconsin's Land Tenure Center in eleven rural communities in all parts of Colombia only reinforced this view. He realized that the agrarian values he once espoused were used by the dominant class to control small farmers and peasants and to rationalize the status quo. Gene's association with Camilo Torres, Orlando Fals Borda and other Latin scholars and students clarified and developed a political-economy and Marxist perspective on social change. While in Colombia he became associated with the Land Tenure Center and moved to the University of Wisconsin in 1964 where he was instrumental in establishing the sociology of economic change program. His later association at the University of Wisconsin with

Maurice Zeitlin, James O'Connor, Eric Olin Wright, and others matured his thinking. These individuals formed the Class Analysis Group. This posed a basic contradiction for the Iowan who as a child had won the state Bible verse recitation contest. The religion Havens received in Iowa on cold hard church benches seemed to him to be juxtaposed to the struggle for social equality. Religion was a rationale for being "poor but clean" and keeping one's place.

Gene's fluent Spanish, deep political and historical knowledge, and command of economic and social theory provided him with insight and empathy on Latin America equaled by few other North Americans. He became extremely influential in the intellectual development of many Latin American students and scholars. He was also respected and sought after as a consultant by many international organizations as well as the Ford Foundation.

In his third phase, Gene "the revolutionary" had made peace with himself but not with social injustice. He was combining the skills he had learned as an organization man with those of the advocate of change to produce a script for change. Gene was serving as department chairperson and rediscovering the U.S. small farmer. Unfortunately, Gene died before knowing that he was elected president of the Rural Sociology Society—a recognition by his colleagues of the value of his sociological perspective and his contributions to a new, innovative and proactive rural sociology.

During the late 1970s, Havens, Eugene Wilkening, and a group of students interested in the sociology of agriculture also formed the "sociology of agriculture study group." This study group focused on issues in U.S. agriculture from a Marxist perspective. Members were engaged in their own research and the meetings of the group acted as a forum for the presentation of research ideas and findings. Upon completing their research, some of the group members had difficulty in finding outlets for publication of their findings. Gene considered these problems unwarranted, given the quality of the work, and he proposed that a number of papers of the group be collected in the form of a book. This volume is the result.

By this time the study group was fairly well established and was seeking to move on to a unified research effort on the sociology of agriculture. Gene had long been interested in the role of the state in agricultural development. He felt that a comparative historical approach was needed to analyze this problem properly. Together with Howard Newby he founded the Center for Comparative Studies in the Sociology of Agriculture as a first step in this endeavor, which was necessarily a long-term project. The attempt to organize such a research project occupied Gene and the group until the time of his death.

The final word on Gene's influence on the discipline will be determined by his students and social events. Current events—President Reagan's farm policy and farm indebtedness—seem to validate his theoretical perspective. Small-farm and small-town protests have mushroomed and the latest farm protest group, Groundswell, berates the economics of the capitalist system while wanting to be petty capitalist—a false consciousness. More and more farmers lose their land, and small businessmen in villages are going out of business—a growing proletarianization. In my last conversation with Gene, he also stressed that a renegotiation of rural sociology's role in the land grant system was needed so that social relevance and critical research could be further advanced, but he worried that the history of the 1940s and the Bureau of Agricultural Economics in USDA not be repeated. He saw the funding sources that had sustained the emergence of critical rural sociology drying up, and he was alarmed by the current administration's negative view of academicians, especially social scientists—the attacks on established change institutions such as the Land Tenure Center by think tanks from the right, censorship measures in the government (especially USDA), budget cuts at the National Science Foundation and the Endowment for the Humanities, and the U.S. withdrawal from global agencies such as the International Labour Organization.

In the meantime, it is difficult for a rural sociologist of my age to speak of Gene Havens in other than personal terms. My first chance meeting with Dean Gene Havens took place in 1959 as an undergraduate with a keg of beer in the fraternity house pool—a heinous act in those days. From this unstructured social situation, in which Gene helped me dispose of the keg, grew a lifelong personal and professional relationship. Many others have their own favorite Gene Havens stories. He was a man who touched the personal and professional lives of hundreds of people. The rural sociological profession, indeed, has lost a great teacher and researcher but many of us have lost a brother. It is appropriate to evoke a commonly heard eulogy from midwest farming communities: "He led a good, hard life."

William L. Flinn
The Ohio State University

1
Critical Rural Sociology of Yesterday and Today

Gregory Hooks

The first section of this chapter offers an historical account of the emergence of critical rural sociology during the 1930s, and a content analysis of the literature of the period.[1] In parallel fashion, the second section of this chapter explores the political and material conditions that nurtured the emergence of today's critical rural sociological research and literature.

In discussing the changes in the context of the discipline, I emphasize the identification of the proximate causes of the emergence of critical rural sociology. For neither the 1930s nor the present generation of critical rural sociology am I seeking to explain the major changes in the political economy, or how and why the U.S. state was transformed. Rather, the emphasis is on the changing options for social scientists during these two periods—especially for rural sociologists. Particularly important in the development of new research and career options for rural sociologists were changes in the administration of the United States Department of Agriculture (USDA) and of academia.

Though the context and the content of the literature of the 1930s and the present are very different, both exhibit the emergence of a critical approach to the subdiscipline. The emphasis on "critical" research means that the literature of present generation and that of the 1930s share several features. First, the term "critical" refers to a movement away from a "condition which anthropologists refer to as 'capture'— adopting a wholly uncritical stance towards the structure and institutions of rural society" (Newby and Buttel, 1980:2). Second, critical rural sociology provides a theoretically and "historically informed critique of the status quo—both in rural sociology and rural society" (Newby and Buttel, 1980:2). In both generations the emphasis is on exposing social inequalities and inequities, not on obscuring them. Though the practitioners of the 1930s and those of the present generation differ in their

1

theoretical grounding, an emphasis on social inequality is shared. A third and closely related shared trait is the link between social research and social reform. That is, critical rural social research is not conducted merely to advance scientific knowledge: it is done to guide and promote significant social reform. On one point, critical rural sociologists of the 1930s and those of today part company. While both generations argue that the state is powerful and that rural society cannot be understood without reference to it, they differ in their view of the state. Practitioners of the 1930s viewed the state as a vehicle for reforming inequalities in civil society. However, the present generation of critical rural sociologists—whether Marxist or Weberian—tend to see the state as integral to the social structure and reproductive of social inequalities.

Part 1 of this paper concentrates on the 1930s. There the basic features of the critical rural sociology that emerged are identified and content analysis is used to explore the changes in the literature over time and across institutional settings. Part 2 explores the present generation of critical rural sociologists in an essentially parallel manner. While the emphasis in the exploration of the present generation of critical rural sociology is similar to that offered in the discussion of the 1930s, no content analysis is used to clarify the arguments made. Instead, the papers in this volume are summarized to emphasize trends in recent critical research. Further, a brief interview with the contributors is used to highlight the authors' own views on the practice of critical rural sociology. Thus, the clarification of the arguments about the emergence of critical rural sociology also introduces the papers to follow.[2]

CRITICAL RURAL SOCIOLOGY OF THE PAST

Critical rural sociology of the 1930s did not emerge simply because of an intellectual dissatisfaction with pre-Depression approaches; rather, the rethinking of those years was made possible by changes in the political context of the subdiscipline. Roosevelt's election in 1932 and associated political changes played the most important role in providing the space for rethinking rural sociology. FDR not only enjoyed a sizeable majority in the Congress, but his ability to secure reelection in 1936 and the crisis conditions of the 1930s provided an opportunity to restructure the U.S. government. These changes included important (if limited) social reform legislation, the Agricultural Adjustment, Social Security, and Labor Relations Acts being particularly important. Roosevelt's policies also brought about a change in the organization of the state, i.e., an aggrandizement of the Federal government at the expense of the states and an enhanced role for the Executive at the expense of the Congress and the courts (Egger, 1975).

The Context

Administering the quickly expanding Federal government posed an important challenge to FDR and the Democrats. In response, they strove for closer coordination among the agencies of the Federal government and relied on social scientists to staff the government to a degree unmatched before or since. During FDR's first administration social scientists provided an analysis of social problems and suggestions for reforms. Further, they were called on to staff the reform agencies— including those in the USDA (Egger, 1975). During the second Roosevelt administration the emphasis shifted to closer coordination among the numerous Federal agencies (Berman, 1979) and to an improvement in the management of each (Egger, 1975). On both counts the goal was to create a powerful and centralized state capable of implementing far reaching social and economic reforms; social scientists were among the most ardent supporters of these changes and dominated the staffing of key agencies.

These same tendencies were in evidence in the arena of agricultural politics. In fact, the USDA of the 1930s was in the vanguard of New Deal agencies. Henry Wallace, Jr., served as the Secretary of Agriculture from 1932 to 1940 and relied on social scientists in the administration, planning and implementation of agricultural policies. In this realm of policy, New Deal reforms represented a direct challenge to the power of the Extension Service and of the American Farm Bureau Federation (AFBF). Though these regional and state based institutions ultimately emerged victorious in the 1940s (McConnell, 1969), the 1930s witnessed an enhancement of the Federal government and of social scientists therein. Wallace's closest administrative assistants played a key role in restructuring the USDA and in the professionalization of public administration in the U.S. The views of one of them on the role of the state and of social scientists gives a sense of the context in which critical rural sociology emerged in the 1930s. Paul Appleby was Wallace's Under Secretary and principal advisor on administration (Kirkendall, 1966:199). In his book, *Big Democracy* (1945), Appleby argues in Hegelian fashion that public and private administration are distinct because private organizations are dominated by shortsighted and particularistic interests while the government serves a broader and more balanced public interest: "It goes without saying that it is to the interest of the public that the powers exercised by government officials be superior within their fields to those of all other parties. For all others would be less representative and less responsible" (Appleby, 1945:38). Not only is government the bearer of the society's broader interest, but it "must be big enough and powerful enough to be definitely superior to any and all special-interest groups" (1945:38).

These public administrators explained the expansion of the U.S. government under Roosevelt in normative and prescriptive terms. J.M. Gaus, a sympathetic student of the social scientists' approach to administering the USDA, argued that the causes of governmental expansion are changes in the "people, place, physical technology, social technology, wishes and ideas, catastrophe, and personality" of society (Gaus, 1947:9). As these factors change, and especially if they become more complex, government must assume a larger role or risk destructive conflict among particularistic private interest groups. These public administrators were not exceptional for the period; they shared with other intellectual descendants of the Progressives a belief that "the study of man and society must become scientific and must tackle pressing social problems. They rejected the theory that man could not control evolution and argued that government action, based upon scientific knowledge, could shape the evolutionary process and promote the general welfare" (Kirkendall, 1966:3). These arguments are important because they were shared by Wallace, and hence guided a systematic restructuring of the USDA, its staffing, and the definition of its role.

One of the most important consequences of the ascendancy of public administrators under Wallace was the emphasis on scientific management of the USDA. These New Dealers made repeated attempts to subordinate the Extension Service and the Agricultural Adjustment Administration (AAA) to the policies of the central USDA (Gaus and Wolcott, 1940:79). Similarly, they resisted the penetration of a public agency (i.e., the USDA) by particularistic interests (i.e., the AFBF). In the same vein, they recruited a staff that was knowledgeable, experienced, and willing to serve the "public interest" (Kirkendall, 1966:199). As a result, social scientists were hired in record numbers to manage existing and newly created agencies. Agricultural economists—especially those reformist and program oriented in the Iowa State tradition—were given key positions in the USDA (Hardin, 1967:227–30). Similarly, the power of the Bureau of Agricultural Economics (BAE) waxed throughout the 1930s. By 1939, the BAE was given responsibility for planning and coordinating the activities of the various USDA action agencies and for national coordination of a county level land-use planning program (Benedict, 1953; Gaus and Wolcott, 1940; Kirkendall, 1966). This broadened role gave social scientists a powerful influence over agencies that were once autonomous while creating a field staff and contacts with farmers that threatened the hegemony of the Extension Service and AAA in the field.

As noted, the expansion of planning and reform and the influence of social scientists depended upon a sympathetic Congress and a President willing to nurture the effort. Within the USDA, Wallace's enthusiastic support during the 1930s was a major factor. These preconditions

Table 1. Agricultural Economists and Rural Sociologists in the
Federal Government and Land Grant System, 1929–30 and 1939–40*

Location	Year	Agricultural Economists	Rural Sociologists	Row Total
Land grant system	1929–30	364	47	417
Land grant system	1939–40	597	91	688
Percent increase		63%	94%	64%
Federal government (i.e., BAE)	1929–30	80	3	83
Federal government (i.e., BAE)	1939–40	661	56**	717
Percent increase		726%	1767%	764%

* Taken from Schultz and Witt (1941). The statistics on the BAE are taken
from Table XXXIII (pp. 276) and those concerning the land grant system are
found in Tables VII–IX (pp. 244–5).

** Schultz and Witt (1941) and Taylor (1939) point out that many of these
rural sociologists had recently transferred from other reformist agencies
(e.g., Resettlement Administration, Farm Security Administration, etc.)
that had been abolished or reorganized.

evaporated in the 1940s—and with their disappearance New Dealer
social scientists came under a powerful attack. That attack was led by
the AFBF and a conservative coalition composed of Republicans and
Dixiecrats in the Congress, and ultimately proved successful (Kirkendall,
1966; McConnell, 1969). By the late 1940s, the role of social scientists
was no longer planning and policy making; rather, it was the implementation of policies chosen by others and technical assistance (see
Hardin, 1955 and 1967 for the views of a disappointed agricultural
economist).

Rural sociologists were not the most powerful of social scientists in
the arena of agricultural politics, but a group of them did support and
participate in New Deal reform efforts. In other words, though the
subdiscipline of rural sociology was not at the forefront of New Deal
reforms, the events of the period did provide the "space" for a rethinking
of rural sociology. This opportunity is reflected most directly in employment opportunities. Table 1 shows the location of rural sociologists
and agricultural economists in 1929–30 and 1939–40.

This table shows two important trends. First, rural sociology was
consistently dwarfed, in both the Federal government and the land grant
system, by agricultural economics. Second, though the practitioners
located in the land grant system remained in the majority throughout,
the 1930's witnessed a dramatic growth in the number of rural sociologists

working in reformist Federal agencies. Schultz and Witt (1941) and Taylor (1939) reported that rural sociologists were spread out among a number of welfare and action agencies from 1933 to 1938. However, with the elimination or decline of these agencies and the growth of the Division of Farm Population and Rural Welfare within the BAE, virtually all sociologists working in the Federal government were concentrated in the BAE by 1939. Though exact statistics are unavailable it appears that the absolute number of rural sociologists in the Federal government stayed roughly the same from 1937 to 1940. And these rural sociologists found the necessary funding to conduct social research. "Let us recognize also that action agencies wrestling with rural social problems have supplied more funds for rural social research in the last six years than all the universities, colleges, and foundations combined have supplied in the twenty-five years during which concrete rural research has been in process" (Taylor, 1940:29). The critical rural sociology that emerged in the 1930s was nurtured by the material conditions discussed here—alternative employment and funding options.

The Literature

Those working in the reform agencies of the 1930s did not inherit a rural sociological tradition well suited for research into governmental social reforms. Prior to the Depression, rural sociology had concentrated on "social problems" peculiar to the countryside, but these problems were seen as located in a deficient rural personality and the underdevelopment of rural social institutions as a result of low population density. Exploitive social relations were beyond the conceptual framework (Hooks and Flinn, 1981a and 1981b). In turn, solving these problems hinged upon improving rural people on the one hand and building rural social institutions on the other, i.e., pursuing the Extension tradition. This tendency was reinforced by the Purnell Act of 1926, which funded rural sociological research for the first time but did so in the context of land grant institutions. The prolonged agricultural depression of the 1920s and 1930s did spark self-doubt among practitioners. These were expressed by E.C. Lindeman: "Either the principles of rural sociology are hot-house products, too fragile to stand transplanting to the rugged soil of actual rural community, or the rural sociologists have failed to develop means of rendering their principles intelligible and useable" (quoted in Danbom, 1979:123). However, prior to FDR's election, the dominant response was to improve the research competence of rural sociologists to overcome the "mania for reform before analysis" (Zimmerman, 1929:260), and to renew the subdiscipline's commitment to the Extension Service (Burr, 1927; Kumlein, 1927).

Throughout the 1930s the traditional view of rural society and of the role of rural sociologists remained influential, but it was challenged by an alternative and critical approach in the Progressive intellectual tradition. While both traditions within rural sociology reflected the important influence of Sorokin and Zimmerman's (1929) *Principles in Rural-Urban Sociology*, they diverged markedly from this common starting point. Dwight Sanderson, who worked in a land grant institution (Cornell University) and was the first president of the Rural Sociological Society (RSS), shaped the thinking of rural sociologists retaining a traditional view. In Sanderson's view (1932), the community was identified as the key sociological category. Furthermore, the role of the sociologist was to "raise community consciousness" (Sanderson, 1932:583) and to subdue conflict. Implicitly, reformist state interventions were downplayed. Taylor (1933), who was a central figure among reformists, took a markedly different position on each of these points. He argued that class was the key sociological category, and that "class consciousness" and struggle were central to valid social reform (1933:658). Not only were state led reforms of the exploitive social order seen as positive, Taylor called on rural sociologists to be actively involved in these reforms.[3]

This reasoning was well received in the central USDA offices. Funding for Taylor's Division of Farm Population and Rural Welfare in the BAE tripled in the late 1930s. In fact, most of the increase in rural sociologists employed in the federal government (as reflected in Table 1) were located in this office. This reasoning struck a note among rural sociologists as well. "Taylor was able to . . . recruit top-flight members of his profession . . . and produce publications that were highly regarded by sociologists outside the USDA" (Kirkendall, 1966:222).

However, several of these studies were used by enemies of the BAE to justify reducing the influence of social scientists. First, Goldschmidt (1947) studied rural California and concluded that large scale capitalist agriculture undermined political and economic democracy. Conservatives in Congress mounted an attack on Goldschmidt's study that was part of the larger assault on planning and reform. But that attack became even more virulent when a researcher into Coahoma County, Mississippi, concluded that:

1. There existed a sizeable gap between white landowners and black share-croppers;
2. Whites had "fairly absolute" control over blacks;
3. White landowners gave constant attention to maintaining the "institutions (particularly established race relations) which underline the plantation system"; and

4. Blacks were turning to the Federal government for security and "militant Negro leadership in the north" was gaining influence among southern blacks (Kirkendall, 1966:235–236).

The response by the AFBF and southern Congressmen was predictably vehement. Congressman McGehee of Mississippi demanded that meddlesome social scientists stay out of the South because "if permitted to work out their problem, the negro will continue to advance to his proper station just as it has taken thousands of years for the white man to reach his present state." The Congressman was particularly hostile to the "long haired, crack-brained, Un-American birds" who conducted the Coahoma County study. He suggested that "the bird that concocted all this rot should be kicked into Kingdom Come, and it should be in the lower regions of purgatory . . . [and that the USDA] had more important work to do in behalf of the farmers . . . than to spend the taxpayers' money by hiring a caste of people to prepare such damned insulting articles" (quoted in Kirkendall, 1966:236). Though the challenges to the BAE were much more fundamental than the issue of rural sociologists' work, the attack on the controversial studies by Taylor's office represented a final and symbolic blow to planning and reform by social scientists (Hardin, 1955).

Earlier, I contrasted Taylor, who worked in a central USDA reform agency, and Sanderson, who was employed by a land grant university and the Extension Service (Sanderson, 1932:v). To determine if there existed a comparable split between the views of rural sociologists in the two settings a content analysis of the articles published in *Rural Sociology* was conducted. Each article published in the journal between 1936 and 1945 was read and categorized according to the following mutually exclusive categories:

1. Location of the author.
2. Use of the concepts of race or class in the argumentation.
3. Promotion of social reform (i.e., state intervention) to resolve a "social problem."
4. Using race or class in argumentation *and* promoting social reform (i.e., 2 and 3 combined).

Using this content analysis it is possible to compare rural sociologists in the various settings with regard to their tendency to analyze rural society in terms of race/class and social reform. While this analysis may not get at the rural sociologists' privately held beliefs, since it relies solely on the opinions and ideas offered in published articles, it is an effective and unobtrusive means to compare their approach to rural

Table 2. Content of Articles Published in <u>Rural Sociology</u> by Location of
          Authors 1936-45 (N=163)*

Content of Article	Land Grant or Extension		Reformist Agencies	
	n	%	n	%
Not relevant (i.e., race, class, and reform excluded from argument)	77	71	21	28
Race or class imbedded in argument	9	8	7	23
Reform advocated	14	13	17	36
Race or class used <u>and</u> reform advocated	8	7	10	13
Column total	108	99**	55	100

DF=7
x^2=14.41
p 0.05

*The 90 articles submitted by non-rural sociologists have been excluded from this content analysis. As such there are only 163 articles under consideration.
**This column does not total to 100 percent due to rounding.

sociological practice. The results of this content analysis are summarized in Table 2.

The X^2 statistic indicates that the distribution in Table 2 differs significantly from chance. The trends exhibited in the table conform to the arguments presented here. While only 29 percent of the articles from land grant university based practitioners mention reform, race, or class, 72 percent of those articles from reform agency rural sociologists did so. Further, rural sociologists in reformist agencies were much more likely to link concerns with race and class to the advocacy of social reform (13 percent versus 7 percent).

As important as this comparison of the content of the articles is, the changes in content over time are equally notable. Reform agency based practitioners discussed race or class in 8 of the 13 articles they submitted in 1936 and linked these arguments to an advocacy of reform in 3 of these submissions. This represents a sizeable portion of the articles addressing these issues by reform agency based practitioners (8 of 17 [47 percent] of the articles addressing race or class and 3 of 10 [30 percent] of those linking race and class to advocacy of reform). After 1936, reform agency based rural sociologists were not only less likely to submit articles, but those articles that were published evince less concern for the controversial issues of race, class and social reform.

Table 3. The Content of the Articles of Land Grant University Based
          Practitioners Over Time, 1936-45 (n=108)

Content of Article	1936-1939		1940-1942		1943-1945	
	n	%	n	%	n	%
Not relevant (race, class, and reform excluded)	37	64	13	59	27	96
Relevant (i.e., race, class, or reform discussed	21	36	9	41	1	4
Column total	58	100	22	100	28	100

DF=5
X^2=11.85
p   0.05

Rural sociologists in land grant settings exhibit a parallel decline in their interest in these issues. Table 3 summarizes the changing content of land grant university based practitioners' articles over time.

Table 3 documents the decline in rural sociologists' interest in reform and other controversial issues as the conservative backlash gained momentum. During the early New Deal years, rural sociologists, including those in land grant universities, showed concern for race, class, and social reform. But this interest virtually disappeared over time. While over 36 percent of the articles published prior to 1940, and 41 percent of those published between 1940 and 1942 treated those issues, only 1 article (4 percent) of the 1942-45 period did so. The decline in the number and prestige of reformist rural sociologists not only undercut their ability to get articles published, but it eroded their ability to force a rethinking of rural sociology and led ultimately to a retrenchment of conservative thinking among land grant university rural sociologists.

After the war, the retreat from reformism continued within the USDA. Not only was the BAE incapacitated, but the increasingly powerful Extension Service deliberately and consistently downplayed reform. Instead, the Extension Service and the land grant system stressed depoliticized "research and education as effective approaches to the solution of human problems" (Hardin, 1955:1976). This attack on the BAE destroyed the niche for rural sociologists in centralized reformist agencies as well. By 1946, the funding for controversial "social surveys" was abolished completely (Hardin, 1955), and the employment of rural sociologists within the BAE, became increasingly rare. The postwar era mirrored the pre-Depression pattern, i.e., rural sociologists were, with rare exceptions, employed in the land grant system. In turn, the job descriptions and career trajectories of rural sociologists were no longer linked to the promotion of populist reforms or critical social research. As a consequence, rural sociologists became convinced of the need to forego "philosophizing" and to concentrate on developing a "technology" for "guiding social action" (Lively, 1943:339). In turn, Blackwell et al. (1948) could report on a new "agreement" with the Extension Service that defined rural sociologists as technicians. "The primary focus of rural sociology as a science is in the structure and function of groups. The primary interest of rural sociology extension must be the same—not as a science, but as a technology working to improve the social order" (Blackwell, et al., 1948:65). As the emergence of the critical rural sociology of the 1930s was tied to broader political and institutional developments, so its decline was shaped by the same factors. The attack on the BAE and reform in the USDA eliminated the institutional basis of this generation of critical rural sociology, hence its marginal impact on postwar rural sociology.

CRITICAL RURAL SOCIOLOGY OF TODAY

The critical rural sociology of the present—as was the case with the critical rural sociology of the 1930s—emerged in the wake of a transformation of the political and economic context of the subdiscipline. The ensuing discussion explores these broader changes and the basic tendencies in the emergent critical rural sociology. We are still in the midst of and close to the latest effort to build a critical rural sociology. Further, we cannot document its rise and fall because this latest effort is still with us. It is, in fact, in the process of growth. Hence this discussion will not provide a statistically based content analysis of the recent literature. Rather, an intimate look at the practice of critical rural sociology is offered. In the tradition of *Doing Sociology* (Bell and Newby, 1977), the contributors to this volume were interviewed to identify their focus and approach to research. The subject matter of each paper is summarized, and the personal choices of the authors and their relationship to critical rural sociology are explored.

The Context

At first glance, the events sparking this latest generation of critical rural sociology are similar to those of the 1930s. In 1960, the Democratic Party recaptured the White House with the promise of getting "the country moving again." Under the Kennedy and Johnson Administrations, social programs and social research were funded on a much vaster scale. "In 1955–56 the total . . . expenditure by all higher educational institutions in the United States was $4.1 billion, of which 12 per cent, including research and development support was supplied by the Federal Government. In 1967 the figure was $16.8 billion of which 23 per cent . . . was from Federal sources" (Seidman, 1976:32–33). However, the parallels between the 1930s and the present break down here. That is, the initiatives of the 1960s did not lead to the creation of the "Great Society"; rather, they were overwhelmed by the political and social turmoil that enveloped the decade. Racial injustices gave rise to a powerful civil rights movement and later to major urban riots. The unpopular Vietnam War led to a politicization of universities and of the younger generation more generally. These protest movements gave rise to still others, the feminist and environmental movements being particularly important. The symbolic culmination of these developments occurred in 1968: the "events" of Paris and those of Prague were matched by the riots in Chicago at the Democratic Party's national convention (Newby, 1981). These social upheavals contributed to the erosion of the legitimacy of the fundamental social institutions of the postwar era.

In marked contrast to the 1930s, reformers of the 1960s did not look to the state's bureaucracy as the solution; rather, it was seen as the problem. The military was particularly suspect given the unpopularity of the Vietnam War; the role of police forces in quelling riots and protests was also seen negatively. But the Federal bureaucracy administering social programs was not much more popular. The key agencies created by FDR during the 1930s had been transformed from the vanguard of social reform to guardians of the social order. The Second World War, and especially eight years of Republican rule, had changed the composition of the staff and the role definition of these agencies. This was true for the White House agencies coordinating the various agencies of the Executive Branch, e.g., the Bureau of the Budget, and for those agencies dealing directly with citizens (Berman, 1979; Schick, 1975). The USDA was not immune from these changes. The New Dealer strongholds within the USDA were destroyed during and shortly after World War II and the Eisenhower Administration purged New Dealers from the Department during its first term in office (Talbot and Hadwiger, 1968:154–56; Hardin, 1955). Those in Congress pushing reform legislation recognized the unreliability of the Federal bureaucracy in realizing their goals. The Bureau of the Budget—once considered the citadel of reformers and "officially" charged with clearing all legislation for the President— was systematically evaded in the creation of the Great Society legislative package (Berman, 1979). Similarly, the emphasis on "maximum feasible participation" reflected the mistrust of the federal bureaucracy, as did the tendency to "vest client status in those who are weak or disadvantaged" (Schick, 1975:156).

These anti-statist and anti-bureaucratic sentiments were not peculiar to reformers in protest and legislative reform movements. If anything they were even more prevalent in universities—with sociology strongly influenced. Western Marxism was revived as was critical theory and leftist readings of Weber. Though the disputes internal to Marxism and between and among these "new" approaches were important and often bitter, they did share some common starting points: first, social inequality and exploitation are not exceptional, they are commonplace; second, the state is seen as the key institution in reproducing an exploitive social order while bureaucracy is antithetical to democracy. Whereas the Democratic administrations of the 1930s expanded funding for social research and were rewarded with the avid support of social scientists, those of the 1960s found the vastly expanded social science institutions contributing to the assault on the government's legitimacy.

Though there was a significant expansion in critical research, such an approach never dominated the parent discipline and made only small inroads into rural sociology during the 1960s. However, the intellectual and material conditions for the development of a critical rural sociology were nurtured during this decade. First, on the intellectual plane, rural sociology students and faculty were not only exposed to the politicization of universities but came into contact with the "critical" theories revived in the parent discipline. Though these influences were not immediately evident in the rural sociological literature, they prepared the ground for subsequent questioning of the consensual view of rural society that dominated postwar thinking. At the same time, important articles were published that criticized the methodological and conceptual underpinnings of rural sociology. Sewell (1965:428–9, fn.3) listed twenty one papers that questioned rural sociology's methods. Though they neither raised the controversial social issues nor promoted a critical alternative, they did stress that "something was wrong" (Newby, 1980). Institutionally, the 1960s witnessed a decline in the subdiscipline's absolute dependence on Extension funding and research. In his Presidential address to the Rural Sociological Society, Sheldon Lowry (1977) pointed out that: "The support rural sociology has had in the Federal Extension Service has diminished, and there appears to be no chance of strengthening it. . . . These changes have taken place almost without notice by the membership of our Society" (Lowry, 1977:470).

Despite the Extension Service's disinterest, the "vital signs" of the subdiscipline were good and membership at an all time high (Lowry, 1977:465–66). Rural sociology's drift from the Extension Service was made possible by the explosion of social science research funding sources in the 1960s and 1970s. With alternative funding sources, rural sociologists also had many more publishing outlets than only a few years earlier

(Lacy and Busch, 1982; Lowry, 1977:67–68). Taking note of the options available to rural sociologists, Newby and Buttel point out that the "funding agencies are not monolithic," and that they have funded the emergent critical research (1980:14). As in the 1930s, critical rural sociology of today is not simply an intellectual dissatisfaction—though there is plenty of that—it is based upon a shift in the funding sources, research options, and job descriptions of practitioners.

The Literature

The most (in)famous of the early calls for a more critical rural sociology came from outside the subdiscipline. Hightower's acerbic dismissal (1973) was among the first of a flood of attacks by non-rural sociologists on the subdiscipline's social (ir)relevance. These criticisms were soon echoed by members and nonmembers of the Rural Sociological Society alike (Benvenuti, et al., 1975; Copp, 1972; Ford, 1973; Friedland, 1979; Nolan and Galliher, 1973; Nolan and Hagan, 1975; Picou, et al., 1978; Stokes and Miller, 1975). By the mid–1970s, the emphasis shifted from criticizing the failures of the past to making a positive contribution by exploring old issues in a new manner or taking up issues long ignored by the subdiscipline. Though these efforts are too numerous to list, some important examples include: Friedland et al., 1978; Friedman, 1981; Goss, et al., 1978; Mann and Dickinson, 1978; and the collection of papers in Buttel and Newby (1980). By 1982, the President of the RSS was calling for a renegotiation of rural sociology's role in the land grant system so that this socially relevant and critical research could be further advanced (Flinn, 1982).

Although the ensuing eight papers in this book reflect the different interests and research agendas of the authors, they are united by four common themes—themes that permeate the critical rural sociology of the present. First, the authors avoid being "captured" by the institutions of rural society they are exploring. Instead, the papers are guided by a theoretical orientation geared toward identifying underlying and historical causal processes—processes that operate "behind the backs" of social actors. Second, the papers approach rural society critically in a deliberate attempt to unmask social inequities. As most of the authors turned to Marxism for theoretical grounding, the structured inequalities and the social dynamics inherent in the U.S. class structure are central elements of the explanation offered. Third, the authors are concerned with processes by which rural society can be improved. Though the papers are not exercises in "applied" social research, the authors are interested in exploring the causes and consequences of social movements and/or the outcomes of state interventions. Though typically implicit rather than explicit, the contributions to this volume suggest a course of action for "reforming" rural society. The final theme that binds the papers in this volume together distinguishes them from the critical rural sociologists of the 1930s. Like others of the present generation, the contributors to this book view the state as a cornerstone of the exploitive rural social order. The critical Marxism and Weberianism that guides these papers clashes with the Progressive orientation that dominated 1930s thinking. The belief in technologically driven and cumulative progress and of the state as above civil society and therefore benign, has been replaced by an approach to sociology that stresses ubiquitous conflict. Progress is a euphemism for changes in the U.S. agriculture's class-based system of exploitation. In turn, the state is seen not as benign and removed, rather it plays an essential role in reproducing the exploitive social order.[4]

Whenever possible, the authors were contacted and asked to explain why they chose the topic of the paper and the conceptual orientation employed in the investigation. As the questions were open-ended, the responses vary significantly. The choosing of topics reflects the influence of the politicization of the past decades on the authors' professional practice. For several authors, the papers in this book reflect an attempt to come to terms with their position in the social structure and other social experiences. Others chose their topics out of more purely intellectual curiosity—answering questions that had been ignored or answered poorly in traditional accounts. As the choice of topics reflected a "critical" approach to rural sociology, so the conceptual orientation reinforced that tendency. Most authors turned to Marxism in an effort to avoid the ahistorical and conservatively biased approaches that had long dominated the subdiscipline. Though the motivations of the authors and their conceptual frameworks reflect some diversity, there does exist a common critical stance. The inclusion of these papers in this book demonstrate that it is possible to pursue critical rural sociology research within the present institutional context.

A.E. Havens paper is the first in the collection to explore U.S. agricultural development—and appropriately so. Havens, as editor, played a central role in bringing this collection of papers together. Additionally, Havens' interest in and involvement with critical rural sociology preceded the prominence of critical approaches in the 1970s. His graduate training and early work on the diffusion of innovations was very much in the postwar consensual theoretical mold. But in the process of working in Latin America in the early and mid-1960s, Havens encountered an "overall context of exploitation that shaped agricultural development and change." Moreover, this class based exploitation was so "stark and apparent" that it became impossible to ignore the limitations of consensual social theories or the irrelevance of the social survey methods so pervasive of the social sciences in the 1960s. During these years in Latin America, Havens worked with older rural sociologists, including those who had contributed to and lamented the elimination of the critical rural sociology of the 1930s and 1940s. Through the personal accounts of Bruce Ryan and T. Lynn Smith, Havens learned of the conservative restructuring of rural sociologists' working conditions in the 1940s at precisely the same time that he confronted the limitations of received rural sociological theories and methodologies.

Havens applied the lessons of his Latin American experiences to the study of the U.S. He turned to both "classical and contemporary sources" (e.g., Marx, Lenin, and Kautsky—and their intellectual descendents of the present generation) to develop a critical analysis of the political economy of U.S. agriculture. Havens argues that the development of modern agriculture is firmly rooted in the triangular relationship between agriculture, the rest of the economy, and the state. From his perspective, the shifts in the social relations governing agricultural production are dependent on commodity producers' relations to loans, commodity markets, capitalist development, and the activities of the state. These relations are based upon the imposition of a dominant set of interests on the bulk of the population through economic and political activity. The state has played an important role in this process as it has successfully repressed threats (such as the agrarian radicals of the Populist revolt) and, at the same time, it has maintained the commercial farmers' position in production through the use of crop subsidies, loans, and technical aid. For Havens, this process has been full of disjunctures and crises. The result has been continued state support of commercial farming and the slow, inexorable decline of the small farm. Havens concludes that even though the number of persons directly involved with agricultural production has declined, the class relations that exist among farmers, their suppliers, food processers, and the state have all grown more complex.

Neil Fligstein investigates the evolution of agriculture in the post-bellum South. His original interest was not the 19th century South, it was the rise of the Sunbelt during the 1970s. But in exploring that issue he became dissatisfied with the existing account of "why people left the South in the first place prior to 1960 or so." The accepted answer to this question was "directly borrowed from economists—mechanization of the cotton fields and the pull of jobs in the North." Trained in sociology, demography, and economics, Fligstein was sensitive to the weaknesses of this account. His contribution to this book looks behind the "accepted wisdom and aggregate data" to examine underlying causal processes. In so doing, Fligstein developed an "historical, structural explanation" heavily influenced by Marxist structuralism (see also his book, *Going North*, 1981).

Fligstein argues that the class structure and dynamics of production in this period resulted from the North's military and political victory in the Civil War. The southern planters of the period, faced with high cotton prices and little capital to grow crops, tried to get the newly freed blacks to work with only a promise of pay. The North did not allow this reenslavement to occur and this forced the reorganization of southern agriculture. This meant the rise of tenant farming, crop liens, and local merchants. The southern economic system became increasingly dependent on the price of cash crops and the credit system. The North came to dominate the South economically by supplying the capital to grow the crops, by controlling the marketing and processing of the crops, and by supplying food and manufactured goods to the South. The Populist movement protested this domination. Its defeat meant that the economic system of the South went unchallenged until it collapsed in the 1930s. Fligstein views this process as a classic case of under-development whereby a developed region organizes and controls an underdeveloped region.

Carolyn Howe's paper provides both a theoretical and an historical account of U.S. farmer movements. Because of this dual concern, it serves as a bridge between the papers in this book which provide historical investigation and those which address theoretical concerns. Howe describes the thinking behind her choice of topic as follows: "There has been a long-standing debate in sociology over the relative importance of social structure and human agency in history. It is the intersection between structure and agency that has inspired most of my research interests." In previous research on these issues, Howe had concentrated on labor history and struggles. In beginning the study of farmers' movements, she used a "class analysis of actors and factions within the movements, and looked for patterns similar to those observable in the labor movement." In this research, Howe reacted to the under-theorization in the literature. "There seemed to be little in the way of a *theory* of farmers' movements and yet the literature was rich in descriptive detail that cried out for such a theory." As her choice of topic was strongly influenced by a larger debate in the parent discipline, she turned to the sociology literature in developing a theoretical frame-work. That is, "the resource mobilization perspective in the social movements literature provided a starting point" for understanding the human agency of farmers. And the "class analysis and the intersection of social struggles and social structure are informed by Marxist sociology." However, hers is a study of farmers. As such, "the new rural sociology, especially the sociology of agriculture" was critically important in situating farmer movements within the changing structure of agriculture. Howe's task, then, was to combine these elements of the diverse conceptual sources into an integrated "theoretical framework suitable to the analysis of farmers' movements under advanced capitalism."

The theoretical section of Howe's paper makes two basic points. First, we must analyze capitalist penetration of the food production cycle and examine the consequences for the grievances, mobilizations, and outcomes of farmers' movements. Second, we must have a class analysis of family farmers and their social movements in order to explain (a) differences between farmers' movements, (b) differences within a movement or its organizational form, and (c) changes in the movements over time. It is suggested that the relationship of farmers to capital is a central determinant of the movements. This relationship is mediated by both the cycles of economic expansion or crisis and interventions by the state. Further, this relationship is linked to the global transformations of agricultural production. In the second and historical section of Howe's paper, this theoretical framework is applied to an overview of farmers' movements in the U.S. Midwest from about 1850 to the present. The basic thesis of the paper is that the changing structure of agriculture gives rise to new class relations in agriculture in ways that account for the internal dynamics and historical transformations of those movements.

The remaining chapters deal with the contemporary agricultural scene and how people have mobilized to influence state policy and changes in agrarian structure. David James chose to explore the institutional basis of southern race relations because he "lived on one side of the color line in the South" as he grew up. James' essay attempts to trace the linkages between political and economic structures and their relation to the transformation of southern agriculture between the 1930s and 1970s. James is not a rural sociologist who turned to critical theories, he is a sociologist who explored rural issues in addressing his broader political sociological question: What accounts for the differential resistance to the southern Civil Rights movement during the 1960s? Southern agriculture became the focus of inquiry because of its fundamental relationship to the class and race relations of the region. In addressing this question, James relied upon Marxist theories of the state and those of social movements to explore the structural impediments and options for the Civil Rights movement. He argues that the racial features of the southern local state structure were organically related to the class structure of cotton plantation agriculture typical of the period prior to the 1930s. The structure of the southern racial state imposed serious constraints on the mobility of black agriculture labor and reinforced coercive methods of labor control on the cotton plantation. Both of these features were functionally compatible with the labor intensive strategies used by cotton planters to cope with commodity market fluctuations. The Farmer Committee system created to administer the price support and acreage reduction programs of the New Deal was also constrained by the class structure of the cotton plantation. Program benefits flowed disproportionately to planters while tenants and sharecroppers were progressively displaced. As this process proceeded over the next thirty years, the class structure of cotton agriculture was transformed into a relationship between capitalist farmers and wage workers rather than cotton planters and sharecroppers. Similarly, the modal response of cotton producers to market vagaries was the adoption of innovation in order to raise the productivity of labor rather than the labor coercive response of the pre-depression planter. Hence, the racial state made the transformation of southern agriculture possible by guaranteeing the docility of the southern agricultural labor force and thereby undermined the organic relationship between the racial state and cotton agriculture. The success of the Civil Rights movement during the 1960s was predicated upon these changes.

Harrington's chapter focuses on the relation between class position and politics in the New Deal in Oklahoma. Before World War II, Oklahoma's economy was based on agriculture and the extraction of minerals and resources like timber. As was the case in the South, New Deal agriculture programs dramatically transformed Oklahoma's economy and polity. Harrington begins by defining the relation between classes and politics. The basic assertion is that classes have immediate and fundamental interests. He argues that classes can be divided into fractions and allied with other groups because of immediate interests. This creates a political arena where immediate interest groups can and will control the definition of political issues, thereby subverting class struggle. Harrington then demonstrates how this process worked in Oklahoma. He argues that Oklahoma had a populist and socialist political history within which workers and tenant farmers were united by radical goals. This alliance came together and was destroyed on several occasions. During the 1930s, New Deal politics permanently destroyed the alliance as the immediate interests of the workers were addressed by the New Dealers while the tenant farmers as a group were being destroyed by the farm subsidies. The tenant farmers' principal reaction was defensive and reactionary. Harrington's paper clearly shows the subtle interaction among class groups, interest groups, and politics.

Pat Mooney's chapter identifies changes in the class structure and in the locus of control in Wisconsin agriculture. The question Mooney addresses is: Have petty bourgeois farm producers survived at all in the face of the market forces working against them? Mooney's choice of topic was influenced by his family experiences. "Having grown up in the Corn Belt, . . . I had always taken an interest in farming and farm life, as they were a vital part of the local economy and many friends were hoping to farm after high school. I suppose I have never really forgiven the banks for foreclosing on my grandfather. I think that all of us study sociology in order to better understand our own location in the social structure." In addressing this broad question, Mooney was influenced by both agricultural history and Marxist sociology.

> There seemed to be an undercurrent running through the rather atheoretical descriptions of the historical transformations of U.S. agriculture but it was difficult to pin down any general processes. On the other hand, Marxist theorizations made sense of the general processes but seemed quite inadequate for explaining specifics. I wanted to tell the story of what happened to all those men and women like my grandparents who had lost their land. Lumping all farmers together—i.e., petty bourgeois—is problematic in any case. But when interested in the historical transformation of agriculture, as I am, it is less acceptable still.

Instead, in his view, the class character of rural society is much more complex. Mooney identifies four classes of agricultural producers: capitalist, traditional petty bourgeois, new petty bourgeois, and proletariat. Capitalist farmers operate large scale, highly mechanized farms that employ wage labor. Traditional petty bourgeois are farmers who own their own land, have little or no debt, do not employ wage labor, do not engage in contract production, and do not work off the farm. Between the capitalist and petty bourgeois exist intermediate groups of farmers who are small scale employers and landlords. The new petty bourgeoisie manage production with heavy dependence on non-family resources. Most likely, this will include hired labor. Farm workers form the rural proletariat. Intermediate between farm workers and petty bourgeois are farmers who are tenants of farm owners deep in debt, doing contract production, or involved in production off the farm. Mooney discusses in great detail how these various positions have arisen over time and how their existence depends a great deal on the activities of the state and capitalist penetration of agriculture.

Max Pfeffer's paper illustrates the distinctiveness of the labor process in agriculture relative to other industries. His interest in the topic emerged from his work experiences of the early 1970s. In his words:

> I worked on a large scale industrial farm in Colorado. It was from this experience that my interest in the role of Mexican workers in U.S. agriculture grew. I was living with my parents at the time, and I had no family to support. Yet, my hourly wage was more than that of my undocumented Mexican co-workers, who had both to pay rent and support a family. I learned to respect the ability and capacity for hard work of these co-workers.

This respect heightened the sense of injustice I felt at the way these workers were exploited.

Pfeffer concentrates on Californian agriculture where corporate agriculture has particular labor needs due to the nature of the labor process. In examining this issue, Pfeffer turned to Marxist theory "because it offered a historical perspective," a perspective that Pfeffer found intuitively appealing and lacking in much of the sociological literature. However, Marxist sociology had concentrated on industrial developments, not on agriculture. This left Pfeffer with the challenge of "applying Marxist theory to the peculiarities of agricultural development." In this effort, Pfeffer's focus was on the labor process, with a special emphasis on the labor needs of capitalist farming operations. These needs are difficult to satisfy and growers have relied on the assistance of the state to supply the necessary work force. U.S. immigration policy on Mexican workers illustrates this relationship. Pfeffer's analysis relates different policies to changing political circumstances.

These papers explore different facets of class forces and political processes in shaping the development of American agriculture. Commercial producers have been most favored by the federal government and it is clear that the New Deal agricultural policies accelerated and transformed the social relations in agriculture. Today, the structure of U.S. agriculture is both complex and fragmented. This structure has developed in response to the needs of capital (in particular, the food processers), the world commodity markets, and the activities of the state and federal governments. While all of the papers begin the task of deciphering those relations, Havens and Newby address this question directly. In the book's concluding paper, an analytic approach for exploring the origins, and especially the consequences, of state interventions into agriculture is offered.

This chapter has made use of the concepts of critical rural sociology to study the activities of practitioners yesterday and today. It is increasingly the consensus that it is time for the discipline to move from introspection and self-flagellation to the creation and pursuit of a positive research agenda. With this in mind we turn to the other papers in this book—from an exploration of our context and ourselves to an investigation of society.

NOTES

1. A more detailed discussion of the critical rural sociology of the 1930s is included in the author's (1983) "A New Deal for Farmers and Social Scientist: The Politics of Rural Sociology in the Depression Era," *Rural Sociology* 48(3):386–

408. The author would like to express his gratitude to *Rural Sociology* for permission to reproduce parts of that article.

2. Interviews with the contributors to this volume were included where possible. However, Dale Harrington and Howard Newby were unavailable for comment.

3. A more thorough discussion of this literature is presented in the author's previously published article on this subject (Hooks, 1983).

4. Though I share the critical orientation found in the other papers in the book, I do differ with respect to the state. In what would represent a middle ground between the practitioners of the 1930s and the more common view of today, I do not see the state as automatically either good or bad. That is, I find the Progressive view of the state overly optimistic and naive with regard to the state's potential for co-opting and suppressing social reform. However, I am no more convinced by the Marxist claim (either structuralist or instrumentalist) that the state is necessarily serving the "interests" of the dominant class. The state's role must be established through careful historical investigation; it cannot be asserted *a priori*.

REFERENCES

Appleby, Paul. 1945. Big Democracy. New York: Alfred Knopf.

Bell, Colin, and Howard Newby. 1977. Doing Sociology. London: Allen & Unwin.

Benedict, Murray. 1953. Farm Policies of the United States, 1790–1950. New York: The Twentieth Century Fund.

Berman, Larry. 1979. The Office of Management and Budget and the Presidency, 1921–1979. Princeton, N.J.: Princeton University Press.

Blackwell, Gordon, Nat Frame, and W.H. Stacy. 1948. "Teamwork Needed in Extension Sociology." Rural Sociology 13(1): 65–70.

Burr, Walter. 1927. "What Contribution Can the Extension Service Make to the Solution of the Agricultural Problem from the Standpoint of a Sociologist?" In Proceedings: Forty-first Annual Convention of Land Grant Colleges and Universities. Chicago.

Buttel, Frederick, and Howard Newby (eds.). 1980. The Rural Sociology of the Advanced Societies, Montclair, N.J.: Allanheld, Osmun.

Danbom, David. 1979. The Resisted Revolution. Ames, Iowa: Iowa University Press.

Egger, Rowland. 1975. "The Period of Crisis: 1933–1945," in F.C. Mosher (ed.), American Public Administration: Past, Present, and Future. University of Alabama: The University of Alabama Press.

Fligstein, Neil. 1981. Going North: Migration of Blacks and Whites from the South, 1900–1950. New York: Academic Press.

Flinn, William. 1982. "Rural Sociology: Prospects and Dilemmas in the 1980's." Rural Sociology 47(1): 1–16.

Ford, A.M. 1973. The Political Economy of Rural Poverty in the South. Cambridge, Mass.: Ballinger.

Friedland, William, Amy Barton, and Robert Thomas. 1978. Manufacturing Green Gold: The Conditions and Social Consequences of Lettuce Harvest Mechanization. Davis, California: California Agricultural Policy Seminar, University of California, Davis.

Friedland, William. 1979. "Who Killed Rural Sociology? A Case Study in the Political Economy of Knowledge Production." Paper presented at the annual meeting of the American Sociological Association, Boston.

Friedman, Harriet. 1981. "The Family Farm in Advanced Capitalism: Outline of a Theory of Simple Commodity Production." Paper presented at the Annual Meeting of the American Sociological Association, Toronto, Ontario.

Galjart, Benno. 1971. "Rural Development and Sociological Concepts: A Critique." Rural Sociology 36: 31–40.

Gaus, John. 1947. Reflections on Public Administration. University, Alabama: The University of Alabama Press.

Gaus, John, and Leon Wolcott, with Vern Lewis. 1940. Public Administration and the United States Department of Agriculture. Chicago: Public Administration Service.

Goldschmidt, Walter R. 1947. As You Sow. New York: Harcourt Brace.

Hardin, Charles. 1954. "The Republican Department of Agriculture," Journal of Farm Economics, (May).

_____. 1955. Freedom in Agricultural Education. Chicago: University of Chicago Press.

_____. 1967. Food and Fiber in the Nation's Politics. Washington, D.C.: Government Printing Office.

Hightower, Jim. 1973. Hard Tomatoes, Hard Times. Cambridge, Mass.: Schenkman.

Hooks, Greg, and William Flinn. 1981a. "The Country Life Commission and Early Rural Sociology." The Rural Sociologist 1(2).

_____. 1981b. "Toward a Sociology of Early Rural Sociology." The Rural Sociologist 1(3).

Hooks, Gregory. 1983. "A New Deal for Farmers and Social Scientists: The Politics of Rural Sociology in the Depression Era," Rural Sociology 48(3): 386–408.

Kirkendall, Richard. 1966. Social Scientists and Farm Politics in the Age of Roosevelt. Columbia, Missouri: University of Missouri Press.

Kumlien, W.F. 1927. "Responsibilities of the Land Grant Colleges in Teaching Agriculture as a Way of Life." In Proceedings: Forty-first Annual Convention of Land Grant Colleges and Universities. Chicago.

Lacy, William, and Lawrence Busch. 1982. "Institutional and Professional Context for Rural Sociology: Constraints and Opportunities." In Dillman and Hobbs (eds.), Rural Society in the U.S.: Issues for the 1980's. Boulder, Colorado: Westview Press.

Lenin, Vladimir I. 1943. "Development of Capitalism in Russia," in Selected Works, Vol. I. New York: International Publishers.

Lively, C.E. 1943. Rural Sociology As Applied Science." Rural Sociology 8(4): 338–49.

Lowry, Sheldon. 1977. "Rural Sociology at the Crossroads." Rural Sociology 42(1): 461–475.

Mann, Susan, and James Dickinson. 1978. "Obstacles to the Development of a Capitalist Agriculture." The Journal of Peasant Studies 5: 466–481.

McConnell, Grant. 1969. The Decline of Agrarian Democracy. New York: Atheneum.

Nelson, Lowry, John H. Kolb, C.E. Lively, Dwight Sanderson and Carle Zimmerman. 1936. "Statement of the Editorial Board." Rural Sociology 1 (1): 5–7.

Newby, Howard. 1980. "Rural Sociology—A Trend Report." Current Sociology, 28(1): 1–141.

———. 1981. "Rural Sociology in These Times." Paper presented at the Annual Meeting of the Rural Sociological Society, University of Guelph (Ontario), August.

Newby, Howard, and Fred Buttel. 1980. "Toward a Critical Rural Sociology," in Buttel and Newby (eds.) The Rural Sociology of the Advanced Societies. Montclair, N.J.: Allanheld, Osmun.

Nolan, Michael, and John Galliher. 1973. "Rural Sociological Research and Social Policy: Hard Data, Hard Times." Rural Sociology 38:491–499.

Picou, J. Steven, Richard Wells, and Kenneth Nyberg. 1978. "Paradigms, Theories, and Methods in Rural Sociology." Rural Sociology 43(Winter): 559–583.

Sanderson, Dwight. 1932. The Rural Community: The Nature and History of a Sociological Group. Boston: Ginn and Co.

Schick, Allen. 1975. "The Trauma of Politics," in F.C. Mosher (ed.), American Public Administration: Past, Present, and Future. University, Alabama: The University of Alabama Press.

Schultz, Theodore W., and Lawrence Witt. 1941. Training and Recruiting of Personnel in the Rural Social Studies. Washington, D.C.: American Council on Education.

Seidman, Harold. 1976. Politics, Position, & Power: The Dynamics of Federal Organization (Second Edition). New York: Oxford University Press.

Sewell, William. 1950. "Needed Research in Rural Sociology." Rural Sociology 15 (June): 115–130.

———. 1965. "Rural Sociological Research, 1936–1965." Rural Sociology 30:428–451.

Skocpol, Theda. 1980. "Political Response to Capitalist Crisis: Neo-Marxist Theories of the State and the Case of the New Deal." Politics and Society 10(2): 155–201.

Smith, T. Lynn. 1957. "Rural Sociology in the United States and Canada." Current Sociology 6(1): 5–19.

Sorokin, Petrim, and Carle Zimmerman. 1929. Principles in Rural-Urban Sociology. New York: Henry Holt and Co.

Taylor, Carl C. 1933. Rural Sociology (Revised Edition). New York: Harper Bros.

———. 1939. "Work of the Division of Farm Population and Rural Life of the Bureau of Agricultural Economics, U.S. Department of Agriculture." Rural Sociology 4(2):221–228.

_____. 1940. "Social Theory and Social Action." Rural Sociology 5(1):17–31.
Talbot, Ross, and Don Hadwiger. 1968. The Policy Process in American Agriculture. Chicago: Science Research Association.
Zimmerman, Carle. 1929. "The Trend of Rural Sociology." in C. Lundberg, R. Bain and N. Anderson (eds.), Trends in American Sociology. New York: Harper and Row.

2
Capitalist Development in the United States: State, Accumulation, and Agricultural Production Systems*

A. Eugene Havens

This chapter provides an historical overview that addresses the following questions: 1) what has been agriculture's role in the accumulation process under capitalist development in the United States, 2) how has state intervention attempted to overcome or avoid accumulation crises, and 3) how have changes in the nature of state intervention affected agricultural production systems? This analysis is guided by the notion that both the nature and the actions of the capitalist state are shaped by class alliances and class struggles that simultaneously limit and transform economic, political and ideological structures.

To understand the role of the state in shaping the food production system and in reproducing class relations, we must first examine the role of agriculture in the process of accumulation. There is a tendency to assume that modern U.S. economic expansion is essentially an urban phenomenon. In this view the expansion is driven by the need for markets for manufactured goods and surplus capital, for raw materials, and for military bases. This view is incomplete. It ignores the historical role of agriculture in foreign policy and the process of accumulation. What follows is an historical overview of this role.

During the second half of the Nineteenth century, U.S. industrialists were striving to become competitive with major European firms. The growing U.S. market was being penetrated by European commodities. Throughout the Nineteenth Century, when foreign credits expanded (1815–1819, 1836–1839, 1850's, 1880's), there was a tremendous influx

---

*Editors Note: A. Eugene Havens passed away before this manuscript was finished. He had used a reference style different than those used by the other contributors. So as to minimize disturbance of his thinking, the reference style he used has been maintained.

of finished goods.[1] The needs of U.S. industrial expansion were clearly stated in the legislation passed by the Northern-dominated War Congress. These included:

1. Central banking
2. High tariffs to protect new industries
3. Contract labor law to provide a steady flow of cheap immigrant labor
4. Homestead Act to gain support of the West
5. Federal Assistance for internal improvements which included the granting of generous loans and free land to build rail links between the industries of the East and the farms of the West, thus unifying the internal market.

To develop U.S. industry, it was necessary to stimulate the growth of the internal market and to protect this market from foreign penetration. At the same time, it was necessary to transfer surpluses from agriculture to industry. Thus, agricultural production was a necessary part of the development process and was stimulated by frontier expansion through land grants and other federal programs.

Due to the distribution of population and the tendency for farm families to produce their own food, the internal market for agricultural products could not absorb all of the agricultural commodities being produced. The majority of the U.S. population was rural at precisely the time that both territorial and industrial expansion were unfolding. In 1870, 74 percent of the total population was rural. In 1900 the rural population still constituted 60 percent of the total. Moreover, with sharecropping emerging as the dominant form of agricultural production in the South immediately after the Civil War, black agricultural workers were producing the bulk of their own food.[2] With the agricultural production increasing, it was necessary to find a way to capture the surplus value embodied in agricultural commodities.

The notion that market-oriented commercial farmers influenced the State to help them penetrate foreign markets runs counter to the myth that independent producers fled the industrial east to avoid market contact and market relations. Like all myths, this one has some foundation in fact. Farmers who eschewed market contact could be found in West Virginia, Ohio, and the Midwest. But large scale, non-cotton agricultural production for export was initially established in the West (Washington, Oregon, California, Wyoming, and Colorado) and Southwest. From the beginning farms in these regions were large commercial enterprises, frequently linked to British capital.[3]

These large units were put together through a variety of control mechanisms and force. The most frequently employed technique was to control access to water and then use public lands for private gain. Many agricultural workers were induced to file homesteads and then to turn them over to their employers.[4] Thus the Homestead Act, usually cited as the prime mover of family farm development, was, in fact, used to control vast territories. The Swamp Lands Act of 1850 and the Desert Land Act of 1877 were conceived as means of carving out large land holdings. If the real ownership and possession of land were revealed, it would become apparent that the United States was much more in need of agrarian reform than were the Latin American countries that, in a later period, the U.S. coerced into adopting agrarian reform laws.

For example, in the 1870's Haggin and Travis carved out what became California's Kern County Land Company, taken over in 1967 by Tenneco. Peter Barnes states that, "Thus by hiring scores of vagabonds to enter phony claims for 640 acres and then transferring those claims to themselves, Haggin and Travis were able to acquire title to 150 square miles of valley land before anybody else in California had even heard of the Desert Land Act. In the process they dislodged settlers who had not yet perfected their titles under old laws and who were caught unaware by the new one."[5]

It was the establishment of capitalist relations of production in agriculture and the concentration of land and capital that accounted for the growing agricultural surplus that sought foreign markets. Thus the class struggle was not so much between independent small producers and an industrial bourgeoisie as between different fractions of the grand bourgeoisie: agrarian, industrial and financial. The agricultural export fraction became increasingly aware of the limits imposed by England's control of the international cereal and cotton markets and the need to directly confront Britain in world markets.[6] Southerners led the agrarian interests for a merchant marine and for the Panama Canal to be constructed and controlled by the United States. As Williams has noted, the Western and Southern-led campaign to remonetize silver was predicated as much upon a drive to weaken Britain's world economic power, and to enter new markets, as by a concern to increase the money supply at home.[7] The drive for new markets was intimately associated with the silver issue. Germany and France were criticized for demonetizing silver because this reinforced Britain's power in world capitalism. The gold standard was seen as the cornerstone to England's economic empire. The remonetization of silver was seen as a way to break London's power and, at the same time, enable U.S. exporters to deal directly with the silver-using countries of Latin America and Asia.[8]

While the silver question appeared to be a struggle between agriculture and industry, it was really a struggle between financiers linked to British banking and entrepreneurs who equated national interests with expansionism. The agrarian bourgeoisie, developed on commercial-export agricultural production, saw the free market not only as a necessity to dispose of surpluses, but also as the key to its political power.[9] But stronger forces were to articulate the interests of these two fractions of capital.

From 1873 to 1900, capitalist cycles recurred with troughs coming in 1873 to 1878, 1882–1885, and 1893 to 1897. With the exception of the 1882 to 1885 period, agricultural exports were crucial to recovery, not only for farmers, but also for economy. For example, export earnings from crude foodstuffs increased from 79 million in 1865 to 94 million in 1876. They grew to 155 million in 1877, 226 million in 1880 and 242 million in 1881. At the same time, income from processed foodstuffs sold in foreign markets went from 110 million in 1875 to 226 million by 1881.[10]

The primary cause of this boom was a five-year period of poor health and disease that sharply curtailed the output of European agriculture. However, it should be noted that the U.S. agricultural producers and processors were able to increase production rapidly, partly because the structure of agricultural export production was based on large land holdings. This response capacity deeply affected the thinking of the U.S. bourgeoisie and political regimes that were able to express their interests through the State. One conclusion drawn from this experience was that the agricultural capitalists, rather than industrialists, were responsible for the famous turn of the trade balance.[11] The effect was to extend and deepen the orientation toward the conquest of overseas markets as a crucial element in the reproduction of capital in general. Such thinking was reflected in the editorial of *Broadstreet* on January 18, 1884: "It is clear that much the most important factor in maintaining the commercial prosperity of the United States during the recent past has been its agricultural industry. It is further clear that if the commercial prosperity of the country is to be maintained in the future, it must continue to find abroad a market for its surplus agricultural products."

These beliefs were reinforced during the depression of 1882–1885. Overproduction of wheat in the United States, coupled with good crop years in Europe, reduced the potential for agriculture to tip the balance of trade in favor of the U.S. and to transfer surpluses from agriculture to other sectors of the economy. Consequently, the 1880's brought about one of the most intense periods of class struggle in U.S. history. The process leading to this period of struggle in which classes tested their capacity to organize is part and parcel of capitalist development: concentration and centralization of capital. Between 1880 and 1884 business failures tripled to 12,000 annually. These businesses were absorbed by big capitalists. The process was aptly described by Andrew Carnegie, "So many of my friends needed money that they begged me to repay them. I did so and bought out five or six of them. That was to give me my leading interest in the steel business."[12]

The problem was even greater in agriculture. With the tremendous effort in frontier settlement between 1855 and 1885 and increased farm mechanization, production soared above world market needs. The result was a sharp decline in prices. Declining prices stimulated overcultivation to increase production, even under the conditions of falling prices, to repay loans and maintain controlling the land. This obvious contradiction not only exhausted the soil but also meant that many small producers could not even meet subsistence needs. The result was a mass exodus from agriculture and a search for jobs in the industrial sector.[13]

However, the industrial sector was also suffering a crisis stemming from overproduction. At the same time, the U.S. railroad system was reaching completion and some 200,000 railroad workers were also looking for jobs.[14] These conditions led to workers organizing to protect their interests. The major events in this struggle were the railway strike of 1877, the Chicago Haymarket Affair of 1886, the Pullman strike of 1894 and Coxey's march of the unemployed upon Washington. Madison's prediction that class war would follow the closing of the frontier seemed to be coming true.

Faced with an increasing capacity of the proletariat to organize and to threaten the accumulation process, the bourgeoisie sought a class alliance with the petty bourgeoisie comprised of independent agricultural producers who had survived the downward price cycle in the Midwest as well as the urban petty bourgeoisie.[15] The open class conflict forced this class alliance to establish a clear cut policy of informal but carefully planned economic domination in Asia and Latin America while maintaining the European market. The Monroe Doctrine would declare Latin America off-limits to European capital and an improved merchant fleet would penetrate Asia with U.S. commodities. Alaska would now be developed into Seward's "drawbridge to Asia." And within the process the productive capacity of U.S. agriculture would play a critical role in conquering new markets and become a weapon to keep hungry nations aligned with U.S. capital. Presumably such action would avoid class struggle at home.[16]

THE STRUGGLE TO RESTRUCTURE CAPITAL: 1900–1940

The beginning of the twentieth century found the United States development pattern in disarray. No significant class alliances or popular mobilizations were promulgating new plans for accumulation that could temporarily resolve the contradictions of overproduction on the one hand and the changing composition of capital induced by technological advances on the other. The processes that defined these contradictions were 1) the concentration and centralization of capital, 2) the reluctance on the part of individual capitalists to move from absolute to relative surplus value extraction, 3) an ideological structure that insisted on a free market economy which severely constrained state intervention in the accumulation process, and 4) increased capacity for labor to organize for struggle to improve working conditions and demand a higher social component of the wage bill to capital. These conditions interacted to present capital with declining rates of profit. All the conditions were present to demand a major restructuring of capital, but there was no coherent ideological justification to buttress this restructuring and no organizational capacity to actually do it. The seeds for a rather long term crisis of hegemony were planted and would not be resolved until the Great Depression and the imposition of the New Deal.

Concentration and Centralization of Capital

This process was based largely on speculative capital seeking windfall profits that could be captured by a few capitalists and reinvested in constant capital. During the mid-Nineteenth Century, key inventions centering on steel, railroad and steamship transportation, agricultural machinery and chemicals had occurred.[17] Even before the full impact of these inventions could be incorporated into new production processes, another wave in the early part of the Twentieth Century brought about further adjustments. These were electrical power, automobiles and the gasoline engine.

An example of the rapid growth and development of these technologies can be demonstrated by the case of the internal combustion engine. In 1873, the most powerful engine could generate 35 horsepower. By 1900, the Paris Exposition included an engine that could generate 1000 horsepower. In the same year, there were 18,500 internal combustion engines in the United States.[18] Of course, the most dramatic effect of the internal combustion engine was the development of the automobile industry. In 1905, there were 121 establishments making cars with about 10,000 wage earners. By 1923, there were 2,471 plants. Similar growth occurred in farm machinery even though wide-scale use of tractors was delayed until the 1940's.

This emphasis on technological growth should not be interpreted as a narrow technological determinist argument. Rather, these technologies provided the basis for a new wave of uneven development wherein small fractions of capital were controlling large industries which gave them a competitive edge. The result was an acceleration in the process of concentration and centralization of capital. In brief, monopoly capitalism was ushered in as the predominant feature of the next stage of capitalist development in the U.S.

The Struggle for Ideological Hegemony

Concentration and centralization of capital had a contradictory impact on the role of the state in accumulation. Most popular classes and the competitive fraction of the capitalist class subscribed to the notion of Jeffersonian democracy. But how could a large number of independent producers be maintained in the face of concentration and centralization of capital? The state would have to intervene. But this intervention was highly circumscribed. The state was not to control effective demand but guard against monopoly. State intervention took the form of trust busting while continuing to repress labor's demands. Thus, effective control over monopoly capital was restricted in such a fashion that concentration was enhanced while centralization was slowed down. This provided the basis for even greater growth in speculative capital. This contradiction reached full expression with the 1929 crisis.

However, monopoly capitalists were beginning to develop their own ideas about how the accumulation process should be changed. Labor struggles in the 1890's pointed toward the need to move from absolute to relative surplus value. Absolute surplus value extraction was based on cheap immigrant labor that was prohibited from organizing to protect workers' interests. This prohibition was reproduced by 1) perpetuating ethnic and linguistic differences which divided the working class, and 2) brutal repression.[19] Monopoly capital's own interests and labor's capacity to struggle would usher in the transition to relative surplus value extraction and the welfare state.

Events such as the Pullman Strike and the Haymarket Riots signalled that workers were willing to face brutal repression to establish a basis for changing the capital-labor relationship for future generations. A group of intellectuals largely centered around the University of Chicago and closely allied with monopoly capital began to forge a new set of ideas that were eventually to coalesce into an ideological hegemony that would be known as corporate liberalism.[20] But it would take a world-wide capitalist crisis to effectively implant this new plan for accumulation and monopoly capital's project for capitalist development.

Labor's Capacity to Struggle

The formation of the working class in the United States was, in some respects, unlike the British experience, where the working class was formed via primitive accumulation internal to Great Britain, the U.S. working class was formed by attracting immigrant workers. Many independent agricultural producers have also been stripped of their means of production since the 1880's. This has contributed to the growth of the working class—not to its formation. The latter was more a result of open door immigration, brutal repression, and deliberate maintenance of social, political and economic rivalry between ethnic groups.[21] The manner in which the working class was formed in the United States made it more vulnerable. It was subject to economic sanction because every boat that docked at Ellis-Island added to the pool of unemployed immigrants. It was easier to repress because of ethnic and social discrimination and uncertain citizenship status. Under these circumstances, it was relatively easy to break strikes.

However, using ethnic differences and police brutality as a means of controlling the working class cut both ways. While such tactics were effective in the shortrun, they highlighted the antagonism between capital and labor.

It is important to recall that, until 1935 workers had no legal right to organize. Consequently, it was a serious matter to form a union and call a strike. It was open warfare and everyone recognized it as such. Victories for the working class came as a result of workers' capacity to make a greater show of power. These shows of power are recognized as key events in U.S. history: 1) the B&O railroad strike (1877); 2) Homestead (1892); 3) Pullman (1894); 4) Cripple Creek (1903); 5) Lawrence (1912); 6) Ludlow (1914); and 7) the Seattle general strike (1919).[22]

The working class made significant gains from 1890 to 1926 as shown in Tables 1 and 2. However, industrial unionism was not established in the United States until the 1930's. In one year, 1934, three major events shaped the future of union struggles. These were the Teamsters Local 574 strike in Minneapolis, the Toledo Auto-Lite strike, and the "West Coast Longshore Strike."[23] The CIO grew out of these three critical events. Labor's capacity to struggle and the New Deal ushered in the ideological hegemony of corporate liberalism.

The "Great Depression"

The neo-classical explanation of what causes depression centers on the rate of capital formation. If saving is essential for investment, investment is essential for prosperity. But the key to understanding investment is the rate of profit perceived by individual capitalists. A recurring overproduction crisis had depressed the rate of profit in key sectors such as agriculture and heavy industry. Thus, investment in the 1920's was speculative. More importantly, much of this speculative investment was based more on a shaky credit structure rather than on production.

Table 1.   Length of the Working Day and Wages in the Manufacturing Sector,
           1890-1926

Year	Total Hr/Wk	Total Wg/Hr	Union Hr/Wk	Union Wg/Hr	Non-Union Hr/Wk	Non-Union Wg/Hr	Farm Workers Wg/Day
1890	60.0	.199	54.4	.324	62.2	.149	0.95
1900	59.0	.316	53.0	.341	62.1	.152	1.00
1910	56.6	.260	50.1	.403	59.8	.188	1.35
1920	51.0	.663	45.7	.884	53.5	.561	3.30
1926	50.3	.647	45.9	1.007	52.2	.488	2.40

Source: Historical Statistics of U.S.: Colonial Times to 1957, U.S. Bureau of
          Census

Table 2.   Labor Union Membership, 1897-1926

Year	Members (1,000)
1897	440
1900	791
1910	2,116
1920	5,034
1926	3,592

Source: See Table 1.

The crash of speculative investment might not have been so disastrous
if the production oriented sectors of the economy had been healthy,
but they were not. One such sector was agriculture. Between 1910 and
1920, while nonfarm output per worker rose by nearly 20 percent,
output per farm worker actually fell.[24] Part of this fall in productivity
was due to natural disasters (especially droughts). Another part was
due to lack of attention to farming production systems and a disregard
for the preservation and conservation of resources. Also, the farming
sector was still highly competitive and was faced with a market structure
for its commodities that rested on an existing distribution of wealth
and income. When food prices fell, the wealthy didn't eat more and the
poor couldn't buy more. Thus increases in output resulted in lower
prices rather than larger cash receipts for the direct producer—the farmer.

This was an example of the basic contradiction that occurs when a
competitive sector is faced with a given distribution of resources that
state policy cannot or will not alter. When the price for farm commodities
started to fall, the individual farmer had no choice but to produce and
sell more to maintain family income and pay debts. This resulted in

aggregate overproduction which further depressed prices. The option for the individual farmer was to produce even more or get out of farming. Many did get out of farming, but where did they go?

They didn't go to manufacturing and mining because even though productivity was increasing in these sectors, employment was not. The organic composition of capital in these sectors had been changing rapidly due to the introduction of labor-displacing technology. Employment increases had been registered in the service sectors: construction; trade and finance and government. But these sectors were heavily affected by the scramble for credit and the crash of speculative capitalist growth.

Not only had the primary sectors of the economy been displacing labor but the workers who remained had also been forced to accept steady or declining real hourly wages.[25] Thus, income distribution was becoming more skewed and this further stressed relations between capital and labor.

Restructuring Capital and Corporate Liberalism

Many argue that the New Deal was nothing more than a hodge-podge of discrete government policies that produced a kind of governmental alphabet soup: NIRA; TVA; AAA; CCC; FERA; FMA; FLSA; etc. In fact it was a basic change. The state could now legitimately intervene in different ways to control accumulation crises.

One important component of this change was the Agricultural Adjustment Act. The effect of the AAA was to permit the state to manage one of the fundamental contradictions of competitive capitalism—increasing production during an overproduction crisis. This was accomplished by paying farmers to curtail acreage and numbers of livestock. Shortrun successes were impressive. In both 1934 and 1935, over 30 million acres of land were taken out of production. As a result, farm income rose from $2.5 billion in 1932 to $5 billion in 1936.

In the industrial sector, the basic thrust of state intervention was to alter the structure of markets. By the time the NIRA was declared unconstitutional, it was already clear that it was not working. The specifics of state intervention then changed, but the general idea remained—it was now legitimate for the state to intervene to ensure the orderly operation of the system. "Social engineering" became the buzz words of state agencies.

By 1939, all indications were that the economy had failed to respond to the packages of New Deal programs. Even though the public debt had risen to $40 billion, which had helped to stimulate consumption expenditures, capital expenditures were still 40 percent below 1929 levels.[26] It is unclear, and historically irrelevant, what the state might have tried next to restructure capital. World War II stopped the theoretical debate about the relative merits of increased state outlays versus a balanced federal budget.

A major consequence of World War II was a new period of capital accumulation: 1945–1980. To explain what makes this period unique, we will first enumerate the major effects of World War II.

1. Government spending soared to a level ($100 billion in 1944) that would not previously have been tolerated by the body politic.
2. Increased government spending was accompanied by unprecedented growth in GNP.
3. Public debt rose to $250 billion in 1945 which showed that the state could sustain a large deficit if accompanied by growing GNP.
4. The destruction of productive capacity in Europe and the immigration of scientists gave the United States an unprecedented monopoly on technology.
5. The decimation of armed forces in Europe and monopoly on atomic weapons gave the U.S. virtually absolute hegemony throughout the non-socialist world. This was true not only with respect to military might, but also with respect to money markets via the internationalization of the U.S. dollar as a medium of exchange and the IMF and World Bank as control mechanisms.
6. The power gained by organized labor in the 1930's was curtailed by emergency war restrictions on strikes and wage increases. Labor lost its initiative and entered into a pact with the Democratic Party that required it to restrain its challenge to basic tenets of capitalism.
7. Agriculture was mechanized because of labor shortages and high demand for food to support the war effort.
8. There was no longer any question about state intervention in the economy. After 1945, state intervention was taken for granted. The question was no longer whether, but how the state would intervene in the process of accumulation.

U.S. HEGEMONY, ITS DECLINE, AND
AGRICULTURAL PRODUCTION SYSTEMS: 1945–1980

The 1945–1980 period was characterized by warfare and deficit spending. As sole contractor for arms buildup to win the Cold War the state gained the unquestioned responsibility to supply capital and manage demand in the name of "national security."

Two mechanisms that were developed to pursue warfare and deficit spending should be highlighted. The first was the cost-plus-fixed-fee contracts. This type of contracting permitted companies to transfer all research and development costs to the state. Second, the state had constructed $17 billion worth of new plant capacity during World War II. At war's end, the state had accumulated about $50 billion in surplus property. The 250 largest manufacturing companies controlled the bulk of these assets. The state sold these assets *to these same companies* at less than one-quarter of their original costs. This enabled these firms to consolidate their oligopolistic position. Thus ideological hegemony was wedded with economic control in a way that allowed monopoly capital to rely on the state to maintain enough effective demand to minimize destabilizing economic crises.[27]

Finally, this period is defined by an unanticipated consequence of warfare and deficit spending that is part of the explanation of current crises. The tremendous increase in deficit spending at all levels of the state required the federal government to compete with the corporate sector and consumers of money. In 1975–76 federal borrowing ate up two-fifths of the nation's total credit market. This tremendous need for credit by the Federal government was occurring precisely at the time that personal borrowing had been encouraged to maintain high consumption levels. By 1975 consumer installment debt amounted to 13 percent of personal income and four-fifths of all consumers were now in debt. This aggregate demand for credit pushed interest rates higher and higher.

World Hegemony, Capital Mobility, and Corporate Liberalism

As capital became concentrated and centralized in the United States, the *laissez-faire* ideology produced by competitive capitalism was no longer adequate to the needs of capital. Capitalism, in all of its phases, must exercise control over labor power, the labor process and resources. Monopoly capitalism must assure this control as well as develop efficient management and marketing systems.[28] To accomplish these new dimensions of control, a more interventionist state was required. The process of creating such a state required power not only in the economic structure but also in the political and ideological spheres.

The generation of support for a more interventionist state involved the articulation and promulgation of a set of ideas which justified certain forms of intervention and ruled out others. This set of ideas emerged as corporate liberalism.

One of the fascinating features of the promulgation of a corporate liberal ideology is that the reforms that were contemplated were originally inspired by "those at or near the bottom of the American social structure" but the actual policies instituted were shaped by capitalists associated with large corporations.[29] The purpose of this ideology was to reshape the state so that it could more appropriately respond to the new needs of the monopoly sector *while deflecting working class dissent.* One of the key concepts embodied in corporate liberal ideology is "responsibility." Responsibility has two dimensions: 1) society should support individuals and underprivileged social classes; and 2) all classes should support, maintain and increase the efficiency of the existing social order. This notion of responsibility allows participation in decision-making for all who have: 1) knowledge of the overall dimensions of the problem (anti-localism—centralization of power); 2) technical competence to deal with the problem (elitism—social engineering); and 3) a commitment not to question the extant social order (trade union pact with capital).[30]

The second critical dimension of corporate liberalism is capital mobility. Capital should have the right to invest wherever profit rates are high. Given that capitalists are "responsible," a reasonable return to labor is assured through collective bargaining. This notion had two effects: 1) it popularized and mystified U.S. imperialism; and 2) ascribed to the state the role of supporting capital accumulation on a global scale via investments in transportation, education, business subsidies, and military might without at the same time telling capitalists where to invest.[31] One indication of the state's growing role in supporting capital accumulation is the increasing proportion of government spending as percent of GNP, climbing from less than 10 percent until 1930 to over 30 percent in the 1970's.[32]

While the roots of corporate liberalism date from the working class struggles of 1890 to 1930 and the centralization of capital that occurred during the same period, it came into full bloom after World War II when the United States clearly could and did police the world to ensure capital mobility.[33] This plan for supporting accumulation on a world scale was strained by the need to rebuild war-devastated capitalist economies[34] and by the challenges of socialist successes. It was at this point that corporate liberalism developed its anti-communist dimension into Cold War policies.[35]

The specifics of state intervention under corporate liberalism has varied from country to country and over time but it has essentially turned around the following notions:

1. The state must help dispose of surplus.
2. As competition increases with the internationalization of capital, the state must continuously mobilize for war to guarantee capital mobility. This also helps dispose of surplus.
3. The state must ameliorate social demands that grow out of poverty and insecurity. This has been a key feature of U.S. welfare policies.
4. The state must provide a growing number of services for both rural and urban populations.[36]

For the purpose of this analysis it is interesting to note that the first large integrated corporations that emerged in the United States dealt with food processing and distribution. Indeed, the prototype vertically linked coporation and its attendant management system was created by Gustavus Swift in 1870 in meat packing which involved manufacturing, shipping and marketing. Andrew Preston began dealing in bananas in 1890; his creation became the United Fruit Company. McCormick's vast agricultural machinery enterprise was built on his own worldwide marketing and distribution organization. Not only did these ventures require new forms of control that had to be guaranteed by the state, they also altered the nature of agricultural production systems.[37]

Some Characteristics of Agricultural Production

While these overall changes were occurring, the nature of agricultural production was also being redefined. As indicated earlier, large sectors of agriculture were slow to incorporate new technology into their production processes before 1930. This was particularly true of mechanization and soil conservation management. Table 3 compares the use of commercial fertilizer with mechanization from 1850 to 1950. Commercial fertilizer use was already widely diffused by 1920 but mechanization's big jump occurred from 1940 to 1950. Two other key changes occurred in the 1930's. These were cross-breeding in hogs and hybridization of corn, both of which yielded large gains in productivity. These new production processes made food cheaper for urban consumers and reduced labor requirements in agricultural production systems. This process released labor for warfare, industrialization and growth in the services sector. Tables 4, 5 and 6 document these changes.

The Current Structure of U.S. Agriculture

One of the most persistent myths about U.S. agriculture is that most farm products and commodities are produced by family units. The family farm concept is so strongly imbedded in U.S. ideology that U.S. AID and other international development agencies, citing productivity as evidence, have attempted to export the family farm form of production to Third World countries as a solution to their food production problems.[38]

As indicated earlier, the leading sectors of U.S. export agriculture have been largely controlled by large production units closely aligned with industrial capital. At the same time, land settlement programs created a large number of small production units and established the family farm as a major farming system. But there has been a pattern of concentration and centralization in U.S. agriculture and it has not been even. The production of some agricultural products remains largely confined to rather small production units. But by 1970, 100 percent of

Table 3. The Use of Commercial Fertilizer and Farm Machinery, 1850-1950

Year	Tons of Commercial Fert. (1,000)	Tractors (1,000)	Combines (1,000)	Milking Machines (1,000)
1850	5.3	--	--	--
1860	164.0	--	--	--
1870	321.0	--	--	--
1880	753.0	--	--	--
1890	1,390.0	--	--	--
1900	2,730.0	--	--	--
1910	5,547.0	1	1	12
1920	7,176.0	246	4	55
1930	8,171.0	920	61	100
1940	8,336.0	1,545	190	175
1950	10,316.0	3,394	714	636

Source: See Table 1.

Table 4. Average Amount of Net Family Income Spent on Food and Other Items, 1967

Expenditure	United States	E.E.C.	Japan
Food	19.0*	31.5	37.8
Clothing	9.2	11.1	11.9
Rent	14.2	9.6	8.6
Durables	11.7	9.8	Included in other
Other	45.9	38.0	41.7

*By 1971, this figure had dropped to 16%; by 1977, it was back to 19%.

Source: See Table 1.

the sugar cane and sugar beets, 97 percent of the broilers, 95 percent of the processing vegetables, 85 percent of the citrus fruits, 70 percent of the potatoes, 54 percent of the turkeys, and 40 percent of the eggs were produced under contracts or integration.[39]

On the other hand, the predominance of grain and general farming, including dairy and hog production, which, at the production level tend to be family operated units, places the North Central States in a distinctive position. The individual farm producers still have some range of decision-making regarding production and marketing. However, the tendency is toward monopoly control of processing and marketing as well as production. Table 7 shows the national pattern of farm organization for 1969.

As can be seen from Table 7, the family farm still appears to be alive and well. However, we should note some important aspects of

Table 5. Employment and Value Added in Agriculture, Selected Countries, 1967

Country	Percent of active labor force employed in agriculture	Number of workers employed per 1,000 hectares of arable land and land under permanent	Value added per worker in agriculture (dollars)	Value added per hectare of arable land and land under permanent crops (dollars)
Turkey	71.0	36.4	330	120
Spain	29.4	17.5	990	170
Denmark	16.6	13.7	2,780	380
Netherlands	8.3	39.7	4,010	1,590
West Germany	10.6	33.5	1,830	620
France	16.6	16.7	2,220	370
Italy	24.1	29.9	1,600	480
Sweden	10.0	12.2	2,020	660
United Kingdom	3.1	10.6	3,180	360
Ireland	30.5	9.0	3,430	400
Canada	9.0	1.5	4,450	80
United States	5.2	2.2	6,350	140
Japan	23.1	199.0	930	1,850

Source: Commission on International Trade and Investment Policy, United States International Economic Policy in an Interdependent World. Washington, D.C.: Government Printing Office, 1971.

Table 6.   Demand for Farm Tractors in the United States

Year	Horsepower (millions)	Man-Hours on Crops (millions)	Cost of Operating and Maintaining Farm Capital (millions of dollars)
1920	5	13,406	n.a.
1950	93	6,922	5,640
1960	154	4,590	8,310
1969	203	3,431	11,500

Source: See Table 1.

the real productive structure of agriculture. First of all, only four percent of the economically active were employed in agriculture in 1974. Second, the family farm myth notwithstanding, recent research shows that the most competitive units in the corn belt control about 5,000 acres. With careful management and the use of available technology, units as small as 1,000 acres can remain competitive. However, for each Corn Belt farmer to acquire 1,000 acres of crop land, about 60 percent of the existing units would have to disappear.[40] And they are disappearing. Table 8 shows scale tendencies in U.S. agriculture. Family farms are also disappearing in another fashion. Many families still own land which they no longer control, and upon which they generate little income.[41]

Those who do produce on the land do so with little labor. The organic composition of capital in U.S. agriculture is tremendously high. For example, in 1967, the value added per hectare of arable land in the United States was $140 while the number of workers employed per 1,000 hectares of arable land was 2.2. That is, $140,000 of value added per 1,000 hectares is produced by 2.2 workers coupled with advanced production technology. Moreover, the productivity per worker is increasing about five percent per year.[42]

This degree of incorporation of machinery into the production process of most farming systems requires heavy investments and incurs high energy costs. Each production cycle requires large advances of money without any return for at least 6 months. In 1975, for example, $82 had to be advanced for each acre tilled. Yet that same year, aggregate net farm earnings were −$6.4 billion. Where did the money come from to start the production cycle? From nonfarm earnings and loans.[43] The small farm unit faces increasing production costs and steady or falling prices which severely restricts its range of decision and creates the objective conditions for yielding control over production through contracts with buyers or credit arrangements with banks and other lending institutions.

Table 7. Percentage of Farms by Type of Organization, 1969

Type of Organization	Percentage of All Farms
Individual or family	85.4
Partnership	12.8
Corporation	
10 or fewer shareholders	1.1
More than 10 shareholders	0.1
Other	0.6
Total	100.0

Source: U.S. Census of Agriculture, 1969.

Table 8. Tendency to Concentrate Agricultural Production from 1929 to 1969
(all values adjusted to 1964 constant)

1964 Census* Class	Percent Total Number			Percent Total Sales		
	1929	1964	1969	1929	1964	1969
1 and 2	1.2	12.7	20.2	14.9	64.4	75.8
3	2.7	14.8	14.5		19.2	14.9
4	7.9	16.0	14.3	17.9	10.6	5.4
5	23.8	14.1	16.7	30.0	4.7	1.9
6	64.4	42.5	34.3	24.8	1.1	2.0

*
Census Class 1 is $40,000 annual sales or more; Census Class 2 is $20.000
to $39,000; Census Class 3 is $10,000 to $19,999; Census Class 4 is $5,000 to
$9,999; Census Class 5 is $2,000 to $4,999; Census Class 6 is less than $2,000
annual sales.

Source: See Table 7.

The corporate structure of the U.S. food industry completes the picture
of the food and fiber production structure. The U.S. food industry is a
$250-billion-a-year industry, bigger than automobiles, steel, oil or even
the defense establishment. Forces in the food industry have already
accumulated the power of shared monopolies and are controlling growth
points to such an degree that they can strip small producers of their
means of production and establish monopoly control in the production
of food and fiber. Two companies share the production of soup, four
control the cereal shelves and one company is dominant in cheese.

A witness at a Senate hearing on corporate control of agriculture
presented the following graphic description about a Thanksgiving dinner

in the United States. "The Smithfield ham comes from ITT, the turkey is a product of Greyhound Corporation, the potatoes are provided by the Boeing Company, and Tenneco brought the fresh fruits and vegetables. The applesauce is made available by American Brands, while Coca-Cola and Royal Crown Cola have provided the fruit juices."[44]

The essence of corporate control of food can be seen in the state of California because of its unique position in controlling crop production. The market value of crops in California is over $17 billion per year. California grows 70 percent of the country's lettuce and is the only significant source in some seasons. United Brands controls the distribution and production of lettuce in California. California produces 65 percent of the tomatoes and 67 percent of the late spring potatoes. This commodity area is also dominated by United Brands. California supplies 92 percent of the table grapes consumed in the United States. Tenneco controls table grape production in California. The list goes on, but the point is clear. Certain food production and most processing in the United States is shaped and regulated by U.S.-based multi-national corporations.[45]

The manner in which food production is controlled varies. One form of control is the cost-price squeeze. Another is concentration of firms on the input supply side. Still another is concentration on the output side. The independent producer confronts markets virtually controlled by food processors and supermarket chains. Finally there is the control over production itself via contracts or direct ownership. Each of these areas will be briefly treated.

In the period 1967–1979, cost of fertilizer increased 80 percent, gasoline costs increased 300 percent, machinery and equipment costs increased 120 percent and pesticide costs went up 250 percent.[46] In all of these areas, monopoly control is present. It is estimated that in 1972, farmers were paying $251.1 million in monopoly rents brought because prices were being set above value.[47] Economic concentration among input suppliers is a major cause of the rising production costs which have forced marginal farmers out of business.

In 1979, for each dollar the consumer spent on food, 32 cents went to the farm producer and 68 cents to all others in the food production chain.[48] However, these "all others" may not be many. In 1979, 44 companies received 68 percent of all food processing revenues and 44 companies accounted for all wholesale and retail food distribution revenues.[49] But in cereal grains, dairy products, bakery products, meat, canned goods, beer, fruits and nuts, fewer than 10 companies receive more than 80 percent of the revenues. The economic concentration among food processors and distributors has enabled them to exert substantial control over the prices received by farmers thus setting the "price" element of the cost-price squeeze.[50]

The image of U.S. agriculture that emerges so far is that of a large number of independent producers sandwiched between a monopoly-controlled input sector and a monopoly-controlled output sector. However, concentration is taking place at the level of farm production itself. In 1970, 17 percent of U.S. food production was controlled by vertically integrated or coordinated corporations[51] via contracts. In 1975, this figure had risen to 25 percent, in 1980 contracts accounted for 50 percent of all food production and the estimate for 1985 is 75 percent.[52] In some areas of agriculture the tendency is to directly own the means of production in agriculture, but no data on actual ownership are readily available. However, we do know that in significant commodity groups the largest 10 percent of the farms control 50 percent or more of production. These commodity groups are eggs, feeder cattle, potatoes, vegetables, oranges, peaches, turkeys, apples, and broilers.[53] These commodities have two characteristics: 1) they are grown in areas where many of the biological conditions of production can be controlled; and 2) they are produced on farms owned by major monopoly corporations.[54]

The potential for large profits in the food industry is a sufficient explanation for multinational corporate penetration. However, other factors may be at work. As indicated earlier, U.S. industry developed through protection from imports. Also, industrial labor's capacity to demand better wage and work conditions assisted in pushing up the wages in U.S. industry so that the U.S. worker has enjoyed a higher real wage than his/her European counterpart. U.S. capitalist industry was able to absorb these higher wages because it was virtually isolated from international competition. This, of course, is no longer the case, yet the higher wages paid to workers and high transfer payments by the state have, until recently, been the tendency in the U.S. industrial development pattern. This has been possible because of a tremendous growth of productive forces stimulated by war production under conditions of labor scarcity since workers have been conscripted for the armed services. Until recently the United States has enjoyed a monopoly control over the technological component of the development of productive forces. However, with monopoly capitalism and the need to find investment outlets for surplus capital, the U.S. has stumbled into a logical contradiction between monopoly capitalism and productivity monopoly. The productivity monopoly created the basis for concentration of capital in the United States. This capital could not be absorbed in the U.S. alone, thus the heavy investment in the industrial sector of other center countries. The very trend of massive capital export diffuses U.S. technology on a world scale, thus tending toward equalization of technological levels among the center countries. Thus, the technological advantage of U.S. industry has virtually disappeared in sectors such as

Table 9.   Labor Productivity in Different Sectors of the U.S. Economy, 1968

Industry or Type of Farming	Labor Productivity[*]
Manufactured tobacco	$ 8.19
Transportation equipment	7.52
Chemicals and allied products	6.88
All services, finance, insurance	6.37
Communication and utilities	6.00
Instruments and related products	5.85
Primary metals	5.61
Construction	5.60
Wheat farming, Washington, Oregon	5.53
Cash grain farming (corn and soybeans)	5.42
Machinery (except electrical)	5.28
Printing and publishing	5.08
All manufacturing	5.07
All mining and extractive	5.04
Average, entire U.S. economy	5.02
All farming	2.96
Electrical equipment	4.81
Manufactured foods	4.53

[*] Total national income by sector divided by total man-hours worked by persons employed in the sector.

Source: Commission on International Trade and Investment Policy, United
States International Economic Policy in an Interdependent World.
Washington, D.C.: Government Printing Ofice, 1971, p. 848.

steel, automobiles, electrical appliances, textiles, furniture, and certain types of industrial machinery. But certain agricultural commodities enjoy high labor productivity and are still highly competitive in world markets. Table 9 shows the productivity of labor by sectors of the U.S. economy.

Such a circumstance sets up two clear needs of U.S. imperialism. One is to attack the wage levels of U.S. workers, and indeed real wages have started to decline in the United States.[55] Secondly, the "comparative advantage" the U.S. enjoys in food production can be used as a weapon to maintain markets for industrial commodities by tying food exports to market protection plans and by encouraging an international division of labor that reduces competition with U.S. food production.

State Policy and Food as a Political Weapon

Earlier, four principal requirements of state intervention under monopoly capitalism were stated: 1) disposal of surplus; 2) military mobilization; 3) amelioration of social demands; and 4) provision of services that private capital can't or won't develop. In agriculture, the state has consistently tried to dispose of agricultural surplus through market signals rather than production controls.[56] While some market signals can act back on production, this has rarely been the case except for the marginal farmer. Indeed, one consequence of state's intervention in U.S. agriculture has been the elimination of the marginal farmer.

A second major feature of state intervention has been its tendency toward welfare rather than income redistribution. Agricultural surplus has assisted state intervention in welfare for urban sectors by providing surplus commodities that are doled out via food stamp programs.

Finally, services to agriculture have taken several forms: 1) vocational education; 2) the Land Grant Educational System and its attendant focus on new agricultural technology production via the Hatch Act and its diffusion via the Cooperative Extension Service; 3) the development of farm to market roads; and 4) rural electrification.

One major consequence of this type of state intervention has been to reproduce the chronic overproduction crisis of U.S. agriculture. And one of the major solutions to this problem, as in the 19th Century, has been the opening and/or expansion of foreign markets. Food has come to be a major component of United States foreign policy.

The declarations of government officials in the 1970's was very similar to the proclamations of their predecessors in the 1880's. Earl Butz, Secretary of Agriculture, declared, "Agriculture has now become our number one source of foreign exchange and it's a powerful factor in maintaining the economic health of this country."[57] Or as Hubert Humphrey declared in April 1974, "Food is power. And in a very real sense it's our extra measure of power. It may be the only thing that we have in greater abundance and in the ability to produce beyond anyone else."[58]

But if food is power, the United States must establish and control foreign markets since agriculture has suffered the chronic problem of overproduction for more than a century. Of course, World Wars I and II and the Korean War provided some relief from the overproduction problem, but during the 1950's and 1960's overproduction tendency was evident. The initial response to the potential crisis in agriculture was for the state to subsidize U.S. farmers rather than to make a frontal assault on world markets. The subsidies were of two major types: 1) paying farmers not to produce; and 2) guaranteed prices for cereals. If the farmer could not obtain a higher price than the government support price, the state would purchase the grain and store it. Similar parity prices were set for milk, milk products and eggs but these costs were usually passed on to the consumer. Government storage of corn, wheat, and soybeans reached gigantic proportions by the middle 1950s. The costs of this program began to impinge on the general process of capital accumulation and reawakened the conflict between different fractions of capital. Moreover, the capacity of the working class to further its immediate interests via higher real wages was increasing. This was a clear signal of a coming crisis. Since the working class spends a significant portion of its income on food, and since its food costs were rising because of monopoly pricing, demands for higher wages were inevitable. Meeting these demands added to the cost of state intervention.

However, an ingenious solution was found in Public Law 480. The importance of P.L. 480 for furthering accumulation was evident. It not only allowed the state to rid itself of stored food, but also increased the indebtedness of other countries and opened new markets for private capital, thus working against the overproduction tendency. Table 10 indicates just how successful P.L. 480 was in establishing new markets. Between 1954 (when P.L. 480 was enacted) and 1970 non-P.L. 480 exports increased from 2.3 billion to 5.6 billion.

The fact that food could be used as a weapon was not overlooked. As Senator Hubert Humphrey observed while arguing for passage of the bill, "I have heard . . . that people may become dependent on us for food. I know that was not supposed to be good news. To me that was good news, because before people can do anything, they have got to eat. And if you are looking for a way to get people to lean on you and to be dependent on you, in terms of their cooperation with you, it seems to me that food dependence would be terrific."[59] But to maintain this dependence, foreign policy had to take new directions.

While the U.S. was conquering new markets in Asia, Africa and Latin America via its P.L. 480 exports and accumulating foreign currencies as payment for the exports (which were loaned to U.S. based multi-nationals in food production to establish foreign-based firms),[60] it was also stimulating production of food crops in the Third World. The general outlines of this contradiction were clearly expressed in the papers submitted to the Commission on International Trade and Investment Policy.

Table 10.   Growth of U.S. Agricultural Exports and the P.L. 480 Program
(millions of dollars)

Year	Total Exports	Commercial Sales	Government Program
1951	3,411	2,215	1,196
1952	4,053	3,430	623
1953	2,819	2,369	450
1954	2,936	2,331	605
1955	3,144	2,309	835
1956	3,496	2,157	1,339
1957	4,728	2,809	1,919
1958	4,003	2,794	1,209
1959	3,719	2,492	1,227
1960	4,628	3,345	1,283
1961	4,946	3,443	1,503
1962	5,142	3,572	1,570
1963	5,078	3,612	1,466
1964	6,068	4,627	1,441
1965	6,097	4,499	1,598
1966	6,676	5,288	1,388
1967	6,771	5,463	1,308
1968	6,313	5,015	1,298
1969	5,741	4,697	1,044
1970	6,646	5,666	988

Source: See Table 5.

The other major recent change in world production affecting U.S. export interests is the technological breakthrough to high yielding varieties of rice and wheat adapted to some of the less developed countries. As a result the world food situation . . . has materially improved and has caused a substantial decline in U.S. concessional sales. . . . This situation provides a major policy dilemma for the industrial countries. We have invested heavily in foreign aid and technical assistance to improve economic conditions in poor countries. Having been successful, in part at least, we now find these countries saying

(1) that they want special or favored access to the rich markets of the industrial countries and (2) that we should not take policy action that will make it more difficult to sell their products on world markets in competition to ours.[61]

The technological advances were stimulated by a series of international centers of agricultural productivity research such as the International Center for Improvement of Maize and Wheat (CMMYT) located in Mexico and financed by USAID, the Rockefeller Foundation, and the Ford Foundation. This center has produced a number of new wheat and corn varieties adoptable to almost all of Latin America.[62] Yet these varieties have never been successfully diffused throughout Latin America. Part of the lack of diffusion is explained by the variety of production systems in agriculture and peasant relations of production.[63] But it is also accounted for by U.S. policy with regard to protecting markets and U.S. accumulation under the guise of "comparative advantage." The comparative advantage the Commission had in mind was not one due to natural conditions of production but one that grew out of an international division of labor that favored the U.S. The aforementioned Commission report was clear on this point. Third World countries should rely on their cheap labor to produce labor intensive crops, such as fruits, vegetables and sugar for export and thus earn money to import U.S. grain and beef. Of course, the report failed to mention that world marketing, including packaging and transport, and in some cases production, in Third World countries is controlled by Del Monte, United Brands, Tenneco, Bunge and Borne, and Grace.

To assure that Third World countries conform to this international division of labor, economic control is coupled with political control. This is expressed through conditions of private bank loans, the World Bank, and USAID. An example of this pressure was expressed clearly by a USAID official testifying before the U.S. Senate. "AID has cooperated with the government of Colombia in carrying out a development strategy that encourages a switch from wheat production into crops other than wheat, which can be produced more economically. As a result, Colombia now imports over 85 percent of its wheat requirement."[64]

The imposition of this international division of labor has definite consequences for the relations of production in the Third World. First, the bulk of the Third World agricultural population is involved in grain production: corn, wheat, barley, millets, rice and beans. However, world markets are closed to them and their internal markets are dominated by the U.S. National government policy provides few effective resources to stimulate production on the large number of small units largely exploited through non-capitalist relations of production. Second, fruit, vegetable and sugar production, to be competitive on the world market, requires capitalist relations of production and advanced technology. Thus, it is susceptible to de-nationalization, i.e. it is a logical field for foreign capital to enter. Thus, international capital can seemingly have its cake and eat it too. It assures a market for its surplus agricultural products and establishes an investment outlet for surplus capital. However, this type of development pattern places objective limits on the accumulation process in Third World countries that can be the undoing of the entire international division of labor and break the relationship between accumulation and surplus value.[65]

A CONCLUDING NOTE

The objective of this overview of the history of capitalist development in the United States and of agriculture's contribution to the process is to explicate the nature of state intervention in the accumulation process. Being an historical overview, this paper has focussed on outcomes and makes no pretense that the policy-making process as defined by class struggle has been analyzed. That is a future task. As a research task it will involve several levels of analysis: 1) the level of the mode of production where the capitalist state is defined; 2) the level of political regimes where process and content of class struggle and its consequences for shaping both state policy and its outcomes can be observed; and 3) the level of specific production processes in agriculture (sometimes called commodity foci) where the concrete behaviors that state policy attempts to reproduce or change are defined. To move across these levels and develop a clearer understanding of historical change, it is necessary to have some preliminary understanding of the specifics of the development pattern. This analysis is meant to be a first approximation of an overview of the U.S. development pattern.

This chapter has indicated that since the AAA, the notion of state intervention in agriculture has been widely accepted. Basically, this intervention has taken the form of market signals to decrease overall production in a given commodity line. However, the cause of recurrent overproduction crises in agriculture is the contradiction between these policies and the need of unorganized competitive producers whose individual interests dictate increasing production even in the face of falling prices due to a skewed distribution of income. Can the state resolve this contradiction?

The answer is unclear. Even though acreages have declined, output has soared. For example, between 1940 and 1970, the amount of harvested acreage declined 15 percent but yield per acre increased by more than 70 percent. Only the coupling of P.L. 480 in the 1960's with world food shortages in the 1970's prevented the surplus problem from exposing its real cause: lack of desire to control production within the current political economic framework. And there has never been a serious attempt by the U.S. state to alter income distribution.[66]

Another question is how much longer will the state attempt to reproduce a competitive sector in U.S. agriculture? As we enter the 1980's, U.S. farmers are carrying a tremendously heavy debt burden. As land values begin to even out and interest rates rise, another mass exodus from farming is occurring. During the first quarter of 1982, more than 2,000 farms were being auctioned *each week*. Who is buying these farms? What sort of production systems will these new owners attempt to develop? How will state intervention affect this process? Of course, some will argue that this loss of farms will merely increase efficiency, since it is the poor manager who is selling out. Even so, the above questions are relevant.

Previous sections of this chapter dealt with the role of cheap food in reducing the necessary labor time component of urban wages. For example, in 1950, 22.4 percent of personal income was spent on food; by 1975 only 17 percent was spent on food. In 1981, this percentage had risen to about 24 percent. How high can this percentage go before urban consumers revolt? Can it reach EEC levels (35%) or Japanese levels (40%)? If so, corporate ownership of agricultural production processes may be perceived as highly profitable. What social forces will define these percentages and profits?

All of this points to the need to focus on the capacity of direct agricultural producers to organize to protect their interests and the alliances they will make with other sectors in this struggle. These class struggles and alliances are the key to understanding the nature and consequences of state intervention in U.S. agriculture. Table 11 is an attempt to summarize these points and indicate the broad outlines of change from 1850 to 1980.

NOTES

1. From 1815 to 1860, imports for consumption rose from $106,457,924 to $336,282,485. Total foreign trade increased from $165,599,027 to $687,192,176. During these 45 years in only 12 was a favorable balance of trade recorded. See *Historical Tables of Commerce, Finance, Tonnage and Immigration of the United States.* Washington: Treasury Department, Bureau of Statistics, 1894. Principal imports were clothing, tea, coffee, sugar, hides and skins and steel. Britain and France alone accounted for over 60 percent of the value of merchandise imported. For complete details of the struggle for industrial and financial independence see Edward C. Kirkland, *Industry Comes of Age: Business, Labor and Public Policy, 1860–1897.* Volume VI. *The Economic History of the United States.* New York:

Table 11. Major Historical Tendencies In U.S. Development Pattern

Historical Period	Major Tendencies in Political Economy	Major Struggles for Hegemony	State Policy in Agriculture
1860-1865 (80% of population is rural)	Frontier expansion; industrial growth; Export agriculture; free labor force via immigration; Circulation of commodities.	Industrial capital; Export agriculture; Foreign capital in agriculture; Control of land; Control of labor.	USDA Homestead Act Public invest- ment in trans- portation.
1865-1890 (By 1890, 65% of population is rural)	Prosperity-depression- recovery-recession- prosperity; Immigration provides cheap labor for industry; Facilitate circulation of commodi- ties: Transportation and monetary policy; Closing of the frontier; Ag commodities to con- quer foreign markets.	Industrial sector displays concentra- tion; Finance capital; Foreign interests; Freeholder: tenants; Large land holder; Alliances with capital.	Eliminate native American claims to territory and foreign interests; Swamp land act; Desert land act.
1890-1914 (By 1910, 46% of population is rural)	Recession-depression; Transformation of industry to relative surplus value; Agricul- ture to provide Cheap wage-goods; Expansion of foreign markets: Panama Canal, Monroe Doctrine, Platt Amendment, Imperialism; Concentra- tion and Centralization in industry; Corporate Liberalism emerges competing ideology.	Competitive capital vs. monopoly capital; Populism and new alliances; Struggle between capital and labor.	USDA becomes depart- ment; Land grant universities; Economic research; Country life commissions; Family farm; Repression of populism.
1914-1930 (By 1930, 44% of population is still rural)	War prosperity-- Recession to boom indus- trial growth. Dry land farming; Recovery in South based on tenant farming; Speculative capital.	Internationalization of capital vs. iso- lationism; Labor movement repressed under war emergency measures; Family farm reinforced as a cushion between and capital- labor.	Protectionism and free market policies for U.S. market.
1930-1941 (By 1940, 44% of population is still rural)	Depression; New deal; State and accumulation; concentration and centralization; Reorgan- ization of labor process; Protectionism; Corporate liberalism as dominant ideology; Reorganization of agricultural production system.	Big capital inter- ests dominate but seriously challenged by industrial union- ism: CIO, UMV, the farm bloc.	Agricultural Adjust- ment Acts of 1933 and 1936; Soil conservation and Domestic Allocation Act; Agricultural Marketing Agreement Act.

Historical Period	Major Tendencies in Political Economy	Major Struggles for Hegemony	State Policy in Agriculture
1941–1950 (By 1950, 36% of population is rural)	War prosparity; Wage and price controls; Machinery in agriculture; Rapid industrialization, Marshall Aid Plan.	Big capital interests dominate; Repression of labor gains.	Stabilization Act of 1942; Failure of the Brannon Plan.
1950–1958 (By 1960, 30% of population is rural)	U.S. hegemony; Cold War; Surplus production in agriculture; U.S. Imperialism reaches zenith.	Capital labor struggles; Farm sector alliance with small business interests.	PL 480; Agricultural Act of 1954– Soil bank.
1958–1982	Recession with inflation; War indebtedness; Waste consumption; End of Kayasian economics; World food crisis; Energy crisis; World capitalist crisis.	Finance capital and industrial capital; Emergence of Multinational Corporation; labor.	Food Grain Act; Food and Agricultural Act; Agricultural Act of 1970; Reganomics and supply side Agricultural Act of 1981.

Holt, Rinehart and Winston, 1951. Worthy P. Sterns "The Beginnings of American Financial Independence." *Journal of Political Economy*, Vol. VI (1897–1898).

2. Data to support the contention that black tenants produced the bulk of their own food are sketchy, at best. I arrived at this conclusion in the following manner. First, black population rose during the reign of tenancy and life expectancy rose slightly. Thus, the black tenant family was able to reproduce its labor power. Secondly, items offered for sale in the infamous merchant stores were either imported or produced by the tenant. Of course, the corn and hogs had to be turned over to the storekeeper and then bought back on "credit" but the producer frequently was a local tenant. For details on how this system worked see George Kirby Holmes, "Peons of the South," American Academy of Political and Social Science, *Annals* Vol. IV No. 2 (Sep) 1893, and T. S. Stribling, *The Store*, London: William Heinemann, 1932. Given the tenants' lack of capacity to control what was produced and how it was marketed, the storekeeper became the pivotal control in the development of local markets. The black workers produced their own food needs, but because of repression did so under overvalued conditions with the surplus going to the storekeeper.

3. For the nature of settlement patterns by region in the U.S. and different farming systems see, Fred A. Shannon, *The Farmers Last Frontier: Agriculture, 1860–1897*. Volume V, *The Economic History of the United States*. New York: Holt, Rinehart and Winston, 1951. For details on British capital involved in agricultural production see Leland Hamilton Jenks, *The Migration of British Capital to 1875*. New York: Alfred A. Knopf, 1927.

4. For a fascinating account of how this process worked see Shannon, *op. cit*. Chapter III. For a detailed account of public land policies see Benjamin Horace Hibbard, *A History of the Public Land Policies*. Madison: The University of Wisconsin Press, 1965.

5. Peter Barnes, "Land Reform I: The Great American Land Grab," *New Republic,* June 12, 1971.

6. The limits imposed by Britain's control of world markets is essentially a reflection of a combination of historical conjuctures and capitalist development on a world scale. The critical feature of the internationalization of capitalism was the uneven development of productive forces and hegemonic positioning which had produced the struggle between France and Great Britain. The U.S. had entered the picture as a result of increased agricultural production via territorial expansion and development of productive forces; e.g. the steel plow, the railroad, the reaper and immigrant labor power. Also, the U.S. jockeying for position in hegemony was largely limited to forming shifting alliances between France and Great Britain. But this was the era of *Pax Britannica* whereby Britain attempted to stabilize the world system. As U.S. production of wheat, corn and cotton increased in the new territories the home market became saturated and the exporting of agricultural commodities became an important dimension of expanded accumulation and industrial growth. But Britain ruled the seas, trade routes and alliances. In effect, Britain was both importer and reexporter of these commodities. For details of these issues: a) U.S. agricultural expansion see Louis Bernard Schmidt, "The Internal Grain Trade of the United States, 1860–1900." *The Iowa Journal of History and Politics,* Vol. XIX, No. 2 April, 1921: 196–245; Louis Bernard Schmidt and Earle Dudley Ross (eds.) *Readings in the Economic History of American Agriculture.* New York: The Macmillan Company, 1925; and Fred Albert Shannon, *Economic History of the People of the United States.* New York: The Macmillan Company, 1934; b) U.S. Foreign Trade Problems see Frank Owsley, *King Cotton Diplomacy.* Chicago: University of Chicago Press, 1931; George W. Norris, "The Tarriff and the Farmer," *The Nation,* Vol. CXXIII No. 3, 191, September 1926: 192–193, and Edward Stanwood, *American Tariff Controversies in the Nineteeth Century.* Boston: Houghton Mifflin, 1903; and c) confrontation with Great Britain see Walter LaFeber, *The Empire— An interpretation of American Expansion 1860-98.* New York: Random House, 1963; Josiah Strong, *Our Country: Its Possible Future and Its Present Crisis.* New York: American Home Missionary Society, 1885; and Alfred T. Mahan, *The Interest of America in Sea Power, Present and Future.* Boston: Little, Brown and Company, 1897.

7. William Appleman Willams, *The Roots of Modern American Empire.* New York: Random House, 1969.

8. The best background to the whole debate on expansionism and fractional money can be found in the multi-volume *Windom Report on Routes to the Seaboard* that grew out of a great convention held in Bloomington, Illinois in January 1873. For specifics on the debate about the gold standard see H. C. Carey, *Monetary Independence.* Philadelphia, 1875. The best overview that details the shifting alliances around expansionism and the silver issue see Williams, *op. cit.* Chaps. 6 and 7.

9. William Appleman Willams, *The Roots of Modern American Empire.* New York: Random House, 1969.

10. *Ibid.,* p. 20.

11. While the home market absorbed an average of 82 percent of all products sold off the farm from 1869 to 1900, foreign trade accounted for about 80 percent of the income from cotton, tobacco, wheat and meat products. These were the products that accounted for the turn of the trade balance. For details see, Frank H. Hitchcock, "Agricultural Exports of the United States, 1851–1902," *U.S. Department of Agriculture Bulletin No. 34.* Washington: Government Printing Office, 1903; and Shannon *op. cit.* who states "It was the balance of trade created primarily by the products of the farms, and especially foods that brought to America a portion of capital for the rapid growth of industries in the cities," p. 190.

12. Broadstreet, p. 6, January 1884, cited in Gareth Stedman Jones, "The History of U.S. Imperialism," in Robin Blackburn, *Ideology in Social Science.* New York: Vintage Books, 1973:220.

13. For example, between 1888 and 1892 half of the population of Kansas left their farms. For complete details see Stephen Thernstrom, "Urbanization, Migration and Social Mobility in Late 19th Century America" in Bernstein (ed.) *Towards a New Past,* 1970, pp. 158–176.

14. Walter La Feber, *The Empire: An Interpretation of American Expansion 1860–1898.* New York: Random House, 1963:20.

15. The best single document that permits one to see just how actively this alliance was sought is Kirk H. Porter, *National Party Platforms.* New York: The Macmillan Company, 1924. The ideological underpinnings of expansion of the empire are traced in Albert K. Weinberg, *Manifest Destiny.* Baltimore: Johns Hopkins, 1935. For a focus on leaders of the debate on expansionism see David Healy, *U.S. Expansionism: The Imperialist Urge in the 1890's.* Madison: University of Wisconsin Press, 1970.

16. The whole notion that class struggle at home could be avoided by expanding the empire was not based on an articulated notion of class struggle and the internal logic of capitalist development but seen as an evasion of the choice between a Christian Socialism which would build American capitalism shorn of its expansionist tendencies versus imperialism. But it was precisely class struggle that closed the debate. For the best overview of this point see the works of William Appleman Williams, particularly his *The Contours of American History,* 1961 and *The Great Evasion,* 1974.

17. Robert L. Heilbroner, *The Making of Economic Society.* Englewood: Prentice Hall, 1975:95–97.

18. Ibid., p. 97.

19. The role of ethnicity in dividing the working class is almost a forgotten issue today in the United States since all recent emphasis is on notions of racial and ethnic harmony perpetuated by terms as "the melting pot," "freedom of choice" and "safety nets." Nevertheless, ethnicity was adroitly employed by capitalists as a control mechanism. Strike breakers were always from different ethnic groups. Police were recruited from one ethnic group and sent to neighborhoods of different origins. For details see, Selig Perlman, *Theory of the Labor Movement.* New York: Augustus Kelley, 1928; Oscar Handlin, *Immigration as a Factor in American History.* Englewood Cliffs: Prentice Hall, 1959; and E. J. Hobsbawm, *Labouring Men.* New York: Basic Books, 1964.

20. Al Geddicks, "The Chicago School and the Rise of Corporate Liberalism," unpublished M.A. thesis, University of Wisconsin, Madison, 1973.

21. It is impossible in this paper to give any detail to the process of forming the working class in the United States. Other points that should be mentioned include: 1) the relative underpopulation of U.S. territory prior to the 1800's, 2) the annihilation of the indigenous population, 3) the lack of a feudal mode of production in the history of U.S. production systems, 4) the nature of the capitalist development pattern in the U.S., and 5) the structure of the U.S. proletariat. The point being emphasized here is that direct confrontation between independent agricultural producers and industrial capital over labor power was postponed due to immigration. By 1880, 62 percent of the economically active U.S. population was salaried and by 1960, 80 percent was salaried. Clearly, the bulk of the salaried employees in 1880 were immigrants and represented a wide range of ethnic backgrounds. See Spurgeon Bell, *Productivity, Wages and National Income*. Washington: Brooking Institution, 1940.

22. For an excellent review and analysis of these events see Vincent Pinto, *Soldiers and Strikers: Counterinsurgency on the Labor Front, 1877–1970*. Chicago: Banner Press, 1972.

23. c.f. Art Preis, *Labor's Giant Step*. New York: Pathfinder Press, 1972.

24. Heilbroner, *op. cit.* p. 142.

25. Production was soaring and employment was sagging. Output per person-hour rose rapidly; it increased 30 percent in transportation, 40 percent in mining and 60 percent in manufacturing from 1920–1929. Meanwhile hourly earnings were falling by as much as 20 percent in manufacturing. In mining, average yearly earnings fell from $1,700 to $1481 from 1920 to 1922 and did not rise again until 1929. This fall would have been even greater had not the cost of living index also fallen 15 percent from 1920 to 1929. At the same time, profits soared from an average for 1916–1925 of $730 million a year to $1,400 million a year from 1926 to 1929. For details see, *Historical Statistics, Series V and Series W*. Washington: Government Printing Office.

26. Heilbroner, *op. cit.* p. 142.

27. Gabriel Kolko, *Main Currents in Modern American History*. New York: Harper and Row, 1976

28. For an elaboration of this point, see Harry Braverman, *Labor and Monopoly Capital*. New York: Monthly Review, 1974, Chap. 12.

29. James Weinstein, *The Corporate Ideal and the Liberal State*. New York: Beacon Press, 1968.

30. *Ibid.*

31. James O'Connor, *The Fiscal Crisis of the State*. New York: St. Martins Press, 1973.

32. Paul Baran and Paul Sweezy, *Monopoly Capital*. New York: Monthly Review, 1966: 146.

33. For details see T. Moran, "Foreign Expansion as an 'Institutional Necessity' for U.S. Corporate Capitalism," *World Politics* Vol. 25 No. 3 April, 1973 and R. J. Barnet and R. E. Muller, *Global Reach*. New York: Simon and Schuster, 1975.

34. For competition between capitalist countries see Ernest Mandel, *Europe vs. America*. New York: Oxford University Press, 1970; and for the U.S. response

to the socialist challenge see Harry Magdoff, *The Age of Imperialism.* New York Monthly Review, 1969.

35. See David Harowitz (ed.) *Corporations and the Cold War.* New York: Monthly Review, 1969.

36. For an elaboration of these points see Braverman, *op. cit.*

37. For two fascinating accounts of food corporations and their early growth see Alfred D. Chander, Jr. Strategy and Structure: *Chapters in the History of the Industrial Enterprise.* Cambridge: Harvard University Press, 1962; and Lewis Corey, *Meat and Man: A Study of Monopoly, Unionism and Food Policy.* New York: Prentice Hall, 1950. What was involved on the management side of these conglomerates was the need to decentralize control within the corporation so that each operating unit could assume its own responsibility while statistics from each unit could be concentrated in the financial division that would allow the "corporation to direct the place of additional capital where it will result in the greatest benefit to the corporation as a whole." This decentralization/centralization dynamic is also reproduced in the state. See Alfred P. Sloan, Jr., *My Years With General Motors.* New York: Alfred Knopf, 1965.

38. This assertion is encountered in almost all U.S. A.I.D. publications on Third World agriculture. For a review of these assumptions and their critique see William Paddock and Elizabeth Paddock, *We Don't Know How.* Ames: Iowa State University Press, 1973; and Alain de Janvry, *The Agrarian Question and Reformism in Latin America.* Baltimore: Johns Hopkins University Press, 1981: Chap. 7.

39. Ronald L. Michell and William S. Hoofnagle, "Contract Production and Vertical Integration in Farming, 1960 and 1970," ERS497, Washington U.S. Department of Ariculture, April 1972.

40. W. B. Sundquist and H. D. Guither, "The Current Situation and the Issues" in *Who Will Control U.S. Agriculture?* North Central Regional Extension Publication 32.

41. There are two dominant trends. One involves rental of land to other small producers or to contract growers. In the latter case, the "owner" frequently becomes a worker by producing on his/her own land but receiving a wage from the contractor. The other trend is to live on the farm but work off-the-farm. In 1980, 62 percent of income of farm families came from off-farm work. See *Wall Street Journal,* July 29, 1982, p. 1.

42. Commission on International Trade and Investment Policy, *United States International Economic Policy in an Interdependent World.* Washington, D.C. 1971: Vol. 1:817.

43. U.S. Congress, Senate Committee on Agriculture and Forestry, *Alternative Futures for U.S. Agriculture.* Washington: Government Printing Office, 1975.

44. United States Senate, "Farmworkers in Rural America, 1971–72." Washington: Government Printing Office, 1972.

45. For a complete picture, see Federal Trade Commission, "The Structure of Food Manufacturing." Washington: Government Printing Office, 1976.

46. A.V. Krebs, *It's Farming! It's Food Production! It's Agribusiness!* Washington: Rural America, 1979.

47. Federal Trade Commission, *The Structure of Food Manufacturing*. Washington: Government Printing Office, 1972.

48. Krebs, *Op. cit.* p. 28.

49. Ibid. p. 27.

50. Perhaps the best single source of information on these tendencies can be found in Kenneth M. Coughlin (ed.) *Perspectives on the Structure of American Agriculture*. Washington: Rural America, Community Services Administration, 1980. This report includes several volumes and each sub-title indicates the subject matter treated by the specific volume.

51. A corporation which owns or operates business in two or more segments of the food system is vertically integrated. A company which *controls* two or more operations is vertically coordinated.

52. Mc Coughlin, *op.cit.* Vol. II, p. 44.

53. Leo V. Mayer, *Farm Income and Farm Structure in the United States*. Washington: Congressional Research Services Report 79–188S, 1979: p. 48.

54. Krebs, *op. cit.*

55. Data on the decline of real wages can be found in all official statistics. The best single source to follow the decline of wages in the U.S. is *Dollars and Sense* published monthly by the Union for Radical Political Economists.

56. See A. Desmond O'Rourke, *The Changing Dimensions of U.S. Agricultural Policy*. Englewood Cliffs: Prentice-Hall, 1978.

57. See G. Nelson and W. W. Cochrane, "Economic Consequences of Federal Farm Programs, 1953–1968," *Agricultural Economic Research*. Vol. 28, April, 1976.

58. U.S. Senate, Committee on Agriculture and Forestry, Hearings, Agriculture and Anti-Depression Act of 1975. Washington: Government Printing Office, 1975:1059.

59. Hubert Humphrey quoted in Harry Cleaver, "Will the Green Revolution Turn Red?" in Steve Weissman, ed., *The Trojan Horse*. San Francisco: Ramparts Press, 1974.

60. For details see NACLA, Latin America and Empire Report: *U.S. Grain Arsenal* (IX, No. 7), October, 1975.

61. Commission on International Trade and Investment Policy, *op. cit.* pp. 823–24.

62. *Ibid.,* Summary Vol., p. 152.

63. See A. Eugene Havens, *Hacia Una Analisas de la Estructura Agraria Peruana* Lima: PUCP, 1976.

64. U.S. Senate, Committee on Agriculture and Forestry, Sub-Committee on Foreign Agricultural Policy, Hearings, *U.S. Foreign Agriculture Trade Policy*, March and April 1973. Washington: Government Printing Office, 1973:160.

65. This relationship between accumulation and surplus value under the conditions of extensive non-capitalist relations of production derives from the necessity of accumulation in the capitalist mode of production. See Karl Marx, *Capital* Vol. I, New York: International Publishers, Chapter X, Section 2 ("The Greed for Surplus-Labor") and Part IV.

66. Some programs have been labeled as income redistribution schemes but in most instances the income distribution has actually worsened while they were in effect. See Heilbroner, *op. cit.*

3

The Underdevelopment of the South: State and Agriculture, 1865–1900

Neil Fligstein

The development of southern agriculture following the Civil War is viewed in light of the military and political victories of the North. The political domination of the South was an immediate outcome of the war, but it took another 50 years for the North to become economically dominant. The problems of southern agriculture in this period and in the 20th century have reflected limits imposed by this domination. The South was like an underdeveloped country with the classic problems of: 1) lack of capital; 2) production for the world markets; 3) dependence on extractive industries; 4) development controlled by outside forces; and 5) the cultural reality and memory of having been defeated.

The problems of the South are viewed here in the context of class struggles and their conjunctural solutions. The northern industrial capitalist class defeated the southern planter class in the Civil War. The struggle for control of the federal government was won by the industrial, banking, and merchantile interests of the North. The federal government then forced the South to undergo economic reorganization by not allowing planters to re-enslave blacks. The South formally capitulated to the North's domination with the Compromise of 1877. In exchange for local political autonomy, the planter/merchant/capitalist class in the South and the rejuvenated Democratic Party accepted northern economic domination. This domination brought into being the agricultural system of the "New South" which eventually brought about severe hardship for most of the southern population. Small farm owners organized and attempted to overcome both northern economic domination and southern planter/merchant/capitalist political domination. Unfortunately, these struggles ended in victory for the planter/merchant/capitalist class. The result was racism as state policy and the disenfranchisement of poor blacks and whites. The South remained an underdeveloped region in the early part of the 20th century. This chapter traces this process and these complex relationships through their development.

It is not of concern here to add detail to the historical record. Instead, the purpose is to synthesize and give a coherent sociological account of events. This synthesis will proceed in roughly chronological fashion through the period 1865 to 1900. The focus is on: 1) problems in southern agriculture and the situation in the world market after the Civil War; 2) the rise of crop liens, sharecropping, and local merchants; 3) the end of Reconstruction and the meaning of "Redemption"; 4) the relationship between the world market and northern control over the South; 5) the dynamics of agriculture in the "New South" and a description of tenant and sharecropping systems, circa 1880; 6) farmers' movements and their political implications in the period 1870–96; 7) the role of blacks in farmers' movements and politics; and 8) the failure of the farmers' movements and the rise of Jim Crow laws and disenfranchisement of blacks and whites. In the end, some conclusions are drawn about the role of the state in agriculture.

SOUTHERN AGRICULTURE AFTER THE CIVIL WAR

The Civil War left the South destroyed, disorganized, and destitute. Since the South was primarily an agricultural region before the war, the first goal of reconstruction was to restore crop production as rapidly as possible. The high price of cotton after the Civil War made this alternative all the more attractive (Brooks, 1914:19; Hammond, 1897:122). In 1865 the average price for cotton on the New York Exchange was over 83 cents per pound (Watkins, 1908:30). Before the Civil War the price had ranged from 9.5 cents per pound in 1852 to 13.5 cents per pound in 1857. It did not drop this low again until 1876. So, for those who could grow cotton, returns were handsome.

The problems facing potential planters/farmers were twofold. First, they lacked money to plant crops and pay laborers. Second, freed blacks—the major part of the labor force—were enjoying their new freedom. Finding workers who would submit to the work gang system was nearly impossible (Hammond, 1897:120–126; Coulter, 1947:92–112; Stampp, 1966:120–126; Ransom and Sutch, 1977:44–47). Building the postwar agricultural system would take time and require new social relations not only between whites and blacks but also between whites and whites.

The problem of securing capital was severe. Most banks failed following the war. Their securities were, on the whole, worthless (Coulter, 1947:4–5). Further, farmers had little to offer as collateral. Land prices plummeted.

Plantations that sold for $100,000 to $150,000 before the war sold for $5,000 to $10,000 after (Hammond, 1925:427; Nevins, 1927:22–24). Before the war, planters used urban middlemen (called "factors") to market crops and supply goods (Gray, 1957:409–433; Hammond, 1897:108–112; Woodman, 1968:8–42). The factor was a banker, a merchant, and a commodity seller. The origins of the crop lien system date from antebellum times. To get loans to plant and sustain a plantation, the planter would commit his crop to a factor. He would use his slaves, land, and the growing cotton as collateral. After the war, the planter no longer had slaves and land was almost worthless. The planter's only collateral was his maturing cotton. The only way he could recover from the war was to get a loan to grow cotton.

Securing a stable labor force was equally vital and difficult. Before the Civil War, plantation owners had a guaranteed labor force. Through close supervision, frequent threats, and physical abuse, slaves were made to work in the cotton fields. It should be noted that slave-holders constituted only 18 percent of the farmers in 1860 (Gray, 1957:529). Twenty-five percent of the slaves were owned by planters who had fewer than ten slaves. Fifty percent were controlled by farmers with 10 to 25 slaves, and the remaining 25 percent were owned by planters with 50 or more slaves (Gray, 1957:530–531). Still slaves and the plantations they worked, produced the bulk of the cash crops in the pre-war South (Gray, 1957:706–710). The freeing of the slaves destroyed these social relations of production.

The discussion so far has been couched solely in terms of a need to secure cash and labor, if southern agriculture were to revive. The role of the freedmen in this revival was complex. The definition of the rights of newly freed blacks and the process by which southern society reorganized were complexly linked. Day-to-day relations between all blacks and all whites had to be redefined, just as relations between landholders and freedmen and white laborers needed to be clarified.

C. Vann Woodward (1966:44–64) has argued that four main philosophies of race relations were put forward in the period 1865 to 1895. The first was extreme racism which demanded total segregation, disenfranchisement, and ostracism of the black population. (This view, of course, eventually won out.) The second was a conservative philosophy which held that blacks were inferior, but stopped short of ostracism and humiliation of the black population. This view was implicitly paternalistic and argued that whites should help and control blacks because they were incapable of doing things themselves. This conservative philosophy was viable for a considerable period (Woodward, 1966:45).

The third approach, that of the southern populists, was radical equalitarianism based on the notion that poor whites and blacks were in the same economic position. This meant that the rights of small landowning or renting white farmers were similar to those of blacks. As a Texas populist put it, "They are in the same ditch as we are" (Woodward, 1966:61). The fourth view was a liberal one which never seriously challenged the others (Woodward, 1966:47). It called for government to treat and protect all citizens equally. It was explicitly against discrimination, segregation, paternalism, and other forms of degradation. Its advocates did not gain a significant following until the 20th century.

The Civil War brought social and economic chaos to the South, putting the governments of the southern states in the hands of the northern military. The period witnessed a fair amount of disorder, much of it involving blacks. Accounts of blacks' behavior express the full range from sympathy to outrage (Woolfolk, 1957; Coulter, 1947:92–112; DuBois, 1964; Reid, 1965: 42–56; Trowbridge, 1966:328–332). It is clear that the newly freed blacks were enjoying their freedom. Many left the plantations, congregated in the small towns of the South, or migrated to the southwest and the border states (Woolfolk, 1957:94–95). Those who stayed behind were not inclined to work for their former masters. If the blacks were to return to work for the whites, it would understandably be under different conditions. Most important to newly freed blacks was the promise of land (Coulter, 1947:109–111; Ezell, 1963:52; Stampp, 1966:126–131). Unfortunately, not enough land was forthcoming.

CROP LIENS, SHARECROPPING, TENANT FARMING, AND THE RISE OF THE MERCHANTS

The high price of cotton following the Civil War provided impetus to a resurrection of the plantation system. But this system needed stable labor and capital. Capital was forthcoming, but the stable labor force never materialized. This section describes how the plantation system was transformed into a sharecropping and tenant farming system. It emphasizes the role of crop liens and of the emerging merchant class.

The capital for postwar expansion of southern cotton crops came from middlemen "factors." Factors received money from people in the cotton trade in New York and Europe. To re-lend it, they needed collateral or some guarantee of payment. This guarantee came in the form of a crop lien. The first postwar crop lien laws were passed in 1867 (Coulter, 1947:211–233; Hammond, 1897:154–160; Brooks, 1914:32–36; Banks, 1905:46–47; Woodward, 1974:179–184; Woodman, 1968:255–268). They allowed planters to get credit by mortgaging their growing crops, to give the factors or others who advanced supplies first claim on their harvests. While some view the crop lien system as fundamentally adverse to the interests of southern farmers, it is difficult to see how they could have operated at all without this system.

By 1868, the plantation system was failing. Freedmen would not be treated as slaves and participate in gang labor. Attempts to legislate gang labor (i.e., the black codes) had failed. Blacks' right to move freely was protected by the federal government and blacks exercised that right. The low wages and forced labor of the plantation system were repulsive in comparison to the option of moving west or living on farms where freedom could rent land or operate under a share system. With bad crop years and a falling price on cotton, more and more planters found that they could not pay off their crop liens. Factors and planters began to sink together and a new farming system was arising (Ransom and Sutch, 1977:56–80).

As early as 1866, farmers in South Carolina were experimenting with the idea laborers should have a share of the crop (Hammond, 1897:132). By 1868, the wage system had been virtually abandoned in Georgia (Brooks, 1914:47). Sharecropping or some form of tenancy was the rule.

As the old plantation system declined the number of farms increased. Large plantations were sold off in small parcels to white and black farmers, though most of these buyers were white. Before the war only 17 percent of those engaged in cotton farming were whites; by 1876, 40 percent were white. Whites took up cotton farming because they believed it would be profitable.

The revolution that took place from 1868 to 1874 was mainly one of organization of labor and the securing of capital. For blacks, the key issue was control over their own labor (Banks, 1905:78–79; Wharton, 1947:58–60; Williamson, 1965:64–95; Brooks, 1914:48–50). Throughout the old South, blacks held the upper hand on this issue. They worked when they wanted to, migrated when they wanted to, and gravitated to farming situations that offered them the most freedom.

Planters had no such alternatives. They tried several schemes to attract immigrants to work in the cotton fields, all of which failed (Hammond, 1897:96–97; Coulter, 1947:102–105; Shugg, 1939:244–249; Woodward, 1974:297–299). The planter could rent out land, sell it, or leave it fallow. All three options were tried, but tenancy arrangements eventually prevailed. Three tenancy arrangements were tried with varying success. These were sharecropping, share-tenancy, and cash rent (Brooks, 1914; Banks, 1895; Hammond, 1897; Schwartz, 1976; Woodward, 1974; Woodman, 1968; Clark, 1944; Ransom and Sutch, 1977). The sharecropper was given land, supervision, tools, seed, animals, and supplies. At the end of the crop year, owner and tenant split the crop equally (Brooks, 1912:48). Share-tenancy was closer to cash rent. The landlord furnished a house and land and the tenant paid with a share of the crop. Three forces made this arrangement popular. First, some planters wanted to move to town and rent their land. Second, some planters had excess land, and preferred to rent it rather than let it lie fallow. Third, and most importantly, blacks wanted to be free of supervision and this arrangement suited them best (Brooks 1912:52). Cash rental arrangements also existed. Renters simply paid a fixed price for the use of the land.

The tenant farming systems adopted after the Civil War, then, have their origins in the inability of plantation owners to secure labor on other terms. To profit from their land, planters had to give freedmen less supervision and/or a stake in the crop they were toiling to produce. The growth of share tenancy and small farm ownership increased the need for credit (Hammond, 1897:144-145). This credit could not come from factors. It was not worth their while to supply small farm owners and tenants (Woodman, 1968:282-284). Financing tenants was not profitable because they could not supervise them or be sure which ones would be good risks.

Changes in transportation and communication also undercut the factor. New railroads reduced the need to ship cotton to intermediate markets and then reship it to larger centers (Woodman, 1968:270-271). Farmers in small towns could use the telegraph to find out the price of cotton and then sell their crop at the closest railroad junction. They could bypass middlemen and increase their profits. By 1880, direct shipping and interior buying had virtually eliminated the factorage system. Every whistle stop became a marketplace (Woodman, 1968:274; Ransom and Sutch, 1977:126-148).

These changes in marketing and credit needs created new opportunities for small town merchants who knew the people with whom they were dealing and could keep track not only of their crop and supply needs, but also of their credit worthiness. The rise of the merchant class is a direct outgrowth of tenancy, small holding and the changing uses of crop liens. The crop lien was created to mediate between factors and planters. As time went on, planters found that it was easier and cheaper to mortgage their crops to local merchants. Supplies were close at hand and direct marketing brought more profits (Woodman, 1968:295-314).

However, relations between merchants, planters/landlords, and tenants became problematic. The conflict was twofold. If a renter were allowed to mortgage the crop to a merchant, the landlord would not have first claim on the crop. This placed landlords and merchants at odds (Woodman, 1968:295-314; Brooks, 1914:35-36; Hammond, 1897:193-195; Schwartz, 1976:57-63). They were also in competition to supply tenants with food, seed, and fertilizer. If the merchant did so, the landlord lost not only potential profit, but also control over the tenant. These conflicts were resolved in three ways: collusion, domination or usurpation.

Sometimes planters and merchants worked out mutually beneficial arrangements. In the first case, the planter would decide with the merchant how much credit to allow and, thereby, retain some control over tenant indebtedness (Brooks, 1914:34). More commonly, the landlord and the merchant competed until one became dominant (Schwartz, 1976:57–63; Brooks, 1914:36; Hammond, 1897:195; Woodward, 1974:180–184; Woodman, 1968:310–314). The third resolution was for the planter to become a merchant, supply the tenants, and profit not only from land rentals but also from interest on debts for supplies.

The credit limit was set by how much cotton was planted. The farmer was thereby in an insiduous circle. The merchant got credit from suppliers in the North on the basis of crop liens. Since cotton was the only commodity that the farmer could sell, it was the only crop for which a merchant could lend money. Merchants could get supplies on loan, only if they had collateral. The only acceptable collateral was the crop lien. So, both farmers and merchants were caught in the need to produce cotton. The crop lien became the tool which allowed cotton production to continue in the south.

It should be noted that the major source of profit for the merchant was the food and supplies sold to the farmer at very high prices and high interest rates (Clark, 1944, 1946; Woodman, 1968; Ransom and Sutch, 1972: 641–669). The merchant kept track of all transactions, but the farmer rarely knew what he was paying for supplies or interest or loans. It was not uncommon for the farmers to find themselves with little profit (or even a debt) at the end of the year.

In sum, the high price of cotton following the Civil War stimulated an attempt to rejuvenate the plantation system. This attempt failed, largely because black laborers refused to be organized into work gangs. Crop failures and the inability of planters to retain resident workers forced them to sell their land or reorganize their enterprises. Many plantations were subdivided and sold. Planters who did not sell were forced to offer their laborers sharecropping or tenancy arrangements. These new arrangements produced a demand for credit that the factor system could not meet. At the same time, the railroad and telegraph systems were allowing cotton producers to bypass the factor. The local merchant arose as the main source of credit for the planter, small farm owner, and tenant alike. In time, the merchant became not only the supplier of goods and supplies, but also the buyer of cotton. The merchant, was in turn, dependent upon the crop lien to secure his credit. Farmers also needed the crop lien; it was their only collateral. It was this dynamic that set up the farmers' revolts of the 1880s and 1890s.

THE END OF RECONSTRUCTION
AND THE MEANING OF REDEMPTION

While attempts to revive southern agricultural production were going through crisis, a political struggle was being acted out throughout the South. Blacks and their rights were at the center of the controversy. This section gives a brief account of the Reconstruction era, and the ways in which its problems were resolved. In many classic accounts of the Reconstruction, the era is portrayed as evil—as a time of abuse of power for personal promotion (Rhodes, 1902; Dunning, 1907; Bowers, 1929; Coulter, 1947). Other historians have questioned this view (Shugg, 1939; DuBois, 1964; Wharton, 1947; Arnett, 1922; Stampp, 1966; Woodward, 1974). Here, the argument is consistent with the interpretations of Stampp (1966) and Woodward (1951, 1974).

After the Civil War, President Andrew Johnson tried to reconstruct the South in line with his vision (Stampp, 1966:50–82). His major difficulty was that he had to deal with Republicans who controlled Congress. Johnson was a Democrat who ran with Lincoln in 1864 to present a bipartisan ticket that was unequivocal in its support of the Civil War. He remained a Democrat and this created a natural tension between him and the Republican dominated Congress. The Republican vision of Reconstruction differed from Johnson's and thus, ultimately, they came into conflict.

To understand these conflicts more clearly, it is necessary to consider the events of 1865–1868. Lincoln's plan for Reconstruction would have restored the southerners' rights very rapidly and would have promoted southern redevelopment. The radical Republicans were determined not to accept an easy peace that would allow southern rebel leaders to regain positions of political and economic power they had held before the war. They were against any such reconstruction (Stampp, 1966:50–51). When Andrew Johnson became president, it appeared he would accept the radical's terms. He was a vociferous opponent of the planters who controlled the South. In 1865, Johnson showed interest in bringing prominent southerners to trial and even considered measures to redistribute the land of the planters (Stampp, 1966:60–70). He had the apparent support of the radical Republicans in these endeavors (Stampp, 1966:52).

The radical Republicans wanted to make re-entry into the Union difficult for the South. They wanted to check southern political influence and try and consolidate the Republican party in America. They supported the civil and political rights of the blacks for both political and idealistic reasons (Woodward, 1974:43–44; Stampp, 1966:89–109). While they were very interested in maintaining political control, they were also concerned with the situation of blacks. They felt that the only way to control the South was to destroy the planter class and its power.

Johnson's point of view was quite different. While he wanted to destroy the planter class, he did not want to replace southern society with an equalitarian society (Woodward, 1951:14; Stampp, 1966:51–82). Rather, he wanted to remove the southern gentry from power and replace them with white yeoman farmers each controlling the labor of a few blacks. While Johnson believed the planter class needed to be controlled, he did not see the elevation of the blacks as the key issue. Instead, he felt that the defeat of the southern planters in the Civil War was complete and the natural heirs to power were the white yeoman farmers who would, with his help, come to control southern governments.

In 1865, Johnson began the Reconstruction. Conventions were held, elections followed, and governments were formed. Johnson decided to go ahead with his notion of Reconstruction without the support of Congress. All over the South, old Confederate officers and officials were elected into positions of power. Johnson's vision of the "New South" did not mesh well with reality. The old southern politicians were not discredited and many of them returned to power. The basic attitude in the South was that while the South had lost the war, the "cause" was still right (Coulter 1947; Woodward, 1974; Stampp, 1966). Congressmen and senators were sent to Washington and they attempted to convince Johnson that the South had suffered enough and that no further penance be demanded (Stampp, 1966:68–70). Johnson was swayed and turned from trying to destroy the planter class to attempting to secure its position. He came out against land redistribution in the South and, further, he spoke against guaranteeing black rights with a constitutional amendment. He became committed to a return to repression of blacks and he did not oppose the black codes which helped planters secure their labor force (Stampp, 1966:80).

The reaction of the radical Republicans in Congress was outrage. The Republican party united for the sake of survival (Stampp, 1966:82–90; Woodward, 1951:16–17). The key to this survival was forcing the planters to surrender political power and upholding the rights of the blacks. The motives of the Republican party were complex. At the core of its position was the place of the free black in American society. Racial equality was the central ideology. It was argued that blacks should have equal protection under the law and all the political rights of other citizens including the right to vote. The Johnsonians and classic historical schools of thought never took these arguments seriously. They believed that the motives of the radical Republicans were more base (Coulter, 1947). It is clear that the radical Republicans thought the best basis of maintaining political power was to organize the blacks. Not all Republicans felt comfortable in an alliance with blacks. More moderate elements in the party dreamed of an alliance with the Southern planters that would promote economic expansion and control black labor. But, in 1865, the Republicans were afraid of a southern and western political alliance that would subvert the Republican cause. Therefore, they sought to prevent this by organizing southern governments that would be friendly to Republicans. Part of the reason for their alliance with blacks was the desire to maintain political power.

Even more practically, the Republican party was the party of northern business (Stampp, 1966:95; Woodward, 1951:246). It was important to control the Congress as aspects of the business environment (laws concerning development, tariffs, incorporation, and money supply) could not be promoted in a Congress dominated by planters and farmers. Stampp argues that all of these motives are present in the actions of the radical Republicans. Perhaps, more importantly, Stampp further argues that if the radical Republicans had not taken this position, the political, legal, and economic rights of the blacks in the South would have been circumscribed (Stampp, 1966:82). If Andrew Johnson had had his way, the plantation system in its post-bellum form would not have been in crisis.

The Congressional election of 1866 produced a tremendous victory for the radical Republicans and a tremendous defeat for Johnson (Stampp, 1966:117). The major issues in the election were clear-cut. Johnson attempted to portray the Republicans as extreme supporters of blacks. He used the banner of racism to denounce the programs of the Republicans. The Republicans countered with arguments that Johnson was going to let the South win the peace by letting them reestablish extreme measures to control blacks and restore governments controlled by disloyal (Confederate) men. The Republican arguments prevailed and in 1867 Congress shaped its own plan for southern Reconstruction.

This program had three major parts: 1) it outlawed the black codes, 2) it passed constitutional amendments guaranteeing black rights, and 3) it established southern state governments that would accept federal rule and promote the rights of blacks. Consideration was given to breaking up southern plantations and giving land to blacks (Stampp, 1966:124–130; Coulter, 1947:66–69, 107–112). This program did not pass Congress for a number of reasons. Many Republicans who supported black political and legal rights did not understand the need to give the freedmen economic support. It would have violated the American principle that one's economic status must be determined by one's enterprise (Stampp, 1966:130). Redistribution of land would have been an attack on property inconsistent with Republican morality (Coulter, 1947:112; Stampp, 1966:13).

While some Reconstruction governments were corrupt, they were no more corrupt than state and city governments in the rest of the country in the period 1865–73 (Nevins, 1927:178–202). In fact, some of the Reconstruction governments were less corrupt than the Democratic Party-controlled governments that followed them (Woodward, 1974:1–23). In Mississippi, for instance, it is clear that this was the case (Wharton, 1947). This was, however, the era of "Grantism," as the Democrats called it (Woodward, 1974:53). There were railroad scandals, cases of state officials embezzling large amounts of money, and state land was given to speculators and other persons in the private sector (Woodward, 1974:51–74; Coulter, 1947:126–142). The Reconstruction governments of South Carolina, Georgia, and Louisiana all had scandals and the Republicans were chased from power.

The major positive accomplishment of the Reconstruction governments was the guaranteeing of the rights of blacks (Stampp, 1966:184–185). The black codes were abolished and the blacks were guaranteed freedom of movement. This political accomplishment forced the plantation system into crisis as protection of black rights made it impossible for planters to coerce black labor. The race policy of the Reconstruction governments as well as the corruption of those governments became the central ideological issues in the struggle over state power.

The end of the radical Republican governments in the South was brought about by two major forces. First, the radical Republican leadership was in decline as early as 1868. Power in the party was shifting from the idealistic, abolitionist elements to the more moderate elements which supported the status quo (Woodward, 1974, 1951; Stampp, 1966). The result of this shift was an increasing uneasiness with the union of "carpetbaggers" (northerners who went South to take advantage of the political and economic chaos), "scalawags" (white southerners who supported the Republican party), and blacks in the South. "The party of abolitionist radicalism had now become the party of vested interests and big business. Yet in the South, the party still appealed to the votes of a propertyless electorate of manumitted slaves with a platform of radical equalitarianism. The contradiction was obvious" (Woodward, 1974:28).

Second, the southern Democratic party was experiencing a resurgence. Their platform was essentially anti-black and anti-carpetbagger. They argued that the North was imposing racial equality and a corrupt government of outsiders on the South. Their race philosophy was the conservative philosophy spoken of earlier. They did not want to make blacks into a brutalized lower caste. They took a paternalistic attitude towards blacks and felt that the inferior black man should be led by his superiors (Woodward, 1966:42–60). The resurgence of the southern

Democratic Party was helped by another force: the extreme racists in the South (Coulter, 1947:162–183; Woodward, 1966:85–86; 1974:55–57; Stampp, 1966:199–202). The Ku Klux Klan and its supporters were terrorizing blacks and white Republicans throughout the South (Horn, 1939; Tannenbaum, 1969). Their racism called for total separation of the races and total subjugation of blacks. Poor whites held that the essential fact of life was skin color. "That I am poor is not as important as that I am a white man and no Negro is ever going to forget that he is not a white man" (quoted in Stampp, 1966:196). The Klan was not the only group which used organized violence against blacks and their white allies. Throughout the South, acts of violence and force were perpetrated against blacks to prevent them from voting, organizing politically, and meeting in large groups.

The ascension of the Democratic Party was due as much to the decline and division of the Republican Party as it was to organization and issues raised by the Democratic Party. As Woodward (1974) and Stampp (1966) have pointed out, the rise of the Republican Party in the 1850s constituted a "second American Revolution." "The party sponsored the policies which hastened the triumph of an urban-industrial capitalist social order over the already declining rural-agrarian interests centered in the South and West" (Stampp, 1966:187). They had passed protective tariffs, created a new national bank system, given federal subsidies for development (especially for the railroads), and provided for the sale of mineral and timber resources to private enterprise. In short, the Republicans were the emerging party of capitalist development. Their southern policy, by 1870, had also succeeded. They had destroyed the succession movement, preserved the Union, and seriously undermined the concept of state's rights. Besides destroying the political influence of the South, they had achieved the abolition of slavery and had written guarantees of civil and political rights for blacks into the Constitution.

Toward the end of the 1860s, the old radical leadership was in decline. Key men like Thaddeus Stevens, Joshua Giddings, Edwin Stanton, and Salmon Chase had died. Others retired or became disillusioned. Replacing these leaders were men brought in by Grant who no longer thought of radicalism and reform but of the status quo. These men were in the service of special interests. Some were the paid retainers of railroad, oil, textile, and steel interests. Nevins calls this an era the "moral collapse in government and business" (1927:178).

The liberals and radicals in the party were appalled at the corruption and became anti-Grant. The Republican alliance almost split apart. The crusade for black rights faded into the background as the party became fractionalized (Woodward, 1974:27–30; Stampp, 1966:186–215). Indeed, by 1876 the blacks in the South were no longer important to the

Republican cause. This was because of the rapid industrialization occurring in the old northwest (Ohio, Illinois, Indiana, Wisconsin, Minnesota, and Iowa). These states had taken a decidedly Republican turn
as the agrarian-based Democratic Party became increasingly superfluous
to the rapidly industrializing region (Stampp, 1966:211). Between 1868
and 1908, these states very rarely delivered their votes to a Democratic
presidential candidate. Eight times the entire region went Republican
(Stampp, 1966:212).

Within the South, the divisions were also becoming apparent. The
Republicans fought one another as ferociously as they fought Democrats.
Through the 1872 elections, blacks remained loyal to the Republicans.
This reflected the fact that the Republicans continued to support black
rights. This support, however, cannot be seen as a total identification
with the business orientation of the national party (Woodward, 1974:28).
A few Republicans, who tended to be "scalawags" (white southerners
who supported radical Reconstruction and the Republican Party), became
alienated from the Republican Party in the early 1870s. These men
realized that using blacks as the basis of the Republican party in the
South was inconsistent with the general conservative tone of the party.
Instead, they argued that the Republicans should form an alliance with
conservative Democrats and defend the rights of property and capitalist
development (Woodward, 1974:28–30). The base of the Republican Party
in the South eroded to the point where it was literally comprised of
only blacks and carpetbaggers (Woodward, 1974:103–105; Stampp, 1966:
190–192).

Another important element in the shift of the Republican Party, was
the racism that always existed in the party. Part of the radical Republican
motive for helping blacks was based on their belief that all men were
equal and the protection of blacks' civil and political rights was essential.
But it is also clear that the support of the black cause was politically
motivated. The black vote had given Republicans a hold on the South
and was a tool to prevent the reascendancy of the planter class (Stampp,
1966:92–94; Woodward, 1974:103–105; Kousser, 1974:11–29). As it became
clear that blacks did not offer enough support to maintain Republican
Party power, a number of Republicans came to support the conservative
Democrats, who wanted to curb the power of black voters. These people
did not believe that the black was equal to the white and felt that
suppressing blacks was quite consistent with Republican principles
(Woodward, 1974:28–30).

The southern Democrats who came to power following radical Reconstruction called themselves "redeemers" (Woodward, 1974:3). They
had two objects: to crush black political power and to remove the
carpetbaggers from their governments (Woodward, 1974:1–22). Beyond

this, their political program was underdeveloped. Who supported this party? On the whole, white men of all socioeconomic strata. In terms of organized forces, there were influential capitalists, merchants, planters, and an emerging middle class (Woodward, 1974:1–22). The southern Democrats were swept to power by a wave of white assaults on blacks that were destructive of both life and property. Those responsible for the violence demanded political, legal, and social subordination of blacks.

As southern Democrats took power all over the South, blacks were becoming more and more isolated. With the Compromise of 1877, the Republican Party officially withdrew its support from blacks and became committed to a policy of conciliation. The crisis which prompted the Compromise of 1877 was precipitated by the election of 1876. Samuel Tilden, the Democratic candidate for president, was one electoral vote shy of victory, and he led the popular vote by over a quarter of a million votes (Woodward, 1951). Rutherford Hayes, the Republican candidate, was behind Tilden in the electoral vote count and he claimed the votes of the three states which had not been decided: South Carolina, Florida, and Louisiana. The compromise entailed a bargain between Hayes and southern Democrats. Hayes told the southern Democrats he would remove the remaining troops from the South thereby ending Reconstruction, as well as withdrawing support from the remaining Republican governments in the South. The southerners, in return, promised to insure Hayes' election (Woodward, 1951:1–21; 1974:24). Hayes felt that by turning southern governments back to indigenous southerners, he would attract white conservatives to the Republican cause. As it turned out, these conservatives remained Democrats (Woodward, 1951: 244).

The implication of the Compromise for settling the regional differences was immense.

> The Compromise of 1877 did not restore the old order in the South, nor did it restore the South to parity with the other sections. It did assure the dominant whites political autonomy and nonintervention in matters of race policy and promised them a share in the blessings of the new economic order. In return, the South became, in effect, a satellite of the dominant region. So long as the Conservative redeemers held control they scotched any tendency of the South to combine forces with the internal enemies of the new economy—laborites, western agrarians, reformers. Under the regime of the Redeemers, the South became the bulwark instead of a menace to the new order (Woodward, 1951:246).

It is necessary to consider the meaning of redemption for the blacks. The desertion of the national Republican Party from the cause of the blacks left them with no Congressional clout and put them at the mercy of the southerners. With the withdrawal of radical Republican support, the political and legal equality of blacks was being threatened. White supremacy was being touted as the racial solution. Blacks were everywhere intimidated by whites. The only whites who did not want to place blacks into a caste from which they could not rise were the upperclass southerners. While they believed in white supremacy, they felt that blacks had rights and that they could be convinced to support conservative Democrats (Stampp, 1966:196–197; Woodward, 1974:79). Planters in black belts came to control black votes and by 1880, blacks were supporting southern Democrats, the party of white supremacy (Woodward, 1974:79). This transition is not hard to understand. The planter elements in the Democratic Party, although paternalistic, did want to maintain political and legal rights for blacks (at least for the time being). Blacks had two options: support the southern Democrats or be at the mercy of more racist elements.

The end of Reconstruction thus brought white southerners back into power, but these new rulers were committed to reunion with the North and the industrial development of the South. They came into office on the issue of white supremacy, but their race policy was not total repression of the black population. The 1880s brought threats to the political system. Before turning to those threats, it is necessary to examine the southern economy and its relation to national and world economies.

THE WORLD MARKET AND THE NORTH'S CONTROL OVER THE SOUTH

Before the Civil War, the South produced more cotton than any other region in the world (Watkins, 1908; Hammond, 1897:291). The British, who were the largest consumers of raw cotton, had tried to find other sources of cotton prior to the war (Hammond, 1897:339). During the war, the British turned to using Indian, Egyptian, and Brazilian cotton. However, with the ending of the Civil War, American cotton was again in demand. This was because Indian cotton, the largest source of imports for the British, was short stapled and therefore more difficult to spin (Hammond, 1898:326). The British began buying long staple American cotton as soon as it became available.

The price was high immediately after the war. But as American production geared up, the price dropped rapidly from an average of 83 cents per pound in 1865 to roughly an average of 24 cents per pound in 1870 (Watkins, 1908:30). The decade of the 1870s saw the price drop to around 10 cents per pound on the average. While the price of cotton dropped, the number of countries consuming cotton increased and the amount of cotton they used also increased. In 1860, Great Britain took 55 percent of the American crop. By 1895, Great Britain consumed only 33 percent of the American crop (Hammond, 1898:340). This percentage decrease occurred while Britain increased its consumption of American cotton from roughly 1.2 billion pounds to 1.6 billion pounds (Hammond, 1897:Appendix 1). The European continent was importing even more cotton. The decade of the 1880s witnessed some very large crop years and the price per pound hovered around 10 cents. The 1890s saw the price plunge to a low of 6 cents per pound by 1899. World consumption of cotton increased roughly 28 percent from 1880 to 1890, while world production of cotton increased about the same amount in the period. Production of cotton increased 12 percent in the period 1890–95, while consumption did not increase at all (Hammond, 1897:337). By 1896, there were roughly 3.9 million bales of cotton unsold. With over-supply, the price plummeted.

Much of the increased production of cotton from 1880 to 1895 occurred in the United States. In 1880, the U.S. crop was 7.5 million bales of cotton, while the rest of the world produced 1.8 million bales. In 1895, the U.S. produced 10.1 million bales and the rest of the world produced roughly 2 million bales. While the U.S. production increased roughly 30 percent, the rest of the world's production increased only 11 percent. The drop in cotton prices affected American farmers the most. The natural question is why did Americans increase their production so rapidly? Here it is argued that overproduction was built into the system of crop liens and the social relationships existing between merchants, planters, and tenants. The cotton farmer was not being overoptimistic about the price of cotton (Hammond, 1897:339). Rather, to repay the debt he was rapidly plunging into, the farmer could only do one thing: produce more cotton. Ironically, the effect of overproduction was to put the farmer further into debt (Ransom and Sutch, 1977:149–170).

While the world price of cotton was of immense importance to the fiscal well-being of the farmer, capitalist development in America impinged directly and indirectly on the farmer's life. Previously, it has been argued that the Republican Party was the party of northern business. This view is held by a number of historians and the only real issue that is debated is the sense in which the Republican party was the Party of northern business. So far, this issue has been skirted and it will be considered here only insofar as it is relevant to understanding how the farmer's life was affected by the state. The view put forward here is that the northern capitalist class was not an organized force at the political level until the emergence of the Republican Party. But the emergence of a party is not a sufficient condition for a "capitalist" class to be organized.

On this matter, the view here is consistent with that of Poulantzas (1968:187–224). The capitalist class, by its very nature, is disorganized. This is because there are a number of competing interests within that class and those individual interests are constantly threatening to tear society apart. The state, in a capitalist social formation, like America, has two functions: accumulation and legitimation. Accumulation refers to acts of the state that aid the accumulation of capital. These acts entail legislation as diverse as tariffs, railroad subsidies, and subsidies to build highways, sewers, and water systems. The actions of the state can aid different fractions of the capitalist class or the entire capitalist class. The legitimation function of the state rests on its ability to convince society as a whole that it is the state of all people and not just the state of the capitalist class. The major mechanisms by which the state does this are both ideological and real. At the ideological level, the state claims to be the state of all citizens and argues that all interest groups in society have equal input into the political system. At the real level, the state supports social welfare legislation and the formation of trade unions that quell a potential class struggle. In an emerging formation like that of 1860–1890 America, the legitimation function is more ideological and the state preaches laissez-faire capitalism (social Darwinism) and practices self-conscious accumulation legislation.

The ascendancy of the Republican Party has been associated with the rise of northern business. The party was the party of business, in that it organized the interests of different fractions of the northern capitalist class (bankers, merchants, industrialists, railroad builders) and placed legislation favorable to those interests on the political agenda. The success of this organization is reflected only later, i.e., from 1870–90. With the proper enabling legislation, and a South that was forced to accept its position in the newly emergent capitalist order, development proceeded rapidly. Spokesmen for the "New South" felt the future of the South lay with northern business. Indeed, without the capital of the North, the "New South" dream of a land industrialized could not emerge. As Woodward and others have argued, "with the aid of the New South propagandists, however, and by frequent resort to repressive or demogogic devices, the right-forkers contrived to keep the South fairly faithful to the Eastern alignment until the advent of the populists" (Woodward, 1974:50). The northern capitalist penetration of the South and its control over the South began after the political domination of the South was completed. With the emergence of the southern Democratic redeemers, an indigenous organized party existed in the South in the 1870s to promote peace with the North and oversee the beginning of the capitalist control over the South at the economic level.

The North and West came to dominate southern agriculture as they provided the cotton farmer with food, supplies, seed, and fertilizer and eventually came to control the marketing of the crop. The crop lien system encouraged farmers to plant as much cotton as possible. One major result of this system was that farmers did not grow their own food (Woodman, 1968:308–314; Arnett, 1922:53–60; Hicks, 1931:45–46; Vance, 1929:200–201; Hammond, 1897:151–160; Banks, 1905:36–38). Food had to be transported to the South. Most came from the Midwest which produced grain, beef, and pork. To produce cash crops, the farmer had to buy food. To buy food from the furnishing merchant, farmers needed a crop lien that was large enough to pay off debts, buy supplies, and eat for eight months. The southern farmer was caught. The beneficiaries of this system were the midwest farmers (although they benefitted the least), the railroad owners (who did the shipping at high rates), and local merchants who charged high interest and prices.

The merchant got his money on credit also. This credit was extended from two sources: 1) the supplier of the goods; and 2) cotton merchants in New York or Europe. Most of the goods suppliers were northerners and these people profited handsomely from their loans (Woolfolk, 1957; Woodman, 1968). The local merchant was interested in securing the largest crop lien available because then he could get more supplies and a firmer grasp on farmers. This increased his potential profit. Cotton merchants extended credit as local merchants promised to sell the crop to those who lent the money. In this way, the entire crop lien system became integrated into the expanding northern business system.

There were two other areas in which the north eventually controlled marketing of the cotton crop: 1) railroads; and 2) the consolidation of the cotton market. Stover (1955), in his monograph on southern railroads, argues that after the Civil War southern railway expansion was controlled almost entirely by southerners (pp. 37–38). As late as 1875, southerners still controlled the southern railways. Northern capitalists were reluctant to invest large sums of money in the South due to the general lack of financial security and the presence of better investment opportunities in the rest of the U.S. (Stover, 1955:55). But this changed in the late 1870s and early 1880s. New railroad building and the consolidation of railroad lines brought northern capital into southern railroads. This trend was gradual and by 1890, 43 of the 58 companies with more than 100 miles of track were dominated by northern interests and these railroads accounted for 88 percent of the total rail mileage (Stover, 1955:279). The depression of the 1890s brought about further merger and by 1900, northern-dominated firms controlled 96 percent of the total rail mileage (Stover, 1955:282). While this was occurring, the number of miles of track increased from 9,167 after the Civil War to 29,263 in 1890 (Stover,

1955:5, 193). The transportation revolution that destroyed the factorage system was related to this increase in railroads and it is not surprising that the northerners who began to control the railway system directed cotton away from the southern ports and towards the northeast.

The actual marketing of the cotton crop also underwent consolidation. With the decline of the factorage system and the rise of the local merchant, a new form of cotton buying evolved. As time went on, cotton buying became concentrated in the hands of a few large American and European firms. By 1921, 24 firms handled 60 percent of the southern crops (Woodman, 1968:289). These firms tended to locate in New York City, although they had representatives all over the South. The post-bellum era also saw the development of a cotton futures market. Merchandise purchased in one market often changed hands several times before delivery.

The "second American Revolution" ended with a South that was controlled by planters, merchants, and indigenous capitalists who strove for the development of the South by northern capital. The southern agricultural system had weathered a series of crises and had obtained some stability at a very high cost. The vast majority of southern farmers were rapidly becoming impoverished as their position in the world market declined due to overproduction. Northern capitalist development supplied the capital and supplies that supported this system and came to control the marketing and transporting of the crop. The white supremacist governments supported the exploitation of white and black farmers under the guise of industrial development. This development brought poverty and constant indebtedness for most farmers. However, forces were emerging in the late 1870s that threatened to bring down these governments—these were the agrarian movements. Before these movements are considered, it is important to examine the crop lien system and the dynamics of the New South agricultural system in more detail.

DYNAMICS OF THE "NEW SOUTH" AGRICULTURAL SYSTEM

A large number of descriptions of the southern agricultural system exist (Banks, 1905; Brooks, 1914; Hammond, 1897; Vance, 1932, 1945; Saloutos, 1960; Hicks, 1931; Arnett, 1922; Shugg, 1939; Woodward, 1974; Raper, 1936; Woodman, 1968; Woofter, 1936, 1969; DeCanio, 1974; Schwartz, 1977; Boeger and Goldenweiser, 1916; Goldenweiser and Trusdell, 1924; to mention a few). Here, the task is to abstractly describe the categories that explain the various relations to the land and give an overview of the arrangements each category entailed. Then, census data will be presented showing gross changes in farming arrangements between 1860–1900 by states. Finally, these changes will be discussed as a function of the agricultural system in which people were involved and the dynamics of the system.

There are six categories to consider: farm laborers, sharecroppers, share-tenants, cash tenants, small farm owners/operators, plantation owners/absentee landlords/merchants and corporation control. While these categories overlap in definition, they appear to cover most of the arrangements that existed.

Farm laborers is the simplest category to describe. These were wage laborers who worked under the direct supervision of a farm owner. If the farm was big enough, laborers would be organized into work gangs. Plantation owners would usually employ a number of laborers whom they would oversee and also have a number of tenants or sharecroppers. Farm laborers were at the bottom of the social structure as they controlled neither land nor their labor.

Sharecroppers worked a part of the plantation, usually 20–30 acres. Their arrangement with the landlord usually had the landlord supplying the land, housing, fuel, tools, work stock, seed, one-half of the fertilizer, and the feed for the work stock. The sharecropper supplied the labor and one-half of the fertilizer. At the end of the year, the crop was split with half going to the landlord and half going to the tenant (Woofter, 1936:10). Central to the sharecropper's situation was the amount of supervision supplied by the landlord. The landlord told the sharecropper what to plant and when to plant it (Brooks, 1914:66–68). Further, the landlord controlled the fertilizer allotment. Often, the sharecropper was almost in the position of the wage hand, except for the fact that he worked a separate land plot.

Share-tenants, on the other hand, were closer to being true renters (Woofter, 1936:92). The landlord supplied the tenant with land, house, fuel, and one-third or one-fourth of the fertilizer. The tenant supplied labor, work stock, feed for work stock, tools, seed, and the rest of the fertilizer. The landlord received one-fourth or one-third of the crop, while the tenant received the remainder. If the share tenant raised cotton and corn, as was often the case, the landlord received a third of the cotton and a fourth of the corn. The share-tenant was a renter and as such, the landlord did not have the right to supervise his daily activity. Share tenants had more status than either sharecropper or wage hands (Woofter, 1936:9–11).

Cash tenants had an arrangement with the landlord similar to that of the share tenant. Typically, the landlord furnished only the land, house, and fuel while the tenant was responsible for labor, work stock, feed for work stock, tools, seed and all of the fertilizer. The landlord in this situation received a fixed rent in cash or cotton lint and the tenant took the remaining crop. These tenants had the most independence and the greatest incentive motivation to raise more crops because they owned all crops produced above the rent.

Small farm owners/operators have been separated from plantation owners as they really occupy different social positions. The small farmer, who owned 20–200 acres, worked the land with his family and possibly one or two wage hands. This farmer tended to be white and, before the Civil War, was mainly a subsistence farmer. After the Civil War, high cotton prices and crop liens from merchants convinced many of these small farmers to produce cotton. It was these small farm owners, called yeoman farmers, who were at the center of the populist revolt.

Large plantations were operated in one of four ways. First, the owner would live on the plantation and work part of the land with wage labor. The rest of the land would either lie fallow or be operated by sharecroppers, share tenants, or cash tenants. It was not unusual for plantations to have mixed arrangements and even have blacks and whites working on the same plantation (Woofter, 1936:10–11). The second arrangement was that of the absentee landlord. Here, the landowner would move to the city and rent the land either to share or cash tenants. His contact with the tenants would be occasional and they would be left largely unsupervised. The third arrangement developed as merchants came to own land. If an owner/operator could not pay the merchant off over a number of years, the merchant sometimes took control of the land. The merchant would then rent the land out, supply those working the land with food, clothes, and goods, while holding a crop lien on the growing crop. Because the merchant owned the land, he would supervise the tenant fairly closely. The fourth situation involved corporate or bank ownership of land. If a planter was unable to repay a loan, the bank took control of the land. The bank might then sell the land to a corporation which would rent out plots.

A number of writers have commented on the division of southern cropland into smaller units after the Civil War (Woodward, 1974; Hammond, 1898; Banks, 1905; Brooks, 1914; Shugg, 1939; Saloutos, 1960). This division was the result of two forces. First, some amount of redistribution of land was occurring. As the plantation system broke down and land values plummeted, smaller parcels of land became available to the small farm owner. The second force, of course, was the rise of the sharecropping and tenant system. Table 1 contains the number of farms and their average size in nine states from 1860 to 1900. There was a large increase in the number of farms throughout the period. Concomitantly, there is a decrease in the average farm size throughout the period. It should be noted that farm, here, refers to any piece of land larger than three acres that was worked by a farmer and his family. Thus, if a 1100-acre plantation had 30 sharecroppers each working 30 acres with the plantation owner working the remainder of the land with wage hands, it would appear in the census as 31 farms with an average size of 35.5 acres. This table does not demonstrate that the concentration of land ownership was decreasing over time; rather, it shows only that the subdivision of land was occurring very rapidly.

How much of this subdivision was due to tenantization and how much was due to new farm ownership? This question is difficult to answer because data on tenure status have been collected only since 1880. Table 2 shows the number of farms in 1880, 1890, and 1900 that were owner operated and rented. Table 3 presents calculations that attempt to suggest how much of the growth in the number of farms was due to the growth of tenant arrangements. In 1860, there were almost no tenant farms in the South, and so the number of farms in 1860 is treated as coterminous with the number of farm owners. By 1880, all states had a sizeable number of tenants. Over 65 percent of the growth in the number of farms is attributable to the growth in tenant farming from 1860 to 1880. Between 1880 and 1890, and 1890 and 1900, tenant farming accounts for over 75 percent of the growth in the number of farms in each decade. In all states, the percentage of owners declined over the period 1860–1900. By 1890, the majority of farmers in South Carolina, Georgia, and Mississippi were tenants. By 1900, the same was true in Alabama, Texas and Louisiana. Over the 40-year span, the number of farms increased by 1,432,574. But, 1,017,687 of these (71%) were operated by tenants. This tenantization grew most rapidly in the old South and by 1900, six of the eight states considered here had more tenants than farm owners. It can be concluded that even though some new land ownership occurred, by far the most important change in land tenure was due to the introduction of tenant farming. The increase in the numbers of tenants is the result of a startling development that can be termed, without overstatement, a revolution.

What is the relationship between cotton growing and growth in tenant farming? Table 4 shows the crop production for the year prior to the census from 1860 to 1900 by state. Table 5 gives the rank order of states by cotton production and by proportion of farmers who were tenants. Of the top six producers in 1880, only one is not in the top six in tenantization. In 1890 and 1900, all of the top six in cotton production are in the top six in tenantization. The Pearson correlation coefficient between the rank orders is .64 in 1880, .78 in 1890, and .76 in 1900. This suggests that cotton growing and the development of the tenant system are intimately related.

Table 1. The Number of Farms and Average Farm Size in Acres in Selected Southern States, 1860-1900

State	1860	1870	1880	1890	1900
Alabama	55,128[1] (349)[b]	67,438 (272)	135,864 (139)	157,772 (126)	323,200 (93)
Arkansas	39,004 (491)	49,333 (301)	94,433 (128)	124,760 (119)	178,694 (93)
Georgia	62,003 (430)	69,964 (338)	138,626 (188)	171,071 (47)	224,691 (117)
Louisiana	17,328 (537)	28,444 (247)	48,29 (171)	69,294 (138)	115,969 (95)
Mississippi	42,840 (370)	67,985 (193)	101,772 (156)	144,318 (122)	220,803 (83)
North Carolina	75,203 (316)	93,565 (212)	157,609 (142)	178,359 (127)	224,637 (146)
South Carolina	33,171 (488)	52,383 (233)	93,864 (143)	115,008 (115)	155,355 (90)
Texas	42,891 (591)	61,125 (301)	174,184 (208)	228,126 (225)	352,190 (257)
Oklahoma	--	--	--	8,826 (182)	62,495 (368)

[a] Number of farms.
[b] Average farm size.

Source: U.S. Bureau of the Census.

Table 2. A Comparison of the Number of Farms Rented and Owned by State for 1880, 1890, and 1900

State	Owner Operated			Number of Renters		
	1900	1890	1880	1900	1890	1880
Alabama	94,346	81,141	72,215	128,874	76,631	63,649
Arkansas	97,554	84,706	65,245	81,140	40,054	29,188
Georgia	90,131	79,477	76,451	134,560	91,594	62,275
Louisiana	48,735	38,539	31,286	67,234	30,755	17,006
Mississippi	82,951	68,058	57,214	137,852	76,260	44,558
North Carolina	131,629	117,469	104,887	93,008	60,890	52,722
South Carolina	60,471	51,428	46,645	94,884	63,580	45,219
Texas	177,199	132,616	108,716	174,991	95,560	65,468
Oklahoma	30,750	8,761	--	31,745	65	--

Source: U.S. Bureau of the Census, 1900.

The next issue to be discussed is a consideration of the relative proportions of blacks and whites who were cotton producers and/or tenants and when they came to occupy those roles. In 1860, only one person in six who worked in the cotton fields was white (Hammond, 1897:130). But the high price of cotton and the end of the slavery/ plantation system brought whites into the cotton fields. Table 6 pieces together the rate at which whites entered into cotton production. In 1876, whites outnumbered blacks in cotton production only in Texas and Arkansas. However, substantial numbers of whites had moved into the cotton fields in every state except Louisiana. By 1900, whites had narrowed the gap between themselves and blacks and were producing cotton almost as frequently as blacks. In Texas, the largest cotton producing state by 1900, whites outnumbered blacks 4 to 1.

As has been shown, most new farm operators were tenants. Further, the number of tenant farmers was related to cotton production. It follows that if whites were entering cotton farming, they must have been tenants. Table 7 presents the numbers of white and black farmers by tenant status and state in 1900. Forty-four percent of the farmers were white owners, while 27 percent of the farmers were white tenants. This is compared with 6 percent of the farmers who were black owners and 23 percent of the farmers who were black tenants. A glance at the table reveals that blacks were much more likely to be tenants than whites. Seventy-eight percent of the blacks were tenants compared to 38 percent of the whites. The largest number of white tenants were in South Carolina, Georgia, Texas, and Oklahoma, while large concentrations of black tenants lived in South Carolina, Georgia, Alabama, Mississippi, and Louisiana. In absolute terms, there were more white tenant farmers in the South than black tenant farmers.

The dynamics of the revitalized southern agricultural system were complex. After the Civil War, cotton production began immediately as the high price of cotton encouraged people to produce. Money for crop production came from two sources: factors and local merchants. Since only planters usually had factors, local merchants increasingly become the source of seed, fertilizer, food, feed, and crop marketing for the small farm owner and tenants. The high price of cotton drew more whites into production and also caused the expansion of cotton production in Texas and, later, Oklahoma.

Tenants or small farm owners were in the position of trying to maximize their profits. Growing food and becoming a subsistence farmer would not yield large profits. Only growing cash crops would do this. So, after the Civil War, many yeoman farmers turned from subsistence farming to cotton farming in the hopes of securing higher incomes. They planted as much cotton as they could and took crop liens to buy

Table 3. An Attempt to Assess the Change in Number of Farms and the Component of that Change Due to the Increase in Farm Owners and Tenant Farmers in Southern States from 1860 to 1900

State	Total Farms	% Owners	% Tenants	Change in Farms	% Change Due to Ownership	% Change Due to Tentantship	Number of New Owners
Alabama							
1860	55,128	100	0	--	--	--	--
1880	135,864	53	47	80,736	21	79	17,087
1890	157,772	51	49	21,908	41	59	8,926
1900	223,220	42	58	65,428	20	80	13,205
Arkansas							
1860	39,004	100	0	--	--	--	--
1880	94,433	69	31	55,429	47	53	26,241
1890	124,760	68	32	30,327	64	36	19,461
1900	178,694	54	46	53,934	23	77	12,848
Georgia							
1860	62,003	100	0	--	--	--	--
1880	138,626	55	45	76,623	19	81	14,448
1890	171,071	46	54	32,445	9	91	3,026
1900	224,691	40	60	53,620	19	81	10,654
Louisiana							
1860	17,328	100	0	--	--	--	--
1880	48,292	65	35	30,964	45	55	13,958
1890	69,294	56	44	21,002	35	65	7,253
1900	115,969	42	58	46,675	21	79	10,196

Mississippi							
1860	42,840	100	0	--	--	--	--
1880	101,772	56	44	58,932	24	76	14,374
1890	144,318	47	53	42,546	25	75	10,844
1900	220,803	37	63	76,485	18	18	14,433
North Carolina							
1860	75,203	100	0	--	--	--	--
1880	157,609	67	33	82,406	36	64	29,684
1890	178,359	66	34	20,750	61	39	12,582
1900	224,627	58	42	46,278	30	70	14,160
South Carolina							
1860	33,171	100	0	--	--	--	--
1880	93,864	50	50	60,693	22	78	13,474
1890	115,008	45	55	21,144	23	77	4,783
1900	155,355	38	62	40,347	22	78	9,043
Texas							
1860	42,891	100	0	--	--	--	--
1880	174,184	62	38	131,293	50	50	65,825
1890	228,126	58	42	178,006	13	87	23,900
1900	352,190	50	50	124,064	35	65	44,583

Source: U.S. Bureau of the Census.

Table 4. Cotton Production by State in Bales (400 lbs.) in Year Previous to Census

State	1859	1869	1879	1889	1899
Alabama	989,955	429,482	669,654	915,210	1,089,519
Arkansas	367,393	247,968	608,256	691,494	705,583
Georgia	701,738	473,934	814,441	1,191,846	1,231,060
Louisiana	777,738	350,832	508,569	659,180	700,352
Mississippi	1,202,507	564,938	963,111	1,154,725	1,237,666
North Carolina	145,514	144,935	389,598	336,261	440,400
South Carolina	353,412	224,500	522,548	747,190	837,105
Texas	431,463	350,628	805,284	1,471,242	2,609,018
Oklahoma	--	--	--	425	71,983

Source: U.S. Bureau of the Census.

Table 5. Rank Order of States by Amount of Cotton Produced and Proportion of Tenants

State	1880		1890		1900	
	(1)[a]	(2)[b]	(1)	(2)	(1)	(2)
Mississippi	1	4	3	3	2	1
Georgia	2	3	2	2	3	3
Alabama	3	2	4	5	4	4
Texas	4	5	1	4	1	6
Arkansas	5	8	6	8	6	7
South Carolina	6	1	5	1	5	2
Louisiana	7	6	7	6	7	5
North Carolina	8	7	8	7	8	8
Oklahoma	9	9	9	9	9	9

[a] Rank order of amount of cotton produced.
[b] Rank order of proportion tenantized.

Source: U.S. Bureau of the Census

Table 6. Proportion of Blacks and Whites Cultivating Cotton by State

State	1860[a]		1876[b]		1900[c]	
	Blacks	Whites	Blacks	Whites	Blacks	Whites
Alabama	83	17	59	41	43	57
Arkansas	83	17	40	60	--	--
Georgia	83	17	66	34	36	64
Louisiana	83	17	77	23	51	49
Mississippi	83	17	68	32	59	41
North Carolina	83	17	65	35	--	--
South Carolina	83	17	68	32	55	45
Texas	83	17	38	62	19	81

[a]Source: Hamond, 1898.

[b]Source: Commissioner of Agriculture, 1876.

[c]Source: U.S. Bureau of the Census; states included were over 70 percent of the farms cultivated cotton in 1889. Figure is based on assumption that black and white farmers are cultivating crop equally.

for and to feed their animals. As the price of cotton dropped in the 1870s and 1880s, tenants and yeoman farmers found themselves in debt. So, the next year the farmer would try to catch up by planting even more cotton. This required buying all food and supplies from the merchant or landlord. As crop prices dropped, the farmers' position continued to deteriorate. They had no choice but to plant more cotton.

Tenant and yeoman farmers were in no position to escape this cycle. If tenants stopped growing cotton or started growing food, the landlord would throw them off the land. To maximize their share of the crop, landlords were most interested in keeping cotton production high. If the landlord was furnishing his tenants, he did not want to see them growing food as that cut into his profits. It was in the interest of the landlord to keep the tenant growing cotton and only cotton. The yeoman farmer also found it difficult to stop growing cotton as the merchant he owed would only give him a crop lien to grow cotton. If the yeoman farmers were in debt and the merchants saw them growing food and thus cutting down on cotton production, the merchant could foreclose on the yeomans' land. After they were in debt, yeoman farmers could not afford to stop producing cotton. The ultimate price was high: they paid with their land. So both tenants and yeoman farmers were caught

Table 7.   Owners and Tenants in Southern States by Race in 1900

State	Whites		Blacks	
	Owners	Tenants	Owners	Tenants
Alabama	79,362 [a] (.61) (.36) [c]	48,973 (.39) (.22)	14,110 [b] (.15) (.06)	79,901 (.85) (.36)
Arkansas	84,794 (.64) (.48)	46,178 (.36) (.26)	11,941 (.25) (.07)	34,962 (.75) (.29)
Georgia	77,154 (.54) (.35)	63,317 (.46) (.28)	11,375 (.13) (.05)	71,243 (.87) (.32)
Louisiana	38,323 (.67) (.33)	18,531 (.33) (.16)	9,378 (.16) (.09)	48,703 (.84) (.42)
Mississippi	61,048 (.66) (.28)	30,253 (.34) (.14)	20,973 (.16) (.10)	107,599 (.84) (.48)
North Carolina	113,052 (.64) (.46)	63,148 (.36) (.27)	21,443 (.32) (.09)	44,139 (.68) (.18)
South Carolina	40,447 (.58) (.26)	28,633 (.42) (.19)	18,970 (.22) (.12)	66,251 (.78) (.43)
Texas	154,500 (.54) (.44)	129,685 (.46) (.37)	30,139 (.30) (.06)	45,306 (.70) (.13)
Oklahoma	50,018 (.53) (.46)	44,265 (.47) (.41)	10,191 (.77) (.10)	2,985 (.23) (.03)

[a] Percentage of whites in each status.
[b] Percentage of blacks in each status.
[c] Percentage of total number of farmers in each status.

Source: U.S. Bureau of the Census.

in a dynamic where their only recourse was to grow cotton. Debt, the lien system, merchants and landlords, and the plummeting world price of cotton placed small farm owners and tenants in a position where they could only produce more cotton, and the increase in production caused prices to decrease even more. Many modern writers have chastised the southern farmer for his dependency on cotton (Woofter, 1969; Vance, 1932; Goodrich, 1934). But the production of cotton was the only logical response to the financial bind in which the cotton farmer found himself. Once the farmer got into debt, there were powerful forces preventing him from changing farming practices. The entire social structure of the South depended on this newly emergent system of agricultural production (Ransom and Sutch, 1972:641–669).

It should be noted that when the price of cotton was high many people made money. In fact, cotton farmers were doing fairly well in this century up until 1922 (Fligstein, 1981). But, as the price of cotton dropped in the 1880s and 1890s, the only people making profit on cotton were local merchants and planters who furnished their tenants as well as renting them land.

The political ascendancy of southern Democrats who favored white supremacy and industrial development were soon to be threatened by a movement that hated that revolution and felt it had nothing to gain from industrial development. As southern Democrats took complete control over all southern governments in 1877, the movement to dethrone them was already taking shape. The Populist revolt would not let this new order come so easily. People were suffering from this revolution and they were going to try and change it.

FARMERS' MOVEMENTS AND THEIR IMPLICATIONS FOR ECONOMIC AND POLITICAL CHANGE

The goal of this section is twofold. First, to characterize how farmers expressed their position on "what was wrong" in America; and second, to examine various efforts to correct this situation and their effects on the economic and political situation. Many excellent studies exist on various aspects of farmers' movements in the South and the rest of America (Hicks, 1931; Hirwan, 1951; Woodward, 1938, 1974; Simkins, 1947; Saloutos, 1960; Arnett, 1922; Schwatz, 1976; Goodwyn, 1978).

In the late 1870s, farmers in the West and South were becoming increasingly angry. Wheat, corn, and cotton prices were all dropping between 1870–1890. Hammond (1897:160) estimated that cotton could be produced for 8 cents per pound. As the price dropped, the profit on the crop became negligible. In the Midwest, farmers were in a similar position (Hicks, 1931:57).

Farmers all over the country were increasingly in debt. Farmers saw three basic enemies: merchants who sold them goods and lent them money; railroads which shipped their goods and charged high prices; and northern capitalists who controlled the grain and cotton markets (Woodward, 1938, 1974; Hicks, 1931; Saloutos, 1960). Further, farmers in general were hostile to the state and federal governments which they viewed as supporting capitalist development at their expense. That is, the government supported tariffs for manufacturers, which held prices of goods artificially high (Hicks, 1931:79–80), and underwrote the cost of railroad construction. While farmers were told that the plummeting price of their crops was due to overproduction, they believed that their share of the profits was dropping while middlemen, like merchants, railroads, and manufacturers were flourishing.

In the South, these general arguments held sway, but they were expressed in different ways. The enemy was the credit system which put more and more people into debt. As long as the price of cotton was high, grievances against merchants, railroads, and tariff-protected manufacturers were muted. But when the price of cotton declined to the point where it was no longer profitable to grow cotton, the protest began. The 1880s and 1890s witnessed enormous growth in the numbers of tenant farmers. Many writers (Arnett, 1922:22; Hicks, 1931:85; Schwartz, 1977:73–89; Hackney, 1969: vii–xii; Hunt, 1934:27–31) attribute this growth to the lapse of small farm owners into tenantry. Arnett, speaking of Georgia, says that in the 1880s and 1890s, "there was a marked tendency toward the concentration of agricultural land in the hands of merchants, loan agents, and a few of the financially strongest farmers" (1922:61). Schwartz suggests that by 1900, land ownership was more concentrated than in 1860 (1977:85–89). The impoverishment of southern farmers was carried further by a system of taxation under which landholders paid a disproportionate share of taxes (Kirwan, 1951: 261–264; Arnett, 1922:72–74; Hicks, 1931:85–86).

Hicks (1931:87) argues that the farmer saw the system of money and banking as his chief enemy. The argument centered on the fact that there was not a lot of money circulating in the economy. Indeed, from 1865 to 1895, the dollar appreciated almost 300 percent (Arnett, 1922:69). The actual amount of money in circulation, meanwhile, had declined (Hicks, 1931:88). For the farmer, who was in debt, this meant that high interest rates abounded. Most farmers paid off their debts in crops. As money appreciated, the price of crops lessened and farmers ended up paying even more to settle their debts.

In the South, farmers were caught up in the dynamic discussed in the previous section. As the farmers' situation deteriorated, organizations with names like the Farmers' Alliance, the Wheel, and the Farmers' Union began. These organizations multiplied until 1889, when the Wheel and the Alliance merged to form the national Farmers' Alliance and Industrial Union (Arnett, 1922:77). By 1889, these organizations claimed three million members in the South alone.

The goals and activities of these organizations were concerned with economic matters. One function of the organizations was educational. They spread information on the use of fertilizers, machines, and seed selection, as well as trying to teach sound business management (Arnett, 1922:78). More importantly, farmers' organizations were out to make the farmers' position more stable in the face of those who were their perceived enemies: bankers, merchants, manufacturers, railway directors, and speculators. Two general strategies were employed in this endeavor:

cooperation was the major strategy and political action only came into play after 1889.

To cut costs, cooperatives were formed to buy fertilizer and other supplies. Also, some crops were sold in the same way. By 1887, it became apparent that a larger scale of business would cut costs even further and state exchanges were formed in most cotton states (Arnett, 1922:79; Hicks, 1931:133–140). These exchanges dealt in almost every commodity that farmers bought and sold. "Encouraged by the success of these enterprises, cooperative stores, cotton warehouses, and gins sprang up like mushrooms over the South" (Arnett, 1922:80). While only members of the various organization could use the cooperative stores, the effect of the "co-ops" were felt by all farmers when merchants in competition with the "co-ops" were forced to cut prices to retain customers.

The rise of the cooperatives was met by opposition from those who had a stake in the old system. Wholesalers, railroads, and money-lenders all charged higher prices and rates to farmers' ventures (Hicks, 1931:138–140; Arnett, 1922:80). Eventually, a large number of them went bankrupt as the farmers' exchanges were often undercapitalized and poorly managed. Merchants in competition with the exchanges would drastically lower prices and the exchanges were unable to hold farmers' loyalty in the face of cutthroat competition (Hicks, 1931:140).

The failure of the cooperative ventures tended to convince leaders of the Alliance that many of the economic ills of the farmers could be corrected only through political action (Hicks, 1931:140–145; Arnett, 1922:81; Kirwan, 1951:93–103). Before turning to a discussion of the politics of the Alliance, it is helpful to consider what kind of struggle was being waged. In the South, white tenant and yeoman farmers were struggling for control of their labor and land. Due to the peculiar dynamics of the cotton situation, these farmers' activities were becoming increasingly controlled by others. This control began with a landlord and then a merchant was added. These local powers controlled credit and the production of crops. More distantly, railroads and cotton merchants, largely from the North, controlled the movement and price of the crop. Finally, federal and state governments supported and abetted this oppression in a number of ways. First, railroads and manufacturers were given loans, land, tax shelters, and tariffs to protect and further their ability to expand and make profit. Second, the federal government controlled the money supply and kept the amount of dollars in circulation tied to the amount of gold in existence. Because the supply of gold was not expanding as rapidly as the demand for money, money was appreciating. This made money scarce and expensive, which affected the farmer adversely. Third, locally, state governments, especially in the

South, supported railroad construction and the crop lien system, both of which worked against the small farm owner and tenant.

This oppression and the struggle which ensued must be considered a class struggle (Hicks, 1931:404–408; Arnett, 1922:81). There were essentially two sets of superordinate/subordinate relationships governing the production of cotton in the South. These were the merchants/small farm owners and the landlord/tenant relations. The landlord/tenant structure, of course, originated in the plantation system of the antebellum South. These producers were always producing cash crops for an export market and were always engaged in capitalist agriculture. The small farm owners, however, before the Civil War, tended to be subsistence farmers. Only the high price of cotton and the availability of credit (in the form of crop liens) drew them into the production of cash crops. The uniting dynamic in the social system was, therefore, twofold: the expansion of the world market for cotton and the availability of credit with which to grow cotton. Once caught in this dynamic, small farm owners became subject to the same forces that affected tenants: the high price of credit and the cyclical price of cotton.

The southern economic system had a clear cut status ordering. At the bottom were wage hands (who could work either for landlords or small farm owners), followed by sharecroppers, share tenants, cash tenants, small farm owners and plantation owners. Booms and busts sent people up and down the scale. For instance, in a boom (high cotton prices), sharecroppers might make extra money, buy a mule and tools and move up to a share or cash tenant status. In a depression small owners might find their land so mortgaged that the local merchant would foreclose and force the owner to move or become a tenant.

It is argued here that shifting statuses within the tenant system does not imply a radical shift in social status as the individual was still operating within the landlord/tenant structure. That is, a shift from one tenant status to another (or even from being a sharecropper to being a wage hand) implied that one was still working someone else's land and therefore one was still subject to a landowners' will and determination. However, the shift from a farm owner to a tenant status (or vice versa) implied a shift in class. That is, the social structure of the South consisted of people who owned land and people who did not. A shift of status across this barrier implied a basic change in one's class position. Put another way, shifting from being a farm owner to being a tenant meant entering into another *kind* of superordinate/subordinate relationship—one whose very character implied more submission to the will of the other. Of course, at all times, small farm owners were in a very vulnerable position. They lacked the money and financial resources to save their land in hard times. At the same time, losing the land would force landowning farmers to 1) migrate or 2) accept renter status. This entailed a real loss of independence and social status.

It is not surprising then, that many of the farmers' movements sprang from groups of small farm owners who were faced, in a depression, with loss of land and a change in class status (Hackney, 1969:vii-xii; Hicks, 1931:104–112; Saloutos, 1960:70–78; Hunt, 1934:27–31; Woodward, 1938: 188, 1974:193). The political movements of the South always reflect this concern and are, in this sense, conservative. That is, small farm owners want to maintain their social position—their *land*—in the face of capitalist development that is causing the prices of goods (including loans) they buy to increase, while depressing the prices for their product. The rural class struggle in the South often implicitly had as its object the preservation of the independent yeoman farmer in the face of the domination of merchants, railroaders, and capitalists. The political program of the organization of yeoman farmers was liberal in that it only sought to mitigate some of the emerging industrial capitalist system's most blatant excesses. The struggle of the tenant farmer fit into this only insofar as the tenant was the victim of these same forces (i.e., the crop lien system and capitalist development).

On the whole, members of the Alliance were small producers or tenant farmers (Saloutos, 1960:76). The role of the large planters in the movement is relatively clear. In most states, planters were in favor of capitalist development as it implied more business opportunities and more effective exploitation of the land (Saloutos, 1960:57–68). These planters had diversified interests as they invested heavily in land, lumber, railroads, and manufacturing. Virginia was an exception. Some of the Alliance's strongest supporters were planters. In most states, however, planters tended to be against this revolt as they supported the New South policy of the southern Democrats.

By 1889 the stage was set for political activity. The founders of the Alliance had stressed that the organization had economic, not political goals. As time went on it became evident to Alliance leaders that economic reform would occur only with political reform (Saloutos, 1960: Arnett, 1922; Kirwan, 1951; Hicks, 1931). The Alliance met in St. Louis to develop a political platform in 1889. At this meeting, the Alliance decided to support only candidates who accepted the principles in the Alliance's platform. The platform had the following goals: 1) abolish national banks and substitute treasury notes "in sufficient volume to do the business of the nation on a cash basis" (Arnett, 1922:84), as well as to expand the volume of money as business grew; 2) outlaw commodity dealing in futures; 3) promote free and unlimited coinage in silver; 4) pass laws outlawing alien ownership of land; 5) eschew taxation as a way "to build up one interest or class at the expense of another" (Arnett, 1922:84); 6) pressure Congress to issue paper currency in large enough amounts to allow exchange through the mail, and 7) government ownership and operation of communications and transportation for all people.

These goals were centrally concerned with increasing the money supply, ending the use of government revenues for railroad and manufacturing development, and nationalizing the railroad and telegraph systems. This program spoke directly to the articulated needs of the small farm owner. In each state, the local Alliance might modify the platform and seek to legislate to specific needs. The Arkansas Wheel, for instance, called for repeal of crop lien legislation (Hicks, 1931:142–143).

A political struggle was brewing across the country. In the South, the struggle was more complex as the role of the Democratic party in this struggle was at issue. The white Alliance leaders sought to carry on the struggle in the Democratic party. The planters, merchants, and industrialists who controlled the party were not about to give up state power and allow agrarian radicals to control state government and enact legislation detrimental to the white ruling elite. The agrarian radicals and the planter/merchant/industrialist faction of the party were in conflict. The balance of power in any election fell to the black voters. Both of these groups realized this, and both tried to woo the black vote.

THE ROLE OF BLACKS
IN THE POLITICAL STRUGGLE

The 1890s saw the rise and fall of the People's Party. Further, they spawned a conservative blacklash against blacks that resulted in his disenfranchisement and subjugation to the whites as extreme racism became state policy with the advent of Jim Crow legislation. In this section, it will be argued that this most overt form of racism provided a natural lever by which southern agrarian radicalism was to be squelched. While the seeds of hatred of blacks predate this ultimate solution, they are brought to nurture relatively self-consciously by the planter/merchant/industrialist faction of the southern Democratic Party.

To understand how this all occurred, one must recall the political situation after the Compromise of 1877. With the rise of the southern Democratic Party as the "white man's party," and the decline of the Republican Party, blacks were becoming politically isolated. While most blacks initially remained Republican, the period 1877–96 witnessed an increasing crossover of the black vote to the Democratic Party. The southern Democrats came to control the black vote through one of four methods: coercion; ballot box stuffing; actual buying of black votes; and fusion (Woodward, 1966:54–57, 1974:79–81; Kousser, 1974:36). In counties through the South with large concentrations of black population, the control of the southern Democrats was most evident. One of the major ways in which black votes were manipulated was coercion and threats. Often, blacks could not find out where voting was to take place and if they did vote, there were a number of whites standing by threatening physical harm for an improper vote. Another favorite tactic was ballot box stuffing. After voting had occurred, it was not uncommon for a new ballot box to appear with only Democratic Party votes. The buying of votes with a bottle of liquor or a small amount of money was also common.

In counties where blacks' political participation was strong, it was not uncommon for southern Democrats to "fuse" with black Republicans (Woodward, 1966:54–57, 1974:79–81; Logan, 1964:57–63; Rice, 1971:53–68). Fusion was the alliance between southern Democrats and black Republicans where black Republicans would support southern Democrats against splinter parties such as the Independent Party, the Greenback Party, and the People's Party, while the southern Democrats would support the black Republicans at the local level. Blacks thus received a share of the county offices in exchange for political support. In these ways, then, the southern Democratic Party maintained control over black votes.

The white southern Democrats, however, were wary of this alliance. They were always afraid that the blacks would split off and ally themselves with more radial agrarian white elements. The conservative southern Democrats were fearful because they saw that the whites could split over fundamental economic issues and the blacks would hold the controlling votes (Woodward, 1966:78–80, 1974:255–259; Kousser, 1974:11–38; Rice, 1971:86–112; Hicks, 1931:334–339; Arnett, 1922:153–155). Because the white small farm owners and tenants would have a program that would appeal to the blacks, the black vote would swing away from the southern Democrats and the poorer white elements would rule in coalition with the blacks.

How realistic was this fear? When the People's Party formed in the South, it was explicitly geared to attract the black vote. It must be remembered that the greatest racial hatred existed among whites who were small farm owners and tenants. As Wharton argues, when blacks were slaves, poor whites made two distinctions between themselves and blacks: they were whites and they were free. After the war, the only distinction left was race (1947:216–218). The poor whites wanted total segregation and subjugation of blacks. By oppressing blacks, poor whites could maintain dignity because they thought they were better than the blacks. In the period 1877–1896, the southern social and political situation was rather fluid. Blacks had some political power and it was not clear that the southern Democrats could stay in power without the alliance with blacks (Kousser, 1974:36–44). But the forces of extreme racism were arising in the 1880s. In 1890, Mississippi became the first state to disenfranchise blacks.

Before considering disenfranchisement and the rise of the Jim Crow laws, it is necessary to consider the role of blacks in the Farmers' Alliance and the People's Party. Blacks were not allowed to join the Farmers' Alliance, but an adjunct organization was formed for blacks called the Colored Farmers' Alliance (Woodward, 1974:192; Hicks, 1931:114). The Farmers' Alliance and the Colored Farmers' Alliance worked together and both organizations approved the platform presented in the previous section. The two organizations were forced to remain separate as white farmers refused to be in an organization with blacks (Hicks, 1931:114).

When the Farmers' Alliance decided to adopt a political strategy, there was some disagreement over how to implement that strategy. In the South, the Alliance stayed with the Democratic Party and supported anyone who accepted its platform. In the Midwest, the Alliance was unable to come to an agreement with the Democrats, so in 1890, the People's Party was formed (Woodward, 1974:233–263; Hicks, 1931:205–237). Whites in the Alliance in the South wanted to remain in the Democratic Party as it was an established party and it was the party of white supremacy. The Southern Farmers' Alliance strategy apparently worked better than the third party (i.e., the People's Party) strategy. People were elected all across the South in 1890 who professed the Alliance platform. As it turned out, Democrats who were elected did not support the Alliance program. They did little, once in office, to further the interests of Alliance members (Hicks, 1931:248–250; Woodward, 1974:235–242).

The final blow that caused certain of the Alliance supporters to join the People's Party came with the Democratic Party's nomination of Grover Cleveland in 1892 as their presidential candidate. Cleveland was a conservative Democrat who supported northern business development and was a foe of the easy money policies supported by the Alliance. At this point, Alliance members who were southern Democrats left the Democratic Party and joined the People's Party. Hicks (1931) estimates that roughly half of the Alliance membership joined the People's Party. Who were the members of the People's Party? Mostly they were white yeoman and tenant farmers. Most were quite poor and saw the Populist movement as a way to attack the most direct causes of their poverty

(Hicks, 1931:85–88; Woodward, 1974:192–194; Arnett, 1922:66–69; Kirwan, 1951:85–93).

The role blacks played in the People's Party was minimal. The Populist leaders, notably Tom Watson in Georgia, tried to appeal to the blacks on the basis of self-interest (Hicks, 1931:114; Woodward, 1938:216–244, 1966:60–64; Arnett, 1922:153–155). The Populist argument was that poor whites and blacks were in the same social position. The only way they could get out of the grasp of landlords, merchants, and railroads, was to organize together and execute legislative action to relieve their mutual ills. The philosophy of race relations underlying this argument was quite radical. It suggested that whites and blacks were equal by virtue of their common oppression (Woodward, 1966:61).

This potentially radical alliance never quite became reality for two sorts of reasons. First of all, much of the hard core support of the Populist movement came from those most prejudiced against blacks. The members of the People's Party who hated blacks were always a force which presented difficulties in any relationship that could exist between blacks and whites in the party.

The second difficulty concerned recruiting blacks into the party. At the outset, the Populists attempted to attract the black vote by ignoring established Republican leadership and trying to appeal directly to the mass of black farmers. This strategy never worked very well and in the end, it only alienated black Republicans from the Populist cause (Woodward, 1966:77–80; Kousser, 1974:35–36; Arnett, 1922:155). Eventually the Populists tried to adopt the strategy of the southern Democrats and attempts were made at "fusion." While these attempts were a bit more successful, all in all, black support of the Populist movement was not strong.

The elections of 1894 and 1896, throughout the South, climaxed the struggle between the Populists and the conservative Democrats. The elections were bitterly fought, and violence was common (Hicks, 1931:321–329; Woodward, 1974:264–290; Kousser, 1974:29–44; Arnett, 1922:183–185). The People's Party only took control of one state government: North Carolina. In Georgia and Alabama in 1894, only very blatant vote fraud prevented Populists from taking power (Hicks, 1931:334–336; Arnett, 1922:183–184). It was ballot box stuffing in the black counties that prevented the Populists from taking control of the state governments. The southern Democrats had weathered the Populist assault, but it took tremendous illegalities to do it.

The Populist revolt lost steam after 1896 as the movement was absorbed into the Democratic Party. Populist leaders became part of the Democratic Party to support the issue of silver-based currency which would have had the effect of increasing the amount of money in circulation. In 1896 the nomination of William Jennings Bryan as the Democratic Party's candidate for president drew the support of the People's Party. But fusing the Populists to the Democrats had the effect of destroying the third party machinery of the Populists and as a result, the party never recovered (Hicks, 1931:378). Not only had the Populists lost the election of 1896, but also they had lost the independent machinery by which they were a force to be reckoned with.

In the South the Populist movement also lost steam. As Tom Watson said, "Our party, as a party, does not exist anymore. Fusion has well nigh killed it" (Woodward, 1974:289). The alliance with the Democrats had once again put the white man's party back together. With the Populists supporting the party of big business and white supremacy in combination with the blacks, it is no wonder that the mass of poor white farmers and tenants became politically apathetic (Woodward, 1974:378).

While political efforts of tenant and yeoman farmers were being thwarted, a new movement was afoot to split the agrarian radicals and ally all whites against the blacks. Many of the Populist rank and file blamed the blacks for their losses and extreme racism began to flare up in the late-1890s. Woodward (1966) argues that the South was poised to react strongly against blacks.

> Economic, political and social frustrations had pyramided to a climax of social tensions. Hopes for reform and the political means employed in defiance of tradition and at a great cost to emotional attachments to effect reform had likewise met with cruel disappointments and frustration. There had to be a scapegoat. And all along the line signals were going up to indicate that the Negro was an approved object of aggression (Woodward, 1966:81).

Blacks would serve as the scapegoat to conciliate the white classes. "The only formula powerful enough to accomplish that was the magical formula of white supremacy, applied without stint and without any of the old conservative reservations of paternalism" (Woodward, 1966:82).

This backlash against blacks took two forms: disenfranchisement and Jim Crow laws. Who was behind the Jim Crow laws and the disenfranchisement movement? Kousser, in his study of southern politics between 1890 and 1910, concludes:

> The new political structure was not the product of accident or other impersonal forces, nor of decisions demanded by the masses, nor even the white masses. The system which insured the absolute control of predominantly black counties by upper class whites, the elimination in most areas of parties as a means of organized competition between politicians and, in general, the nonrepre-

sentation of lower class interests in political decision-making was shaped by those who stood to benefit most from it—Democrats, usually from the black belt and always socioeconomically privileged (Kousser, 1974:238).

Kousser goes on to argue that disenfranchisement operated not only against blacks, but also against whites. He argues convincingly that at the center of the movement to remove blacks from the political arena were whites who were part of the planter/merchant/industrialist elite who wanted to protect the Democratic Party from further threats to its continued conservative form.

While the southern Democrats did not invent the extreme racist attitudes sweeping the South in the 1890s, it is clear that they were quite willing to use them to rebind the poor whites into the Democratic Party, the white man's party. The social function of the Jim Crow laws and disenfranchisement was to establish the social order once and for all. Blacks were placed firmly on the bottom and the poor whites had one consolation: at least they were not black. The class struggle of the 1880s and 1890s was resolved ideologically by the emergence of extreme racist pronouncements that were to be made into law. The political domination of the southern Democrats became a fact and the agricultural system that was in crisis was offered no real relief. The broad outlines of southern poverty in the 20th century were set into place.

CONCLUSIONS

The underdevelopment of the South throughout much of this century cannot be viewed in isolation from events beginning with the Civil War. The rise of an eastern-based capitalist class and the emergence of a federal government controlled by that class placed the first limits on the development of southern agriculture. The crisis of labor and capital immediately following the Civil War in conjunction with the high price for cotton in the world market brought about fundamental changes in the social relations of production in the South. Sharecropping and crop lien systems were the primary mechanisms by which an impoverished, defeated South sought to resume production of cotton.

However, the dynamics of these shifts in the social organization of cotton production brought forth new crises. By 1877, many white yeoman farmers were producing cotton utilizing the crop lien mechanism. As the world price of cotton fell, these farmers went further into debt, and many lost their land. They perceived that bankers, merchants, railroads, and industrial capitalists were their enemies. They organized, first at the economic level, then at the political level. Their defeat signalled a resolution of the southern crisis that insulated future political events from future economic crises. Local state governments were firmly held by local indigenous planters, merchants, and capitalists. With the defeat of populism, no hope of relief was in sight for those laboring under southern agriculture's social relations. Only the collapse of the credit system in the early 1930s would bring change to the South. And it should be noted that this change came from the federal government and wealthy landowners and was not a result of political action of the southern masses (Fligstein, 1981). The underdevelopment of the South in the 20th century is the result of the crisis of agriculture and their relations to political practices at the state and national levels. In turn, the state itself had its activities directed and manipulated by the needs of the capitalist class, both in the South and in the North, which reflects these complex relations and indeed, cannot be understood without a knowledge of them.

REFERENCES

Arnett, Alex M. 1922. The Populist Movement in Georgia. New York: Columbia University Press.

Banks, Enoch. 1905. The Economics of Land Tenure in Georgia. New York: Columbia University Press.

Beard, Charles and Mary Beard. 1933. The Rise of American Civilization. New York: Macmillan Co.

Boeger, E. A. and E. A. Golderweiser. 1916. "A Study of the Tenant Systems of Farming in the Yazoo-Mississippi Delta." U.S. Department of Agriculture Bulletin 337. Washington, D. C.: U.S. Government Printing Office.

Bowers, Claude. 1929. The Tragic Era: The Revolution after Lincoln. Cambridge, Mass.: Houghton-Mifflin Company.

Brooks, Robert. 1914. "The Agrarian Revolution in Georgia, 1865-1912." Bulletin of the University of Wisconsin History Series, Vol. 3.

Clark, Thomas D. 1944. Pills, Petticoats, and Plows. Norman, Oklahoma: University of Oklahoma Press.

———. 1946. "The Furnishing and Supply System in Southern Agriculture Since 1865." Journal of Southern History, XII (February):28–46.

Coulter, Ellis M. 1947. The South during Reconstruction, 1865–1877. Baton Rouge: Louisiana State University Press.

DeCanio, Stephen J. 1974. Agriculture in the Postbellum South: The Economics of Production and Supply. Cambridge, Mass.: M.I.T. Press.

DuBois, W.E.B. 1964. Black Reconstruction in America. Cleveland: World Publishing Co.

Dunning, William A. 1922. Reconstruction, Political and Economic, 1865–1877. New York: Harper Bros. Inc.

Ezell, John. 1963. The South since 1865. New York: Macmillan Company.

Fligstein, Neil. 1981. Going North. New York: Academic Press.

Goldenweiser, E. A. and Leon Truesdell. 1924. Farm Tenancy in the United States. Washington, D. C.: U.S. Government Printing Office.

Goodrich, Carter. 1934. Migration and Economic Opportunity. Philadelphia: University of Pennsylvania Press.

Going, Allen. 1951. Bourbon Democracy in Alabama, 1874–1890. Montgomery: University of Alabama Press.

Goodwyn, Lawrence. 1978. Democratic Promise. Chapel Hill: University of North Carolina Press.

Gray, Lewis. 1957. History of Agriculture in the Southern U.S. to 1860. Washington, D. C.: Carnegie Institute of Washington.

Hackney, Sheldon. 1969. Populism to Progressivism in Alabama. Princeton, N.J.: Princeton University Press.

Hammond, Mathew. 1897. The Cotton Industry: An Essay in American Economic History, Part I: The Cotton Culture and the Cotton Trade. New York: Macmillan Co.

Hicks, John D. 1931. The Populist Revolt. Minneapolis: University of Minnesota Press.

Horn, Stanley. 1939. Invisible Empire: The Story of the KKK 1866–1871. Montclair, N.J.: Patterson Smith Co.

Hunt, Robert L. 1934. "A History of Farmer Movements in the Southwest, 1873–1925." Unpublished Ph.D. dissertation, University of Wisconsin-Madison.

Key, V. O. 1949. Southern Politics in State and Nation. New York: A. A. Knopf Co.

Kirwan, Albert. 1951. Revolt of the Rednecks: Mississippi Politics 1876–1925. Lexington: University of Kentucky Press.

Kousser, J. Morgan. 1974. The Shaping of Southern Politics, 1880–1910. New Haven: Yale University Press.

Logan, Fremise. 1964. The Negro in North Carolina. Chapel Hill: University of North Carolina Press.

Myrdal, Gunnar. 1944. An American Dilemma: The Negro Problem and Modern Democracy. New York: Harper Bros. and Co.

Nevins, Allan. 1927. The Emergence of Modern America, 1865–1878. New York: Macmillan Co.

Poulantzas, Nicos. 1968. Political Power and Social Classes. London: New Left Books.

Ransom, Roger and Richard Sutch. 1972. "Debt-peonage in the South after the Civil War." Journal of Economic History, 32 (September):641–669.

————. 1977. One Kind of Freedom. Cambridge: Cambridge University Press.

Raper, Arthur. 1936. Preface to Peasantry: A Tale of Two Black Belt Counties. Chapel Hill: University of North Carolina Press.

Reid, Whitelaw. 1965. After the War. New York: Harper Torchbooks.

Rhodes, James F. 1902. History of the United States from the Compromise of 1850 to the Final Restoration of Home Rule at the South in 1877. New York: The Macmillan Company.

Rice, Lawrence. 1971. The Negro in Texas, 1874–1900. Baton Rouge: Louisiana State University Press.

Saloutos, Theodore. 1960. Farmer Movements in the South, 1865–1933. Berkeley: University of California Press.

Schwartz, Michael. 1976. Radical Protest and Social Structure. New York: Academic Press.

Scott, Emmett. 1920. Negro Migration during the War. New York: Oxford University Press.

Shugg, Roger. 1939. Origins of Class Struggle in Louisiana. Baton Rouge: Louisiana State University Press.

Simkins, Francis Butler. 1947. The South, Old and New, a History, 1820–1947. New York: A. A. Knopf.

Somers, Robert. 1973. The Southern States since the War of 1870–71. New York: Arno Press.

Stampp, Kenneth. 1966. The Era of Reconstruction, 1865–71. New York: Alfred Knopf Co.

Stover, John F. 1955. The Railroads of the South 1865–1900. Chapel Hill: University of North Carolina Press.

Tannenbaum, Frank. 1969. Darker Phases of the South. New York: Negro Universities Press.

Tindall, George. 1967. The Emergence of the New South, 1913–1945. Baton Rouge: Louisiana State University Press.

Trowbridge, John T. 1956. The Desolate South, 1865–1866: A Picture of the Battlefields and of the Devastated Confederacy. New York: Sloan and Pearce.

U.S. Bureau of the Census. 1864. 8th Census of the United States, Agriculture. Washington, D. C.: U.S. Government Printing Office.

———. 1872. 9th Census of the United States, Compendium. Washington, D. C.: U.S. Government Printing Office.

———. 1883. 10th Census of the United States, Compendium. Washington, D. C.: U.S. Government Printing Office.

———. 1896. 11th Census of the United States, Report on Farms and Homes. Washington, D. C.: U. S. Government Printing Office.

———. 1902. 12th Census of the United States, Population, Vol. II. Washington, D. C.: U. S. Government Printing Office.

———. 1902. 12th Census of the United States, Agriculture, Vol. VI, Part II. Washington, D. C.: U. S. Government Printing Office.

Vance, Rupert. 1929. Human factors in Cotton Culture. Chapel Hill: University of North Carolina Press.

———. 1935. Human Geography of the South. Chapel Hill: University of North Carolina Press.

———. 1945. All These People. Chapel Hill: University of North Carolina Press.

Watkins, James L. 1908. King Cotton: A Historical and Statistical Review, 1790–1908. New York: J. L. Watkins and Sons.

Wharton, Vernon L. 1947. The Negro in Mississippi. Chapel Hill: University of North Carolina Press.

Williamson, Joel. 1965. After Slavery. Chapel Hill: University of North Carolina Press.

Woodman, Harold D. 1968. King Cotton and His Retainers. Lexington, KY: University of Kentucky Press.

Woodson, Carter. 1924. A Century of Negro Migration. New York: Russell and Russell.

Woodward, C. Vann. 1938. Tom Watson, Agrarian Rebel. Savannah, Georgia: The Beehive Press.

_____. 1951. Reunion and Reaction: The Compromise of 1877 and the End of Reconstruction. Boston: Little, Brown, and Co.

_____. 1966. The Strong Career of Jim Crow. New York: Oxford University Press.

_____. 1974. The Origins of the New South. Baton Rouge: Louisiana State University Press.

Woofter, Thomas. 1936. Landlord and Tenant on the Cotton Plantation. Work Progress Administration Research Monography, Vol. V. Washington, D. C.: Work Progress Administration.

_____. 1969. Negro Migration: Changes in Rural Organization and Population in the Cotton Belt. New York: Negro University Press.

Woolfolk, George. 1957. The Cotton Regency. New York: Bookman Associates.

4
Farmers' Movements and the Changing Structure of Agriculture

Carolyn Howe

INTRODUCTION

While a richly descriptive but disparate literature on farmers' movements in capitalist countries exists, there has been an underemphasis on macro-theoretical issues and a failure to link the many historical studies into a unified body of knowledge. This has left us with an inadequate understanding of the relationship between these movements and the changing structure of agriculture.

This chapter presents a theoretical framework for understanding social movements among family farmers in advanced capitalist countries. By elaborating the elements of a theoretical framework, it is hoped that it can then be applied to our understanding of the development of agriculture, its changing class structure, and the role of farmers' movements in effecting and being affected by those changes. In the recent literature on farmers' movements, controversies have arisen over the class position of farmers and peasants and the conditions under which agricultural workers mobilize into radical social movements. Many of these theories attribute the rising discontent of farmers to economically bad times (Hofstadter, 1971). Paige (1978) and Wolf (1969) go beyond the assumption that as individuals experience hard times, their discontent leads them to collective action. They have theorized the variability of agrarian movements by positing which strata of agrarian workers are more likely to join radical or conservative movements. While they differ as to which strata are likely to be most radical, both authors suggest that agrarian producers respond from their own economic position to economic changes and the development of a commercialized agriculture. Their work suggests the need to examine the effect of changes in the structure of agriculture on agrarian movements and to analyze the differential impact of such changes on different strata or class "fractions" of farmers. Both, however, fall short of presenting a class analysis of farmers and neither attempts to account for transformations of agrarian movements themselves.

In an attempt to develop a more comprehensive theoretical framework, I argue that as the structure of agriculture changes it transforms and fragments the social base of agrarian social movements. The new class relations that emerge account for the internal dynamics and historical transformations of farmers' movements. In part one I develop the theoretical framework by emphasizing two elements that must form the core of a theory of farmers' movements: First, we must analyze the changing structure of agriculture as capitalist relations penetrate the entire food production cycle and examine the effects of these changes on the grievances, mobilizations, and outcomes of farmers' movements. Second, I argue that a class analysis of family farmers and their social movements is needed in order to explain (a) differences between farmers' movements, (b) different orientations within a movement or its organizational form, and (c) changes in the farmers' movement over time. I argue that the relationship of farmers to capital is a central determinant of the movements. This relationship is mediated by cycles of economic expansion or crisis, on the one hand, and interventions of the state, on the other hand.

In part two I illustrate the applicability of the theoretical framework through a brief historical overview and periodization of Midwestern[1] farmers' movements from 1850 to the 1940s. This history establishes the background against which present day farm politics must be understood. In the conclusion three hypotheses are developed which should be the basis of future research.

ELEMENTS OF THE MODEL

The Changing Structure of Agriculture

There are two important aspects to the analysis of the structure of agriculture and its relationship to farmers' movements. The first involves, at the most abstract level, an analysis of the forces and relations of production of agricultural commodities. The technological development of the forces of production, the various forms of land tenure, the nature of the labor force, and the relations of ownership and control are all included in this aspect of the analysis. The last hundred years have witnessed a transformation within the general form of capitalist agriculture as evidenced by the penetration of capital in incremental and new ways. The "ideal-typical" form of agricultural production is the simple commodity form in which relations determining productive consumption and distribution are class relations, while relations within the enterprise are family relations (Friedmann, 1981). Mooney, in Chapter 7 of this volume, has elaborated various deviations from the ideal type reflecting a shift in family farming to a more proletarianized form involving increased debt financing, tenancy, contract production, and off-farm employment. There has also been an increase in pure capitalist relations involving the employment of agricultural wage laborers as primary cultivators. These changes, along with the growing capital-intensification of production over the last century indicate some of the most fundamental changes in the structure of agriculture.

 The second aspect of the analysis broadens our understanding of agriculture to include the entire production process involving the production and circulation of agricultural commodities. Goss, Rodefeld, and Buttel (1980:97) divide the agricultural production process into three stages. The first stage is the provision of farm inputs such as machinery, fertilizers, insecticides, seeds, etc. Second is the food and fiber raising stage, when actual farming occurs. The third stage is that of processing and marketing of farm products. For the analysis of farmers' movements it is useful to note subdivisions within each stage. Stage One, for example, includes financial as well as technological inputs. Stage Three includes processing, transportation and marketing. It is around various issues related to each stage of the production cycle that farmers have mobilized to express grievances throughout the history of farm movements. By understanding the different stages of the production cycle and the timing and sequencing of capital penetration and state intervention in each stage, we can better understand the uneven and combined development in agriculture as it relates to the mobilization and organization of farmers.

The general thesis regarding the changing structure of agriculture is that agriculture has periodically been restructured to maintain the conditions of capital accumulation. The *political* form of that restructuring has involved uneven forms of state intervention into the various stages. The *economic* form of restructuring has involved capital penetration into the three stages of the production cycle. While the restructuring of agriculture has generally followed the pattern of general capitalist accumulation and crisis, the penetration of Stage Two has been indirect, at best, resulting in the persistence of the family farm up to World War II. Nevertheless, changes in Stage One and Three have had ramifications for Stage Two, and it is in response to the former changes that farmers have mobilized.

Weisskopf (1981) has recently outlined a historical account of the development of capitalist crises, presenting a "long wave historical framework" which takes into account both domestic and international contradictions in the capital accumulation process. His periodization yields six approximate cycles of growth and crisis: 1850–1870 (growth); 1870–1890 (decline); 1890s–1920s (growth); 1920s–1940s (decline); 1950s–1960s (growth); 1970s–present (decline). This periodization roughly fits changes that occurred in the structure of agriculture, although the period from 1890 to 1900 had characteristics reflecting both its preceding and its succeeding decades. To understand changes in agriculture, however, we must understand the intersection of periods of growth and decline with the three stages of the agricultural production cycle.

The period of 1850 to 1870, for example, was a period of growth reflected primarily in Stage Two of the cycle, as the westward territorial expansion and government policy stimulated the proliferation of family farms and large-scale farming in certain geographical locations and within certain commodities. The most extensive penetration of capital into Stage Three of the cycle took place during the last twenty-five years of the nineteenth century. The value of capital invested in flour mills, canned goods, and packinghouses increased most dramatically during these decades (U.S. Department of Commerce, 1976). The development of the food processing industries, plus the tremendous expansion and growing power of railroads and grain companies during these years transformed the nature of agricultural production. The result was the loss of control by farmers over their products and the prices received for those products. Not surprisingly, farmers during this period focused their grievances on the growing power of monopolies, including the railroads and the grain elevators.

With the advance of monopoly capital in the twentieth century, the small changes that had occurred in Stage One during the previous decades reached new proportions. The development of horsedrawn power equipment affected both the productivity and the labor process on family farms. By the turn of the century, those who wished to survive had to adapt to the new methods of farming or face marginalization. The growth period of 1900 to about 1920 was experienced by those farmers who were able to go into debt and expand their operation either extensively or intensively. The introduction of machinery like the gasoline engine tractor further transformed the production process on the farms. While prices fluctuated during this period, the average income of farmers increased as did the value of their farms. Perhaps the greatest change was the capital-intensification of farming, which increased the outstanding debt, and became an impediment to accumulation in the next period when farm and bank foreclosures threatened the entire agricultural economy (U.S. Department of Commerce, 1976). Speculation in the grain trade and other industries contributed to the sense of prosperity in the decade 1910–1920, but stimulated the onset of crisis during the 1920s.

This led to new levels of state intervention in the economy during the 1930s, in an attempt to reestablish favorable conditions of accumulation. World War II stimulated production in agriculture, created new markets for farm products, and resulted in the further capital-intensification of the industry. As a result, one of the greatest changes in the post-war period was the concentration and centralization of farming, reflected in fewer, larger, and more profitable farms. It also was reflected in a new class structure in agriculture, involving more capitalist farmers and hired farm laborers. It was primarily in the Midwest that the small, commodity-producing family farm survived to any significant extent.

Social Movement Theory

Four interrelated questions suggest the essential elements for an analysis of social movements. These questions are underemphasized in the literature which asks which sectors of the agrarian population are likely to mobilize (Paige, 1978; Wolf, 1969) and penetrates the debate over the relative progressive or conservative nature of farm movements (Hofstadter, 1971; Hicks, 1961) without resorting to historical simplifications. The questions are: (1) What determines the issues or grievances around which a social movement arises? (2) How is a population mobilized to act upon its social environment to remedy the grievances? What determines the extent of mobilization? (3) What determines which courses of action, ideological orientations, and long term strategies are employed by a movement, once mobilized? (4) Finally, what determines the outcomes of a movement? While looking to the resource mobilization perspective for answers to these questions, I argue that the application of a class analysis provides a more complete and adequate understanding of farmers' movements.

1. *The emergence of grievances:* Based in part on a Marxian notion of class interest and class conflict, recent theorists have attempted to examine the conditions that give rise to grievances and collective actions. Most resource mobilization theorists accept the Marxian emphasis on structural contradictions or transformations as the major source of grievances (Tilly, 1978; Useem, 1979). In the Marxist view, classes are the main actors of history, and the conflict between classes accounts for the structural contradictions (Castells, 1978; Useem, 1979). Following this view, I suggest that farmers' grievances arise as the structure of agriculture changes. The grievances generally reflect either changes in class relations[2] or a heightened awareness of those relations, made more transparent by changes in the structure of agriculture.

2. *Mobilization of a population:* The problem of mobilization has been extensively analyzed by Pickvance (1977) who, using Castells' (1978) terminology, asks how it is that a "social base" becomes a "social force."

Pickvance argues that conflicting forms of consciousness (e.g., value orientation, ethnic consciousness) may prevent the transformation of a social base into a social force organized around class issues. It is the role of social movement organizations to overcome these barriers and facilitate the mobilization of the base into a force. Gamson and Fireman (1979) argue that solidarity is facilitated to the extent that people are linked together in ways that generate a sense of common identity, shared fate, and general commitment to defend the group. The essential element in these theories is their emphasis on the structural bases of solidarity and the organizational manifestations of those bases. This analysis constitutes a starting point for understanding the ways in which farmers are *pre-organized* such that their commonality can serve as a basis for mobilization. This is an essential ingredient in the analysis of farm movements, given the particularly isolated and individualist character of farming (see Wilson, 1978).

3. *Orientations and actions of a social movement:* Wilson (1978) and Lipset (1968) both see a conservative tendency in farmers' movements aimed at preserving what appears to be an idyllic past. I argue, however, that when farmers resist the "progress" that leads to their own marginalization, there can be progressive elements in their backward-looking goals and demands. The anti-monopoly movements of farmers at the end of the last century are a case in point. Several common sources of grievances have provided fertile ground for powerful farmer-labor alliances. Nevertheless, farmers have never fully embraced either the capitalist class or the working class as their ally; they have fought for the right to remain small commodity producers, giving them contradictory interests as both producers and owners. I have differentiated between (1) those movements that pursue a "politics of inclusion"—seeking greater access to the system, hoping to become more like capital to reap the benefits of capitalism—and (2) those that pursue a "politics of resistance"—attempting to resist capital's economic and political penetration of agriculture. Those which pursue the politics of resistance may seek political reforms attempting to harness capital or increase their survival capacity, or may seek genuine transformations of the system in order to change the conditions within which they work and live. Those which pursue the politics of inclusion will generally acquiesce to the changes, although they may pursue minimal reforms to enhance their economic survival. The reforms sought, however, are reforms within the boundaries of the system, not reforms of the system itself (see Chart 1).

On a theoretical basis alone, we might expect farmers' movements to assume a politics of resistance during periods of economic crisis; the politics of inclusion should be most visible during periods of economic

Chart 1. Strategies and Tactics of Farmers' Movements

Tactical Arena	Strategic Goals and Orientations		
	Politics of Inclusion	Politics of Resistance	
		Reform	Transformation
Political focus	Lobbying: support for traditional parties	Formation of third party movement: demand for direct primary, referendum and recall, women's suffrage	Election of a farmers' government (e.g., the Non-Partisan League of North Dakota; support for socialist and communist parties)
Economic focus	Against government intervention in economy; for protective tarriffs for agriculture; support for laissez faire marketing; support for traditional banking system	Demand for parity in prices; development of farmer-controlled cooperative businesses; demand for government credit facilities	Demand for state-owned banks, elevators, utilities, and means of transportation
Collective actions	American Agricultural Movement tractorcade to Washington, D.C.	Withholding actions; boycotts; collective bargaining (characteristic of NFO).	Farmers' Holiday blockades and resistance against mortgage foreclosures
Political allies	Most capitalists excluding agricultural monopolies; rural petit bourgeoisie; strategic alliance with conservative labor leadership	Petty bourgeoisie; labor; strategic alliances with consumer and enviromental groups	Labor; progressive petty bourgeoisie; consumer and environmental groups

expansion where farmers' economic conditions are most likely to improve. This expected tendency is limited, however, by the contradictory class location of farmers and their dependence on market conditions for their survival. During periods of expansion, for example, farmers must go into debt to expand their productive capital. Only those farmers with sufficient collateral can afford such expansion. Thus, farmers' standard of living may increase during an expansionary period, while their relative class position may remain unchanged or become increasingly subordinate to capital. A complete analysis of movement orientations would have to examine the changes in class position as well as standard of living or economic well-being. The political or ideological orientation of a movement reflects changes in farmers' economic well-being and class position. The more the social base experiences a trajectory of subordination to dominant classes, the more likely its social force will reflect the politics of reform or transformation and build alliances with other subordinate groups. Similarly, those who move towards positions of dominance and power vis-à-vis other agricultural workers and farmers will tend to adopt a politics of inclusion.

4. *Outcomes of a social movement:* Movements undergo changes for a number of reasons. Wilson (1980), Lipset (1968), and Taylor (1953) argue that as a movement grows, it develops a professional bureaucratic leadership structure which loses its organic connection with and concern for the membership of the social force or the population of the social base. I suggest an alternative analysis which emphasizes the internal struggles within the organization reflecting different interests represented in the social base. As new cleavages cut through the social base, new social forces are likely to emerge with altered goals and perhaps even latent opposition to the initial movement goals. This helps cause the movement to disintegrate because the composition and goals of the social base, social force, and/or official leadership no longer correspond to each other. As the historical evidence summarized below suggests, new divisions within the farmers' movements emerge—often along class or class fraction lines—as the structure of agriculture changes.

Concurrent with changes taking place internal to the social force of a movement are the relations between the movement and factors external to it. Different factions of a movement or organization with opposing political orientations will appeal to its corresponding allies in an attempt to strengthen itself against its opposing faction. At times authorities may facilitate the growth or demands of a less threatening movement in order to draw attention away from more militant movements seeking systemic transformations.

In summary, the importance of an integrated theoretical framework analyzing the interrelationship between the structure of agriculture, the state, and the social movements of farmers has been emphasized. Changes in the structure of agriculture follow changes in the larger political economy; crisis and transformations in the broader economy necessitate transformation in the structure of agriculture. As small commodity producers, farmers' interests neither directly correspond to those of capitalists or the working class, and at times are different from those of the traditional petty bourgeoisie. Consequently, farmers' movements have generally tended to resist the economic and political power of capital while never fully embracing the working class as an ally. Generally, such movements have tended to lean either in one direction or the other, at times fully adopting the politics of inclusion and at times rallying behind a politics of resistance. As suggested in the historical overview, the state became an increasingly central figure in shaping both the structure of agriculture and the mobilization, ideological orientations, and political power of farmers' movements and organizations.

HISTORICAL SPECIFICATION OF THE MODEL

Having specified the elements of a framework needed to analyze farmers' movements, this section turns to a discussion of the early history of the farmers' movement in the U.S. While most of the discussion focusses on the fifty-year period between 1870 and 1920, I have broken down the time span from 1850 to the 1940s into the periods suggested in part one of the paper. By focussing on the periods of decline and growth bordering the turn of the century I hope to illustrate the usefulness of the framework as outlined.

1850–1870: A Period of Transition

The changes that took place during this period set the stage and gave rise to the issues that were to dominate the farmers' movement thereafter. In the early part of the nineteenth century, agriculture had largely been a regionally self-sufficient enterprise, with the three stages of agricultural production under the control of farmers or local merchants (Bogart, 1923). The Westward territorial expansion of both farmers and capital helped to sever Stages One and Three from farmer and local control. Between 1850 and 1870 there was, in the Midwest, an increase of 156.8 percent in the number of farms (U.S. Department of Commerce, 1976:458). Before the Civil War, cotton had been the chief export of the country, but the settlement of the corn and wheat-growing country was increasing the economic and political importance of grain. Some of the earliest mechanical improvements in farm machinery, begun in the 1830s and 1840s, were in widespread use in the grain areas by mid-century. The processing of farm products was rapidly being transferred from the farm home to city factories.

Prior to 1860, farmers had organized themselves into small educational and social clubs and societies where they traded ideas about improving the methods of farming. There was little concern about the issues of credit, transportation, and monopolies that dominated the farmers' movement during the remainder of the century (Buck, 1969; Taylor, 1953). Much of this changed with the financial panic of 1857. The speculation in the grain trade and the expansion of railroads and railroad capital contributed to the economic crisis, which, in turn, mobilized farmers. One of the greatest periods of railroad construction occurred between 1856 and 1857, converting a regionally self-sufficient agriculture into a national and international commercial enterprise. As farmers began to feel the demands placed upon them by competition in an international market, they began to seek ways of expanding production and increasing the value of their own labor power. In hope of expanding the market for their products, farmers began investing in railroad securities and actually helped to finance the building of the roads. Nevertheless, farmers were beginning to experience their impotence at dealing with the powerful railroads and grain elevators; in the largest grain growing state, Illinois, farmers issued a "Farmers' Platform of 1858" which raised, for the first time in a concerted manner, demands regarding prices, markets, credits, and the growing power of "nonproducers." Also for the first time, there were calls for a "union of farmers" to engage in economic and political activities—many of which were taken up by later movements (Taylor, 1953:84–87).

One of the earliest forms of state intervention affecting agriculture reflected a conflict over land policy. Hamiltonians hoped to obtain lands in the West and sell them to proprietors in order to increase the national treasury. Jeffersonians, on the other hand, hoped to secure western land for the development of small, family farms (Benedict, 1953). Beginning with the Louisiana Purchase in 1803 and culminating in the Gadsden Purchase of 1853 following the war with Mexico, the state pursued an expansionist policy which provided land for both capital and small farmers. The 1860s signalled a new form of state involvement with the passage of several acts which set the stage for the future development of agriculture. The Pacific Railway Act of 1862 provided authorization for the building of a transcontinental railroad and gave land grants to the railroad companies all along the route. In the same year the Homestead Act made land available to settlers who could obtain title to the land they worked. Loopholes in the law made it possible for land speculators to obtain title to large land tracts which were then sold to settlers at an inflated price. The government established a land grant college system through the Morril Act of 1862, which provided states land for the establishment of agricultural colleges. Recognizing the increasing importance of agriculture to the economic health of the system, the U.S. Department of Agriculture (USDA) was created in the same year, to be made a regular department in 1889. The significance of these state policies was the new nature of state intervention as a facilitator of private accumulation in agriculture. Symbolic of its embryonic accumulation function was a practice by the USDA to provide seeds to Congressional legislators to distribute free to their constituents. Meanwhile, the state pursued laissez faire policies towards land and wheat speculators, and virtually ignored the unfair practices of railroads. Not surprisingly, many of the farmers' demands by the end of this early period were for a more regulatory state, recognition of the plight of the farmer, and more direct access to governmental decision-making.

In summary, the interventions of the state during this period seemed to focus mainly on facilitating capitalist economic development. Interventions in Stage One centered around monetary policies (e.g., acts authorizing the issue of legal-tender notes), the establishment of a National Bank (1863), and protective tariff legislation. Interventions in Stage Two focussed on giving farmers, railroads, and businesses access to cheap or free land in the west. Interventions in Stage Three were characterized by the granting of lands to the railroads, which then gained control of major distribution mechanisms (Benedict, 1953). State power during this period represented the varied interests of old merchant capital, old Southern plantation agriculture, and emerging industrial capital. The victory of the North in the Civil War indicated the emerging power of industrial capital and set the stage for the period of monopoly capitalism which was to come. The period can be summarized as having set the preconditions of growth and generated the embryonic forms of state intervention which were to influence the subsequent period when agriculture underwent important structural change.

1870–1900: A Period of Industrialization, Crisis, and Agitation

The most visible force of change in this period was the changing structure of agriculture. This was a period of severe and recurrent crises in which the economy was restructured to favor monopoly capital and the penetration of capital into agriculture (Dowd, 1974). This state was too weak to regulate business or to come to the defense of the victims of the crises, who included capitalists, farmers, and workers. The economic crises adversely affected workers and small farmers who mobilized and struggled against often violent repression. The state intervened both to repress that radicalism and to take embryonic steps to put some order into the anarchy of capitalism.

The history presented below describes in some detail how the grievances of farmers developed in response to the changing structure of agriculture. The small, rural communities provided a pre-organizational basis for the tremendous mobilizations that occurred during this period. Midwest farmers became increasingly dependent on monopoly control of the distribution and storage facilities in Stage Three of the production cycle, establishing the conditions for a strong alliance with workers— most notably in the railroad unions. The farmers' movement of this period generally reflected the politics of resistance—resisting the penetration of capital via the railroad industry and grain trade. The political climate was a volatile one. As the labor movement gained strength, and sectors of it assumed an anti-capitalist ideological orientation, the business community responded with charges of socialism and anti-Americanism (Boyer and Morais, 1965; Foner, 1975). Farmers involved in some of the more radical agrarian movements also became subject to "red-baiting" attacks (Foner, 1975). This raised the costs of participation in a radical movement allied with labor. As the farmers' movement turned towards political reform by forming the People's Party, the social base became so broad that heterogeneous class interests in the larger society came to be reflected within the party. Ultimately, the cleavage between the social base of farmers and workers and the small business and capitalist interests represented within the social force of the People's Party became too great and the farmers' movement was temporarily weakened.

This period, representing the growth of monopoly capitalism, was characterized by the concentration and centralization of capital and a dramatic increase in the penetration of capital into Stage Three of the production cycle. There was, for instance, a 212.5 percent increase in the capital invested in the canning industries, and a 164.8 percent increase in investment in the milling and packinghouse industries, respectively (U.S. Department of Commerce, 1976). These figures indicate the growing importance of the "middleman" in the agricultural economy, which, when coupled with the growing power of railroads during this period, accounts for many of the grievances expressed by farmers, who were growing increasingly critical of monopolies. Following the Civil War there had been a steady decrease in prices. The war had increased the demand for farm products and prices had skyrocketed, creating serious overproduction problems. Immediately after the war prices began to drop, contributing to the problems farmers faced during the depression which spanned the next thirty years (Taylor, 1953:91). The war, however, had helped produce changes in the entire agricultural production cycle which could not be undone with the depressed conditions. The drafting of men into the army contributed to a shortage of labor power on the farms, which encouraged the development and implementation of farm machinery. Between 1860 and the turn of the century the value of farm implements and machinery in use on farms increased by over 200 percent (Bogart, 1923:117). The loss of the South as a market during the war and the overproduction which followed the war gave rise to changes in Stage Three of the cycle involving the penetration of capital into that stage. The control of the railroads over terminal elevators and granaries contributed to the growing power of the grain and railroad trusts. The invention of the refrigerated box car, first put into use in 1869, gave impetus to the rapid development of the slaughtering and meat-packing industry. The total value of products from these industries increased 947 percent between 1860 and 1880, and 160 percent over the next twenty years (Bogart, 1923:126). Much of this growth took place during the 1870s.

The decline in prices, the increases in farm debt, and the growing economic and political power of creditors, railroads, and grain companies, all contributed to farmer unrest during the last three decades of the nineteenth century. It should be no surprise that the farmers' movement during the period 1870 to 1890 concentrated its demands on credit policies, regulation of the railroads, and attempts to gain more control over terminal elevators, freight charges, and pricing. Because railroad companies were the most visible source of farmers' oppression, the farmers of this period expressed grievances with an anti-monopoly character, reflecting the politics of resistance and reform. In fact, farmers formed the nucleus of an anti-monopoly, reform-oriented social movement that transcended the narrow economic interests of farmers. In many cases farmers formed alliances with railroad and other workers in struggles against a common enemy.

Two farmers' organizations represented the farmers' movements of this period. The Order of the Patrons of Husbandry (Grange) was organized in 1867 and peaked around 1875. The Farmers' Alliance emerged from disparate origins beginning around 1872 and became the major force behind the organization of the People's Party in 1892 (Goodwyn, 1978; Hicks, 1961).

The Granger Movement: The Grange was organized as a secret, rural fraternity, primarily concerned with the social and educational concerns of farmers. Men, women, boys, and girls (age 14 and over) were admitted on an equal basis (Tontz, 1964). Initially the Grange was a top-down organization, with no grass roots locals and little grass roots control. Grange founder, Oliver H. Kelley, had been an employee of the USDA for a short time, and although he was a Minnesota farmer by profession, he was working for the U.S. Post Office Department at the time he organized the Grange. The organization was launched in Washington with six members, all of them from Washington and some of them USDA employees (Taylor, 1953:118). They developed an elaborate ritual for a secret organization, initially opposed to organizing around political issues or economic action. Concomitant with worsening economic conditions and the growing concentration of power in the monopolies, the Grange began to address political and economic interests. In 1873 the Grange split into two factions: the Minnesota faction was anti-monopoly and concentrated on attacking railroads and other monopolies; the Iowa faction urged farmers to emulate rather than attack the business system (Saloutos and Hicks, 1951). It was the anti-monopoly faction, however, that harnessed the grievances of farmers, and in the mid–1870s the membership increased dramatically as the Grange began to focus on issues related to the railroad transportation problems: unfair freight rates and policies; scandals involving railroad financiers and speculators; free passes to political candidates and representatives. The Grange also pursued cooperative business ventures, including cooperative buying and selling warehouses, cooperative stores, and cooperative industries for manufacturing farm equipment. Politically, the Grange organized a lobby in Washington, demanded the popular election of U.S. Senators, and advocated anti-trust legislation. The Grange rise to power took place during years of severe depression and high unemployment. While farmers organized to fight the railroads, industrial workers in the textiles, mines, and railroads held long and bitter strikes which were crushed by federal troops (Foner, 1975). Both farmers and workers were learning that their interests could not be protected as long as the state was controlled by or served the interests of capital. The Grange provided the major leadership for independent political action during the 1970s (Foner, 1975), and, by some accounts, industrialists feared farmers more than the workers (Boyer and Morais, 1965). The Grange united with the Knights of Labor to help form the Greenback Party in 1875, which joined with the short-lived United Labor Party in 1877 to become the National Greenback-Labor Party. As the Grange turned its energies to party politics, the class membership of the farmers' movement was diluted to include politicians, professionals, and even businessmen whose interests were sometimes opposed to those of farmers. Differences between farmers and workers, and accusations of "communism" in the press contributed to the decline of the Grange (Buck, 1969). The Grange dropped from a membership of 858,050 in 1875, to 124,420 in 1880 (Taylor, 1953:137).

Despite its short-lived heyday, the Grange and other smaller organizations managed to get legislatures in several states to pass laws regulating railroad fares, freight rates, and warehouses. The most effective laws were passed in Illinois, although Minnesota, Iowa, Wisconsin, and Missouri passed similar, but less effective laws (Benedict, 1953:101). The important national legislation came in the next decade, with the passage of the Interstate Commerce Act of 1887 which gave the federal government the power to regulate interstate traffic. Other issues raised by the Grange were implemented in the 1880s, including rural free mail delivery and the Hatch Act of 1887 which initiated state agricultural experiment stations. When the Grange began to revive after the turn of the century, following twenty-five years of decline, it began to again serve primarily as a social and educational organization, pursuing a politics of inclusion when it pursued any politics at all. The more transformative issues of ballot reform, women's suffrage, protection of the environment, and opposition to monopolies were taken up by new farm organizations, most notably the various permutations of the Farmers' Alliance.

The Farmers' Alliance: Because of its central importance in the history of the progressive farmers' movement, the origins, growth, and decline of the Farmers' Alliance are treated in some detail below. The Alliance history shows the class basis of a movement, its demands, and the basis upon which it forms class alliances. The decline of the Farmers' Alliance illustrates the interconnection between its internal class dynamics and the changing structure of agriculture.

The Farmers' Alliance had several origins, the earliest being an anti-horse-thief and anti-land-grab organization in Texas, which was started in 1873 and became known as the Texas Grand State Alliance in 1878 (Taylor, 1953:194–5). The Texas Farmers' Alliance and the Louisiana Farmers' Union (formed in 1880) united in 1887 to become the National Farmers' Alliance and Cooperative Union of America, later to change its name to the Farmers' and Laborers' Union. In 1889 the organization attempted to merge with the Northern Farmers' Alliance, officially named the National Farmers' Alliance, and the name was again changed to the National Farmers' Alliance and Industrial Union. Only Kansas, North Dakota, and South Dakota joined with the Southern organization, which was popularly known as the Southern Alliance. The key issues preventing the union of the two alliances were the questions of secrecy and the admission of blacks into the Alliance. The Southern Alliance prohibited the membership of blacks, and instead had organized a parallel organization known as the Colored Farmers' National Alliance and Cooperative Union. It also originated as and remained a secret organization, much as the Grange had been. The Northern Alliance members objected to both the segregation and the secrecy, and, thus, amalgamation never occurred (Hicks, 1951; Taylor, 1953).

The organization of the Northern Alliance is generally attributed to the efforts of Milton George, the editor of a farm journal known as the *Western Rural*. He had once been a farmer and had experienced first hand the discriminatory practices of the railroads, which he criticized openly in his journal. On April 15, 1880, he brought together a number of farmers and organized the Cook County Farmers' Alliance Number One. The idea for such an alliance came from a previous attempt to organize the New York Alliance, which was the political mouthpiece for the Patrons of Husbandry in New York, seeking railroad regulation, tax reform, and the legalization of Granger insurance companies. The New York Alliance, in turn, is reported to have stemmed from a Kansas squatters organization, organized in about 1874 to defend squatters' land against the railroad claimants. The Settlers' Protective Association formed cooperative enterprises and appointed an eastern purchasing agent, from whom the New Yorkers learned of the Kansas group (Hicks, 1961; Benedict, 1953).

Throughout the summer of 1880 charters for local Farmers' Alliances were granted to farmers' groups across the Midwest. On October 14 a "Farmers' Transportation Convention" was called and about 500 farmers— many of them representing local alliances, farmers' groups, or Granges—

attended the meeting in Farwell Hall in Chicago (Taylor, 1951:215). A national organization was formed, composed of local, state, and the national alliance, with the national body having little more than a coordination function. A constitution was passed which stated the following objectives:

> To unite the farmers of the United States for their protection against class legislation, the encroachments of concentrated capital, and the tyranny of monopoly; to provide against being imposed upon by swindlers, and swindling advertisements in the public prints; to oppose, in our respective political parties, the election of any candidate to office, state or national, who is not thoroughly in sympathy with the farmers' interests; to demand that the existing political parties shall nominate farmers, or those who are in sympathy with them, for all offices within the gift of the people; and to do anything, in a legitimate manner, that may serve to benefit the producer (Taylor, 1953:215).

The railroads were singled out as the chief enemy of both producers and consumers, and resolutions were passed calling them oppressive, defiant of the law, corrupting to politics, "a hindrance to free and impartial legislation, and a menace to the safety of our republican institutions" (Hicks, 1961:99).

Within a year of its founding, the National Farmers' Alliance claimed to have 1,000 locals. By its second convention it claimed a total membership of 24,500. At the third convention, in October 1882, the organization claimed 2,000 locals and a membership of 100,000. By 1887, the membership was four times as large (Taylor, 1953:216). Between 1883 and early 1885, however, the Alliance went into a period of decline, due in part to improved economic conditions resulting from good crops and a rise in prices. By the winter of 1884–1885, wheat prices dropped and hard times set in for farmers. By 1887 a new constitution was passed, dues were collected for the first time, state leaders became more active in the national affairs, and new demands were made including government ownership of the railroads and the unlimited and free coinage of silver. The growth of the Alliance following the 1887 convention has been attributed to the "complete and thoroughgoing awakening of class consciousness among the farmers . . ." (Hicks, 1961:104). The Southern Alliance was at the same time making more political demands, including higher taxation on lands held for speculation, prohibition of alien landownership, more taxation of railways, and new issues of paper money (Goodwyn, 1978; Hicks, 1961:106). Both Northern and Southern Alliances made conscious statements proclaiming their alliance with working people, and both Alliances had friendly exchanges with the

Knights of Labor. Throughout the 1880s, the Knights of Labor expressed their solidarity with the demands of farmers for regulation and government ownership of the railroads and for new monetary policies; farmers, in turn, gave food to striking workers. The Knights of Labor reached its membership peak in 1886, following a successful strike against railroad baron Jay Gould. Farmers' Alliance locals and members contributed money and food to the strikers, insisting that labor's fight against Gould was their own fight (Foner, 1975:301).

The growth of the Farmers' Alliance can be attributed to a number of factors. Hicks' (1961) argument that low prices accounted for the Alliance's growth is true, in part, in that declining prices were perhaps the major grievance of the farmers. However, the structural changes and contradictions that gave rise to this and other grievances involved more than changing prices. Farmers were angered by the fact that, while they followed the rules of laissez faire capitalism—utilizing the latest machinery and technology, producing regional crops for an expanding market, and increasing their yields—the prices for their products remained low. The market for agricultural goods increased, due in part to the growing strength and competitiveness of the United States in the international economy, the influx of immigrant workers (12 million between 1870 and 1900), and the declining proportion of farmers to other workers (Benedict, 1953:87). When, by 1876, the U.S. achieved a favorable balance of trade—primarily through an expanded market in Latin America and the Pacific—farmers reaped few of the benefits and there was little incentive for anyone but farmers to demand a higher price for food and grain (Benedict, 1953; Williams, 1966). Farmers became increasingly conscious of the power of railroads, banks, and other monopolies as they were forced to pay exorbitant prices for farm inputs, were denied easy access to credit, and were forced to take the prices offered them by the elevators which were often owned or controlled by the railroads. Thus, despite the expansion of capital during this period, it was a period of recurrent crisis, intense class struggle, frequent "red-baiting," and violent repression of worker and farmer militancy. The Farmers' Alliances advanced demands including government ownership of the railroads, although they never questioned the right to own private property itself.

The organizational strategies used by the Alliances were similar to those used by the Grange. Neighborhood gatherings were common and there were frequent lodge meetings (once or twice a month), picnics, and conventions. In the South, secret rituals were a part of gatherings; in all regions there were efforts made to have music, speeches, and debates. Hundreds of farmers attended conventions of county, district, and state Alliances; on special anniversaries and holidays all-day picnics or rallies were held, bringing farmers together from all over a region. Alliances met the needs of the sick, destitute, and afflicted by appointing committees to bring aid and comfort to these people. The impact of these social activities was to build solidarity among the farmers; this was an essential organizational feature for building unity among farmers, who worked and lived individually and isolated from one another. Farm journals and newspapers educated farmers along political lines, and an intellectual climate developed whereby farmers discussed numerous political and economic issues (Goodwyn, 1978; Hicks, 1961). Local organizations usually had an officer who was responsible for suggesting topics of discussion at meetings and for disseminating information to farmers about the subject. Farmers thus learned to express themselves in public and to search in books and journals for information supporting their positions. In many places local study groups were organized and circulating libraries were formed. In addition to information about political and economic issues, the Alliance distributed scientific agricultural information and made it a point to inform farmers about issues such as crop rotation, the use of new machinery, careful seed selection, and other information that met the immediate production needs of farmers (Goodwyn, 1978; Hicks, 1961).

A slogan that became a part of the program of the Alliance was "Let the Alliance be a business organization for business purposes" (Hicks, 1961:132). The business ventures of the alliance were of both an alternative and a competitive nature. Cooperative stores, elevators, and gins were attempted, and many of them were successful for a while. Cooperative marketing ventures were also attempted, where Alliance members attempted to market their products directly to the city buyers. The efforts failed, however, because buyers from far away didn't come to the established selling place, preferring to pay the higher cost and have the goods delivered by the railroads. In addition to the alternative strategies represented by cooperative ventures, the Alliance set up business agencies which paralleled, and attempted to compete with, established business institutions. They formed purchasing agencies to replace the "middleman"; the most ambitious of these was the Farmers' Alliance Exchange in Texas, which marketed cotton and grain, purchased farm implements at a discount, and sold dry goods, groceries, and other goods, all at reduced rates. The Exchange attempted to compete with banking institutions by extending credit to farmers who signed promissory notes which the regular banks refused to accept, except at a ruinous discount, and the Exchange credit system proved unsuccessful (Hicks, 1961).

The refusal of the banks to extend credit to farmers or to accept their own system of creditation, and the difficulty of establishing successful businesses that attempted to by-pass the power of the elevators and railroads, contributed to the ultimate failure of those institutions.

As economic strategies were tried and failed, the farmers turned increasingly to the political arena, hoping to find solutions to their grievances there. The repeated frustrations of the farmers' movement to address the structural inequalities they experienced ultimately led them to place demands on the state as the only agent that could regulate and transform structural relations. Initially Alliance members worked through existing parties or small independent parties to put pressure on legislators. Eventually, however, the Northern Alliance sought independent, third-party action to capture the state machinery, after having been disappointed time and again by the existing parties. In the South, control of the Democratic party was the strategy. The elections of 1890 were a tremendous victory for the Alliance in both the North and the South. Alliance candidates won positions in local, state and national elections. However, due to the inexperience of the elected farmers, the strength of the opposing lobbies, and the power of the traditional party machines, the Alliance programs were only partially realized through legislation. The program had been pushed on a local and state-wide basis, and its failure pointed the way towards a national third party organization that could coordinate efforts and exert real clout at the level of national politics (Hicks, 1961).

During the 1890s farmers expanded the social base of their movement by taking a major role in organizing the People's Party, giving rise to what came to be known as the Populist Movement. Present at the founding convention of the party were the National Farmers' Alliance and Industrial Union (246 delegates), the National Farmers' Alliance (97 delegates), the National Colored Alliance and Cooperative Union (97 delegates), the Knights of Labor (82 delegates), and several smaller delegations with 25–50 additional delegates (Hicks, 1961:226). The American Federation of Labor refused to ally with the party, which contained "employing farmers." The first party platform endorsed government ownership of railroads and telephone and telegraph lines. It also demanded that railroads and other corporations return lands to the government that were not being used by them, and it condemned alien ownership of land. It sought the unlimited coinage of silver, a graduated income tax, savings banks, shorter hours for labor, direct election of U.S. Senators, and single terms for the President and Vice-President. The "Populist" vote was strong in the 1892 and 1894 elections, but by 1896 the silver issue had become primary, and the party fused with the Democratic party in support of the election of William Jennings Bryant. Farmers began to lose interest in the party, which struggled along weakly until the 1904 election (Hicks, 1961).

The decline of the People's Party is attributed to many factors. Both Hicks (1961) and Taylor (1953) emphasize the farmers' turn to party politics as a major cause of the decline of the Farmers' Alliance. Two other factors, however, provide a deeper explanation. One is the opposition experienced by the movement. The other relates to the changing class composition of the social force and the social base and the resulting conflicts between these. These differences were ultimately expressed as political, economic, and ideological cleavages which led to the split in the party.

On the issue of opposition, the press warned farmers and workers of the dangers of "atheistic Socialists" who were trying to wean them away from traditional values and politics (Foner, 1975:324). This kind of "red-baiting" had a strong impact on the less committed and potential party members.

The second factor was even more decisive. As the party broadened its social base by reaching out to all classes of people, it lost its strength as a party of farmers and workers. While the initial goal of the party was to unite all producers—workers and farmers alike—into a coalition to protect their interests against monopoly power, the movement was not anti-capitalist per se; capitalists and conservative business leaders were able to join the party and eventually helped eliminate the pro-labor, anti-monopoly demands from the platform, leaving only the free silver plank as an issue (Foner, 1975). The financial panic of 1893 and the ensuing depression united eastern workers and western farmers under the party banner, but also helped raise the currency issue to primacy. The increased production of gold in the late 1890s, however, took the steam out of the free silver issue, leaving the third party movement weaponless. The need for a stable U.S. dollar on the international market had long been supported by industrialists and encouraged the production of gold. The demands of capital for new markets and its new political and economic power to create such markets contributed to the expansion of the U.S. Navy. The entrance of the U.S. in the war against Spain for an independent Cuba was part of the effort to establish U.S. hegemony in Latin America; this signalled the beginning of the new, "anti-colonial imperialism" which sought favored access for U.S. products in a competitive world market (Dowd, 1974:159).

In summary, the power of the railroads over the distribution of farm products represents the major form of capitalist penetration of agriculture during the 1870s and 1880s. The growing monopoly control over Stage Three of the cycle was experienced as a new and devastating phenomenon by farmers, and gave the farmers' movement of that period a militant, anti-monopoly character. The proliferation of agricultural machinery reflected the embryonic penetration of capital into Stage One of the cycle. With the expansion of markets and the new, mechanized techniques of production, farmers were dependent on unregulated mortgage companies, railroads, and grain elevators for credit with which to purchase the new machinery. The major form of state intervention involved the development of protective tariff policies and the creation of an inflated currency. The state was too weak or disinterested to regulate big business, and farmers and workers were not sufficiently organized to overcome the old party machinery and have an immediate impact on state policies. Farmers' demands were not met until the succeeding period, when a corporate liberal state began to intervene with the two-fold purpose of regulating capital to save it from its own destructive competition and granting reforms to farmers and workers to stave off revolution.

1900–1920: Consolidation of Monopoly and Political Reformism

In the period from 1900 to 1920 farmers became visibly active in their attempts to intervene in the political process to influence state policy toward agriculture. Their attempts to resist the adverse effects of the changing structure of agriculture centered primarily on building alternative institutions, such as marketing cooperatives, to bypass monopoly control of the distribution of farm products. In general these attempts reflected the politics of inclusion, although the alternative and sometimes militant methods used had a lasting impact on the nature of farmers' organizations and the relationship between farmers and the market. The turn of the century brought greater capital penetration of the manufacturing and processing aspects of agriculture. This contributed to the polarization of the class structure in agriculture, which in turn contributed to the factional polarization in the overall farmers' movement. The state's interventions helped to strengthen the pro-capitalist faction, which proved to be useful during the economic crisis that followed.

The political and economic conditions of the 1890s contributed to the development of a strong capitalist class and a more powerful state. In the early decades of the twentieth century the state's intervention in agriculture focussed mostly on Stage Three. During this period, state structure was reorganized slightly, giving more access to "common people" through the direct primary, direct election of Senators, and women's suffrage—all demands that farmers' organizations supported. The repressive apparatus of the state was also bolstered during this period. Following the railroad strike of 1877, during which farmers supported striking workers with food and rail boycotts, the state militias and National Guards were strengthened and equipped with new weapons and National Guard Armories (Boyer and Morais, 1965). Federal troops were used against striking miners in Colorado in 1914. Arrests were made during the "Palmer Raids" in 1919 and suspected radical aliens were deported. While these interventions mostly affected the working class, a police apparatus was established which could be used against farmers if necessary (as in the 1930s police actions against the Farmers' Holiday Association). In the legislative field, the Sherman Anti-Trust Act of 1890 was used against farm cooperatives as well as against labor unions, in an attempt to limit their power (Boyer and Morais, 1965; Saloutos and Hicks, 1951).

Not all of the changes during this period were as dramatic as women's suffrage or the Palmer Raids. It was during the first two decades of the twentieth century that the government began to regulate industry and commerce in ways that protected farmers from big business and protected capital from its own destructive pursuit of immediate interests. Most of the changes were initial steps at regulating the economy in ways that would maintain the conditions of capital accumulation while protecting small producers and consumers from the inequitable excesses of monopoly capitalism. The Americanization movement attempted to create peaceful, hard-working citizens out of militant, immigrant workers. The advertising industry flourished to replace class consciousness with consumer consciousness (Ewen, 1976). In 1922, farm cooperatives were made exempt from the Sherman Anti-Trust laws; the effect of this law was to allow business cooperatives to flourish at the expense of more radical farm experiments (such as state ownership as practiced in North Dakota). Beginning in 1897, the USDA began to develop demonstration farms and adult education programs for farmers to teach them more productive farming techniques. It worked with the Country Life Commission to help create a more educated, patriotic, and dependable rural populace. In 1906, it was given its first regulatory role, being placed in charge of enforcement of the Food and Drug Law of 1906. Numerous other regulatory acts were passed, regulating the processing and distribution of food. A system of Federal Land Banks was established in 1916 making access to credit easier for farmers. In summary, state intervention in Stage One and Three of the agricultural production cycle, largely in the form of regulation, marked the beginning of a new relationship between the state and agriculture.

The period from the late 1890s until about 1920 was one of general growth and prosperity during which the small changes begun during the previous decades reached new proportions. The value of non-manufactured food output increased 85 percent from 1900 to 1920, and 104 percent in the next decade. Manufactured food goods increased in value by 84 percent and 170 percent over the same decades. Capital investment in food manufacturing industries increased only slightly less rapidly in this period than in the decade of the 1880s (U.S. Department of Commerce, 1976). There was an increasing concentration and capital intensification of all manufacturing and processing aspects of agriculture. Farmers were forced to go into debt and expand their operations in order to survive during this period of prosperity. This was made necessary by the capital-intensification of farming that originated with the introduction of the gasoline engine tractor. While the farm population of the Midwest dropped slightly in the first two decades of the century, the size and net value of farms increased. Thus, farmers experienced a sense of prosperity as they invested in new capital, expanded the size and value of their farms, and received some concrete benefits in the form of better farm prices. The prosperity was a two-edged sword, however: farm debt increased 163 percent between 1910 and 1920 (U.S. Department of Commerce, 1976). This increase in outstanding debt became an impediment to accumulation in the next period when farm and bank foreclosures threatened the entire agricultural economy. Farmers' increasing dependency on finance, processing, and manufacturing capital would ultimately undermine their tenuous prosperity.

In part because of the new market conditions, the grievances of farmers shifted during this period from a focus on monopolies and transportation problems to a focus on credit and marketing issues (Saloutos and Hicks, 1951). The combination of general economic prosperity and the inequitable distribution of wealth led farmers to organize to increase their share of the prosperity. The new forces that shaped the political economy of U.S. capitalism shaped the structure of agriculture, and when new farmers' movements emerged at the beginning of the new century, their strategies were attempts to survive within, rather than to transform, the system. In part because of the new market conditions, the grievances of farmers shifted during this period from a focus on monopolies and transportation problems to a focus on credit and marketing issues. The combination of general economic prosperity and the inequitable distribution of wealth led farmers to organize to increase their share of the prosperity.

During this period farm organizations began to reflect divergent political and economic strategies. Some groups emphasized their alliance with labor while others emulated the business methods and goals of capital. Two polar economic strategies emerged; one advocated the self-organization of farmers through cooperatives and one advocated state ownership of banks and distributional facilities upon which farmers were so dependent. Farmers became increasingly involved in legislative politics, reflecting the greater involvement of the state in the regulation of agriculture. The state was a major actor in the outcomes of the farmers' movements of this period; it facilitated the development of and legitimated a conservative business-oriented farmers' organization that it hoped would draw support away from more radical or reformist groups. This political intervention by the state severed whatever direct correspondence there may once have been between economic change and the orientations and outcomes of social movements.

The American Society of Equity, the Farmers' Union, and the Cooperative Movement: Two farmers' organizations were begun in 1902. The more conservative of these was the American Society of Equity. The Equity was founded and organized by J. A. Everett, an Indianapolis editor of the newspaper *Up-to-Date Farming*. He planned to help farmers become a "third power" equal to business and labor. He clearly advocated the politics of inclusion, arguing that farmers should use business people and business organizations to insure "controlled marketing to compel profitable prices" (Taylor, 1953:366). The strategy was opposed to the reform and transformative politics of the Farmers' Alliance and the Grange before it; rather, farmers were encouraged to regulate their own rather than the other person's business. Everett advocated a coalition of farmers and business men and was opposed to governmental intervention or legislation affecting agriculture. The organization advocated the building of cooperative elevators, stockyards, dairies, and tobacco warehouses, although it eventually expanded into other business ventures. It encouraged farmers to withhold farm products from the market in order to raise prices, calling for the first "Hold Your Wheat" action in 1903 (Taylor, 1953:372). The organization was split in 1907 between the crop-holding business faction and a group which favored cooperative exchanges and sought alliances with labor unions. Following the split in 1907, Equity locals were established in most areas, and members began to pass resolutions on political issues such as the direct vote for Senators, women's suffrage, and legislation affecting farmers. While initially strongest in the tobacco and eastern wheat growing areas, the Equity soon spread to Wisconsin and the northern states of Minnesota, Montana, and the Dakotas. Wisconsin eventually became the strongest Equity region; there Equity promoted farm-labor cooperation and established consumer cooperative stores where "middlemen" were bypassed completely.

Another farmer's organization was founded in 1902 by a former Alliance member in Texas. The Farmers' Educational and Cooperative Union, commonly called the Farmers' Union, spread rapidly throughout the cotton states of the South, organizing grass-roots locals in every southern state by 1908. The Union was concerned with tenancy and farm credit problems and was active in the education of farmers on these and other technological and economic issues. It organized many cooperatives for the purchase and sale of farm supplies and products. Ideologically, it attacked organizations of middlemen, chambers of com-

merce, and boards of trade. Economically, it set a level of prices below
which farmer-members were not to sell (Saloutos and Hicks, 1951). By
1903, some locals were able to negotiate a contract with cotton ginners.
A year later, members withheld one out of every five bales of cotton
throughout Texas in order to demand a price of 10 cents per bale. Other
tactics included acreage reduction, plowing under surplus cotton, and
building warehouses to control supplies on the market. Through its
business agencies, the Union obtained contracts with merchants who
offered a 10 percent discount on products sold to Farmers' Union members.
In Colorado, the Union bought and operated a coal mine. In Mississippi,
it attempted to establish a Farmers' Union Bank and Trust Company.
Innumerable business ventures were attempted throughout the agricultural region, many of them successful to this day. After 1912, the Farmers'
Union began moving into the wheat states, and throughout most of the
decade to 1920, Kansas, Nebraska, and North Carolina contributed 52
percent of all the national Union income (Taylor, 1953:347–355).

Initially, the Farmers' Union attempted to stay out of politics, although
it kept representatives at several legislatures trying to influence votes
on important issues. The political demands were different than those
of the previous decades, however. Rather than transportation, monopolies,
and cheap money, the Farmers' Union demanded rural credits, direct
government loans, and an equitable distribution of wealth. In later years
it began to demand government ownership and control of all natural
resources, although its main focus remained on price and marketing
problems. In most cases, Farmers' Union supporters saw themselves as
members of the laboring class and allied with labor unions on several
issues.

The Farmers' Union and the American Society of Equity grew during
a time of relative agricultural prosperity. They had similar goals and
strategies, although the Equity seemed to project an image of farmers
as small business people while the Farmers' Union emphasized the role
of farmers as producers. The Equity was initially strongest in the tobacco
and hard spring wheat states of the northern grain belt. The Union was
stronger in the cotton states and the hard winter wheat belt of Kansas,
Nebraska, Colorado, and parts of Texas and Oklahoma. Both the northern
and the western hard wheat regions were growing in importance as
modern milling conditions made the use of hard wheats for bread flour
more efficient than the soft wheats previously used in the eastern regions
(Saloutos and Hicks, 1961). The growth of this region as the new
agricultural center probably accounted for the growth of both the Equity
and the Farmers' Union, although it is not clear why the Equity gained
strength in some states while the Farmers' Union grew in others. Nor
is it clear why the Farmers' Union continued to grow and survives up

to the present, while the Equity ceased to be an important factor in the farmers' movement by 1920, except in Wisconsin where it remained strong until the 1940s.

The phenomenon that most characterized the farmers' movement in the first two decades of the twentieth century was the cooperative movement. Besides the cooperatives organized by the American Society of Equity and the Farmers' Union, many business cooperatives were organized on a local basis. Some were organized along the principle of the English Rochdale cooperatives, where each member received one vote and surplus income was distributed according to how much business that person did with the cooperative. Others distributed profits according to the amount of stock owned in the joint-stock corporations. The "big business" approach to farming was most apparent on the West Coast. The California Fruit Growers Exchange was organized in 1895 and became one of the largest business cooperatives in the country (Benedict, 1953:136). Its growth is attributable to the large Western produce farms, made possible by the Reclamation Act of 1902 which helped fund, set up, and provide the necessary resources for irrigable lands in the arid regions. Settlers could receive free farm land, although they had to repay the government for irrigation structures within ten years (Benedict, 1953:126). Because large farms could most efficiently use the irrigation systems, the Reclamation Act, more than any other piece of legislation in this period, stimulated the early development of capitalist agriculture in California (Benedict, 1953).

The Nonpartisan League: At the other extreme from the California Fruit Growers Exchange was the Nonpartisan League of North Dakota, a radical departure from the norm of that period. Organized in 1915, it pursued an aggressive membership campaign drive with the major objective of taking over the state government of North Dakota. Rather than farmer-owned cooperative businesses, the League advocated state ownership of elevators, banks, utilities, and other industries throughout North Dakota. While it denied that its program was socialist, it nevertheless challenged the very foundations of the private property system— at least as it affected the property rights of big business. Not surprisingly, the League program was opposed by banks, lumber companies, grain houses, implement dealers, and mail-order houses; these joined together to organize the "Better Farming Movement" to try to convince farmers that their grievances could be addressed by improving their farming methods (Taylor, 1953:425). This "blame the victim" approach did not deter the organizers of the Nonpartisan League who went throughout North Dakota and into adjacent states, driving their Ford motor cars, organizing farmers who initially paid annual dues of $2.50.[3]

One of the important variables affecting the success of a mobilization drive is the ability of organizers to communicate effectively. The spatial difficulties confronting the Nonpartisan League organizers were minimized by the early decision to use some of the membership dues to stockpile a fleet of Ford cars in which organizers would travel about the state enlisting members. Organizers were given a commission for every member they enlisted. The organizers received instruction on the best line of argument and how to deal with opposition. This instruction came from experienced organizers or from the League's founder, Arthur C. Townley, himself a bankrupt farmer. Communities and organizers were matched up so that Catholics went to Catholic communities, Scandinavians to Scandinavian communities, etc. Townley held meetings with organizers each week, where stories were traded, and the most successful organizer for the week presented his (they were all men) "sales pitch" (Taylor, 1953:433–4). Between February, 1915, when Townley and a friend went out in the first Ford car, and July, 10,000 farmers were enlisted as members of the League. Among the issues raised by the organizers was the "system" controlled by the farm machinery companies, money lenders, and grain speculators. Railroad control of all transportation and of elevators, and their unfair grading practices were also major grievances. The major organizing issue revolved around taking control of the state government; it was argued that farmers were a majority of the population in North Dakota and should therefore be a majority of the government. The failure of the state legislature to heed the mandate of the people on two previous occasions certainly contributed to the successful mobilization effort of the League. In 1912, the voters had ratified an amendment providing for the erection of a state-owned terminal elevator outside of North Dakota (presumably to be built in Minneapolis, St. Paul, or Duluth). Two years later a similar amendment was passed, allowing the elevator to be located inside of North Dakota. The legislature authorized $75,000 for the project and told the State Board of Control to proceed with the plans. The Board, however, did no more than prepare a report showing that the elevator was unnecessary. Farmers petitioned the 1915 legislature to carry out the people's mandate, but it refused the demand. Consequently, a social base, which included more than farmers, developed around the issues addressed by the Nonpartisan League. By September 1915, the League paper claimed a circulation of 22,000. By the following year, it claimed 40,000 members, and by 1917 it claimed 10,000 members outside of North Dakota (Taylor, 1953:424–437).

In its first few years, the Nonpartisan League was surprisingly successful. Members campaigned vigorously for their selected candidates, ultimately electing 3 members of the state supreme court, 87 members of the lower house, and 18 members of the upper house. The "Farmers' Legislature of 1917" passed many reforms regulating industry, although it failed to get a terminal elevator bill. It proposed a "Farmers' Bill of Rights" which would redraft the state constitution to provide the legal basis of the League's state-ownership program. The League and its members in the legislature were accused of being anarchists, destructive, extravagant, socialistic, and even revolutionary. The less-than-total success in the legislature caused the League to re-energize its organizing campaign, seeking two-year, paid-in-advance membership dues of $16.00 (Taylor, 1953: 438–9).

In 1918 the League elected what came to be known as the "League Legislature" of 1919. Controlling both houses and all major state offices (including the governorship), the League finally passed a comprehensive program of state-owned industries, including an Industrial Commission to oversee those industries. Its Bank of North Dakota was the sole depository of all public funds, and provided the financial basis for all other projects. The North Dakota Mill and Elevator Association oversaw the manufacturing and warehousing businesses including any state-owned warehouses, flour mills, and elevators that would be built. A Home Building Association was to promote home building and ownership throughout the state. In addition, a state hail insurance program was started, workmen's compensation laws were passed, and numerous other laws were enacted addressing tax, freight rate, and grain grading grievances. The League held nightly sessions in a Bismarck hotel where its farmer-legislators were briefed and de-briefed in secret sessions. Some newspapers railed against "bolshevistic, red-radical Townleyism" and the anti-Leaguers strongly attacked the state bank as a symbol of the entire state-ownership program. Numerous articles, pamphlets, and booklets were published inside and outside of North Dakota, accusing the League of socialism, pro-Germanism, pacifism, and sympathy with the Industrial Workers of the World (I.W.W.). In Minnesota, an opposition organization was started with the name Minnesota Nonpartisan League, Inc. Within North Dakota, an Independent Voters' Association was organized to publicize the League's political sympathies and its mistakes, and to help tie up the legislature and the courts with referenda and law suits. Through a coalition effort of anti-League Democrats and Republicans, the League lost the governor's seat in 1922, and the opposition managed to weaken the League's position within the legislature. By 1924, the League ceased to be an important factor in North Dakota politics; its progressive role in the state was taken up by the Farmer's Union, which came to North Dakota in 1926 (Taylor, 1953:458–469; Conrad and Conrad, 1976:1).

The Early Origins of the American Farm Bureau Federation: Among the opponents of the Nonpartisan League in both North Dakota and in other states, were people who later became leaders in the American Farm Bureau Federation. Although the Farm Bureau was not organized until 1919, establishing itself in North Dakota in December of 1920, its roots belong to the first two decades of the century. Unlike the other farm groups organized around the politics of inclusion, the Farm Bureau was organized with the partial but explicit goal of undermining the more radical elements in the farmers' movement—most notably the Nonpartisan League. In North Dakota, for example, the first president of the Farm Bureau was a progressive Republican who lost his bid for a legislative seat to the Nonpartisan League victors. Although he later became disillusioned with the Bureau's conservatism, the president initially hoped to provide a unified, non-political farmers' organization. The farmers of North Dakota were too radical for the Farm Bureau, however, and it virtually disappeared from the state by 1924 (Conrad and Conrad, 1976:10).

While the American Farm Bureau Association is generally associated with the farmers' movements of the 1920s and 1930s, its origins date back to 1903, and understanding those origins is a key to the entire period leading up to 1920. The Farm Bureau roots stem back to the county extension service programs, organized in 1903. In that year, USDA began to organize community demonstration farms and send out "county agricultural demonstration agents" to help farmers, especially in the South, adopt new farming methods that could help them survive under adverse conditions. Shortly after the county agent system was begun, the Rockefeller-endowed General Education Board began to contribute a large part of the funding for the education, and later, the demonstration work. The county extension "movement" gained tremendous support from bankers and businessmen. The American Bankers' Association formed a Committee on Agricultural Development and Education in 1911 to try to establish a better rapport between farmers and bankers, and to help farmers become "more successful producers, a better credit risk, and a more contented and prosperous people" (McConnell, 1953:31, quotation from Proceedings of the American Bankers' Association). The National Implement and Vehicle Association and corporations such as John Deere and Company, International Harvester, various railroad companies, Chambers of Commerce, and other business associations joined the bankers in urging the passage of the Smith-Lever Act, which allowed the county agent system to continue operating with the dual funding and sponsorship of business organizations and the USDA. According to McConnell (1953:31–35), the land grant colleges generally opposed the provisions of the bill which would cause them to lose control of the extension programs.

In general, county agents operated by organizing local farm bureaus through which they carried out their programs and gained an audience for their demonstrations. In many cases the local farm bureaus were directly organized by a chamber of commerce or business organization. As agricultural expansion blossomed with the preparation for war, the bureaus grew in membership; the Emergency Food Production Act of 1917 was passed which increased the money available to the extension programs. Some states began to organize state federations to coordinate the activities of the local bureaus. A large number of agents had already begun working as managers of local cooperatives, although they were increasingly being paid from public funds. When the American Farm Bureau Federation was finally organized in 1920, it was largely a creation of the USDA and private business organizations. Shortly after its organization, it was decided, for public relations reasons, that the activities of the county agents within the Farm Bureau should be limited. In 1922 the Secretary of Agriculture intervened to formally order that county agents cease their participation in the farm bureaus (McConnell, 1953:50–4). Despite this order, agents continued to operate in many bureaus, sometimes taking an active leadership role. Even where the official ties were severed, however, the stage had been set for the dilution of radical politics during the depression which was to come. A conservative, business-oriented farm organization had been created which would be capable of playing a major role in the politics of the farmers' movement during the potentially volatile decades that followed. The conservative role played by the Farm Bureau will be explored in the next section.

In summary, the period from 1900 to 1920 was one of growth and agricultural prosperity, although farmers were forced to organize in order to reap their share of that prosperity. Perhaps the additional security provided them the time, money, and confidence with which to pursue alternative survival strategies. The period was also one of intense class struggle, marked by successful unionization efforts on the part of workers and interventions by the state and private militias to repress all forms of radicalism. The image of prosperity was marred by two major recessions (Dubofsky, 1969:9–10), the penetration of capital into all aspects of life, a world war, and an unprecedented amount of red-baiting, arrests, and deportations of suspected radicals and radical aliens. In Wisconsin, farmers rallied around Robert M. La Follette, Sr., whose Progressive Party symbolized the more moderate and characteristic reformism of that period. While the American Society of Equity and the Farmers' Union tried to stay out of politics and reap the harvest of the agricultural prosperity, the Nonpartisan League reflected the spirit of discontent and the belief that a better system could be created. Despite the relative prosperity of the period, North Dakota farmers remained dependent on finance and grain capital. As with many northern wheat farmers, the emerging class relations in agriculture were becoming transparent. The failure of old tactics and legitimate channels to alleviate the impact of these class relations contributed to the mobilization of farmers. The attacks against the Nonpartisan League were characteristic of the red-baiting that took place. This, coupled with the polarization of the class structure in agriculture contributed to the fractional polarization in the overall farmers' movement. The state's interventions helped to strengthen the pro-capitalist faction, which proved useful during the economic crisis that followed.

1920–1940: Economic Crisis and State Intervention

The economic crisis that covered most of the period from 1920 to 1940 led to a restructuring of the economy involving new levels of state intervention and the further concentration and centralization of capital. While the state intervened with allocative and productive strategies, it attempted to thwart the development and influence of radical farmers' movements and working class struggle by imposing various limitations on that struggle. These ranged from limiting access to the state by channeling such efforts through the conservative American Farm Bureau Federation to direct repression of militant actions by the Farmers' Holiday Association. The impact of the mobilization and class struggle of that period was felt as liberal legislation was passed and as farmers and the working class gained new capacity for struggling for their demands. The farmers' movement was generally weakened during this period, and, in proportion to its abandonment of opposition to monopoly capitalism, capital continued to penetrate agriculture, leading to displacement, marginalization, and new class relations in agriculture.

The farmers' movement of this period was more divided than ever before. While the Farm Bureau can hardly be characterized as a social movement, it nevertheless represented the interests of a sizeable group of farmers who hoped to emerge victorious from the restructuring process taking place during the economic crisis. Besides the Farm Bureau, which represented the politics of inclusion, the Farmers' Union and the American Society of Equity continued to pursue alternative strategies to survive the depression. The grievance all farmers had in common was the economic crisis, which for many meant foreclosures, declining incomes, and plummeting farm values. The most active mobilization of farmers was the Farmers' Holiday Association which successfully transformed a social base of distressed farmers into a militant social force. This period of history suggests the contrast between the militant mobilization of such farmers, who, having all other alternatives blocked, engaged in direct action tactics to resist the effects of the depression and the failure of the state to protect their interests; on the other hand, a group of farm leaders became the legitimized voice of farmers within the state, pursuing strategies that qualitatively reorganized the relationships between the state, agriculture, and farmers.

During the decades of the 1920s and 1930s, the farm population dropped slightly. Although the proportion of hired farm workers and tenant farmers to the total remained roughly constant both nationally and in the South, dramatic changes took place regionally. In the South, for example, there was a 26.3 percent decrease in the total number of farms worked by black farmers, including a 20.5 percent decrease in fully owned black farms, and a 28.0 percent decrease in black tenant farms. For Southern whites, there was a 6.2 percent increase in tenant farms and a 3.4 percent decrease in fully owned farms. These figures compare to national decreases of 8.4 percent and 3.8 percent for fully owned and tenant farms respectively (U.S. Department of Commerce, 1976:465). During the 1930s, 300,000 Southern farm families migrated to California as agricultural workers, joining the ranks of Mexican and Japanese migrant workers already there (Vogeler, 1981:219). During the 1920s, there was a drop in the national average farm income of 45.6 percent. The average net value of farms in the Midwest dropped nearly 35 percent in each decade (U.S. Department of Commerce, 1976). During the 1920s, farmers continued to go into debt to survive. While trying to maintain the value of their farms, farmers faced a decreasing market and falling prices. While farm exports had more than tripled during the period 1910–1920 they dropped 61 percent in the 1920s, and 51 percent the following decade. Farmers in the wheat states suffered as the physical output of wheat flour decreased during this period for the first time in at least sixty years (U.S. Department of Commerce, 1976).

While most farmers suffered dramatically in the 1920s and 1930s, some were able to expand the value of their farms by investing in tractors and grain combines. In 1920, an average of 3.8 percent of all farms had tractors, compared to 14.6 percent in 1930, and 25 percent in 1940 (U.S. Department of Commerce, 1976:469). The stratification between larger, more capital intensive farms, and smaller, labor intensive farms was reflected in the differences between and within farm organizations. Those who could tried to intensify their production techniques, which meant going further into debt. The county extension services of the U.S.D.A. continued the practice begun in 1903 of teaching farmers about new, improved, and more mechanized farming techniques (McConnell, 1953:24). Farm machinery manufacturers often donated equipment for the demonstration work of the extension services, thus helping to build a market for their products. Even the larger, more successful farmers faced the problem of finding markets for their products and getting a fair price for that marketed. Many of these farmers joined in the movement to establish a powerful and coordinated system of business marketing cooperatives in an effort to survive the economic crisis as victors, rather than as victims. These farmers represented the social base of the American Farm Bureau Federation, the conservative farmers' association that began not as a social movement, but as a bureaucratic organization with a professional, salaried leadership and close ties to the government and sectors of big business (Saloutos and Hicks, 1951: McConnell, 1953). The largest membership in the Farm Bureau came from the corn-growing states of Iowa, Illinois, Indiana, Ohio, and Michigan (Tontz, 1961:156, Table C).

In the wheat states of Kansas, Nebraska, Minnesota, North Dakota, and South Dakota, the Farm Bureau never obtained a large membership until after World War II (Tontz, 1961:156, Table C). There, farmers continued to express grievances toward the large grain monopolies centered around the Twin Cities and Duluth. In these states farmers continued to demand lower freight rates, easier access to credit, and new ways to secure more equitable prices for their products. After the decline of the Nonpartisan League, the Farmers' Union became the progressive voice of farmers in North Dakota. Nebraska and Kansas had long been strong Farmers' Union states. In Wisconsin, the Society of Equity was still strong, and it was there that Robert M. LaFollette mounted his campaign for the Presidency in 1924, running on the Progressive Party ticket. In that election LaFollette captured 13 electoral votes and 17 percent of the popular vote. Fifty-two percent of his 4.8 million votes came from the Midwestern states (U.S. Department of Commerce, 1976: 1073). Meanwhile, in Minnesota, the Farmer-Labor Party attempted to revive the third party movement among farmers and workers, and with some help from the Nonpartisan League, became a powerful force in Minnesota, and a lesser force nationally.

The more influential farm organization of the 1920s and 1930s, however, was the American Farm Bureau Federation. The leadership of the Farm Bureau seldom came from the social base of farmers, and the organization was often accused by the Farmers' Union and other more progressive farm groups of being a tool of big business used to wipe out a progressive farmers' movement. Indeed, the events in North Dakota and Minnesota seem to confirm the accusations, for it was the North Dakota Better Farming Association (the anti-Nonpartisan League business group) that helped begin county agent work in Minnesota and helped to build the local farm bureaus. There were real fears among business and government leaders that organizations like the Nonpartisan League and the Farmer-Labor Party of Minnesota would bring back the radicalism they had tried to crush during the teens. At the convention which launched the Farm Bureau, resolutions were passed stating opposition to the Industrial Workers of the World and endorsing the American Legion as a "soldier citizenry for law and order" (Saloutos and Hicks, 1953:269). The new organization was opposed to all forms of radicalism, against the Nonpartisan League, and in favor of cooperation with business (McConnell, 1953).

Initially the Farm Bureau was divided over whether to continue its emphasis on local educational programs, favored by the Eastern and Southern delegates, or to advance a dual program of building commercial cooperatives while pursuing legislative action, favored by the Midwestern delegates. The latter program came to dominate, and in the first few years of the 1920s the Farm Bureau had its greatest success, organizing and working through the powerful Farm Bloc to pass legislation which had been on the agenda of farm organizations for many years (McConnell, 1953:56). Such legislation included packer and stockyard control, regulation of grain exchanges, extension of the War Finance Corporation's power to lend money for export of farm products, and legalization of farmers cooperatives. After its initial success, the legislative program subsided due in part to the diffuse issues that had formed the Farm Bloc's program and to the lack of a central and clear focus in the Farm Bureau (McConnell, 1953:58).

As the Farm Bloc's clout and importance declined, the Farm Bureau realized that in order to survive it had to begin speaking for farmers in some unique way. In the early days, it had taken concrete steps to pursue large-scale marketing through cooperatives but a debate soon arose within the organization over whether to pursue a policy of service to cooperatives or to develop surplus disposal legislation. By the 1925 convention, the surplus control advocates achieved a clear-cut victory: the Farm Bureau began to devote itself to the passage of the McNary-Haugen bill, which sought to obtain a government guaranty of farm product prices. The bill advocated export of farm surpluses at world prices while domestic prices were maintained at an acceptable level. A government export corporation would buy up commodities at the accepted price whenever prices for that commodity fell below that level. After several unsuccessful attempts to pass the bill in Congress, the fourth McNary-Haugen bill was passed, only to be vetoed by President Coolidge (Benedict, 1953).

While the Farm Bureau can be credited with helping to pass much beneficial farm legislation in the early 1920s, the Bureau has come under attack both contemporarily and in scholarly analyses since that time (Danbom, 1979; McConnell, 1953). McConnell (1953:64) argues that by adopting the McNary-Haugen program as its major focus in the mid-1920s, the Bureau narrowed its focus to those commercial producers of crops with large surpluses whose complex of problems came to be defined as the "farm problem." This focus circumscribed its future development, concentrating its strength primarily in the Midwestern corn and hog producing areas and secondarily in the cotton South. Throughout the 1920s the Bureau's membership declined, except in these areas (Tontz, 1961). The Bureau's early educational focus diminished and a bureaucratic structure was established with large salaries given to its officials and professional staff. While the Bureau attempted to solve the "farm problem" as it applied to large-scale producers of surplus crops, it never sought to become a mass organization or address the needs of small farmers and tenants. The major concern underlying all of its efforts was to put agriculture on a par with industry.

As a result of its organizational strategies and program, the Bureau was often accused of conspiring with business against the interests of farmers, as when Senator LaFollette of Wisconsin accused it of working with railroad, coal, steel, and lumber capital to prevent the repeal of sections of the Esch-Cummings Transportation Act of 1920 (which had guaranteed railroad companies a 5 1/2 percent return on the value of their properties). The Transportation Act had given the Interstate Commerce Commission authority to establish rates that were fair to the railroads, and in some cases it had allowed increases of 35–40 percent (Benedict, 1953:170). The Farmers' Union and the American Society of Equity accused the Bureau of assisting railroad companies, machine manufacturers, and bankers. They charged that while the Bureau pursued legislation for better credit facilities, it ignored the farmers' main problem, which was obtaining a fair price to get them out of debt. The Union accused the Bureau of allying with big business, maintaining, along with the Nonpartisan League and the Farmer-Labor Party, that the working class was a more natural ally of farmers. In spite of attacks against it, the Farm Bureau pointed to a membership of 456,000 on the day it was born, and by 1921 claimed over 1 million members (Saloutos and Hicks, 1953:272). When family memberships alone are counted, the 1921 membership was probably closer to 500,000 (Tontz, 1964:156). The large membership is accounted for by the fact that so many farmers were "members" of the local farm bureaus in the teens. However, for reasons noted above, the membership dropped steadily between 1921 and 1933, when it again began to rise.

The class orientation of the American Farm Bureau Federation is revealed most effectively when its role in the demise of the Farm Security Administration (FSA) is examined. The FSA emerged out of the Resettlement Administration which was established by Executive Order in mid-1935 to handle the problems of poverty in agricultural areas; by 1937 the name was changed to the Farm Security Administration (see Baldwin, 1968, for a detailed history). The political origins of the Resettlement Administration and the subsequent FSA were typical of many New Deal programs. In 1935 testimony supporting the creation of a Farm Tenant Homes Act, Agricultural Secretary Wallace noted the seriousness of the problem of farm tenancy:

> The present conditions, particularly in the South, provide fertile soil for Communist and Socialist agitators. I do not like the bitterness that is aroused by this sort of agitation, but I realize that the cure is not violence or oppressive legislation to curb these activities but rather to give these dispossessed people a stake in the social system. The American way to preserve the traditional order is to provide these refugees of the economic system with an opportunity to build and develop their own homes and to live on the land which they may call their own and on which they can make a modest living year after year (quoted in Baldwin, 1968:135).

Wallace went on to note that the problem of farm tenancy was exacerbated by the crop restriction program of the Agricultural Adjustment Act (AAA)—which led many farm owners to reduce their acreage by taking their rented land out of production—and he added that rural stability and health would be impossible unless the country were to "convert tenants of this sort into owner-farmers" (Baldwin, 1968:135).

The compromise measure that eventually came out of Congress was the Bankhead-Jones Farm Tenancy Act, passed in mid-1937. This Act authorized many of the activities carried on by the Resettlement Administration, which soon became the FSA and was placed under the direction of the USDA. The FSA became heir to a large number of programs for rural rehabilitation and welfare. The idea of rural rehabilitation was to make needy families self-sufficient through educational and loan programs designed to educate farmers and help those with viable farms become more efficient and self-supporting. The farm ownership aspect of the FSA originated with the Bankhead-Jones Act and was also conducted through a loan program. The resettlement programs dealt with displaced farm families and even industrial workers by providing them with plots of land for full or part-time farming; a few cooperative farms were organized; in some cases the program tried to bring industrial establishments to rural areas to provide employment for part-time or displaced farm families (Baldwin, 1968; Benedict, 1953; McConnell, 1953).

The FSA had a number of problems, not the least of which were administrative and bureaucratic in nature. Ultimately, its major problem was the attacks it incurred from business interests, conservatives in Congress, and the Farm Bureau. In the Great Plains area, large grain dealers in Minneapolis were hostile to FSA-sponsored loans to enable cooperatives to purchase failing grain elevators. The Farm Bureau itself was a central initiator of the attacks on the FSA. McConnell (1953:97) makes the strong accusation that the Bureau "was the agency which destroyed the FSA." The Bureau mounted its offensive against the FSA in 1941 by calling for a complete reorganization of the Department of Agriculture. The Bureau advocated decentralizing various functions of the USDA, particularly those of the FSA; it urged that the farm and home management services be turned over to the Extension Service and the loaning functions be given to the Farm Credit Administration. With the onset of World War II, a joint Congressional committee was organized to find ways to reduce nonessential government spending and the FSA was one of the first agencies summoned to justify itself before the committee. The Farm Bureau hastily put together material for its testimony against the FSA, and although much of the evidence was sketchy and based on hearsay, it exerted an inordinate amount of influence over this and subsequent committees. The Farm Bureau found allies which joined in its attack on the FSA. Among these was the Irrigated Cotton Growers which objected to the FSA's support for a minimum wage for Mexican labor used in cotton picking. In 1943 a separate subcommittee of the House Committee on Agriculture was set up specifically to investigate the FSA. The committee was "amenable to Farm Bureau suggestions in its probing, and either was unaware of the objectives of the FSA or was hostile to them" (McConnell, 1953:107; Baldwin, 1968).

While Baldwin (1968) concurs that the AFBF played a major role in dismantling the FSA he insists on the need to understand the FSA's rise and fall within the context of "time and political change." Baldwin views the FSA as something of an anomaly, whose success must be considered in the context of favorable internal and external contexts, the latter including amicable relations with Congress, the urgency imposed by the Depression, the influence of the President and the New Deal movement, and the indifference or acquiescence of government people and farm organizations hostile to its programs. The ideological commitments of the FSA's leaders were also important. By contrast, the onset of the war and with it the growing opposition to New Deal programs and accusations of "communism" within liberal governmental agencies established a climate favorable to the attack on the FSA (Baldwin, 1968:323). These factors contributed to the decline of the FSA and had nothing to do with the AFBF. Thus, Baldwin concludes, while the Farm Bureau attack does not entirely explain the demise of the FSA, McConnell may be correct in arguing that the Farm Bureau's attack on the FSA is explained largely by its desire to maintain the county agent system of the Extension Service. As long as the latter was organized in a decentralized manner, the Farm Bureau could ensure its control and power at the local level (Baldwin, 1968:410–11).

The role of the Farm Bureau throughout the 1920s and 1930s supports the contention that the organization pursued a politics of inclusion. While the Bureau supported some of the price support programs of the New Deal, it sought economic and political power for itself as an organization, and for its members whose economic situation was relatively privileged in the context of a major depression. The conservative tenor of the Bureau's policies and actions has been explained in part by its origins in a period of relative prosperity, where its constituency—its social base—was a group of farmers whose participation in the economic prosperity of the time made them susceptible to the problems of food surpluses in later years. The price support solutions to the food surplus problem had the ironic effect, on the one hand, of reducing production at a time of depression with its concomitant unemployment and hunger, and, on the other hand, of encouraging government economic support for precisely those farmers who, as a group, were perhaps the most capable of surviving the depression. While a number of alternative and more "radical" organizations arose during the 1930s to address the problems of farmers, only one will be discussed here in an effort to show the contrast between the politics of inclusion and reform during the 1930s.

While the farmers' movement of the 1930s was never as explosive as the workers' movement to build the Congress of Industrial Organizations (CIO), and the Communist Party never became a major force among farmers (Dyson, 1982), the Farmers Holiday Association, the Southern Tenant Farmers' Union, and efforts to organize agricultural laborers in California were radical influences during this period. The most militant organization in the Midwest was the Farmers' Holiday Association, led by Milo Reno of the Iowa Farmers' Union. The Farmers' Holiday advocated a program of direct action. For a number of years in the early 1930s the Farmers' Holiday Association engaged in militant, and occasionally violent action to prevent foreclosures of farms, to prevent authorities from condemning livestock on the basis of questionable tuberculosis tests, and to prevent farmers from taking their products to market in violation of various farmers' strikes which were called. Farmers held numerous demonstrations, blockaded roads to a governors' conference held in Sioux City, Iowa; held a mass march and rally in Des Moines; and, in one case, forced a judge to sign an agreement not to execute any more foreclosure sales. In cases where foreclosure sales were held, usually through an auction, members of the Farmers'

Holiday Association gathered to bid no more than a few pennies for hundreds of dollars of goods. They threatened any outsider who joined in the bidding in hopes of obtaining cheap property. The auctioned property was then returned to the original owner by the Farmers' Holiday people (Dyson, 1982). The Farmers' Holiday movement was strong in Iowa, Minnesota, Wisconsin, Nebraska, and South Dakota. In North Dakota and Minnesota the governors defended the indebted farmers by calling for moratoriums on foreclosure sales. Other states were also forced to pass anti-foreclosure legislation (Saloutos and Hicks, 1951:435 ff.). While the Farmers' Holiday movement was the radical edge of the Farmers' Union, it was never repudiated by the parent body (McConnell, 1953:68).

The legislative importance of the Farmers' Holiday Association was that it contributed to the general anxiety about unrest which helped the more liberal and conservative farm programs get passed. The collective actions of the Farmers' Holiday Association and efforts of tenants and agricultural laborers to organize forced legislators to attend to the demands of poor farmers and contributed to the passage of more liberal laws regarding foreclosures, rehabilitation assistance, and loans to small and tenant farmers and croppers.

The legislative history of the 1920s and 1930s is central to understanding the politics and economics of agriculture in the post-World War II period. Four of the major changes in state policy that developed in the New Deal are summarized here.

First, the state became involved in a variety of production-control measures, signifying its intervention into Stage Two of the production cycle. Second, the state expanded its intervention into Stage Three by setting marketing quotas to regulate prices and by directly intervening to adjudicate disputes over freight rates. Third, the state became a purchaser of farm commodities, thereby insuring a market for a portion of the surplus. Fourth, the state intervened in Stage One by providing crop insurance, more direct loans, and encouraging the use of certain agricultural input commodities—such as fertilizer—for the sake of "conservation" of the soil. All of these marked a more direct intervention of the state into the economy as regulator, planner, and subsidizer. Among the implicit goals of the entire New Deal program was the important one of appeasing enough farmers to prevent the perfusion of the kind of radical farmers' movement which had characterized earlier periods and which was then mushrooming within the working class. By granting a number of concessions that had been fought for in earlier periods, the radical potential of that depressed and volatile period was contained to a large degree.

Excluded from the legislation of the New Deal period were the agricultural laborers, who were explicitly left out of both the National Labor Relations Act (Wagner Act) of 1935 and the Fair Labor Standards Act of 1938. More struggle and further polarization of the class structure in agriculture were needed before agricultural laborers could either successfully organize against capitalist growers or bring themselves under the protection of the law. Such changes would gradually come after World War II, when a second wave of capitalization and intensification penetrated Stage Two of agriculture.

In conclusion, the period of 1920 to 1940 represented the gradual, but qualitatively significant intervention of the state into all three stages of the agricultural cycle. At the beginning of the period, two distinct and qualitatively different farmers' organizations represented the politics of inclusion, on the one hand, and the politics of resistance and transformation, on the other hand. In previous periods with a generally high level of class struggle, the farmers' movement had turned towards an alliance with labor, seeking transformations or reforms in the social structure. When economic conditions began to improve, a large number of farmers found themselves included in the economic expansion and were susceptible to a politics of inclusion. The decisive factor in preventing an outbreak of a mass movement of farmers and workers during the depression of the 1930s was the state, which had intervened previously to promote the American Farm Bureau Federation, thereby limiting more radical farm organizations' influence on and access to the state. The legitimacy of the Farm Bureau was weak, however, among those farmers whose class position became more transparently dependent on capital. The continued efforts of those farmers to organize around a politics of reform or transformation, and the use of direct action tactics to address their grievances forced both the state and the conservative Farm Bureau to take them seriously. As World War II approached, the agricultural situation improved and the stage was set for new levels of capital penetration of agriculture that would make earlier transformations in the structure of agriculture seem modest by comparison.

World War II and Beyond

Dramatic changes occurred in the structure of agriculture following World War II. The chemical and electronics industries were stimulated by military production needs; as the post-war conversion of industry took place, new developments in the production of chemical fertilizers and herbicides created a revolution in the area of agricultural inputs. The capital penetration of the chemical industry into Stage One of agriculture reached new proportions. As in World War I, the capital intensification of agriculture that took place during the World War II forced farmers to expand their debt to go along with the new methods of production, or become marginalized and proletarianized. Between 1940 and 1970 the number of farms dropped 52 percent and the farm population dropped from 23 to less than 5 percent of the total population. While roughly 47 percent of the total land area remained farm land, the average farm size went from 175 to 373 acres (U.S. Department of Commerce, 1976:457). Meanwhile, farm debt increased nearly 117 percent during the 1950s, and 135 percent the following decade. The class structure in agriculture became more polarized during these years, reflected in the proletarianization of small farmers and the expansion of capitalist relations in most fruit and vegetable growing areas (see Mooney, Chapter 7 and Pfeffer, Chapter 8 of this volume). One of the most significant changes in the class politics in agriculture has been the development of farm-worker unions in the capitalist farming regions. Throughout the 1930s, 1940s, and 1950s there were repeated attempts to organize migrant farm workers, particularly in California. These efforts met with limited success until, in 1962, the National Farm Workers Association was organized following three years of patient effort to build a grass-roots based organization. Throughout the 1960s farm labor strikes received considerable publicity as well as broad-based support (McWilliams, 1971). Majka and Majka have examined the nature of state interventions into this new form of agrarian class conflict, arguing that state interventions generally sought to regulate the supply of farm labor in the interests of growers, and yet labor insurgency played a pivotal role in forcing the state to play a mediating role and generate reforms beneficial to farm labor.

The period of 1940 to the mid–1970s was a period of internationalization and economic growth. Both the U.S. state and U.S. capital expanded their power and hegemony, especially in the early part of this period. The concentration and centralization of Stage Two of the agricultural cycle was stimulated by the penetration of Stage One and Stage Three capital into the business of food and fiber production. As family farmers were forced to seek off-farm employment, go further into debt, or engage in contract farming, they experienced first hand the changing structure of agriculture. Farm organizations like the Farm Bureau continued to emulate capitalist organizations and goals, the Farmers' Union and newer organizations like the National Farmers' Organization continued to seek alliances with and emulate the policies and practices of organized labor. These organizations maintained a reformist outlook while attempting to help their members benefit from the greater productivity in agriculture.

One of the interesting changes in the farmers' movement since World War II is the development of international organizations of farmers. The

International Federation of Agricultural Producers (I.F.A.P.) was started in 1946 with major support from the Farmers' Union. Originally designed to help push the U.S. Marshall Plan in Europe, this organization has advocated national and international programs and policies intended to increase export markets for U.S. agricultural goods. The Farmers' Union, through the I.F.A.P. helped develop policies designed to use food as a weapon of U.S. foreign policy.

The 1970s brought on a new period of crisis, and we are witnessing the restructuring process during the eighties. The crisis is characterized by stagflation, the failure of Keynesianism, austerity economics, and the decline of U.S. military, economic and political hegemony in the world. Within agriculture, there has been a notable decline in the number of farms, rendering farmers a small minority of the work force; black farmers have virtually become extinct. A 1983 *Business Week* special report on the farm crisis noted that, for the first time in 13 years, farm exports declined by 11 percent; the agricultural sector's assets had begun to shrink for the first time since the early 1950s; farm debt had quadrupled since 1970, reaching $215 billion by the beginning of 1983; and the U.S. was expected to lose a bitter trade war with Europe. The "average U.S. farm family" now relied on outside jobs for two-thirds of its income (*Business Week*, 1983:112). Across the country, hundreds of farms have been facing farm foreclosures and thousands face bankruptcies or liquidations for financial reasons. It is estimated that the nation's overall farm loan delinquency rate is 25 percent (Orr, 1982:3). Farmers have shown a willingness to engage in collective actions that parallel those of earlier periods. Recently, farmers and union members from Ohio to Colorado and as far north as Canada have joined forces to stop farm foreclosures and seek legislative reforms to aid small farmers (*New York Times*, June 5, 1983), although a radical-populist uprising has yet to emerge. If anything can be learned from the history of farmers' movements it is that the presence or absence of that uprising, and the political-ideological form it takes will be a decisive factor in the outcome of the present restructuring process in agriculture.

CONCLUSION

The arguments developed in this paper should be read more as propositions than as conclusions. The historical data presented suggests three basic hypotheses regarding the relationship of farmers' movements to the changing structure of agriculture.

The first hypothesis is that the class relations between farmers and other classes or class fractions—especially the capitalist class—is the major determinant of the orientations and transformations internal to farmers' movements. As the class structure of agriculture changes, differences between established capitalist farmers, small commodity producers, and proletarianized farmers are exacerbated. These differences are then reflected in the social force of the movement and account for the conflicting efforts to expand the social base into an alliance with either workers, small business people, capitalists, or state bureaucrats. Changes internal to the movement can lead to uncertainty or conflict over who, exactly, constitutes the social base, and who can or should be mobilized into the social force. Thus, what is often noted as a separation of the (bureaucratized) leadership from the mass base (Lipset, 1968; Wilson, 1978) may very well reflect the intrusion of a new class element into the social force that has little to do with the initial social force or social base of the movement. Alternatively, it may reflect transformations within the social base that distance it from the original social force.

A second hypothesis is a modification of the first. It is argued that the dynamics of class relations suggested in the first hypothesis are mediated by cycles of economic expansion or crisis in capitalism. In a general way the politics of inclusion have their greatest strength during an expansionary period. By contrast, more militant, reform-minded farmers' movements, pursuing the politics of resistance, have a tendency to be strongest during periods of crisis or when the nature of the restructuring of agriculture is still contested. Harrington's analysis of Oklahoma in the 1930s demonstrates this point (Chapter 6).

A third hypothesis is that the state becomes a factor affecting farmers' movements in direct correspondence to its increasing role in the agricultural economy. While the early farm movements actively sought modest forms of state involvement in agriculture, the use of the state against them was not anticipated by reform-minded farm movements. The opposition to government intervention often expressed in farm circles today reflects, on the one hand, the laissez faire philosophy of the Farm Bureau Federation. It reflects, on the other hand, a latent form of ideological resistance to the capitalist state which has facilitated the marginalization of many family farmers. Mooney's analysis of family farming in Wisconsin in Chapter 7 elaborates this point.

Whether the present economic crisis will contribute to a progressive mobilization of farmers remains to be seen. A decisive factor will rest on the balance of class forces at home and abroad and the ability of farmers to learn from their own history and make conscious choices about which side to be on. Part of that decision will depend on whether farmers will join a broader social movement that includes an alliance with labor and consumers and whether they pursue more than their own narrow and immediate economic interests. Quite possibly the failure to do so will mean abandoning the progressive movement within agriculture to the workers in the agricultural fields and the factories of this country. If agricultural production units continue to expand, wage laborers may become an increasingly important class of agricultural producers. Two factors mitigate against the successful mobilization of these farm workers: if agricultural workers are undocumented foreign workers, their capacity to struggle is severely limited (see Chapter 8); secondly, marginalized farmers entering the work force may bring with them conservative orientations characteristic of the petty bourgeoisie. Counteracting these negative factors is the experience farmers and workers are gaining in current struggles against foreclosures and corporate domination of agriculture. These new agricultural workers and part-time farmers may bring with them shared grievances, political orientations, and previous experience in organizing struggles around immediate interests that will become the basis for class alliances between direct producers in agriculture and urban industry.

NOTES

1. Throughout this paper, reference to the Midwest includes the following states: Illinois, Indiana, Iowa, Kansas, Michigan, Minnesota, Missouri, Nebraska, North Dakota, Ohio, South Dakota, and Wisconsin.

2. When the farmers' alliances of the 1880s and 1890s turned to organizing the People's Party, they maintained their earlier alliance with labor. The issues were broad, including political reforms, demands for the regulation of monopolies, and structural changes benefiting farmers and workers. As the party grew it incorporated a broader social base and small business people and even capitalists joined the party. Many joined with the silver capitalists to push the party platform to adopt the single issue of the free and unlimited coinage of silver—an issue pushed as a panacea for farmers' financial dilemmas (Foner, 1975). As this faction came to dominate the party, the social base of farmers and workers drifted away, causing the party to fold.

3. The dues were soon raised to $6.00, then $9.00, and eventually to $16.00 for a two-year period.

REFERENCES

Benedict, Murray R. 1953. *Farm Policies of the United States 1790–1950: A Study of Their Origins and Development.* New York: Twentieth Century Fund.

Bogart, Ernest Ludlow. 1923. *Economic History of American Agriculture.* New York: Longmans, Green & Co.

Boyer, Richard O. and Herbert Morais. 1965. *Labor's Untold Story.* New York: United Electrical, Radio & Machine Workers of America. (c. 1955).

Buck, Solon Justus. 1969. The Granger Movement: A Study of Agricultural Organization and Its Political, Economic and Social Manifestations 1870–1880. Lincoln: University of Nebraska (c. 1913, Harvard University).

Castels, Manuel. 1978. City, Class and Power. London: Macmillan.

Conrad, Charles and Joyce Conrad. 1976. 50 Years of North Dakota Farmers' Union.

Danbom, David. 1979. The Resisted Revolution, Ames, Iowa: Iowa Univ. Press.

Dowd, Douglas F. 1974. The Twisted Dream: Capitalist Development in the United States Since 1776. Cambridge: Winthrop.

Dubofsky, Melvyn. 1969. Industrialism and the American Workers, 1865–1920. Arlington Heights: AHM.

Dyson, Lowell K. 1982. Red Harvest: The Communist Party and American Farmers. Lincoln, Nebraska: University of Nebraska.

Ewen, Stuart. 1976. Captains of Consciousness. New York: McGraw-Hill.

Fine, Nathan. 1961. Labor and Farmer Parties in the United States 1828–1928. New York: Russell & Russell (c. 1928).

Friedmann, Harriet. 1981. "The Family Farm in Advanced Capitalism: Outline of a Theory of Simple Commodity Production in Agriculture." Paper presented at the Annual Meeting of the American Sociological Association, Toronto.

Foner, Philip S. 1975. History of the Labor Movement in the United States. Volume II: From the Founding of the American Federation of Labor to the Emergence of American Imperialism. New York: International.

Gamson, William A. and Bruce Fireman. 1979. "Utilitarian Logic in the Resource Mobilization Perspective." In M. Zald and J. McCarthy, ed., The Dynamics of Social Movements: Resource Mobilization. Beverly Hills: Sage.

Goss, Kevin F., Richard D. Rodefeld, and Frederick Buttel. 1980. "The Political Economy of Class Structure in U.S. Agriculture: A Theoretical Outline." In Buttel, Frederick H. and Howard Newby, eds., The Rural Sociology of the Advanced Societies: Critical Essays. Montclair, NJ: Allenheld, Osmun.

Goodwyn, Lawrence. 1978. The Populist Movement. New York: Oxford.

Hicks, John D. 1961. The Populist Revolt: A History of the Farmers' Alliance and the People's Party. Lincoln: University of Nebraska, Bison (c. 1931, University of Minnesota).

Lipset, Seymour Martin. 1968. Agrarian Socialism: The Cooperative Commonwealth Federation in Saskatchewan. A Study in Political Sociology. Garden City, NY: Anchor (orig. 1950, University of California).

McConnell, Grant. 1953. The Decline of Agrarian Democracy. New York: Antheneum.

Mooney, Patrick. 1985. "Class Relations and Class Structure in the Midwest." In A. E. Havens, with Gregory Hooks, Patrick H. Mooney, and Max J. Pfeffer, eds., Studies in the Transformation of U.S. Agriculture, Boulder: Westview Press.

Olson, Mancur, Jr. 1965. The Logic of Collective Action: Public Goods and the Theory of Groups. Revised Edition. New York: Schocken (orig. 1965, Harvard University).

Pfeffer, Max. 1985. "The Labor Process and Corporate Agriculture: Mexican Workers in California." In A. E. Havens, with Gregory Hooks, Patrick H.

Mooney, and Max J. Pfeffer, eds., Studies in the Transformation of U.S. Agriculture, Boulder: Westview Press.

Pickvance, C. G. 1977. "From 'Social Base' to 'Social Force': Some Analytical Issues in the Study of Urban Protest" in Michael Harloe, ed. Captive Cities. Studies in the Political Economy of Cities and Regions. London: John Wiley & Sons.

Saloutos, Theodore and John D. Hicks. 1951. Agricultural Discontent in the Middle West 1900–1939. Madison: University of Wisconsin.

Smelser, Neil J. 1962. Theory of Collective Behavior. New York: Free Press.

Taylor, Carl C. 1953. The Farmers' Movement 1620–1920. New York: American Book Co.

Tilly, Charles 1978. From Mobilization to Revolution. Reading, Mass.: Addison-Wesley.

Tontz, Robert L. 1964. "Memberships of General Farmers' Organizations, United States, 1874–1960." Agricultural History XXXVIII 3(July): 143–55.

U.S. Department of Commerce. 1976. Historical statistics of the United States: Colonial Times to the Present. Washington: U.S. Printing Office.

Useem, Michael. 1970. Protest Movements in America. Indianapolis: Bobbs-Merrill Educational Publishing.

Weisskopf, Thomas E. 1981. "The Current Economic Crisis in Historical Perspective." Socialist Review No. 57.

Williams, William Appleman. 1966. The Contours of American History. Chicago: Quadrangle.

Wilson, Graham. 1978. "Farmers' Organizations in Advanced Societies." In Howard Newby, ed., International Perspectives in Rural Sociology. London: John Wiley.

Vogeler, Ingolf. 1981 The Myth of the Family Farm. Boulder: Westview Press.

5
Local State Structure and the Transformation of Southern Agriculture

David R. James

> For this much all men know: despite compromise, war, and struggle, the Negro
> is not free. In the backwoods of the Gulf States, for miles and miles, he may not
> leave the plantation of his birth; in well-nigh the whole rural South the black
> farmers are peons, bound by law and custom to an economic slavery, from which
> the only escape is death or the penitentiary.
>
> —W.E.B. DuBois
> (1903:41)

INTRODUCTION

Almost all contemporary studies of southern economic development mention the passing of the old, labor-intensive methods of producing cotton and the demise of sharecropping and tenant farming as a way of life for the majority of southern farmers of both races. The increased use of tractors and other agricultural machinery coupled with the replacement of the large class of sharecroppers and tenants with a much smaller class of agricultural wage laborers is often referred to as the transformation of southern agriculture. Most accounts of this transformation have ignored DuBois' argument that southern racial politics were intimately related to the plantation economy. Some view economic and political change as independent processes and, therefore, analyze economic development with almost no mention of southern politics (e.g., Day, 1967). Others suggest that political and economic changes have many causes but make little attempt to establish linkages among causes or attach differential importance to them (e.g., Bass and DeVries, 1976; Matthews and Prothro, 1966). A few who theorize connections between economic and political change tend to emphasize the effects of economic development on regional politics but essentially ignore the possibility that politics might affect economic change (e.g., Wilson, 1978; Mandle, 1978).

In this chapter, I will argue that there were intimate connections between southern political structures and class structures which led to the transformation of southern agriculture. The transformation began during the 1930s with the implementation of the New Deal farm programs, but national farm policy was not the decisive element. The crucial factor was the way those national policies were implemented at the local level throughout the South. The domination of local politics, particularly the farmer committee system of the Agricultural Adjustment Administration (AAA), by the cotton planter class ensured that the major portion of the benefits of the AAA programs went to white owners of large farms rather than to small owners, tenants and sharecroppers of either race. The progressive displacement of tenants and small farmers from the land after the 1930s was a direct result of the political efficacy of planters with respect to small farmers, tenants and sharecroppers.

First, I will discuss the salient features of the rural class structure typical of the cotton South around 1900 as compared to that existing about 1975. Second, I will introduce the concept of "local state structure"[1] and will analyze the relationship between it and the rural class structure of the South before 1930. The key element of southern local state structure was its racial nature. Racial segregation and black political disfranchisement were not merely aspects of the value system of southern whites nor a primordial sentiment that led whites to discriminate against blacks. Racial segregation and black disfranchisement were components of a state structure that rewarded discriminatory behavior and rendered the black population politically impotent. This state structure was organically related to the class structure of cotton plantation agriculture. The economic viability of labor intensive cotton agriculture was predicated upon the political docility of the agriculture labor force, especially black sharecroppers and tenants.

Third, I will present some evidence which suggests that this transformation began during the Great Depression rather than during or after World War II as many authors suggest (e.g., Day, 1967; Mandle, 1978). This point is a crucial element of my argument. If, contrary to my thesis, the transformation did not begin with the initial implementation of the New Deal farm programs, then the prime cause of the transformation cannot be attributed to their implementation at the local level. Finally, I will present evidence that the implementation of the Federal farm programs, through the farmer committee system of the AAA and its lineal descendent, the Agricultural Stabilization and Conservation Service (ASCS), led to the transformation of southern agriculture especially with regard to cotton.[2]

The domination of the farmer committee system in the South by cotton planters and their allies created a structure that rewarded the displacement of tenants and sharecroppers and funded the adoption of capital-intensive farming methods. This result is somewhat ironic because the official purpose of the cotton subsidy programs was to relieve the distress of the agricultural classes in the South, not to displace tenants and sharecroppers. Rather than the finest example of "grass-roots democracy" as proponents have argued since the New Deal, the farmer committee system was an effective instrument of southern planter oligarchy (Grodzins, 1966). The devotion of the farmer committee system to the satisfaction of planter interests had the unanticipated consequences of transforming the production relations of cotton plantation agriculture from those of planter and tenant to those of capitalist farmer and wage worker. The transformation of southern agriculture was at its core a politically determined transformation of the rural class structure of the South.

RURAL CLASS STRUCTURE DEFINED

Three principal agricultural classes existed in the South at the turn of the century. These were: 1) landlords who had tenants or sharecroppers working the land for them; 2) independent yeomen who owned land and for the most part worked it themselves with the assistance of unpaid family labor; and 3) sharecroppers and tenants who had to enter into an agreement with landlords in order to gain access to the means of production and subsistence. These three classes comprised the poles of a triangular class structure which is illustrated in panel A of Figure 1.

The so-called agricultural ladder from cropper to independent farmer are intermediate positions between two of the principal classes based upon the degree to which the tenant owns and supplies the means of production and can control the production process. Cash tenants, for example, pay a fixed rent, provide all of the factors of production except land, and decide all aspects of the production process including the crop mix. Sharecroppers, by contrast, own neither work stock nor implements. They must rent all of the factors of production from a creditor, usually the landlord. For their labor, sharecroppers received a share of the crop produced, typically half, from which they must pay all of their debts including the food and clothing loans extended to them during the time that the crop was being produced.

Notice that the "wage cropper" category occupies the same structural position as the sharecropper. This is consistent with the fact that cotton planters often shifted individuals in this lowest tenure category to wages or shares depending upon the price of cotton. High prices for cotton

FIGURE 1. Rural Class Structure of the Cotton South

Panel A. *About 1900*

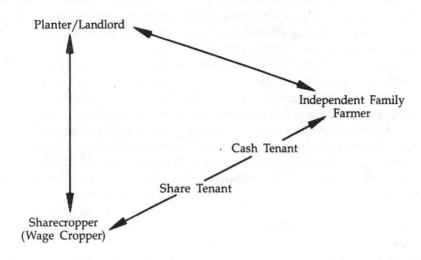

Panel B. *About 1975*

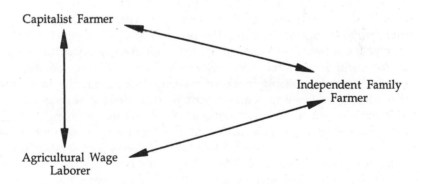

yielded greater returns to the planter (landlord) if the cropper were paid a fixed wage rather than shares. Shares, on the other hand, shifted more of the risk toward the cropper when prices were low. The systematic pattern of the mode of payment indicates the similarity of the two cropper types (Langsford and Thibodeaux, 1939). Whether they were paid wages or shares, croppers resided on the plantation and usually had some access to land for the cultivation of subsistence crops.

By 1975, tenants and sharecroppers had virtually disappeared as a form of land tenure in cotton agriculture (Beale, 1976; James, 1981). In place of sharecroppers, there remained a class of wage workers who were primarily machine operators, more skilled in the operation and maintenance of complex machinery than were the typical wage croppers of the past. The old planter/landlord class was also replaced. A new class of capitalist farmers appeared. These farmers were forced to continually increase the productivity of their labor force by the introduction of improved machinery, techniques, and cotton varieties.

This new class structure is illustrated in panel B of Figure 1. Despite its apparent similarity to the structure depicted in panel A, it is different in a very important way: it contains a structural imperative, well understood from the perspective of both neoclassical and Marxist economics, that compels capitalist farmers to adopt labor-saving innovations. If a capitalist does not continually find new production methods and technologies, he or she will lose the competitive struggle to others who are more successful in that search. This imperative is not reducible to the psychological disposition or personality of the capitalist. Because the capitalist has no option for obtaining the necessities of life and new means of production (e.g. seed, fertilizer, fuel, machinery) but to enter the market, the failure to maintain satisfactory profit levels means that the capitalist can no longer exist as a farmer. The adoption of innovations is the only viable long term strategy for survival as a capitalist farmer.

By contrast, the rural class structure of the South prior to 1930 contained no such imperative to innovate. There were several factors that mitigated against it. First, the possibility of subsistence agriculture as a yeoman farmer was not completely removed as an option available to the rural labor force until relatively late in the period before the Great Depression. Rising levels of tenancy throughout the first third of this century indicate that attainment of this alternative was becoming increasingly difficult. Nevertheless, to the extent that farmers could grow their own foodstuffs, they insulated themselves from market pressure to obtain credit or to enter into less advantageous tenant contracts with landlords. Second, the technical solution for the mechanical picking of cotton was not commercially available until the early 1940s, although the principle upon which it was based had been known for at least 15 years (Street, 1957). Until a commercially viable mechanical cotton harvester became available, it made little economic sense to mechanize the preharvest. Because an adequate labor supply had to be available for the harvest, leaving it idle during the rest of the season would have been costly. Finally, the disfranchisement of blacks and the institutionalization of racial segregation in all spheres of public and private life in the South had the effect of maintaining a guaranteed labor force for cotton agriculture. Racial segregation prevented blacks from responding to the higher wages of the growing capitalist industry of the South.

The planters' inability to substitute capital for labor made labor repressive techniques the modal response to competition and the vagaries of the cotton market. Blacks were the preferential targets of this coercion, of which two types should be distinguished. The first and most pernicious was the continuing everyday subordination of blacks through institutionalized segregation and discrimination. The second type—the type which is most informative of the nature of the class relations between planter and tenant—was the overt physical coercion that was triggered by conditions of the cotton economy. The complaints of planters concerning the shortage of labor were always intensified during periods of peak labor demand, particularly during the harvest period and especially during years which yielded bumper crops. At those times, agencies of the local state, particularly the police and the courts, cooperated to provide planters with an adequate supply of labor (Cohen, 1976). The use of coercion will be discussed in more detail below as part of the analysis of local state structure.

LOCAL STATE STRUCTURE DEFINED

The distinction between local and non-local state structures is not strictly a matter of the physical location of organizations. Neither the location of the buildings typically occupied by an organization, the residences of organization members nor the operating terrain of an organization are sufficient to classify that organization as an element of "local" state structure. In this essay, the appellations "local" and "non-local" refer to the location of interest groups, in this case, representatives of classes, which effectively control a particular state structure, or to which particular state structures must be responsible. In other words, the terms refer to the operating terrain of the interest groups which dominate state structures. Which interest groups are the most important is an empirical question depending upon the state structures under investigation. A principal contention of this chapter is that the domination of certain crucial state structures by the southern planter class was the key causal factor in the transformation of the southern rural class structure.

Depending on the strength and/or size of the interest group in question, its operating terrain may be restricted to a very small geographic area or it may be national or even international in scope. Class representatives such as large corporations and labor unions have the resources to directly and indirectly place effective constraints on State and federal state structure, but the control of state structures is always an object of contention and conflict. The power and organization of parochial interest groups, in this case, the southern planter class, may prevail within certain geographically proscribed areas even if they cannot protect their interests throughout the nation.

Cotton planters were unevenly distributed across the South. Certain counties, for example, the counties of the Mississippi Delta,[3] had very high concentrations of cotton plantations as compared to other types of farming and business activity. In these areas, the domination of local state structures by the class of cotton planters was more effective and complete than it was in rural areas less suited for cotton production and in urban areas. Because of its regional concentration, the planter class was able to influence politics at the national level, usually through elected representatives in Congress, as well as the State and local level.[4]

The mechanisms of control of state structures are both through the selection of personnel for positions of authority and constraints on the behavior of persons who occupy those positions. For example, the disfranchisement of blacks made it unlikely that persons sympathetic to black political participation would be elected to public office. Even if such persons were elected to office or hired to fill non-elective positions, they had to enforce a policy of black subordination if they wished to remain in office.

The term "state structure" refers to the relatively stable formal organizations that authoritatively maintain the distribution of power in society. These organizations may be of local, regional or national importance. The means available to the state for maintaining the existing distribution of power are of two broad types: those which exercise force and coercion, and those which control the collection and distribution of public funds and resources. The first type consists of those organizations which exercise the monopoly of the means of violence. In the United States, however, coercive organizations are not perfectly coordinated. Police activities, for example, are performed by communities and cities, counties, States and the federal government and are far from being uniformly applied across the country. Local and non-local police organizations have frequently pursued different policies with regard to the policed population, and the outcomes experienced by various groups have varied from place to place depending upon the local distribution of power. For example, the treatment blacks could expect from southern police and courts was very different from that which they experienced in the North for much of this century. Even within the South, there were great differences between urban and rural areas and cotton and non-cotton growing areas (James, 1981).

Police activities as well as most other local governmental activities such as the operation of the courts and the provision of public services are typically left to local organizations. Only in unusual circumstances have the military or other federal law enforcement agencies been used by the national government to settle domestic confrontations.

The second type of local state structure consists of those organizations which raise public revenues and put them to use. Throughout most of this nation's history, the uses to which public funds could be put were typically restricted to paying for the maintenance of policing and administrative organizations and the construction of public works. With the coming of the New Deal, not only were these functions expanded, but the federal government began to make large financial payments to large numbers of private individuals. These payments took the form of welfare and relief as well as those designed to induce individuals to conform to certain aspects of national policy such as reducing the production levels of selected agricultural commodities. In cases such as the payments made to farmers through the farmer committee system of the AAA, and in later years, the ASCS, the federal revenues distributed to individuals dwarfed those raised and expended by agencies of community and county government. The impact of the implementation of these programs is the main subject of this chapter.

Excluded from this definition of state structure are those organizations that are not immediately involved in maintaining the existing distribution of power in society. Thus, organizations which are formed to influence or transform formal state structures, for example, political parties and movement organizations such as the Ku Klux Klan, White Citizens' Councils, and civil rights organizations, will not usually be considered to be part of state structure. Of course, this distinction is partially artificial. Throughout post-civil war southern history, the Ku Klux Klan often operated as a branch of the local state and directed much violence and coercion against blacks with the approval, if not the explicit cooperation, of the local policing organizations. The legitimate exercise of police power by the Ku Klux Klan and other such white supremacy organizations was a southern expedient designed to preclude the intervention of the federal government on behalf of the subordinated black minority. In fact, one of the central issues addressed by the southern civil rights movements was whether white supremacy organizations would continue to exist as legitimate extensions of local police authority or whether they would be branded as outlaws and suppressed by the police.

LOCAL STATE STRUCTURES: FORCE AND COERCION

By 1910, all of the institutional structures which came to be known as the "solid South" were in place. Blacks had been disfranchised, along with a large number of poor white farmers from the hill counties which had been the base of agrarian radicalism. Jim Crow segregation had been established in virtually all spheres of public and private life. Blacks were disproportionately relegated to the most menial and lowest-paying jobs and were especially prominent among the farm tenant classes. Black sharecroppers were the preferred form of labor on the cotton plantation. Because of the low productivity of agricultural labor, black tenants and sharecroppers were often targets of force and coercion by planters as the only possible response by planters to the vagaries of the cotton market. Local state structures reinforced and protected this discriminatory behavior toward blacks. For example, black tenants were sometimes subjected to beatings by planters or their managers. "In past decades, the sheriff seldom went on large plantations, minor discipline being one of the manager's undisputed prerogatives. The broad leather strap was the principal instrument of discipline" (Woofter, 1936:32). This quote illustrates the futility of seeking legal redress through the courts as well as the presence of the abuse. Southern courts were heavily biased against the black complainant in cases against white defendants (Davis, Gardner and Gardner, 1965:322–333). Blacks were excluded from jury duty and employment as police officers. In fact, police often beat blacks as a form of punishment when they thought that the courts had not punished them with the severity appropriate for particular infractions, real or imagined (Davis, Gardner and Gardner, 1965:299–300) and even joined lynch mobs on occasions (Raper, 1933). The possibility of obtaining redress through the courts, clearly perceived by the black population as the "white man's justice," was not a viable alternative for most infractions by whites against blacks.

Some aspects of the state structure were clearly designed to regulate the supply of black agricultural labor. Two types of laws evolved after the Civil War for this purpose: those regulating the behavior of landlords and potential employers and those regulating the behavior of tenants and sharecroppers. Laws regulating the behavior of landlords and potential employers included: 1) "enticement statutes (that) established the proprietary claim of employers to 'their' Negroes by making it a crime to hire away a laborer under contract" (Cohen, 1976:33); 2) and emigrant agent laws that discouraged labor recruiters from hiring tenant labor by imposing prohibitively expensive license fees on them.

Laws regulating the behavior of laborers, primarily black tenants and sharecroppers, came in several varieties: 1) contract enforcement statutes; 2) vagrancy statutes; and 3) the criminal surety system. The heart of the contract enforcement statutes was to make breach of contract a criminal rather than a civil offense. To make the contract system work, blacks had to be forced to enter into a contract in the first place. Broadly drawn vagrancy statutes performed this service. During periods of labor scarcity, virtual round-ups of blacks were conducted to supply local planters. For example, in August 1930, the Macon, Georgia, Chief of Detectives "asked all those who wanted work in the fields to get in touch with him. Simultaneously, he warned: "There is no excuse for loitering and loafing . . . and we are going to arrest all who do not go to work at once" (Cohen, 1976:51). Similar incidents occurred in Memphis in 1936 and in Columbia, S.C., in 1942 and on a less dramatic scale throughout the cotton belt. Those who went to work were immune from the charge of vagrancy; highly publicized round-ups were unnecessary in most cases (Raper, 1939; Cohen, 1976; Davis, Gardner and Gardner, 1965; Zeichner, 1940).

Criminal surety laws reinforced the other laws that regulated the supply of black labor. Persons arrested for minor offenses such as vagrancy, drunkenness and lesser criminal offenses could choose to have their fines paid by an employer. In return, the miscreant was contractually obligated to repay the benefactor. Labor services were the only possible means of repayment. This pattern of obligation was wide spread and well known (Davis, Gardner and Gardner, 1965:318–321; Woofter, 1936:293–294; Cohen, 1976:53–55).

The alternative to accepting the offer of a potential employer was the chain gang or southern prison system. There is some evidence that the practice of bailing out tenants continued well into the depression when labor was in abundant supply. As late as 1934, Woofter (1936:32) reports that 11 percent of the landlords in his sample had acted "as a parole sponsor for tenants and 21 percent had paid (tenants') fines."

White aggression and violence against southern blacks were ubiquitous and virtually certain of being condoned by the police. Invasions of privacy, abusive language and other forms of intimidation such as compulsory caste etiquette were common place. The most extreme form of violence against blacks was the practice of lynching, and lynch mobs were seldom punished for the most blatant acts of cruelty and murder. Between 1900 and 1930, fewer than one percent of lynchings resulted in the conviction and punishment of the lynchers (Chadbourn, 1933:13).

The extent to which blacks were politically disfranchised and subordinated to the needs of cotton agriculture by 1930 is adequately documented elsewhere and need not be explored in greater detail here. It is clear that the local state structures which used force and violence as the principal means of maintaining order had the effect of providing an agricultural labor force which was both tractable and adequate to the needs of cotton planters. It is anomalous, therefore, that mechanization of the cotton preharvest would begin during the Great Depression, a period during which the political subordination of blacks was not under serious challenge and the price of agricultural labor was lower than it had been in decades or would ever be again.

The key to this puzzle is the intervention of the AAA during the New Deal. New local state structures were created which controlled the distribution of enormous funds to local farmers. Cotton planters were extremely influential in the creation of those structures and in their operation during the next 30 years. Throughout this period, the principal local financial state structure, namely, the local committee system of the AAA, was extremely responsive to the immediate needs of cotton planters and other large farmers. The political subordination of blacks enforced by the coercive local state structure ensured that there would be little effective resistance to planter oriented policies. The unanticipated consequences of this process, which will be analyzed in the following section, was the transformation of the planter class into a class of capitalist farmers.

Local State Structure: The Creation of the Farmer Committee System

Pressed into action by the low farm commodity prices of the depression, Congress quickly passed legislation proposed early in 1933 by Franklin D. Roosevelt. The intent of the legislation was to raise farm prices by removing farmland from production, thereby creating scarcity in agricultural commodities.

To implement the legislation, individual contracts had to be negotiated with some three million individual farmers across the nation. The only federal agency in existence at the time that could perform this enormous task was the Agricultural Extension Service which had field representatives in about two-thirds of the agricultural counties of the nation (Hardin, 1967:63–68; McConnell 1953:202). The Extension Service had been created by the Smith-Lever Extension Act of 1914 to provide farmers with practical educational demonstrations of the most efficient and profitable ways to produce crops.

The Extension Service field representatives who teach new farming techniques to farmers are called county agents. To succeed, the county agent had to demonstrate to his superiors that large numbers of farmers had adopted the methods being promoted. County agents soon learned that the quickest way to reach the largest numbers of farmers was to convince the larger and more successful farmers to use the new methods (McConnell, 1953:19–47). To guarantee the diffusion of the new farming techniques, a local private farm organization was required. Out of this necessity was born the long, intimate association between the Extension Service, a governmental agency, and the Farm Bureau, a private organization of farmers. For several decades after 1914, the first practical task of all new county agents was to organize a local Farm Bureau. Part of their salaries was often provided by the Farm Bureau. By 1920, the local Farm Bureaus had federated on the state and national level and were becoming a powerful national lobby (McConnell, 1953:47–48).

The relationship between county agents and the Farm Bureau has been analyzed by others (McConnell, 1953; Campbell, 1962; Hardin, 1952; 1967; Block, 1960). The most important aspect of this relationship as far as this study is concerned is that Farm Bureau membership has always been disproportionately drawn from the more successful commercial farmers and that the county agents have served this constituency in a variety of ways. They tended to sympathize with the needs of the more prosperous farmers. Gunnar Myrdal (1944:258) stated "it is our impression, based upon a large number of interviews, that the county agents in the plantation South, to a great extent, have an attitude on economic, social, and racial questions which is similar to that of the large landowners. Some of them are planters themselves."

Both the Farm Bureaus and Extension Service of the cotton belt counties were dominated by whites. In the case of the Farm Bureaus, State Federations set their own membership requirements. Some southern Federations admitted blacks; others did not (Campbell, 1962:24). Even if blacks were admitted to the Farm Bureau, they were relegated to subordinate roles and often exploited by whites (Myrdal, 1944:1253). Southern local Farm Bureau meetings were usually segregated if blacks were allowed to attend (Campbell, 1962:26). Blacks almost never had local voting rights in the Farm Bureau and planters sometimes charged black tenants for Farm Bureau dues without their knowledge (Henderson, 1947:108). This led midwesterners to complain that southern delegations benefited from artificially inflated delegate strength at national meetings because they took credit for their black members (Campbell, 1962:25, 101).

Since its beginning, the Extension Service also incorporated racial distinctions within its structure. It practiced segregation at both the State and county level; a white land-grant college was always chosen to administer the program at the State level. Black extension agents were typically undertrained and underpaid, had larger case loads and were often little more than assistants to white county agents.[5] These conditions continued until late in the 1960s (Campbell, 1962; Henderson, 1947:51; U.S. Commission on Civil Rights, 1965a:25–26; Mercier, 1921:6; Georgia State Advisory Committee, 1967:17).

The Agricultural Adjustment Act of 1933 empowered the Secretary of Agriculture to "establish state and local committees or associations of producers" to assist him in discharging his duties of taking cropland out of production. This provision for local "democratic" control would partially defray critics' charges of bureaucratization as well as obtain the cooperation and assistance of "persons familiar with local conditions" (Nourse, Davis and Black, 1937:34–35). Because the act become law on May 12, 1933, after most crops had been planted, a great sense of urgency attended the actions of the AAA in its first months. The county agents were pressed into service and, to avoid the further delays which democratic elections would have required, the Secretary ordered county agents in the cotton belt to appoint the community and county committees.

In 1934, county agents again appointed the local committees in the cotton counties, but were instructed to retain the original committeemen "insofar as possible" (Richards, 1936:75–76). Local committees were allowed to elect the county committeemen from among themselves with the provision that at least two of the three men would be selected from the three who has served as county committeemen in 1933. This restriction was justified by the AAA on the grounds of retaining experienced men to administer the program (Richards, 1936:76).

Beginning in 1935, local committeemen were elected by the producers in each community. County committees were then elected by local committees from among their number. The Agricultural Act of 1938 provided a legal framework for the local committee structure adopted by the AAA in 1935. That basic structure, without substantial change, has prevailed to the present (Hardin, 1967:63–68).

The county committeemen, with the assistance of local committees, were the people who approved the historical records of cotton production for local farmers on which all allotments, production quotas and subsidy payments after 1934 were based.[6] The importance of the power vested in these committees was not lost on the Farm Bureau Federation. The authority to control or at least shape the distribution of the vast sums of money flowing to farmers, certain amounts of which were deducted for per diem payments to committeemen, guaranteed the organizational stability of the committee system. Such an organization with the resources to mobilize large numbers of farmers might deliver them to a rival farm organization and thereby jeopardize the Farm Bureau's membership base. The Farm Bureau had not forgotten that its success was based upon its ability to capitalize on the mobilizing power of an earlier federally funded organization, the Extension Service.

The southern Farm Bureaus were relatively weak compared to the midwestern organizations. To counter the threat of the formation of a rival farm organization, a vigorous membership drive was begun with particular emphasis on the South. In areas where the Farm Bureau was not organized, the AAA production control committees were invited to assist in the formation of local Farm Bureaus. Hopefully, the chairman of the committee would become the president of the Farm Bureau and other committee members would constitute its board of directors. "They would be asked to serve, 'not in their capacity as committeemen, but as leaders in whom the farmers have confidence'" (Campbell, 1962:88–89).

The intimate connection between the farmer committee system and the Farm Bureau, both of whom were disproportionately composed of the most prosperous white farmers and planters in the South, was completed. Farm Bureau membership increased from 163,000 in 1933 to 410,000 in 1938 (Hardin, 1967:74). A study of the county committeemen in eight representative cotton belt counties indicates that the majority had enough acres under cultivation to be classified as planters in both 1933 and 1934. Those committeemen who were dropped from the committees between 1933 and 1934 tended to have much smaller holdings or were not engaged in farming (Richards, 1936:79). Even the local committeemen in these 8 counties had relatively large holdings: the 228 who served in both 1933 and 1934 held an average of 473 acres under cultivation; the 148 who were replaced held an average of 195 acres as compared to 264 acres held by their replacements (computed from Richards, 1936:79). Hardin (1952:119) summarizes AAA unpublished studies of county committeemen in the east central and southern divisions before World War II which found that the committeemen tended "to be farm owners . . . , to operate larger acreages, to have more education, and to have joined more farm organizations" than the average farmer.

A study of the farmer committee system commissioned by the Secretary of Agriculture in 1962 found that conditions had not changed much (U.S. Department of Agriculture, 1962). Southern county committeemen tended to be successful farmers who produced cotton (49%), corn (63%), and livestock (75%). They owned medium- to large-sized farms and 75 percent of them were members of the Farm Bureau. In fact, at least a third of them had held offices in the Farm Bureau in addition to their duties as county committee chairmen (James, 1981:325). Morton Grodzins, a member of the study committee dissented from the majority opinion that the committee system was basically good, with only minor deficiencies. Noting that committeemen had strong links to the communities which they served, Grodzins stated

> The very fact of intimate acquaintanceship with and participation in the local community may lead not to even-handed justice but to subservience to the powerful and neglect of the weak. . . . it is worth nothing that in all the county committees of the South there has never been, as far as I can discover, a single Negro member. . . . Justice . . . may be hindered by intimacy and

fostered by aloofness. This is especially so in a rural community where powerful people have a great opportunity to punish their local opponents with a wide range of economic, social, and political weapons. The linkage in many counties between political (or farm) organizations and ASC committees is also prejudicial to justice. (U.S. Department of Agriculture, 1962: 46G).

Farmer Committees and Tenant Displacement

The previous section indicates that the planter class was in a position that would allow it to dominate the farmer committee system to the disadvantage of white and black sharecroppers and tenant farmers of the cotton belt. This section shows that the New Deal farm subsidy programs created a decision environment which gave the planter class an interest in displacing and/or reducing the tenure status of their tenants. In fact, tenants and sharecroppers, both black and white, were progressively displaced and reduced in tenure status from the 1930s until the 1960s when the sharecropper class disappeared almost completely. In place of the planters, sharecroppers, and tenants who produced the cotton crop in the 1930s, there remained much smaller classes of capitalist cotton farmers and wage laborers who produced crops with the aid of complicated machines.

Both tenants and landlords soon realized that the AAA program was vulnerable to two types of abuse at the local level: 1) the displacement of tenants as cotton acreage was reduced; and 2) an unfair division of benefits between landlord and tenants when the tenants were retained. In 1933, these abuses were probably not as extensive as they were to become later because the correct division of benefits between landlord and tenant was made clear by the tenant's contract (either written or understood) at the time the "plow-up campaign" began. After 1933, crop reductions were accomplished by planting less rather than destroying crops already planted. This plan could be implemented before a landlord made a contract with his tenants.

The lower the tenure status of the farmer, the smaller the proportion of benefits received, with wage workers being ineligible for any benefits at all. Sharecroppers on halves were entitled to 50 percent of the cotton produced but only 1/9 of the AAA benefit payments on the acreage taken out of production. Managing share tenants, entitled to 3/4 of the crop by the contract with their landlords, were entitled to 5/9 of the benefit payments on the idle cotton land. Cash tenants received all of the crop and all of the benefit payments. One contemporary analyst concluded that "(i)t must be evident . . . that the potential gains of landlords from displacing some of their tenants or from reducing their tenure status were fairly large" (Richards 1936:145).

As required by the Bankhead Cotton Act of 1934, the AAA tried to "protect the interests of sharecroppers and tenants" by requiring landlords to agree to reduce acreage "as nearly ratably as practicable" among the tenants on his farm and to maintain, "insofar as possible, . . . the normal number of tenants and other employees" (USDA, 1934:72; Richards, 1936:140–141) as part of the cotton reduction contracts with the government. Nothing revealed the class nature of the committee system of the AAA with as much clarity as did the nature of the protests which arose in response to the administration of this program.

In 1934, numerous complaints came from tenants all over the cotton belt alleging that they had been evicted or suffered a reduction of their tenure status in violation of the cotton contracts (Richards, 1936:146). The most famous and effective of these protests came from a section of Arkansas near Memphis, Tennessee, where the protests were given an organizational voice through the Southern Tenant Farmers Union (STFU)(Grubbs, 1971; Thomas, 1934; Mitchell, 1979; Kester, 1936). In response to these complaints, the AAA sent representatives into the field to investigate. In the words of Henry Richards (1936:146), "The representatives worked closely with the county agents and (county) committees." Attempts were made to resolve the disagreement between the landlord and tenant. After an internal struggle within the AAA in which the liberals lost, the AAA decided that the maximum sanction which could be applied to a landlord was to terminate his contract (Grubbs, 1971:30–62). If the contract were cancelled, the tenant was surely not protected from the landlord's anger.

After three months of field investigations, the complaints were referred to the county committees for investigation (Richards, 1936:147). Thus, the people who were the defendants under the complaints gained effective control of the investigation and adjudication of the complaints (Johnson, Embree and Alexander, 1935:51–56; Grubbs, 1971:40–41). Grubbs cited one case as being typical, in which the committeeman who signed the committee report which exonerated an accused landlord was the same person who had submitted a statement in favor of the landlord's position and was also accused of contract violations by his own tenants (1971:41).

Secretary of Agriculture Wallace and other officials of the AAA argued that few tenants were being displaced or otherwise adversely affected by the new programs (Grubbs, 1971:58–60). The conclusions of other contemporary observers were mixed. Two studies by the Brookings Institution concluded that some displacement had occurred but that tenants had benefitted as a class (Nourse, Davis and Black, 1937:347–349) or sustained little injury (Richards, 1936:160–162). Studies by sociologists were less sanguine (Frey and Smith, 1936) or very critical (Johnson, Embree and Alexander, 1935), while studies contracted by the STFU argued that the AAA programs as administered by the county committees were devastating for the tenants and led to huge numbers of them being displaced (Kester, 1936; Amberson, 1934). Given the resulting demise of cotton sharecropping and tenancy, it is now clear that the tenants were not exaggerating the magnitude of their problem.

Few longitudinal studies of cotton plantations were performed during this period. Two of the best are of cotton farms in Arkansas, although some non-plantations were included in the study (Osgood and White, 1945; McNeely and Barton 1940). The farms studied were larger than average and owned continuously during the periods of 1932–1938 or 1932–1944. Some 86 of the farms studied were located in three counties characterized by plantation agriculture. Of these 86 farms, 20 had fewer than five tenants and would not be classified as plantations; the non-plantation farms were larger and more successful than most farms during these periods, however.

Pertinent information from these studies is presented in Figure 2. The first panel shows that the trend toward the increasing use of tractors began before World War II. Curves in the first panel also indicate how the amount of cotton cultivated varied with AAA policies. When strong acreage controls were in effect, total cotton acreage was dramatically reduced and the amount assigned to each sharecropper declined.

Cotton acreage reductions led to the displacement of some families, but of greatest importance is the effect they had on the tenure of plantation workers. Notice that the proportion of wage families increased dramatically up to about 1936 (Panel 2 of Figure 2). The number of sharecropper families stabilized at about 45 percent because greater reductions would have jeopardized the labor supply during the cotton harvest. Mechanization of the preharvest proceeded steadily during this period; less than 2 percent of the families studied had no access to a tractor (Osgood and White, 1945:24).

As mechanization of the preharvest continued, tenant incomes declined. Croppers were charged for the preharvest tractor work whereas they used to perform that work themselves with mule power. Wage family income was less than cropper income ($273 vs. $311 per year) and the value of food produced on the tenant plots ($55) increased the difference between them. Notice that the acreage allowed sharecroppers declined during periods of strong controls, implying a more intensive cultivation of the plots and more surplus labor available to pick cotton for wages on the landlord's acreage.

With the beginning of World War II, wage families and wage workers responded to the higher incomes provided by industrial jobs. Many were shifted back to sharecropper status to guarantee their presence during the harvest season. Access to land, even under the dependent

FIGURE 2. Arkansas Cotton Farm Trends

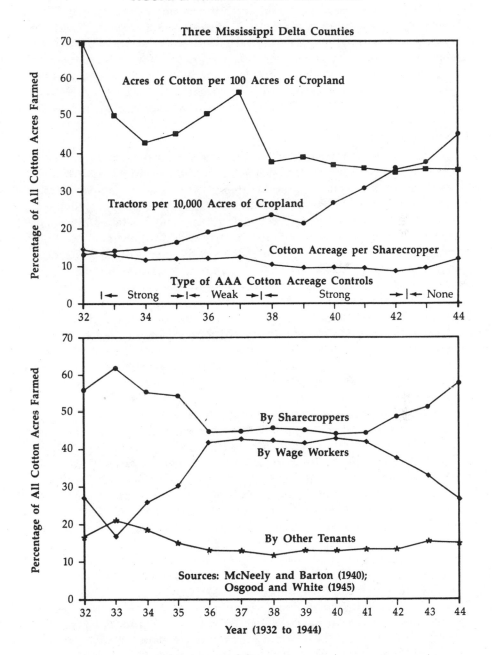

conditions of sharecropping, appeared to many to be more attractive than migration in search of non-agricultural employment. Panel 2 of Figure 2 indicates that the sharecropper proportion approached the level that existed before 1934, the first year that AAA policies affected the number of tenants. More importantly, the tenants of 1944 were retained only because of the labor requirements of the harvest. Mechanization of the preharvest was accompanied by increasing cultivation of other crops on land that had been diverted from cotton. The principal bottleneck to the continued capitalization of cotton agriculture was the lack of a viable mechanical cotton harvester.

Other studies support the claim that the transformation of southern agriculture began during the 1930s rather than during World War II, but space considerations prevent their review here (Langsford and Thibodeaux, 1939; Raper, 1936; Bureau of the Census, 1940; Fligstein, 1981). Mandle (1978) is correct that black agricultural labor moved in response to wartime demand for labor but this movement did not "trigger" technological change. It merely continued a process that was well underway by 1940. The AAA acreage reduction programs of the New Deal reduced the number of acres of land devoted to cotton cultivation and magnified the rewards for increasing the per acre yield of the cotton produced. The AAA benefits for cotton land diverted to other crops provided the capital required to mechanize those new crops. This machinery was also useful for mechanizing the cotton preharvest operations. With the great supply of cheap labor available during the depression, planters incurred little risk of serious labor shortages during the harvest season as a result of discharging tenants no longer needed for preharvest operations. Consequently, tenants were increasingly displaced or converted to wage laborers as cotton acreage was reduced and the preharvest was mechanized. In contrast to previous post-bellum experience, agricultural laborers were increasingly separated from the means of subsistence on the land. Rather than residing on the plantation in much the same condition as sharecroppers, wage labor was recruited on a day hire basis during periods of peak labor demand. Throughout the rest of the year, these laborers were not subject to the authority of planters.

The success of cotton allotments in restricting cotton acreage is illustrated in Figure 3. Farmers were ineligible for production loans from the Commodity Credit Corporation (CCC) and could not sell their cotton on the domestic market without penalty if they planted more cotton than Acreage diversion payments under a variety of programs were in addition to the price support programs and were the principal reason that planted acreages were not closer to allotted acreages. During World War II, government programs made other commodities more profitable

FIGURE 3. Cotton Alloted and Planted
Source: USDA (1974, 1978)

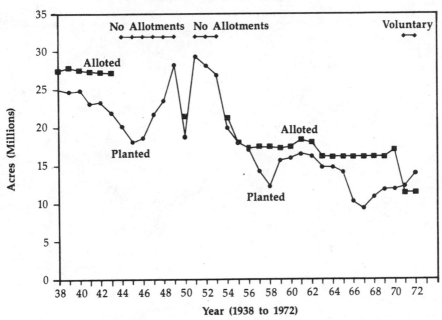

than cotton and the cotton planting shortfall increased until 1943 when allotments were discontinued. When wartime programs expired in 1947, cotton production increased until allotments were reimposed in 1950. Increased demand for cotton during the Korean War made controls unnecessary for three years but in 1954 allotments with marketing quotas were reimposed and remained in effect until 1971 when quotas were suspended. Allotments ended in 1978.

Crop diversion payments in 1950 were based upon the average production of cotton during 1946, 1947 and 1948 (United States Department of Agriculture, 1950:4). County committees were instructed to give primary allotment consideration to 1954 cotton farms on the basis of the "farm's proportion of the total county cropland" (United States Department of Agriculture, 1953:7); thus, larger farmers were given an advantage in obtaining allotments. Allotments were not to be reduced on farms growing five or fewer acres of cotton and provisions were made to provide allotments for new farms; but, of course, new farms might be large as well as small (U.S. Department of Agriculture, 1953:5–8). Control of committees remained in the hands of white farmers who were primarily large farmers (U.S. Commission on Civil Rights, 1965a; Hardin 1967).

FIGURE 4. Mississippi Cotton Harvested
Source: USDA (1974:71,218)

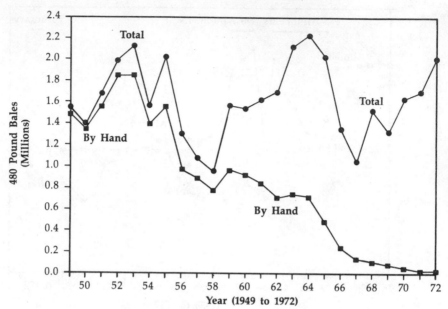

Notice that very large shortfalls were experienced in 1957 and 1958 (Figure 3). These large reductions were obtained because of extremely high participation in the Soil Bank (U.S. Department of Agriculture, 1957a, 1958). This program was discontinued after two years because of its high cost and planted acres again approached allotted acres (Whitaker, 1967:134). In 1966, another very attractive diversion program was initiated by the Department of Agriculture and diverted acres jumped to over 4.5 million acres (Whitaker, 1967:136–137). This program remained essentially unchanged until 1971 when production quotas were abandoned.

Figure 4 indicates the effects of the cotton acreage control programs on the mechanization of the cotton harvest in Mississippi. The experience in other states was similar. Notice that the amount of cotton harvested by hand tends to mirror the total harvested until after 1958. The curves differ most during peak harvest years when labor shortages stimulate mechanization. These differences tend to persist as cotton acreage was progressively reduced through 1958. With wages already severely depressed, the Soil Bank programs of 1957 and 1958 coupled with the production ceiling imposed by the allotments pushed large numbers of tenants off of the land. A USDA study of the effects of the comparatively modest reduction required in 1954 and 1955 found decreases in the numbers of sharecroppers and share tenants ranging from 17 percent in the Southern Piedmont to 34 percent in the Delta (USDA, 1957b:43). The main reason given by tenants for leaving was the reduction in cotton acreage required by the cotton program. Incomes of croppers who remained tended to be depressed under the new programs whereas owners experienced income gains in 1955 over 1953 as high as $4214 for the "typical" farm in the Delta (pp. 48–50). Butler (1956) confirmed these results for the Piedmont area of Georgia and South Carolina reporting that croppers, and particularly black croppers, had suffered most under the program and that many small farmers had to supplement reduced farm incomes through off-farm work.

By 1957, the USDA could candidly report, without creating a controversy, that the cotton programs were displacing tenants. Tenant displacement continued throughout this period even though the pertinent section of the Agricultural Adjustment Act of 1938 requiring the Secretary of Agriculture to protect the interests of sharecroppers and tenants was still in effect. By the early 1940s, the STFU ceased to be an effective lobby for the interests of tenants and sharecroppers (Grubbs, 1971). No counter-force to planter domination of the cotton programs appeared and, by 1969, only 10,000 of the half million black sharecroppers of 1930 remained on the land.

Between 1959 and 1965, farmers planted about 14 to 16 million acres of the 16 to 18 million allotted (Figure 3). During this period, the black civil rights movement reached its peak. In 1964, civil rights workers in Mississippi even expanded their voter registration drive to include attempts to elect blacks to the local Agricultural Stabilization and Conservation Service (ASCS) committees, the new name for the old AAA committee system. For the first time, blacks served on local committees in six Mississippi counties. In December 1964, only about 75 of the 37,000 community committeemen and alternates in the Deep South were blacks (U.S. Commission on Civil Rights, 1965b:91; 1968:26).

Figure 4 indicates that the greatest increase in the machine harvesting of Mississippi cotton occurred during the period of greatest civil rights protest. Other southern states had similar experiences. The political enfranchisement of blacks was inconsistent with the old, labor intensive methods typical of the cotton plantation. By 1970, only two percent of the cotton produced in the United States was hand harvested.

These data support the argument that the cotton programs of the USDA as administered through the local farmer committee system have been a powerful force in requiring tenant farmers, both black and white, to leave cotton agriculture. The racial structure of the system guaranteed that blacks were disproportionately displaced by these programs, but white tenants and croppers were also displaced. The race issue, inscribed in the texture of the southern racial state, divided the tenant classes, contributed to their political weakness, and blunted their efforts to resist displacement.

Control of the committee system by successful white owners of large farms precluded redistributive policies designed to shift resources to the agricultural underclasses. Cotton acreage reductions displaced tenants and depressed the incomes of those who remained. When acreages were increased again, planters had no choice but to invest in more advanced machinery in response to labor shortages experienced during the harvest season. The labor shortages resulted from the attempts of tenants to find solutions to their chronic underemployment during the rest of the year and especially when cotton acreages were the most depressed. Whereas sufficient labor had always been available prior to 1930, job opportunities off of the farm coupled with shifts to more capital intensive crops on the farm had combined to force the underclasses to leave cotton agriculture by the 1960s.

CONCLUSION

Rather than resulting from the vagaries of commodity and capital markets, the process that transformed cotton agriculture in the South was politically determined from beginning to end. First, landlords reduced cotton acreage about forty percent in accordance with original AAA policy. Second, landlord control of the farmer committee system permitted both steady displacement of tenants and reduction of tenants to wage laborers as landlords attempted to find profitable ways to exploit the acreage removed from cotton production. Shifting land to the production of crops such as soybeans, oats, corn and other small grains reduced the annual labor requirements on the plantation. In many cases, the land diverted from cotton was left idle because farmers had insufficient land or capital to shift to another cash crop (U.S. Department of Agriculture, 1957b; Butler, 1956; Welch, 1943).

Third, landlords used their cotton program benefits to invest in the tractors and associated equipment necessary for the profitable production of the new crops. Fulmer (1950:72–75) found a strong relationship between the number of tractors per county and the number of non-cotton farms between 1920 and 1945. This result is consistent with the argument offered here because reduction in the number of tenants is also a reduction in the number of cotton farms. Finally, much of the machinery purchased could also be used in the cultivation, planting, and other preharvest operations required in cotton farming. The result of this process of crop shifting was to make the maintenance of sharecroppers "uneconomic" throughout much of the year (Day, 1967:439).

Thus, the crop reduction programs of the AAA led directly and indirectly to the displacement of tenants and the conversion to wage workers of those who remained. The descendants of these programs, administered through the farmer committee system, continued the process of tenant displacement until its completion in the 1960s.

The local state structure of the cotton South was constrained by the class structure typical of the cotton plantation to reinforce and protect planters' labor-coercive strategies in maintaining the economic viability of their plantations. This coercion was directed primarily toward black agricultural laborers but the political capacities of the tenant classes of both races were severely weakened because of it. Consequently, the farmer committee system created during the New Deal period became a functioning component of the racially repressive local state. Because the farmer committee system was constrained to act in the interests of the planter class, the implementation of national crop reduction and farm subsidy programs through this system meant that planter class interests would be satisfied whenever they conflicted with those of tenants and sharecroppers. Hence, local implementation of national farm policy led to the demise of cotton sharecropping and tenancy in the South. Cotton planters became capitalist cotton farmers who had no need for the services of sharecroppers and tenant farmers.

Capitalist cotton farmers have more flexibility in responding to the vagaries of the cotton market than did planters dependent upon labor intensive methods. For example, capitalist farmers can lay off wage workers during a market downturn whereas planters must continue to provide support for their croppers and tenants. Accordingly, the transformation of southern agriculture was accompanied by a steady reduction in the use of coercion as a strategy for controlling the black agricultural labor force. It is not difficult to find extensive evidence of the use of coercion during periods of labor shortage before World War II. In fact, the police in Columbia, S.C., were still using vagrancy laws to provide planters with a labor supply during the harvest until the mid–1940s. Extradition of sharecroppers accused of breach of contract under criminal laws was still being sought from Northern authorities. Even the most blatant forms of coercion (including severe whippings and chaining of blacks to prevent their escape) were still being practiced (Daniel, 1972; Myrdal, 1944; Columbia Record, 1942; Raper, 1939). Evidence of widespread use of these forms of abuse during and after the 1950s is difficult to find.

The modal response to labor unrest and shortages in the late 1950s and throughout the 1960s was to substitute machines for human labor. Of course, the more subtle forms of coercion such as economic sanctions and verbal threats continued to be used but the reasons for their use was changing (U.S. Commissions on Civil Rights Hearings, 1965b, 1968). Control of the agricultural labor force by coercive means was no longer a viable long term strategy as it had been prior to 1930.

Physical coercion and violence against blacks in the late 1950s and 1960s was increasingly applied in attempts to prevent blacks from exercising political and civil rights rather than efforts to enforce labor discipline in cotton agriculture. The repressive aspects of local state structure that were necessary for the reproduction of plantation agriculture had not changed although the limits imposed on them by the structure of southern agriculture had been dramatically transformed. The local state structures created during the New Deal imposed a decision environment on planters that eventually led to the transformation of the planter class into a class of capitalist cotton farmers. The weakness of the tenant classes, maintained by the repressive aspects of local state structure, insured that they would be an ineffective force in preventing their own displacement as the planters pursued their private advantage.

NOTES

1. In earlier versions of this chapter, I used the phrase "local political structure" instead of "local state structure" to designate the concept of interest here. The term "state" more accurately represents the type of political institutions being analyzed and distinguishes them from those political organizations which are attempting to influence or control state institutions. I will capitalize the word "State" when referring to a State of the United States and use the lower case when referring to organizations of the state in the generic sense.

2. Throughout this chapter, I emphasize the importance of landlord control of the local AAA (ASCS) committee system in determining the timing and nature of the transformation of southern agriculture. A similar story could be told with respect to other local state structures which have influenced the implementation of national agricultural policy. The more important ones are the Soil Conservation Service (SCS) which provides technical assistance and encourages farmers to divert land from "soil depleting" to "soil building" crops (the SCS committee system is distinct from the ASCS system which has soil conservation programs of its own); the Extension Service, which I will discuss in some detail below; and the Farmers' Home Administration (FmHA) which provides low interest loans to farmers for farm operating expenses, farm and home purchases, and for emergency needs. These agencies also contributed to the transformation but I believe that their contribution was subsidiary to that of the AAA (ASCS), especially during the early years of the farm commodity programs. The Farm Security Administration (FSA), on the other hand, retarded the transformation. It is significant that the power of the southern planter class through southern representatives in Congress were able to dismantle the FSA by the early 1940's. See James (1981:307–318) for a discussion of these agencies and their effects on southern agriculture.

3. A region shaped approximately like the Greek letter delta bounded on the East and West by the Mississippi and Yazoo rivers and on the North and South by Memphis, Tennessee, and Vicksburg, Mississippi.

4. Again, Mississippi provides the archetypal example. Today, Congressman Jamie Whitten, long a favorite of planters from the Delta region of Mississippi, is the Chairman of the United States House of Representatives Appropriations Committee.

5. There were notable exceptions to this pattern. Some of the black agents, such as Frank Pinder and Charles L. Davis became world famous. There is no doubt, however, that black county agents operated under severe handicaps because of racial discrimination and because of the political impotence of their principal constituency, the black farm operators.

6. In cotton, 1928–1932 was the base period from which average historical production was calculated. Payments were then made on reductions from that average production. Base production periods were changed in future years but were greatly influenced by the original acreages established under the old AAA. In 1933, the number of acres of cotton harvested was reduced by 25 to 40 percent of that prevailing during the 1928–1932 base period (Richards, 1936:47–52; Hardin, 1967).

REFERENCES

Amberson, William R. 1934. "Report of Survey Made by Memphis Chapter L.I.D. and the Tyronza Socialist Party." Pp. 1934 in Norman Thomas, The Plight of the Sharecropper. New York: League for Industrial Democracy.

Bass, Jack and Walter DeVries. 1976. The Transformation of Southern Politics: Social Change and Political Consequence Since 1945. New York: Basic Books.

Beale, Calvin. 1976. "The Black American in Agriculture." Pp. 284–315 in Mabel Smythe (ed.), Black American Reference Book. Englewood Cliffs, NJ:124–132.

Block, William J. 1960. The Separation of the Farm Bureau and the Extension Service. Urbana: University of Illinois Press.

Bureau of the Census. 1940. Special Study: Plantations. Washington, D.C.: U.S. Government Printing Office.

Butler, Charles P. 1956. "Some Economic Effects of Cotton Acreage Diversions in the Piedmont Area of Georgia and South Carolina, 1953–1955." South Carolina Agricultural Experiment Station Bulletin 440 (September). Clemson, S.C.: Clemson Agricultural College.

Campbell, Christiana McFayden. 1962. The Farm Bureau and the New Deal. Urbana: University of Illinois Press.

Chadbourn, James Harmon. 1970 (1933). Lynching and the Law. Chapel Hill, North Carolina: University of North Carolina Press.

Cohen, William. 1976. "Negro Involuntary Sevitude in the South, 1865–1940: A Preliminary Analysis." Journal of Southern History 42:31–60.

Columbia Record. 1942. "Sharecropper Fights Return: S.C. Farm Worker Charged with Breach of Trust for Leaving Crops." Columbia Record, August 28, 1942, p. 8. Columbia, South Carolina.

Daniel, Pete. 1972. The Shadow of Slavery: Peonage in the South 1901–1969. Urbana: University of Illinois Press.

Davis, Allison, Burleigh B. Gardner and Mary R. Gardner. 1965. Deep South: A Social Anthropological Study of Caste and Class. Abrid. ed. Chicago: University of Chicago Press.

Day, Richard H. 1967. "The Economics of Technological Change and Demise of the Sharecropper." American Economic Review 57 (June):427–449.

DuBois, W.E.B. 1961 (1903). The Souls of Black Folk. New York: Fawcett.

Fligstein, Neil. 1981. Going North: Migration of Blacks and Whites from the South, 1900–1950. New York: Academic Press.

Frey, Fred C., and T. Lynn Smith. 1936. "The Influence of the AAA Cotton Program Upon the Tenant, Cropper, and Laborer." Rural Sociology 1 (December):483–505.

Fulmer, John Leonard. 1950. Agricultural Progress in the Cotton Belt Since 1920. Chapel Hill: University of North Carolina Press.

Georgia State Advisory Committee to the U.S. Commission on Civil Rights. 1967. "Equal Opportunity in Federally Assisted Agricultural Programs in Georgia." Washington D.C.: U.S. Government Printing Office.

Grodzins, Morton. 1966. The American System. Chicago: Rand McNally.

Grubbs, Donald H. 1971. Cry from the Cotton: The Southern Tenant Farmers' Union and the New Deal. Chapel Hill: University of North Carolina Press.

Hardin, Charles M. 1952. The Politics of Agriculture: Soil Conservation and the Struggle for Power in Rural America. Glencoe: Free Press.

———. 1967. "Food and Fiber in the Nation's Politics." National Advisory Commission on Food and Fiber Technical Papers, Volume 3. Washington, D.C.: U.S. Government Printing Office.

Henderson, J. Lewis. 1947. "In the Cotton Delta." Survey Graphic 36 (January):48–51; 108–111.

James, David R. 1981. "The Transformation of Local, State and Class Structures and Resistance to the Civil Rights Movement in the South." Unpublished Ph.D. dissertation. University of Wisconsin: Madison, Wisconsin.

Johnson, Charles S., Edwin R. Embree and W. W. Alexander. 1935. The Collapse of Cotton Tenancy. Chapel Hill: University of North Carolina Press.

Kester, Howard. 1936. Revolt Among the Sharecroppers. New York: Covici Friede.

Langsford, E. L., and B. H. Thibodeaux. 1939. "Plantation Organization and Operation in the Yazoo-Mississippi Delta Area." U.S. Department of Agriculture Technical Bulletin No. 682 (May). Washington, D.C.: U.S. Government Printing Office.

Mandel, Jay R. 1978. The Roots of Black Poverty: The Southern Plantation Economy after the Civil War. Durham, N.C.: Duke University Press.

Matthews, D. R. and J. W. Prothro. 1966. Negroes and the New Southern Politics. New York: Harcourt, Brace and World.

McConnell, Grant. 1953. The Decline of Agrarian Democracy. Berkeley: University of California Press.

McNeely, J. G. and Glen T. Barton. 1940. "Land Tenure in Arkansas II: Change in Labor Organization on Cotton Farms." Arkansas Agricultural Experiment Station Bulletin No. 397 (June). Fayetteville, Ark.: University of Arkansas.

Mercier, W. B. 1921. "Extension Work Among Negroes: 1920." United States Department of Agriculture Department Circular 190. Washington, D.C.: U.S. Government Printing Office.

Mitchell, H. L. 1979. Mean Things Happening in This Land: The Life and Times of H. L. Mitchell, Co-Founder of the Southern Tenant Farmers Union. Montclair, N.J.: Allanheld, Osmun.

Myrdal, Gunnar. 1944. An American Dilemma: The Negro Problem and Modern Democracy. New York: Harper and Row.

Nourse, Edwin G., Joseph S. Davis and John Black. 1937. Three Years of the Agricultural Adjustment Administration. Washington, D.C.: The Brookings Institution.

Osgood, Otis T., and John W. White. 1945. "Land Tenure in Arkansas IV: Further Changes in Labor Used on Cotton Farms, 1939–1944." Arkansas Agricultural Experiment Station Bulletin No. 459 (August). Fayetteville, Ark.: University of Arkansas.

Raper, Arthur F. 1969 (1933). The Tragedy of Lynching. New York: The New American Library, Inc.

_____. 1936. Preface to Peasantry: A Tale of Two Black Belt Counties. Chapel Hill: University of North Carolina Press.

_____. 1939. "Race and Class Pressures." Notes for the Carnegie-Myrdal Study, Schomberg Collection, New York Public Library on microfilm. Wisconsin State Historical Society: Madison, Wisconsin.

Richards, Henry I. 1936. Cotton and the AAA. Washington, D.C: The Brookings Institution.

Street, James H. 1957. The New Revolution in the Cotton Economy: Mechanization and Its Consequences. Chapel Hill: University of North Carolina.

Thomas, Norman. 1934. The Plight of the Share Cropper. New York: The League for Industrial Democracy.

United States Commission on Civil Rights. 1965a. Equal Opportunity in Farm Programs: An Appraisal of Services by Agencies of the United States Department of Agriculture. Washington, D.C.: U.S. Government Printing Office.

_____. 1965b. "Hearings Held in Jackson, Mississippi, February 16–20, 1965: Volume I, Voting." Washington, D.C.: U.S. Government Printing Office.

_____. 1968. "Hearings Held in Montgomery, Alabama, April 27–May 2, 1968." Washington, D.C.: U.S. Government Printing Office.

United States Department of Agriculture. 1934. "Compilation of the Agricultural Adjustment Act as Amended and Acts Relating Thereto." Washington, D.C.: U.S. Government Printing Office.

_____. 1950. The Cotton Situation CS-127 (January, February, March).

_____. 1953. The Cotton Situation CS-149 (September, October).

_____. 1957a. The Cotton Situation CS-170 (May).

_____. 1957b. "Effects of Acreage-Allotment Programs, 1954–55." Agricultural Research Service ARS 43–47 (December). Washington, D.C.: U.S. Government Printing Office.

_____. 1958. The Cotton Situation CS-176 (May).

————. 1962. "Review of the Farmer Committee System." Report of the Study Committee (November 28). Washington D.C.: Agricultural Stabilization and Conservation Service.

————. 1974. "Statistics on Cotton and Related Data." ERS Statistical Bulletin 535. Washington, D.C. (October).

————. 1978. ASCS Commodity Fact Sheet/Upland Cotton. (March)

Welch, Frank J. 1943. "The Plantation Land Tenure System in Mississippi." Mississippi Agricultural Experiment Station Bulletin 385 (June). State College, Mississippi: Mississippi State College.

Whitaker, Rodney. 1967. "The Cotton Surplus Problem, 1930–1966." Pp. 81–166 in National Advisory Commission on Food and Fiber Technical Papers, Volume 2 (July). Washington, D.C.: U.S. Government Printing Office.

Wilson, William Julius. 1978. The Declining Significance of Race: Blacks and Changing American Institutions. Chicago: University of Chicago Press.

Woofter, Jr., T. J. 1936. Landlord and Tenant on the Cotton Plantation. W.P.A. Monograph V. Washington, D.C.: U.S. Government Printing Office.

Zeichner, Oscar. 1940. "The Legal Status of the Agricultural Laborer in the South." Political Science Quarterly LV (September): 412–428.

6
New Deal Farm Policy and Oklahoma Populism

Dale Harrington

Oklahoma in the 1930s is an interesting example of agricultural politics because the state was in a time of transition from an agricultural society to one with a diversified economic structure. Before World War II, agriculture had furnished most of Oklahoma's domestic income. (Oklahoma's petroleum industry, which had grown steadily all through the 1920s, was dominated by eastern corporations that transferred most of their industrial profits out of the state.) During the 1930s, Oklahoma was transformed in two ways that had importance to the political structure. First, the severe devastation of the agricultural economy by the Great Depression transformed the structure of Oklahoma agriculture by ending tenant farming and the destroying of the cotton economy of southern Oklahoma; this transformation in turn caused mass migration of population from rural areas to the larger cities or to other states. Second, the introduction of major federal (mainly defense) employment to the state in the late 1930s and early 1940s provided the first mass nonagricultural employment in Oklahoma.

These changes rang the death knell to a whole tradition of politics in Oklahoma—agrarian populism. First populism, then liberalism, and finally a resurgent conservatism became important electoral forces, but not all these ideologies fielded candidates in every election of the decade. Therefore it's possible to assess whether the appearance and disappearance of different political programs affected the alignment of interest groups behind particular programs and candidates. The aim of this chapter is to provide an understanding of the relationships among changes in Oklahoma's agricultural structure, its voting patterns, and its economic interests.

THEORETICAL APPROACH

Every class society is organized around both *fundamental* and *immediate* interests. Fundamental interests involve issues that call into question the social relations of a society. For example, a demand for worker control of the investment policy of corporations is a fundamental issue. Immediate interests, on the other hand, include those issues centered on reforms, improvements, or rectifications of inequalities within the existing context of society. For example, a demand for unemployment insurance for all workers laid off during a recession is an immediate political issue. In general, immediate interests are those that strengthen the power of a particular social group without directly calling into question the basic relations of a society.

Since voting is an individual act, the typical voter will tend to emphasize his or her immediate concerns in making voting decisions. The crucial problem for politicians is getting elected, and in order to win elections, politicians must center on promises that they can deliver. Working class politicians, for instance, might emphasize an immediate issue such as government contracts to provide jobs for the home district. The fundamental interests embodied by a candidate of a particular political program tend to be compromised by the need to stress the immediate interests of individual voters. In addition, in order to win elections, politicians must usually reach out beyond the boundaries of the particular interest group they may wish to represent. To organize an election coalition, politicians tend to tone down their rhetoric and compromise their programs.

Capitalist democracy is thus an ideal setting for examining the potential conflicts between fundamental and immediate interests. First, the structure of the parliamentary system functions to put immediate issues at the top of everyone's list of demands regardless of the congruence or incongruence of immediate and fundamental interests of a particular class. Politicians' tendencies to compromise in order to stress immediate interests and maintain an electoral coalition reorganize voters of a given social class into competing fractions with a variety of immediate interests. These competing fractions combine with fractions from other classes into nonclass political interest groups.

In this analysis political interest groups are defined as *informal* organizations at the political level. A political interest group is an informal organization in that it is not limited to the members of any particular formal association but includes all individuals who subscribe to the demands of the interest group. Although a political interest group is organized primarily at the political level, this does not mean that an interest group's demands are only political. Its interests may be situated at economic or ideological as well as political levels. Each political interest group has a set of demands upon the institutions of government according to its immediate interests, whether economic, political or ideological.

Political Interest Groups and Voting Patterns

The main focus of this chapter is the relationship between political interest groups and voting patterns for various political candidates in specific Oklahoma elections. The three central terms used are:

1) Patterns of Interest Groups: the particular combination of different political interest groups that explains voting patterns for a particular candidate.
2) Voting Patterns: the distribution of votes for a particular candidate across the subdivisions of a political arena. The value of voting patterns lies not in discerning the overall strength of a candidate but rather in discerning the areas (not necessarily geographic) in which he or she was politically strongest.
3) Structure of Political Choices: the types of political programs available in a given election as vehicles for expressing interest groups' demands.

Immediate interests will ordinarily determine voting patterns. However, this determination is modified by the types of political programs and candidates available in the political arena. Interest groups are not a datum prior to political and ideological practice but are in fact the result of political forces in struggle to maintain or alter existing social relations. The set of interest groups that will vote for a particular candidate is not predetermined by that candidate's political program but is shaped by the various alternative political programs that are available in an election.

THE HISTORICAL BACKGROUND OF OKLAHOMA'S ECONOMIC INTEREST GROUPS

This chapter will examine voting patterns and immediate interests of the state of Oklahoma's gubernatorial elections of 1930, 1934, 1938 and 1942. Those elections attracted the most attention from Oklahoma voters and the largest percentage of registered voters; moreover, they are the only elections of the period for which there is sufficient historical information to permit analysis.[1]

To understand Oklahoma's elections, however, some key political and economic factors of the state's political scene must be described. The primary task is to provide historical background on the interest groups and political choices that were of consequence in the 1930s: the political and economic events that brought those interest groups and political choices into being. This historical description will be divided into two parts: (1) an examination of the economic history of early twentieth-century Oklahoma until the U.S. entrance into World War II, and (2) a survey of the political scene and political programs of the same period.

The Economic Setting

Before Oklahoma became a state in 1907, Americans knew it best as a dumping ground for displaced Indian tribes and a new frontier lately opened to furious land rushes. On the west side of the present state, the tribal reservations that had existed since the end of the Civil War were extinguished by 1900, and the land was thrown open to settlement by non-Indians. Well over 300,000 people soon occupied the best parts of 25 million acres on the western side of the state. From the 1830s until the early 1900s, the Five Indian Nations (Cherokees, Creeks, Choctaws, Chickasaws, and Seminoles) had led an autonomous existence as United States protectorates in what is roughly the eastern half of the present state. In the years after the Civil War, the governments of these Indian nations leased land to white developers, who laid railroads and sank coal mines between 1870 and 1890. The whites soon set up a clamor for the dissolution of the tribal lands. The results of this clamor were predictable. Between 1900 and 1910, the Indians saw their governments disbanded, their lands allotted to whites, and their society torn apart (Burbank, 1976: 3–4).

The destruction of the Indian Nations and white settlement of the western prairies brought intensive farming to the state. In the northwest and north central parts of Oklahoma wheat became the principal cash crop while in the southern half of the state cotton was first in importance; together these two crops accounted for 80 percent of the cash value of all crops in 1929 (see Map 1). This division between wheat in the north and cotton in the south was the result of both historical and geographic factors. The northern half of the state was exploited primarily by farmers from Kansas and other northern plains and midwestern states, while the southern half was settled by farmers (both black and white) from Texas, Arkansas, and Louisiana. Both northern and southern settlers brought their familiar crops to these new lands. Also, the northern half of Oklahoma to the west of Tulsa is a vast rolling plain with relatively fertile soil rainfall of between 20 and 35 inches per year; these are excellent conditions for the cultivation of wheat. Further south, rainfall increases to 30 to 45 inches a year, the growing season becomes longer,

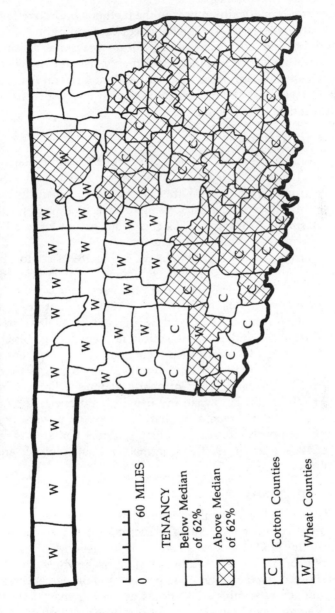

MAP 1. TENANTS AS PERCENT OF FARMERS IN 1930
AND MOST IMPORTANT CROP COUNTY

and the winters are not quite so harsh; conditions are better for cotton than for wheat (Morris, 1952: 25–29).

There were dramatic differences in the methods of production between the wheat and cotton areas. Oklahoma cotton farming in the 1930s was a highly labor intensive kind of agriculture practiced by small tenant farmers operating with low capital investments. In contrast, wheat farming was capital intensive agriculture by independent farmers. This agricultural division was paralleled by differences in the cultures and social structures of the two areas, as we shall see.

Cotton and Tenancy

Except for the adoption of the horse drawn plow in the nineteenth century, the implements used in cotton farming remained substantially unchanged from the 1700s until after World War II, when the mechanical picker was introduced. The tractor might have had an important effect on cotton farming during the 1920s and 1930s except for another feature of cotton farming in Oklahoma: tenancy.

Cotton farmers moving to Oklahoma in the 1890s could obtain land for little or nothing, and southern Oklahoma by 1895 was covered by small, owner operated farms. However, the percentage of owner operated farms dropped quickly to 60 percent by 1900. It continued to decline rapidly to 49 percent in 1920, and 38 percent in 1930 (Harlow, 1961: 527). Replacing the independent cotton farmers were tenant farmers, agricultural laborers who furnished their own farm equipment and work animals and obtained use of land by agreeing to pay a fixed percent of their crop to the landowner, or share-croppers who had everything furnished to them by the owner and usually paid one half of their crop to the owner. Whether tenant or share cropper, they were poor, uneducated, and malnourished. A typical tenant farmer had an average income of only $240 a year in 1933 and farmed a small plot of land with a horse (Johnson, 1935: 6–31).

Cotton and Credit

The disappearance of small independent farmers was not limited, of course, to the cotton counties of Oklahoma, but it was concentrated in those areas. In 1930, the state's cotton region (see Map 1) had a mean tenancy rate of 46 percent while the state as a whole and the wheat counties showed tenancy rates of 41 percent and 30 percent, respectively. The dependency of southern Oklahoma as well as many other southern states on a single cash crop—cotton—caused severe problems after about 1890, when American cotton agriculture entered continuous crisis because of domestic overproduction and expanding foreign competition in world markets. These two factors brought wild fluctuations in cotton prices from year to year, depending upon the quantity of cotton on the world market. These fluctuations had uneven effects on cotton farmers. Large farmers could more easily weather these yearly swings in prices since they often had cash reserves to cover their losses and could also shift the burden of price declines onto the shoulders of their tenant farmers. In contrast, small non-tenant farmers often had no alternative when the price of cotton fell except to redouble their efforts to increase output. However, when all small farmers succumbed to a personal need for greater production, the price fell that much faster. Eventually most small farmers went bankrupt or looked for credit.

The depressed cotton market was aggravated, for these small independent farmers, by the pervasive system of local credit. Bank credit in the south had always been inadequate and this forced reliance upon other more costly sources. The two most important sources of credit for the small farmer in Oklahoma were large landowners and credit merchants, both of whom demanded that the small farmer stake an entire year's crop as security for the loan. In addition, the growing crop offered such uncertain collateral and there were so few alternative sources of loans that creditors demanded extremely high interest rates (Johnson, 1935: 25–29).

The depressed nature of the cotton market and the usurious credit system combined to take land out of the hands of small farmers and put more and more of it into the hands of large landowners. The newly landless farmers had to feed their families; their choice was to move away or become tenants of the large landowners. Most became tenants. Over the years between 1890 and 1930, small cotton farmers lost their lands and cotton fields of southern Oklahoma became more and more concentrated in large holdings. In four cotton counties (Bryan, Choctair, Marshall and Love), for example, 75 percent of the landowners held fewer than 200 acres, but the remaining 25 percent of owners controlled well over half of the total farm acreage.

Wheat and the Tractor

Tenancy was more rare in the wheat areas of Oklahoma because of the methods of wheat farming. The introduction of the mechanical reaper allowed owner operated farms to be more profitable than the leasing of lands to tenants in the wheat areas. In the wheat counties the crop-lien tenant system was not so profitable as it was in southern counties because tenant farmers, closer to alternative jobs and industrial wage rates in the cities of the midwest, were able to demand a bigger part of the shared crop. By the 1920s, social conditions in Oklahoma's wheat belt were amenable to reliance on mechanized, capital-intensive farming: a tractor, a large tract of land, and access to a mechanical reaper were necessary for wheat farming to be profitable.[2] By contrast, the southern Oklahoma cotton farmer needed only a small piece of land and a mule to start production. By 1926, the small farmer was becoming a rarity in the wheat belt because low market prices dictated that the individual farmer produce more bushels at less cost in order to show a profit. A survey among 61 owners of combines in that year showed that the mean farm size among them was 419 acres (Green, 1977: 73). Most Oklahoma wheat farmers were economically better off than the state's cotton farmers, with the mean farm value being $10,500 in 1930 for the wheat counties but only $5,000 in the cotton counties. Also, the mean family income in wheat counties was $2,260 per year in 1930 but only $1,590 per year in cotton counties, while the mean illiteracy rate was 5.7 percent in wheat counties versus 10.7 percent in cotton counties, according to the 1930 census.

Industry

The most important point in analyzing industrial production in Oklahoma is its lack of significance in the lives of most Oklahomans until World War II. In 1940, only 20 percent of the labor force was employed in the industrial sector of the state's economy, and much of this industry was concentrated in four counties. In addition, a large proportion of industrial production was concerned with the processing of farm products by flour mills, cotton gins, meat packing plants, etc. Of course Oklahoma was fully integrated into the industrial economy of the United States and changes in industrial production had direct effects on agricultural production in Oklahoma. However, the effects of industry on *people* in Oklahoma were indirect, mediated through effects on agriculture. Political demands focused on agricultural issues even if problems in agriculture were related to problems in industrial production. Political interest groups directly concerned with industry were few and relatively unimportant in the electoral arena since they could command the votes of only a few individuals, although such industrial interest groups could be (and often were) powerful and effective in protecting their interests through lobbying, providing campaign funds, or other forms of political influence outside the voting booths. Until the 1960s Oklahoma's industries were principally providers of raw materials (especially petroleum, lumber, zinc, and coal) for the industrial processors of the northern and eastern U.S. (Litton, 1957: 194–200). Thus there were only local areas in the vicinity of the oil and coal fields and in the timber districts where the populace depended on the well-being of these extractive industries. This local dependence did provide the conditions for industrially related interest groups in a few parts of Oklahoma.

Oil

Petroleum was the basis of Oklahoma's industry until World War II, and the entire industrial base of Oklahoma was dependent on the well-being of the petroleum industry. During the 1920s Oklahoma was the major petroleum producing state in the nation and Tulsa was built on oil money from the fields that lay beneath it. People called Oklahoma "the state that oil built." This motto might have been more accurate had it read "the oil companies that the state built," for although the oil industry did contribute $200 million in state taxes between 1907 and 1943, this tax came from reported sales of $8.5 billion. In other words, the oil industry paid in taxes at the most 2.5 percent of the total value of the petroleum sales (Litton, 1957: 194). Most of the remaining wealth in oil was transferred out of the state to the headquarters of eastern corporations. Furthermore, although oil workers were some of the most highly paid workers in the state, the petroleum industry was highly automated and did little to provide employment. Even in 1940 the state's petroleum industry was employing only 75,000 Oklahomans from a labor force of 800,000.

Lumber

Oklahoma's major logging and sawmilling activities were located in Oklahoma in the mountainous southeastern region. Large-scale lumber production began about 1910, and soon became consolidated in the hands of one firm, Dierks Lumber Company. Lumbering, although the third largest industry in the state, employed only about 10,000 people in four southeastern counties. In these four counties Dierks was the dominant economic power and two of the county seats were company towns. Most workers were only part-time employees, and wages could be kept low so long as hill farmers and other seasonal workers were relying on the lumber industry for supplemental rather than basic income (Litton, 1957: 73–74).

Coal

Commercial mining of coal in Oklahoma appears to have had its beginning about 1872 with a mine in Pittsburg County. Until about 1920, coal mining in Oklahoma was not unattractive. The wages paid in the Oklahoma coal fields were higher than in the eastern fields; day wages at one time averaged about 20 cents higher than in the east. The workers were well organized and membership in the United Mine Workers reached 16,000 (about 95 percent of all miners) by 1908.

However, after about 1922, the fields in Oklahoma became unprofitable for the coal companies because of competition with petroleum fuels and the expense of extracting Oklahoma's coal, which lay in very thin veins that made mechanization difficult. At first the coal companies attempted to overcome their difficulties by reducing wages and breaking the unions. A prolonged strike between 1924 and 1927 severely damaged the union and marked a definite change in the employment pattern in the coal fields. Before then more than two-thirds of the miners had been paid as skilled workers, but after the strike most miners were reduced to the level of unskilled laborers. The union scale of wages was destroyed and many miners left the state to work in the expanding automobile and rubber industries of the midwest (Litton, 1957: 158–170).

In the long run, this reduction of wages sustained the Oklahoma coal industry for only a few years. Production dropped from 4,800,000 tons in 1920 to 1,200,000 by 1934. Production in Oklahoma was just not competitive with cheaper eastern coal. By the mid-1930s coal mining was important in only two or three counties in the southwest.

Unions

Although organized labor was quite influential in the drafting of labor legislation in the early years of statehood, it had been relatively ineffective in electoral politics except in a few urban centers and mining districts. Union membership was always low; Oklahoma ranked well below the national average in proportion of the labor force in labor unions. In the 1920s and 1930s few unions had much strength in the state except for the railroad workers and some of the craft unions.

Depression: Agricultural Disaster and Industrial Slump

In Oklahoma as elsewhere during the Great Depression of the 1930s business floundered, farm prices were extremely low, and unemployment was high. The market for one of Oklahoma's principal crops, cotton, collapsed in 1929 and never recovered. The entire Great Plains suffered drought in which high winds stripped away thousands of acres of fertile topsoil and whipped up huge dust storms. Much of western Oklahoma became part of the Dust Bowl; many counties there saw large declines in population. Oklahoma was one of the most economically devastated of the states during the Depression.

Agriculture: Rural Calamity

During the Great Depression, farmers of the southern plains suffered a five year drought (1932–1936) that devastated the land. New record lows for rainfall were established in Oklahoma and nearly 4 million acres of farmland were abandoned in Texas and Oklahoma. The western wheat counties of Oklahoma, which were most affected by the drought and dust, lost 20 percent of all crops planted in 1935, even though many acres of parched and eroded cropland were not even planted that year. In 1935–36 average wheat yields in the state were only 8–10 bushels per acre (versus 17 in the pre-drought year of 1930) (Litton, 1957: 51–52); in Cimmarron County in the Oklahoma panhandle not a single grain of wheat was harvested in 1935.

Nine months after the stock market crash of 1929, the price of wheat in Oklahoma had dropped from $1 a bushel to 70 cents a bushel; by August 1931, the price was down to 30 cents, and many farmers were broke. Yet when autumn came the tractors were in the fields plowing up new lands. If farmers thought it good business to expand wheat acreage in good times, it was absolutely necessary in hard times to expand production to pay overdue debts and mortgages. Of course, more production did not help matters. The price of wheat did not rise above $1 per bushel until 1936 (Litton, 1957: 54–55).

After this short rise in 1936–1937 due to price supports, the price dropped again to around 60 cents and did not return to $1 until 1941. This long slump in prices was related to two factors particular to wheat production within the context of the financial and production crisis of the U.S. economy as a whole. After the mid-1920s American wheat farmers lost their foreign markets to European and other competitors. That first problem exacerbated the second: increased production. Wheat was produced in greater quantities than it could be profitably sold in the domestic market. The large fixed costs of mechanized wheat production made it profitable only if supply was below demand and prices stayed high. In the late 1920s, as foreign markets dried up and the depression brought a drop in domestic demand, oversupply of wheat became chronic.

The eastern part of the state did not escape the agricultural disaster either; the region just had its own variety based on the toppling of King Cotton. Oklahoma had produced more than 1 million bales of cotton per year between 1924 and 1929. The rolling hills of eastern and southern Oklahoma are subject to flash rains of great intensity and the soil-robbing nature of cotton combined with this climate to slowly destroy the land's productivity. By the early 1930s the top soil had washed away, leaving nothing but a red subsoil that would grow little. Yields fell off to less than 100 pounds per acre, not even half what they had been earlier. Cotton was not really suited to the fragile soil of Oklahoma unless the land was well treated through large amounts of fertilizer, crop rotation, and contour plowing (which required a tractor). The small penniless tenant farmers of Oklahoma could never afford to make these investments, and even if they could, it is unlikely that they would invest in someone else's land. Tenant farmers abandoned thousands of eroded acres.

Shrinkage in the domestic and world cotton markets because of the onset of worldwide depression meanwhile produced a huge surplus of cotton and dropped Oklahoma cotton prices, by 1931, to a low of 5 cents per pound (Litton, 1957: 50). In county after county there were foreclosures on cotton-farm mortgages.

Agriculture and the New Deal

Relief for farmers did not come until Congress enacted the Agricultural Adjustment Act of 1933 during the first weeks of the presidency of Franklin Roosevelt. Under the direction of Secretary of Agriculture Henry Wallace, the USDA launched an emergency plow-up campaign as a means of bringing about a rise in prices. Oklahoma growers, who saw the potential federal payments as a salvation of their operations, enthusiastically signed up to participate in the government programs. They plowed up approximately 1.2 million acres of cotton and wheat in exchange for $11,730,000. For thousands of cotton and wheat producers, government aid became the key to their survival as farmers.

In spite of the support of many farmers for the federal programs, there were frequent charges that small cotton growers in Oklahoma had been shortchanged in allotments and quotas. The Agriculture Adjustment Act and other federal programs of acreage restrictions and payments did also have damaging impacts on small farmers, especially tenant farmers, in Oklahoma. On many farms the acreage allotments on cash crops were too small for tenants to make a living, so they left the land. On other tenant farm owners reclaimed their property, took the federal payments, bought tractors, and did the farming themselves. There is no doubt that the New Deal farm program was a success for large landowners. With the price of cotton and wheat fixed at a high enough level by government regulation, grower profits went up considerably, in some cases doubling between 1933 and 1936 (Green, 1977: 52–55)

But, with farm tenancy at 80 percent in some Oklahoma counties, only a fraction of farmers benefited from New Deal programs.[3] Landowners got the benefits of government subsidy while tenants were left open to continued risks. The reason for the neglect of the tenant lies in the fact that the New Deal organized its program under the direction of large landowners (Raper, 1936: 136). Most tenant farmers in Oklahoma did not like the New Deal; they got little from it, and had their farm production restricted. Higher production was the only way to increase tenant farmers' incomes.

The combination of erosion, depression, and government programs had profound impacts on cotton farming in Oklahoma. Between 1929 and 1945, the number of cotton farms declined by 33,639 units and cotton cropland harvested dropped by almost 2.8 million acres. Even in southwestern Oklahoma, center of the state's cotton production, the percentage of cropland devoted to cotton dropped from 47 percent to 26 percent. These changes spelled the end of cotton and cotton-growing tenants as important factors in Oklahoma agriculture (Green, 1977: 52–55).

Industrial Production

The depression of the 1930s severely damaged the industrial economy of Oklahoma. Since very few farmers were then counted in unemployment statistics, the unemployment rate is a good indicator of this slump in industrial production. Unemployment climbed steadily in Oklahoma throughout the early 1930s; it peaked in 1933 at 30 percent, and did not drop below 10 percent until late 1941. In some counties the unemployment rate was 60 percent of the labor force during the height of the depression in 1933. Many thousands went on welfare rolls or joined WPA work projects in Oklahoma; people "on relief" soon came to be an important political group in the state because their well-being was directly connected to the state's implementation and administration of social welfare legislation (Dangerfield and Flynn, 1936: 100).

Also tied to the slump in Oklahoma's industrial production was the effect of the Depression on the petroleum industry. When factories shut down in the east and automobile production plummeted, the bottom fell out of the oil market. Overproduction in Oklahoma oil fields soon became critical. The price of oil dropped below 20 cents a barrel in the summer of 1931, and the total annual value of all oil production in Oklahoma was less than half its 1930 level throughout the 1931–33 years (Litton, 1957: 198). Low prices brought havoc in the oil industry and the state government shut down the oil fields in August 1931, in order to raise the price and make oil production profitable once more.

The decline of the petroleum industry was the key item in the downslide of the budding industrial base of Oklahoma. The coal mines of southeastern Oklahoma, as well as the lead and zinc mines of the northeast, shut down. The saw mills of southeastern Oklahoma closed as the home building industry sank. Food processing and milling plants ran at half speed as crop production dropped off. The entire industrial economy of Oklahoma stagnated for a decade, and was not revived until the construction of major military and defense installations between 1940 and 1945.[4] The politics and the political programs that arose in the context of this agricultural and industrial catastrophe will be the focus of the next section.

The Oklahoma Political Scene

Two major facts about Oklahoma's politics in the 1930s stand out: (1) Oklahoma was predominantly a Democratic state; and (2) there had been a history of agrarian political revolt since statehood. I will examine these two facts, and show how they dominated the political choices of the 1930s in Oklahoma. In a broader sense, this section will describe the "political scene" of Oklahoma: the complex set of relations that characterized the struggle between social forces as organized in political interests.

In Oklahoma in the 1930s the main political disagreement concerned the role of the state as a vehicle for reorganizing the American economy. This political division was manifested in two opposing sets of political programs. "Conservative" political candidates promoted policies that provided subsidies to business, kept taxes low, avoided government regulation of business, favored corporate resistance to the growing union movement, and limited social welfare expenditures to a practical minimum. In contrast, "liberal" candidates favored government social welfare programs, government intervention in the economy, government expenditures to promote inflationary growth, and the acceptance of the union movement. On the basis of their adherence to one of these two sets of political programs, Oklahoma's non-populist candidates are here divided into liberals and conservatives.

Populism, by contrast, is a particular ideological form in which a distinction between the "people" and the "bosses" is presented as an antagonistic relationship. A power bloc's ideology and culture and its control of political and economic institutions is seen as destroying the mode of existence of the "people." Opposition to the power bloc may or may not be radical; it can appear in the politics of the most divergent classes and still be called populism. The emergence of populism is historically linked to such general social crises as the Great Depression. In Oklahoma, populism surfaced primarily among small farmers, although certain populist sentiments were to be found in New Dealism, as discussed below. Populist programs of the 1930s combined the small farmers' faith in the independent landowning farm society as the best of all possible worlds and their protest that this society was being destroyed by corporate capitalism. The populist appeal was a result of the economic devastation endured by the small farmer of Oklahoma and the ensuing breakdown of the ideological hold that corporate capitalism had over these farmers. No longer did small farmers believe that industrial capitalism was the way to bring prosperity to their lives.

The populists offered programs for the restoration of small farms and small businesses of a mythical golden age of the past. In Oklahoma in

the 1930s, populists were reformers looking backward rather than rev-
olutionaries looking forward, and populist candidates are here defined
as those who: (1) were strongly opposed to the established political
order; (2) attacked business, bankers, and financiers as the main enemy
of people; (3) wanted to minimize the power of the government and
return power to the small farmer and storekeeper; and (4) promoted
policies to help small farmers.

A categorization of Democratic candidates in Oklahoma's gubernatorial
primaries, 1930–1942, as populists, conservatives, and liberals, is presented below.

	Populist	Conservative	Liberal
1930	Murray*	Buttram	————
1934	Anglin	King	Marland*
1938	Murray	Phillips*	Key
1942	Smith	————	Kerr*

*Denote winners; the Democratic primary winner won every gub-
ernatorial election in this period.

In Oklahoma, as in much of the South, the Democratic party dominated
state politics. The Democratic party had controlled the Oklahoma Legislature since statehood in 1907 except for the years 1921–23, and the
party had elected every state governor. Political interest groups which
might otherwise have been more comfortable within the Republican
party were factions within the Democratic party. In Oklahoma's state
government, such factions of the Democratic party played the role
assigned elsewhere to political parties (Key, 1949: 298–311).

Oklahoma's political system was constructed in a way that insulated
state party politics from national politics. At the national level, the
Republican and Democratic parties were clearly identified in the 1930s
with the conservative and liberal politics, respectively. Within the Oklahoma Democratic party, however, this division was blurred. The state
party sometimes presented the voters a liberal candidate and sometimes
a conservative candidate. In national elections the state's voters had
often backed Republican presidential candidates, who had carried the
state in 1920 and 1928 and had run a close second in 1908 and 1924.
Yet in state elections the Republican party was a weak minority party
with little voice in the determination of state policy.

The structure of state government was such that it was difficult for
a minority party to wrest control from the entrenched majority party,
the Democrats. For example, all state election officials—who determined
voter registration and who counted election returns—were appointed

by the state election board. The state election board was, in turn, appointed by the governor, and this structure gave the Democrats the opportunity to manipulate elections in their favor. A 1916 referendum to change the means of appointing these election officials was probably "fixed" by the Democrats. The Democrats were charged with creating a ballot shortage of 20,000 in counties where anti-Democratic opposition was strongest (Scales, 1949: 189). In summary, the structure of politics in Oklahoma was two-tiered, with national political and state political groupings.

The Democratic Leadership

Who were these Oklahoma Democrats and what did they believe? In a sample of Democratic political leaders active between 1921 and 1930, a disproportionate number of small business and professional men were found. Since the counties in this sample were among the most rural in the state, the underrepresentation of farmers in the Democratic leadership is striking (Burbank, 1976: 92).

The composition of the Democratic leadership had political significance in the types of political reforms the party supported. In the terms of the day, most of Oklahoma's Democratic leaders would qualify as progressives of the William Jennings Bryan and Woodrow Wilson varieties. As small businessmen, they were deeply suspicious of eastern corporate business, and as southern Democrats, they were fearful of the federal power exercised by corporate "tools" in Washington. They therefore favored legislation to limit the power and influence of eastern corporations. Yet these Democratic leaders were property holders and they were generally hostile to legislation that affected property rights. In addition, a number of the most influential members of the legislature were also large landowners; they favored the maintenance of the tenant system and opposed any reform of lending practices. These newly successful Oklahomans revered people "who made their own way" and were unsympathetic "with the great masses of the plain people" (Ibid: 92–93). This antipathy toward the poor amongst party leaders gives some insight into the history of the other major factor in Oklahoma politics of the time: agrarian revolt.

Agrarian Revolts: Three Movements of the Poor

Agrarian radicalism in Oklahoma politics before World War II is well illustrated by three different movements. The first was the Socialist Party U.S.A., which entered the state in 1905 and immediately began to gain membership. Its strength was drawn chiefly from the coal miners and the many tenant farmers in rural Oklahoma. The Socialists appealed to these voters with a two-fold platform. For industrial workers, they demanded legislation to regulate hours, working conditions, and wages. For farmers, the Socialist platform proposed a "Renter's and Farmer's Program" that was strongly agrarian in its insistence upon various measures to put land into "the hands of the actual tillers of the soil."

Although the Oklahoma Socialists never attained a plurality in any statewide election, they increased their vote in the state in every election from 1907 to 1914. The share of votes cast for the Socialist party steadily climbed from 4 percent in 1907 to 11 percent in 1910, 17 percent in 1912, and 23 percent in 1914, and Oklahoma became the most important state in the Socialist movement. The Socialists elected 5 state representatives, 1 state senator, a few county officers, and numerous rural township officers. Without doubt the leaders of the Socialist party had created an effective organization in their first decade in Oklahoma. The party's secretary could happily report to the convention in 1913 that there were 3,015 paid party members, and 342 locals in good standing in Oklahoma. Party leaders hoped to gain control of the state government in 1918 (Burbank, 1976: 7).

However, the success of the Socialist movement in Oklahoma ended with America's entry into World War I. The party opposed the war and took up the cry of "rich man's war and poor man's fight." This gave opportunity to the State Council of Defense, appointed by the Democratic state administration, to encourage popular suspicion of "dangerous" political attitudes. Socialists were silenced, and suspected sympathizers were run out of the state by vigilante groups. Many were jailed, although they had committed no legal offenses, and the Socialist movement had been effectively smashed in Oklahoma by 1920 (Scales, 1949: 173–75).

The second significant illustration of agrarian unrest, in August, 1917, is known as the "Green Corn Rebellion," an armed revolt by rural people of 3 adjacent southern counties of Oklahoma. In the eastern part of the state during the two previous years, many farmers had been organized into a group called the "Working Class Union." This organization existed to fight for the legal rights of tenant farmers and opposed the draft of working people into the army. Throughout 1916 these militant agrarians of eastern Oklahoma carried out sporadic violent attacks upon their "enemies" and their opposition to the draft broke into massive violent resistance when there was an attempt to enforce the draft laws in Oklahoma in the summer of 1917. People in 3 counties gathered in numbers and fired upon sheriffs, captured banks, and attempted to stop a railroad train. The national guard was called into the area and major resistance was soon broken, although some fighting continued into October. Almost 1,000 persons were arrested for sedition, conspiracy, and resisting the draft. Several hundred were sentenced to long prison terms, including the Socialist candidate for governor in 1910, J. T. Cumbie (Scales, 1949: 191).

The third illustration of agrarian unrest was the rise and fall of the Farmer-Labor Reconstruction League between 1921 and 1923. The drastic deflation policies of the Federal Reserve Board had exacerbated the post-war agricultural depression and many farmers were ruined. Agricultural prices had fallen sharply, farm incomes had dropped, and farmers' debts were beginning to pile up. The farmers, together with allies in organized labor, met in Shawnee in September 1921 to form the Farmer-Labor Reconstruction League of Oklahoma. These Oklahoma radicals had conceived of a new political stratagem for the purpose of redeeming the cotton tenant and other afflicted farmers. The League decided not to form a third party but instead to capture the Democratic primary in 1922 (Burbank, 1976: 157–58). J. C. Walton, the liberal mayor of Oklahoma City, was picked to run for governor by the League. The League's candidates, especially Walton, were received with enthusiasm by the rural people of Oklahoma.

The League's appeal derived from a platform that combined socialists' and farmers' demands. These included government ownership of railroads and utilities, the establishment of a state bank, warehouses, and insurance system, state grain elevators, a state operated cooperative marketing system, and state credit for small farmers (Scales, 1949: 230–258). After a bitter campaign in which farmer-labor candidates were often maligned as reds, Walton won the primary, defeating a Klan-endorsed candidate in the primary election (Burbank, 1976: 158). Walton was elected governor in the fall of 1922 and the demands of the League seemed on the verge of accomplishment. However, the Reconstruction League did not control the state legislature and its program was frustrated at every turn by hostile legislators. The League and its governor met their downfall in the fall of 1923, when they attempted to crush the Ku Klux Klan (Scales, 1949: 230–258).

The Klan had become a powerful force in Oklahoma by the early 1920s and had more than 80,000 members in 1923. Their numbers included the county sheriff of Oklahoma county, the speaker of the state's House of Representatives, a U.S. senator, the state's Attorney General, and many members of the state legislature. In the early 1920s Oklahoma was a racial powderkeg; in a major race riot in Tulsa in 1922, 100 people died. When Governor Walton began demanding laws to suppress the Klan, there were rumblings of of Klan mobilizations in several counties. Finally, in October 1923, the state legislature impeached Walton and quickly undid all the administrative reforms that he had been able to enact in his one year in office (Scales, 1949: 230–268).

The cause of the poor farmer was set back for eight years and the presence of a radical party in Oklahoma permanently was ended.

Alfalfa Bill, Populism and the New Deal

With the coming of the 1930s and economic disaster in Oklahoma, a new force arose in Oklahoma politics—"Alfalfa Bill" Murray. William Henry Murray was born in Texas, where he taught school, edited newspapers, and practiced law before coming to Oklahoma in 1895. He was active in early Oklahoma politics and served as the first speaker of the Oklahoma House of Representatives. However, he dropped out of politics in 1916 and left the country for Bolivia, not returning to Oklahoma until August 1929. Amazingly, he was overwhelmingly elected governor little more than a year later. Murray was successful because he tapped the agrarian unrest of rural Oklahoma, just as Walton and the Socialists had done (Scales, 1949: 321–23).

Murray was something of a political anachronism, a 1930 model of Nineteenth century populism. He believed that by reducing taxes on farmers, making credit available for small farmers, and putting an end to "tax dodging" on the part of the railroads and utility companies, he could solve the state's economic problems. His administration was the first to make a real attempt to block the drain of taxable wealth from the state by large corporations (Ibid: 327–328). Yet he was not a full blown populist of the Nineteenth century, for his demands for change were limited. Although "Alfalfa Bill" had the characteristics of a populist, his social program was not radical. Murray certainly shook up the power system of Oklahoma with his many declarations of martial law and his use of the state national guard. He made enemies of many state corporations, including most of the state's oil industry. However, his policies were aimed at a return to the Oklahoma of the 1890s and early 1900s. He did not envision a new society, but an old utopia of small farmers and an egalitarian spirit of American rural society before the coming of corporate industrialization.

Murray's main program was a restructuring of the Oklahoma tax system so that more revenue could be obtained from the large corporations that operated in the state. Yet this tax program did not take into account the problem of corporations passing their taxes onto consumers through higher prices. This oversight is best exemplified by the sales tax on gasoline introduced by Murray's administration. The tax was aimed at extracting revenue from the oil industry, but it was collected at the gas pump, so in reality the consumer paid the tax. In addition, Murray demanded a reduction in state expenditures in order to lower taxes and a reduction in appropriations for education; neither measure was very helpful to poor people in Oklahoma (Scales, 1949: 329). Alfalfa Bill's political philosophy is nicely expressed by this verse from his 1932 campaign song:

> Give us back the good old days, give us the good old days,
> Give us back the old familiar scenes.
> Then we'll have money to pay the rent. (Bryant, 1968: 224)

The good old days were gone and Murray could not turn back the economic clock. Although he often irritated big business, he never really threatened their interests. His policies rarely touched the structure of business. His program was aimed at the small yeoman farmer he loved so dearly.

Murray was an important figure in the 1930s not only because of his own career but because he was the central figure around which other candidates with similar politics grouped under the banner of populism. These politicians included 2 major candidates for governor: Tom Anglin in 1934, and Gomer Smith in 1942. In addition, 2 U.S. senators, T. P. Gore and Elmer Thomas, wore a populist coat, as did many lower level state officials or candidates between 1930 and 1942. These populist candidates, although not always successful, were to be a major force throughout the 1930s.

The populist faction was a major wing of the Oklahoma Democratic party in the 1930s. By the end of 1932, Oklahoma's unhappy citizenry desperately hoped for an end to hard times. "We are losing our home, our family's in need . . . Russian communism would look good with lots of red-blooded Americans that can't make or have a dollar, . . ." complained a Tulsa woman (Green, 1977: 101). Populist candidates were symbols of discontent among the poor farmers of Oklahoma and the people who depended on these farmers, such as the small rural store-keepers. Characterized by the large metropolitan newspapers as "rabble rousers," they were able to turn such criticism to their own advantage and appear as the champions of the down-trodden farmers (Dangerfield and Flynn, 1936: 99). Yet, the populists did not win any state elections after 1936. This failure at the polls was the result of two interventions in the political scene, both tied to a long term economic transformation of Oklahoma.

These two political interventions were the change in the content of populist platforms after about 1938 and the introduction of "New Deal" politics to Oklahoma. The key to understanding the change in content of the populists' demands is the New Deal.

The Intervention of the New Deal

The failure of populist candidates to win Democratic primaries after 1936 was linked to the introduction into Oklahoma politics of New Dealism. The New Deal came late to Oklahoma as a political program. It did not become prominent until the gubernatorial campaign of Ernest Marland in 1934. He ran on the slogan "Bring the New Deal to Oklahoma," and demanded massive state expenditures to end the depression. Marland was elected governor in 1934 on the issue that the money and expertise of the federal government were not coming to Oklahoma because of Governor Murray's less than wholehearted endorsement of the New Deal (Scales, 1949: 362–363). Marland and other New Deal candidates were identified with urban industrial interests and one of their major campaign promises was to transform Oklahoma into a prosperous industrial state (Scales, 1949: 371–373). From Marland's election until the 1940s, the endorsement by the national administration of a gubernatorial candidate as the bona fide New Deal candidate was an important plus in his chances for election. Murray's chances of being reelected governor when he ran again in 1938 were ruined by Roosevelt's personal attack on his candidacy. The New Deal as a platform was the dominant issue in Oklahoma from 1934 onward; a candidate either ran on the New Deal platform or against it (Scales, 1949: 408).

The New Deal program disrupted the populists' coalition of mid-size and small farmers, rural small businessmen, and urban workers. The New Deal moved into the political territory of the populists by providing a more satisfying political program to two major components of the political base of most mid-to-small non-tenant farmers.

Populism: Radical to Reactionary

In 1930 the populist Murray ran on a strictly anti-big business, anti-Republican, and pro-small farmer political platform. He pledged to appoint only honest officials, and promised to embark upon an extensive road building campaign. His platform included planks advocating economy in government, greater control over public utilities, and equal rights for all, including blacks. Murray in 1930 was the first Democratic politician in 10 years to seek black support for his campaign. He promised that "the poor and weak shall have my especial care for the rich and strong can usually protect themselves." He advocated a state minimum wage law, the eight hour day for women, and a program of old-age assistance. His anti-corporate campaign is summed up in his inaugural address: "I shall honestly and honorably represent those who choose to call themselves the 'better element,' but this is one time when Oklahoma Indians, niggers, and po'white folks are going to have a governor too" (Bryant, 1968: 177–190).

Compare this 1930 campaign platform with Gomer Smith's 1942 campaign after the entrance of the New Deal as a force in Oklahoma politics. Smith promised the same type of economic program as Murray, but he emphasized other issues. Always an exciting and vivid orator, Smith surpassed anything that the Republicans said in their denunciations of the New Deal bureaucracy. He aroused fears of a vicious federal police state, which he foresaw as a consequence of the passage of New Deal legislation. Smith introduced a Red Scare into his speeches, telling crowds that the New Deal legislation was designed by the Communist party. After losing the Democratic primary, Smith endorsed the New Deal candidate's Republican opponent on the grounds that the country needed a strong coalition government in time of war (Scales, 1949: 431–439). The program of the Oklahoma populists, which had originally been so anti-big business, became rapidly anti-New Deal and essentially reactionary with the barest bones of an anti-capitalist platform. This reactionary trend toward right-wing extremism was already evident in Murray's 1938 campaign, but did not come to fruition until 1942.

This political reversal was the result of the New Deal's usurpation of the political program of the old Oklahoma populists. No longer was populism the vehicle for the expression of these views. With the loss of working class support and the migration of many poor tenant farmers out of the state, the populist candidates were stripped of the majority of their political base. Their response was a dramatic rightward shift in order to maintain a hold on their remaining base of support among small-town businessmen and the dwindling numbers of tenant farmers. Both of these groups were highly suspicious of federal New Deal programs because the New Deal favored large farmers in its agricultural programs and because federal business regulation hurt small business proportionately more than big business. Eventually, even this rightward shift in political orientation was not enough to maintain the populists' political base, and populism disintegrated as a political force in Oklahoma by the end of World War II. This disintegration was linked to the industrialization of the Oklahoma economy during the war and the demise of tenant farmers as an important economic group in Oklahoma, but the entrance of New Deal politics into Oklahoma was the triggering mechanism that made it impossible for populism to adapt itself to the changing economic situation.

In summary, the two major factors in the "political scene" of Oklahoma in the 1930s were (1) the predominance of the Democratic party in state politics; and (2) the existence of a powerful agrarian populist movement. These two factors—the "givens" of Oklahoma politics at the beginning of the 1930s—were transformed by the entrance of a new political force, New Dealism, and by concomitant economic change, especially the end of tenant farming's significance and the building of a large military-industrial sector in the state.

CONCLUSIONS

The two important generalizations suggested by this historical analysis are: (1) the narrowing of the populist base of support; and (2) the fluctuation of the social base of the various candidates from election to election. These concluding remarks discuss the meaning of these two points in relation to Oklahoma and to the general study of voting.

The Collapse of Populism

The key question of this study is why the powerful agrarian populist movement in Oklahoma collapsed in the early 1940s and has not reappeared on the political scene. Agrarian populism had been a powerful political force since statehood and although it had suffered several setbacks it kept reappearing under different cloaks (Socialists, Farmer-Laborites, Murrayism). Yet, after the death of Murrayism, agrarian populism vanished from the political arena of Oklahoma and the state's whole political discourse changed. The major political division in Oklahoma since World War II has been between liberal and conservative ideologies, with conservatism usually the dominant political force. Oklahoma had once been an overwhelmingly Democratic state, but it has had its first two Republican governors since 1960 and as of 1978 both of Oklahoma's U.S. Senators are Republicans. In addition, the conservative wing of the state's Democratic party has dominated that party since the mid-1960s.

The disappearance of agrarian populism as a third political choice in Oklahoma is the result of the conjuncture of two factors: (1) the destruction of the social base on which agrarian populism was anchored, (2) the introduction of New Dealism into the Oklahoma political arena in the 1930s. Neither of these two factors is sufficient by itself to explain the collapse of agrarian populism: the specific *conjuncture* of these two factors in Oklahoma resulted in the collapse. In some other southern states this conjuncture did not occur and the conservative/liberal redefinition of politics did not happen in the 1940s, as it did in Oklahoma.

The Destruction of Populism's Social Base

This study has indicated the primacy of tenant farmers in the social base of the populist candidates. The demise of the tenant farmer as an interest group in Oklahoma in the 1930s and particularly the 1940s is directly connected to the end of populism. Without the tenant farmer populist candidates had to alter their political programs drastically to reach out to other interest groups. The reorganization of Oklahoma agriculture through government legislation, mechanization, and migration of the rural laborer to the better paying jobs of the cities or to California, took with it, literally or figuratively, the tenant farmers who were the social base of the populists. Between 1935 and 1950, half of the tenant farmers of Oklahoma left the land; the tenancy rate dropped from 60 percent to 31 percent of all farmers. These small farms were taken over by the large-scale landowning farmers who had seldom been supporters of the populists.

The social base of the populists, the tenants, was not truly gone until the mid–1950s. Yet the populists collapsed much earlier, no later than 1944. Although the tenants were the keystone to the populists' success, what is of central importance, is that tenants were never a majority of the voting population: the populists had to attract other interest groups to be viable candidates. In the early 1930s they successfully organized some workers and rural merchants to win elections. However, the populists lost these groups by the late 1930s, even though economic conditions were ripe for populist candidates throughout the decade: unemployment was high, farm prices low, and people were blaming big business—all conditions which had led to successful populist movements in Oklahoma in the past. It is apparent that the economic transformations in Oklahoma are not sufficient to explain why the populists collapsed in the 1930s.

Destruction of the Political Coalition

I have already pointed out the important realignment of interest groups that took place with the introduction of New Deal politics. The New Deal ideology of regulated industrial growth, high farm prices, and social welfare programs all attracted interest groups who had voted for populist candidates in the past. New Deal liberalism contained certain populist elements in its attack on big business and corporate wealth, and these elements provided an appealing program to many interest groups, especially industrial workers. The New Deal did incorporate many of the populist demands that had originally attracted these groups to populist candidates. The populists' social base was narrowed to tenant farmers as other groups fell away and backed the liberal New Deal candidates.

The populist's first response (1934–36) was to attack the New Deal as anti-small farmer in hopes of dividing the state along rural/urban lines as they had done successfully against the conservatives. However, there were never enough non-tenant small farmers to provide a voting majority for the populists. Without some support from industrial workers or larger farmers they could not win elections. The second political strategy of the populists (1937–42) was an attempt to be the rallying point for all anti-New Deal sentiments, whether these were the sentiments of small farmers, merchants, or disgruntled small capitalists. The populists' political discourse became more right-wing but conservatives' own attacks on the New Deal blocked the movement of other anti-New Deal groups to the populist banner.

Although populism remained an important ideology in Oklahoma through the 1930s into World War II, it was of only secondary importance after 1934. In a sense, the populists' role was to block the total domination of the state by the liberals during the 1930s. For instance, the populist candidate's presence on the ballot allowed a narrow margin of victory for the conservatives in the 1938 gubernatorial campaign. However, the populists' gradual shift to the political right undermined even this limited role. With each election, the populists were less successful and in the 1942 Democratic primary, the populist, Gomer Smith, was crushed by the liberal, Robert Kerr. Smith received only 30 percent of the vote and carried only 6 counties.

However, just as the economic transformation of Oklahoma cannot be considered the sole cause of the collapse of the agrarian populists, neither can the introduction of New Deal liberals in 1934 be seen as the sole cause. New Deal liberalism was clearly important in undermining the populists' social base but only when linked to the economic characteristics of Oklahoma in the 1930s. The importance of this linkage is demonstrated by comparing Oklahoma with other states.

New Deal liberalism was not an all-conquering political ideology in every state, particularly in southern states. Both Louisiana and Texas also have a history of populism. Louisiana in the 1930s had a strong populist movement centered on the state governor, Huey Long (1928–35). Although Long's organization reached others (e.g., small merchants), the core of his strength was small farmers (Perry, 1971: 243). As did Murray in Oklahoma, Long made violent attacks on the New Deal and he too was a personal enemy of President Roosevelt (Perry, 1971: 212–225). New Deal politics entered Louisiana, through the candidacy of Dudley J. LeBlanc, at the same time they reached Oklahoma. What is strikingly different about Louisiana's populism is that, unlike Oklahoma's it did not collapse in the 1930s. In fact, populists dominated the state government until about 1956 and are still an important group in Louisiana (Perry, 1971: 251–290).

The major reason for the maintenance of the populist presence in Louisiana is found in the disjuncture between the economic transformation of Louisiana and the ascendancy of liberal politics in America. Unlike Oklahoma, Louisiana did not have any significant industry such as Oklahoma's oil industry (petroleum did not become important in Louisiana until the late 1940s with the development of offshore drilling); nor did Louisiana have any agricultural system comparable to Oklahoma's wheat farms. A populist candidate in Louisiana did not have to reach out to other interest groups to be a viable candidate; he could rely on a narrow base of farmers. The dominant form of agriculture in Louisiana was plantation production of cotton, rice, and sugar cane, by tenant farmers who were predominantly black and therefore disenfranchised (James, 1978). As a result, populist candidates in Louisiana depended on independent, small-scale, white hill farmers, rather than tenant farmers, as their main base of support. The collapse of tenancy in the 1930s and 1940s did not undermine the populists' social base as it did in Oklahoma. Combining this different social base with a single firm base of populist support made the populist relatively immune to political losses to New Deal liberalism.

Texas, on the other hand, has developed a political structure very similar to Oklahoma's with liberals and conservatives as the principal political choices since the 1940s (Key, 1949: 255–260). As in Oklahoma, the years from about 1890 to World War I saw continual political dispute over regulation of corporations and support for small farmers. Populism had several cycles of success in Texas (1890–98, 1906–10, 1915–17), much as it did in Oklahoma. In the 1930s populism in Texas was centered on the governorship of Amanda (Ma) Ferguson (1932–36), although the state was actually run by her husband James (Pa) Ferguson. The counties that consistently gave the Fergusons their highest majorities were the highly agricultural counties of eastern Texas (Key, 1949: 264–265). Like Oklahoma, Texas had few black people, a large number of white tenant cotton farmers, and a growing industrial base centered on oil. Just as in Oklahoma, the introduction of New Deal politics in the 1930s spelled the end of populism in Texas. As early as the Texas Democratic convention of 1944, the state's political division for president was between the liberals and the conservatives (Key, 1949: 256).

These two comparisons, of course, cannot bring out the full complexities of a state's politics. Their usefulness is exemplification of the structural relationship between the economic characteristics of a state and the introduction of liberal politics. In southern states where agrarian populism was a significant political force, the effect of the introduction of liberal politics in the 1930s was shaped by the economic characteristics of that particular state. Liberalism's introduction undermined and eventually destroyed populism in some states. In other states liberalism could establish no permanent place in the political arena. Finally, in a few states, such as Louisiana after 1956, both liberalism and populism maintained strong followings in the political arena.

NOTES

1. All of the text's statistical data on Oklahoma elections were obtained from Samuel A. Kirkpatrick and David R. Morgan, *Oklahoma Votes 1907–1962*, Norman, Oklahoma: University of Oklahoma Press, 1970.

2. The mean number of tractors in wheat counties in 1930 was 35 per 100 farms compared to a mean of 5 per 100 farms in non-wheat counties. In 1940 these figures were 61 per 100 farms and 14 per 100 farms, respectively, according to the 1940 Agricultural Census.

3. Although tenancy rates declined 7 percent between 1935 and 1940, major declines did not take place until the 1940's with a 23 percent drop between 1940 and 1950. The availability of nonfarm employment at high wages in military production brought many tenants off the land. The 1967 Census of Agriculture reports tenancy rates for 1930–1950.

4. Between 1940 and 1945 some 28 army camps and 13 naval bases were built in Oklahoma. Tinker Air Force Base in Oklahoma City became the largest air force base in the United States. In addition, several private war production plants were built in Oklahoma (Litton, 427–428).

REFERENCES

Bryant, Keith. 1968. Alfalfa Bill Murray. Norman, Oklahoma: University Of Oklahoma Press.

Burbank, Garin. 1976. When Farmers Voted Red. Westport, Connecticut: Greenwood Press, 1976.

Dangerfield, R. J. and R. H. Flynn. 1936. "Voter Motivation in the 1936 Oklahoma Democratic Primary." Southwestern Social Science Quarterly.

Green, Donald E. 1977. Rural Oklahoma. Oklahoma City: Oklahoma Historical Society.

Harlow, Victor E. 1961. Oklahoma History. Oklahoma City: Harlow.

James, David. 1978. "The Transformation of Local Political and Economic Structures and Resistance to the Civil Rights Movement in the South." Unpublished Manuscript.

Johnson, Charles. 1935. The Collapse of Cotton Tenancy. Chapel Hill: University of North Carolina Press.

Key, V. O. 1949. Southern Politics in State and Nation. New York: Knopf.

Litton, Gaston 1957. History of Oklahoma. Oklahoma City: Lewis Historical Society.

Morgan, David R. 1970. Oklahoma Votes 1907–1962. Norman Oklahoma: University of Oklahoma Press.

Morris, John W. 1952. Oklahoma Geography. Oklahoma City: Harlow.

Perry, Howard. 1971. Political Tendencies in Louisiana. Baton Rouge: L.S.U. Press.

Raper, Arthur. 1936. Preface to Peasantry. Chapel Hill: North Carolina Press.

Scales, James R. 1949. Political History of Oklahoma 1907–1944. Unpublished Ph.D. Dissertation. University of Oklahoma.

7

Class Relations
and Class Structure
in the Midwest[1]

Patrick H. Mooney

INTRODUCTION

Who are the Midwestern family farmers? Traditional images portray them as an independent commercial producer who, together with their families, work hard and enjoy a moderate lifestyle, free not only from city strife but also free from bosses and wage-labor. Other images, more often of their own making, portray them as victims of exploitation by the infamous "middlemen" and the monopolies who also victimize consumers. This divergence is reflected in most analyses of the American farmer. While one study will find the family farmer thriving (Nikolitch, 1965), another will find the family farmer in great trouble (Hightower, 1975).

Most analyses of American class structure leave farmers in a residual category, by-passed as if they were "non-existent, historically speaking." Yet if they are no longer politically powerful, they are certainly economically powerful as producers of food and often as the legal owners of valuable land. Their location in the class structure and struggle may often prove crucial. Friedrich Engels noted the importance of this "intermediate" class in the determination of the political, referring to "this class" as "a most important one in every modern body politic, and in all modern revolutions." Engels contended that, in Germany, the petty bourgeois class "generally played the decisive part" (1973: 304).[2]

Analysis of the class structure within the agricultural sector sheds light on the issue: "who will control U.S. agriculture?" By transcending notions of class that focus on age, education, income, etc. (which merely quantify status) the control of agriculture is revealed in a class analysis which focuses on the social relations within the actual processes of production and the objective structural conditions of control over capital and labor.

The family farm can be characterized as a simple commodity mode of production. Though this mode of production has never existed by itself as a social formation, it ideally refers to "a society in which each producer owns his own means of production and satisfies his manifold needs by exchange with other similarly situated products" (Sweezy, 1942: 23). It is necessary to emphasize the importance of exchange in this mode of production. The petty bourgeois producer, as we shall refer to simple commodity producers, differs from the subsistence production typified by some peasantry. The petty bourgeois producer is actively engaged in production for a market. Thus they produce a surplus in order to enter into various exchange relationships with other petty bourgeois producers and, since simple commodity production never exists alone, with actors in completely different modes of production. In short, the petty bourgeois production unit differs from the subsistence household insofar as it cannot, by definition, shelter itself in subsistence isolation but remains dependent on market conditions for exchange of its surplus product. It is this surplus which is the beginning point of our investigation.

> Analysis of a concrete social formation must therefore be organized around an analysis of the way in which the surplus is generated in this formation, the transfers of surplus that may be effected from or to other formations, and the internal distribution of this surplus among the various recipients (classes and social groups) (Amin, 1976: 18).

The processes of producing and marketing this surplus allow the penetration of influences of the dominant mode of production through the interaction and dependency of exchange. The dynamics of capitalist development provide, on the one hand, that petty bourgeois producers may be incipient capitalists. That is, their (slow) accumulation of wealth in a capitalist society offers a chance of joining the capitalist class. The development of monopoly capitalism, on the other hand, constrains such chances. Not only is their bid to join the capitalist class inhibited, but market-dependency raises the possibility of subjection to proletarianization in the squeeze between increasingly monopolized costs of production and monopolized prices paid for their products on the market.

Marx noted this role of petty bourgeois producers in forming a portion of the "reserve army of labor": "Part of the agricultural population is therefore constantly on the point of passing over into an urban or manufacturing proletariat, and on the lookout for opportunities to complete this transformation" (1977: 796).

Both the agricultural market and the labor market formed the basis for the massive reduction of the petty bourgeois agricultural producers following World War II. Ironically, one potential mechanism by which the flow of this reserve labor supply could be regulated was created in response to an earlier demand of the farmers themselves. Price supports were generally based on the parity ratio or the farmer's return on his investment of capital and labor. Parity reflects closely the cost-price squeeze which many farmers indicate as a reason for leaving farming. Could the state use its ability to support or not support farm prices to partially regulate the flow of the farm population to the city and to proletarian status?

The Eisenhower Administration's decision to effectively abandon price supports followed several years of low unemployment (3.3 percent to 2.9 percent in 1951 and 1953). The next phase of low unemployment (3.8 percent to 3.5 percent in 1966 and 1969) was also followed by a period of low parity prices (69 percent in 1971) after which there appears to have developed a relative stability of farm population with increasing unemployment and, until recently, an upsurge in exports of agricultural products and higher farm prices. The present period is unique (in the post-Depression period) in the coincidence of low farm prices and high levels of unemployment. The agricultural economist, Theodore W. Schultz, made explicit the possible use of the relationship between price supports and proletarianization as a regulatory mechanism for filling the ranks of the unemployed when he proposed that in the post-war period, price support payments be made only when the economy "was at less than full employment (defined as 5 percent unemployment). Under full employment conditions, no payments would be made" (Halcrow, 1977: 165).

Low unemployment may temporarily raise wages and opportunities to a level that "pulls" marginal farmers toward proletarianization while low parity prices "push" them out of agricultural production. However, the "push" factor is probably stronger than the attraction of proletarianization. A 1978 survey of Wisconsin farmers, for example, found 71 percent of those leaving farming or unsure about their continuation in farming citing the cost-price squeeze as the main issue, while only 5 percent cited the attraction of another job (Mooney, 1985). This is contrary to agricultural economists' attempts to focus on the "pull" factors with the concept of "opportunity costs" which evaluates the farmer's self-employed labor time in comparison to what he could otherwise obtain by employment in town. Such a concept not only assumes formal rationality but also ignores the fundamental shift in class relations by preferring to quantify labor rather than to qualify it.

While the view of petty bourgeois agricultural producers as a portion of the reserve army of labor provides some explanation of the reduction of the rural farm population in the post-World War II era, it does not explain the survival of what appears to be a petty bourgeois class of agricultural producers among the remaining farm population, especially in the Midwest. This is a numerically smaller petty bourgeois class in control of larger, more productive units. How and why this simple commodity mode of production appears in a world of capitalist relations seem to be the strategic questions which follow from the present concerns of the diverse array of interests in the (belated) preservation of the "family farm." If one wishes to preserve what is left of this mode of production one must understand how it has survived the development of capitalist relations to the extent that it has.[3]

How does the dominant capitalist mode of production affect the petty bourgeoisie? What is their specific location with reference to class struggle in a predominantly capitalist social formation? Only by asking this can we begin to ask: Who are their allies? or perhaps, more importantly: Who are their antagonists?

Marx provides a particularly concise and useful discussion by raising for himself the question: "What then is the position of independent handicraftsmen or peasants who employ no laborers and therefore do not produce as capitalists?" (1969: 407)

The utility of his response consists in the fact that the commercial family farmer has characteristics of both the handicraftsman (in terms of the level of skill development, market-orientation, and possession/ ownership of the instruments of production) and the peasant (in terms of agricultural production). In dealing with both groups simultaneously Marx provides a statement which is particularly applicable to the population in which we are interested. Marx strips away the usual equation of the peasant with non-market-oriented subsistence production by referring at the outset to both independent handicraftsmen and peasants as "producers of commodities" (1969: 407). Marx clearly designates such production as existing outside the capitalist mode of production:

They confront me as sellers of commodities, not as sellers of labor and this relation therefore has nothing to do with the exchange of capital for labor; therefore also it has nothing to do with the distinction between *productive and unproductive labor*. . . . They therefore belong neither to the category of productive nor of unproductive laborers, although they are producers of commodities. But their production does not fall under the capitalist mode of production. (1969: 407)

The designation of such production as occurring outside the capitalist mode of production does not, however, mean that such producers are incapable of producing surplus value, only that such surplus value is appropriated by the direct producer himself: "It is possible that these producers, working with their own means of production, not only reproduce their labor-power but create surplus-value, while their position enables them to appropriate for themselves their own surplus-labor or a part of it (since a part of it is taken away from them in the form of taxes, etc.)" (1969: 407).

This statement is of particular significance to the theoretical framework at hand. In acknowledging the existence of surplus value in this mode of production Marx opens the door to questions concerning the distribution of this surplus value.

The independent peasant or handicraftsman is cut up into two persons. As owner of the means of production he is capitalist; as laborer he is his own wage-laborer. As capitalist he therefore pays himself his wages and draws his profit on his capital; that is to say, he exploits himself as wage-laborer, and pays himself, in the surplus-value, the tribute that labor owes to capital. Perhaps he also pays himself a third portion as landowner (rent), in exactly the same way, as we shall see later, that the industrial capitalist, when he works with his own capital, pays himself interest, regarding this as something which he owes to himself not as industrial capitalist but qua capitalist pure and simple (1969: 407–8).

However, transformations occur which literally, rather than figuratively, cut the independent producer into two persons. When an actual second person, rather than the first, comes to receive wages for labor, rent for land-use, or interest for capital-use we must question whether or not such production remains outside of the capitalist mode of production as it does when one "pays oneself" wages, rent or interest.

Following Marx, the analysis of the historical transformation to capitalism focuses on the ownership and possession of the means of production by the producer: "The means of production become capital only in so far as they have become separated from the laborer and confront labor as an independent power . . . in the case referred to the producer—the laborer—is the possessor, the owner, of his means of production" (1969: 408). As long as this case pertains, the separation (the payment of wages, rent or interest to oneself) is only an appearance; the means of production are: "not capital, any more than in relation to them he is a wage laborer. Nevertheless, they are looked on as capital. Separation appears as the normal relation in this society . . . in this society unity appears as accidental, separation as normal; and consequently separation is maintained as the relation even when one person unites the separate functions" (1969: 408–9).

Thus we take a step back from the question: "How has the 'family farm' (petty bourgeois/simple commodity production) survived?" and ask, instead, the prior question: "Has it survived?" To answer this question we must penetrate appearances and examine the objective socio-economic relationships in this mode of production. We must abandon the view with which many of the "save the family farm" interests understand capitalist development. These interests generally look for the appearance of characteristics of capitalist agriculture as typified by California's "factories in the fields." Such an ahistorical approach excludes the observation of the subtle and devious means which capital develops to penetrate other modes of production in various specific historical circumstances.

Behind the appearance of a surviving petty bourgeois class, capitalist relationships may have been established or are being established in entirely new forms or thinly disguised old forms. The analysis of these forms begins with "clearing up the problems of the generation and circulation of the surplus within this formation" (Amin, 1976: 23), the ways in which surplus value is extracted, realized and redistributed throughout the formation, and the extent to which the appropriation and distribution of surplus and surplus value coincide with interference in the petty bourgeois producer's control over his own labor process and means of production.

This chapter is intended as a preliminary step toward a model for the more complete analysis of class formation. The economic level is emphasized because the examination of the political and ideological levels is contingent upon the theoretical development of the economic base. The first section of this chapter attempts to work within a neo-Marxist problematic, focusing particularly on the class structure theory of Wright (1978) and adapting it to the specific nature of production relations in agriculture. There are, however, limitations in this approach to class analysis. Aside from the focus on "class-in-itself" rather than "class for itself," there is a neglect of the subjective component generally. Nevertheless, certain aspects of this neo-Marxist class analysis yield fundamental insights not found in traditional analysis of the structure of agriculture. Of particular interest will be: 1) the examination of relations of production rather than gradations of size, income, etc.; 2) a focus on the exploitative rather than the symbiotic character of these relations; 3) an emphasis on the issue of control over agricultural production; and 4) the development of the concept of "contradictory class location" for agriculture. The second section of the chapter attempts to address some of these limitations through speculation on the political implications of contradictory class location and then analyzing the transformation in light of the Weberian concepts of rationality and rationalization.

CLASS RELATIONS

Marxian class analysis often takes as its starting point the abstract category, "mode of production" and moves toward the concrete concept of "social formation." As Poulantzas writes: "The mode of production constitutes an abstract-formal object which does not exist in the strong sense in reality . . . The only thing which really exists is a historically determined social formation. . . . The social formation itself constitutes a complex unity in which a certain mode of production dominates the others which compose it" (1978:15).

In the post-World War II United States the capitalist mode of production is clearly dominant. This social formation, however, also exhibits vestiges of simple commodity production as a subordinate mode. In the interaction or exchange between these "pure" modes of production the problems of class analysis arise.

Two works of particular influence in the development of neo-Marxist class analysis in the U.S. have been Braverman (1974) and Wright (1978). Central to Braverman's analysis is the appropriation of surplus value from direct producers. He uses Marx's concepts of productive and unproductive labor which refer to labor's production of surplus value under capitalist relations of production. For Braverman, the decisive criterion for class distinction is the production of surplus value for capital, not the nature of the labor process nor the utility of the product. The discussion of productive and unproductive labor "is in reality an analysis of the relations of production and, ultimately, of the class structure of society" (Braverman, 1974: 411). Thus, the process of proletarianization consists of the incorporation of labor into forms in which surplus value may be appropriated. As Braverman writes: "The transformation of unproductive labor into labor which is, for the capitalist's purpose of extracting surplus value, productive, is the very process of the creation of capitalist society" (1974: 413). Wright, on the other hand, focuses on "three central processes underlying the basic capital-labor relationship: control over the physical means of production; control over labor power; control over investments and resource allocation . . . these three processes are the real stuff of class relations in capitalist society" (Wright, 1978: 73). At the highest level of abstraction, the mode of production, the capitalist class is defined by its control over each of these processes, while the proletariat is defined by its exclusion from such control. At the level of social formations, however, the analysis of class structure becomes more complex. First, other modes of production coexist, in a subordinate role, with the capitalist mode. The subordinate mode of production in which we are interested is simple commodity production represented by the petty bourgeoisie in the class structure. Wright defines the petty bourgeoisie "as having no control over labor power (since no labor power is employed)" (1978: 74).

A second complication which appears with analysis of social formations is the imperfect coincidence of these three processes. This non-coincidence gives rise to the concept of contradictory class location. Wright points to three contradictory class locations: 1) between capitalist and proletariat (e.g. managers and supervisors); 2) between petty bourgeoisie and capitalist (e.g. small employers); and 3) between petty bourgeoisie and proletariat (e.g. semi-autonomous employees). With respect to the latter two categories Wright appears to follow Braverman in distinguishing simple commodity production from capitalist production: "The distinctive feature of capitalist production is the appropriation of surplus value through the exploitation of workers in the labor process. In simple commodity production, on the other hand, there is no exploitation" (p. 79, 1978).

Thus, four criteria form the basis for the development of a theoretical model of class structure in agriculture. First, the appropriation of surplus value from direct producers via relationships which traverse household or immediate family boundaries indicates a proletarianization process. The retention of surplus value within the household or family indicates the reproduction of simple commodity production. The direct producers' control over the physical means of production and investments indicate petty bourgeois class location. Loss of such control implies proletarianization. Finally, control over the labor power of others indicates transformation toward the capitalist mode of production with the party exercising control being nearer a capitalist class location to the extent that direct production is performed by hired labor.

Our task is to identify relationships in agriculture in which these processes are actively reproducing or transforming the class structure. Five relationships which involve one or more of these class criteria will be discussed. These will then be integrated into a model for the analysis of agricultural class structure. The social relations of production to be discussed are: tenancy, indebtedness, off-farm work, contract production, and hired labor. Elsewhere (Mooney, 1983, 1985), I have provided more extended theoretical discussion of each of these social relations. The following section will, therefore, emphasize empirical analysis of the character and transformation of these social relations of agricultural production particularly as they occur in a selected Midwestern state: Wisconsin.

Tenancy

Stinchcombe's influential essay "Agricultural Enterprise and Rural Class Relations" (1961) drew attention to the family-size tenancy. Stinchcombe's focus on property systems as the point of differentiation in rural class structure yields a typology of five property systems of which only two, the family-size tenancy and the family small-holding, are generally found in the midwest. The distinctive characteristic of the family-size tenancy is the lost income due to the payment of rent, encouraging instability through the antagonism between landlord and tenant. This hostility may be exacerbated by the tenant's possession of the technical knowledge and skills that not only make the landowner appear as redundant but perhaps even as a constraint on efficient production.

The extraction of rent payments from direct producer tenants constitutes an appropriation of surplus value. Share crop arrangements increasingly give way to cash rent where the producer himself must realize the value of the product before surrendering a portion of it. In this sense the tenant farmer's labor becomes productive labor, as the landlord exchanges the use of his capital-land against the capacity of the producer's labor to generate surplus value.

The question of control is more complex. Generally, the tenant retains ownership of means of production other than land and buildings. The extent to which landlords exercise control over these means of production is highly variable, seemingly dependent on their own knowledge and skills and perhaps their physical proximity to the site of production. The centrality of land and buildings as means of production mean that decisions made by the landlord with respect to these will circumscribe the range of control exercised by the tenant within the production cycle. The net effect is that the landowner makes major (organizational) decisions, such as the quantity of any commodity to be planted/grazed or work that affects the land itself, particularly its productivity or its conservation while day-to-day possession (operational decisions) rest with the tenant. Such routine may, in part, disguise the extent to which the landlords' decisions structure both the use of the tenants' own instruments of production and their labor process. An increasingly important form of tenancy, in which the rented farm supplements a farm that is owned by the operator, creates particular problems around the issue of control. As Sublett (1975) points out, these "part owners" need to control managerial processes in order to coordinate with their home farm production.

As absentee landlordism increases, particularly with urbanites seeking tax or inflation shelters, a form of organization which is becoming more important further threatens the autonomy of tenant farmers. This is the farm management company, employed by absentee landlords to manage farms in which they have invested. The tenant's managerial role is substantially reduced, while in some cases the direct producer is actually an employee of the firm. The management company form of organization appropriates surplus value in the form of a fee or percentage of the value generated. This suggests a renewed relevance of Marx's concept of ground rent. The management company must obtain for itself an average rate of profit from the labor power of its tenant-employee. The absentee landlord's return then constitutes ground rent in Marx's sense of surplus profit. This is, again, a specific production relation within the general tenant form of production. It is not the norm, though it may become a tendency as nonfarm people continue to invest in farm land.

Finally, control over investments in tenancy is split between real estate and non real estate inputs. Many basic production decisions reside primarily with the landowner since land is a major investment. The tenant's investment in equipment is dependent upon the amount of land accessed through rental relations and the intensity with which the land is to be farmed. The tenant has little incentive to invest in the maintenance of land and buildings since lease agreements are often short-term.

In summary, engagement in tenancy negates the direct producer's location in simple commodity production. On each of the four criteria, the tenant is subject to processes characteristic of the capitalist mode of production that reflect proletarianization. This process of proletarianization remains incomplete until access to land is terminated. Without complete expropriation, the process leaves the tenant in a "contradictory class location" between simple commodity and proletarian production.

Some analysts of tenancy wish to minimize this antagonism. Dunaway and Morrow (1980), for example, open their book with the implication that the landlord-tenant relation is characterized by "mutual trust," a sharing of goals, even "friendship." Ironically, the rest of the book is devoted to devising means by which the conflicting interests of the parties may be minimized. Not surprisingly, the legal device of a detailed, written lease and intricate calculation of each actor's costs and benefits are the instruments for ensuring that this "team" can develop a relationship that "works." In this sense, rationalization proceeds as a mechanism in the amelioration of an inherently conflictual relationship.

A study of Illinois landlord-tenant relations (Soltwedel, 1967) found substantial participation of landlords in management, particularly in organizational decisions. Soltwedel also notes the less conspicuous interventions of landlords into the managerial process. Interventions include the imposition of limitations on the carrying capacity (e.g. the number of livestock, or intensity of cultivation) of the rented production unit. Soltwedel found that the negotiating position of Illinois landowners is strong enough that they are often able to restrict the tenant from farming other rented land or even from engaging in off-farm work. Such restrictions need not be spelled out in a lease but may be implemented through the landlord's selective elimination of potential tenants to include only those who will fit the landlord's needs.

The history of tenancy in Wisconsin can be roughly broken into three periods: settlement (1840–1920); Depression and war (1920–1945); and post-war (1945–). Our primary concern here will be this latter period though we recognize the critical role played by policies developed during the period of depression and war in structuring the subsequent period.

Until 1920 the percentage of full tenants in Wisconsin was rising along with the percentage of mortgaged farms and continued increase in the number of farms. During this period, capital, in the form of indebted and tenant relations of production, was making inroads against simple commodity production although the ranks of simple commodity producers were continually being replenished. This replenishment took two forms. First, of course, was the settlement of new land for farming as agriculture penetrated the central sands area and then the northern forests. By 1910, however, nearly all of the land (21,060,066 acres) that was to be used for agricultural purposes had been settled and the increase in the number of farms could no longer be attributed to the frontier but rather to the entry of more farmers to existing agricultural land. This is indicated by a decline in average farm size between 1910 and 1920 (decrease of about 2 acres) and again between 1920 and 1925 (decrease of about 4 acres).

The second period began with the farm depression of the 1920s which eliminated a number of the mortgaged farms between 1920–25 and then forced a number of other farms into mortgage debt in the latter 1920s. Foreclosures during the Great Depression again forced a decline in the percentage of farms under mortgage. The elimination of these units paved the way for an increase in the number of farms as the unemployed and underemployed sought the security of the land in the 1930s, again driving down the average size of farms by about 3 acres. Throughout this second period tenancy in Wisconsin increased to a peak of 23.0 percent in 1940 after which World War II and a new era of agriculture began the process of eliminating tenancy. This second period is characterized by a break of the simultaneous and parallel development of tenant and debtor forms of agricultural production, forms which likely corresponded to life cycle or the "agricultural ladder." The wave of depression foreclosures reversed this cycle, transforming many owner-operators into tenants, if not into outright proletarians or unemployed.

Table 1. Percent of All Farms in Each Tenure Status Category

Year	Full Owners	Part Owners	Full Tenants
1940	ND	ND	23.0
1945	67.4	11.5	20.4
1950	71.6	12.4	15.6
1954	69.3	15.8	14.5
1959	69.2	18.8	11.4
1964	70.8	19.6	9.1
1969	73.3	19.6	7.1
1974	67.6	26.3	6.0
1978	62.1	30.3	7.6
1982	59.0	32.4	8.6

Source: U.S. Census of Agriculture, various years.

Following World War II tenancy more completely gave way to the debtor form of production. Debt is a formal rationalization of agricultural production relations insofar as the relationship is much more readily calculable in monetary terms. The tenant form, which may also undergo rationalization in itself, has traditionally carried elements of substantive rationality in the paternalism characteristic of the landlord-tenant relation.

Aggregate data disguises considerable regional variation within the state. Although tenancy in most areas of the state has consistently declined since World War II, most of the regional differences have been maintained. In 1945, the southwestern corner of the state was heavily operated by tenants (40 to 50 percent). Moving northward or eastward the percentage of tenancy gradually declines. The counties near Milwaukee appear to have declined less than in the rest of the state. This may be partially due to higher land prices of an urban fringe and to the specialty crop production in this area. The northern part of the state has long had the lowest tenancy rates (around 5 percent in 1945 and becoming lower). In 1974 tenancy was still highest across the southern tier of counties but especially in the southeast and southwest.[4]

Table 1 shows the decline in the percentage of full tenants in post World War II Wisconsin. Immediately following the war, relatively high commodity prices allowed the percentage of mortgaged farms to drop off in coincidence with a sharp drop in tenancy from 20.4 percent in 1945 to 15.6 percent in 1950. The decline in tenancy during the 1950s and the relative stability of the percentage of mortgaged farms allow the inference that many tenant farmers joined the massive off-farm migration of this period (40,000 farms were eliminated in Wisconsin between 1950 and 1960). This characteristic of the process is further reflected in the near halving of the percentage of tenants in this period (1945–59) while the percentage of full owners actually increased. The data suggest that a number of tenants became full owners of very small farms in the period following the war.

Full tenancy continued to decline after 1960, at least until the later 1970s. Corresponding to this trend was an increase in the percentage of fully owned farms throughout the 1960s. In the 1970s however, the percentage of fully owned farms began to decline from 73.3 percent in 1969 to 62.1 percent in 1978. (Full ownership of commercial farms likewise declined from 68.5 percent to 57.7 percent.) Most of this decline can be attributed an increase of 10.7 percent (10.5 percent in the commercial farm sector) in the part owners category. The part owners category not only increased relative to the other categories but also absolutely, by nearly 8,000 farms.

Tenancy may be an artifact of life cycle. The consistently lower average age of tenants indicates that it is a step on the "agricultural ladder." The average age of full owners and part owners shows remarkable stability over the period, but full tenant average age fluctuates. The range of 4.5 years in the average age of tenants does not exhibit any particular directional tendency over time. This fluctuation may result from tenants seizing the opportunity to step up the 'ladder' during periods of prosperity.

Tenancy also varies considerably both within commodity groups across time and between commodity groups at any particular point in time. Not until after 1969 did full ownership begin to decline among dairy producers. Prior to the 1970s full farm ownership in dairy production was comparable to several other commodity groups. In both 1974 and 1978, however, full ownership was lowest in the dairy sector. This decline in full ownership did not give way to full tenancy but to partownership. The absolute number of part owner dairy farms increased by 3,359 while the overall number of dairy farms decreased by 14,375. Further, while part-ownership accounted for only 14.0 percent of dairy farms in 1950, by 1978 it comprised 43.3 percent, a much higher percentage than any other commodity group. In cash grain production full ownership has declined since the end of World War II. In 1978, only tobacco had a higher percentage of full tenants. In 1950, full ownership was lowest in livestock production. By 1978, only poultry and "fruit and nut" producers had higher percentages of full ownership. Full ownership has also been the dominant form of tenure among "vegetable and melon" producers.

Debt

Despite the enormous dependence of today's agriculture on credit, surprisingly little attention has been given to this relationship; although

Stinchcombe does note the equivalence of rent and debt: "The formal title to the land may not be held by the non-cultivator—it is quite common for the 'rent' on the land to be, in a legal sense, the interest on a loan secured by the land" (1961:169).

Interest payments can be argued to also constitute an appropriation of surplus value from direct producers and therefore fulfill the first criteria by which to evaluate the proletarianization process. Control over capital itself in the debtor-creditor relation resides with the creditors by the very nature of the relation. The autonomy of the producer will vary relative to the availability of credit; creditors enjoy a greater capacity to intervene in managerial processes when credit is tight. The producer's capacity to "possess" the free usage of credit will also vary with the creditor's evaluation of his capacity to secure a profit.

The intervention of "professional" farm management services in tenant production parallels the same development with respect to debtors. Many of these farm management firms emanate directly from banks with agricultural interests. As in tenancy, the routinization of day-to-day possession may mask the extent to which critical decisions of creditors structure the producer's routine possession of both means of production and labor process. The appearance of being one's "own boss" is reproduced, while the basis of that autonomy is undermined. As in eviction, the authority to foreclose, or even the threat of foreclosure, is the power from which the control over the producer is derived. The transformation of the simple commodity producer toward proletarianization via the debt relation remains incomplete without foreclosure. Thus, the producer falls into a contradictory class location between petty bourgeoisie and proletariat. Barriers to complete proletarianization appear to issue from both the economic advantage to the creditor in perpetually extracting interest as against acquisition of the land and the debtor's capacity to generate enough surplus value to pay such interest. The penetration of these barriers is conditioned by the sanctity of private property in capitalist social formations. As Kautsky wrote: "bourgeois property recognises only one basis for expropriation—default. As long as the peasant repays the capitalist and the state, his property is sacrosanct" (1980:65).

The empirical analysis of debt as a social relation involves analysis of the direct producers' "partners" in that relationship, i.e. the creditors. The credit market thus becomes a focal point of analysis. The diversity of credit sources runs from the private to the public with the cooperatively organized Farm Credit System falling in between. Each form implies a different set of social relations.

Whatever its source the input of capital in the form of credit transforms not only the social relations of agricultural production but the very structure of agriculture itself. This occurs at the most fundamental levels.

The capital intensification of agriculture substitutes capital for human labor requirements at the point of production. At the societal level these labor requirements are merely displaced from the farm to the industrial input sector (e.g. manufacture of tractors, chemicals, etc.). In so far as credit is used to finance this capital intensification it is clear that this structural transformation is not entirely in the hands of farmers themselves, though that may appear to be the case. Boulding makes this point quite clear:

> The principal function of the financial system is to separate the ownership of real capital from its control, that is to enable people to administer real capital without owning it, and to own it without administering it. . . . If there were no financial system . . . every person would have to administer the real assets which he owned, no matter how incapable he might be at such a task (Boulding, 1950).

The "invisible hand" of creditors is masked in two ways. First, and less subtle, is through their capacity to determine what loans are used for. Here their interests in generating profit-maximization through cash volume rather than production efficiency per se will enhance tendencies toward increasing the scale of production and hence the capital intensification of agriculture.

> In the U.S., conventional wisdom states that increased profitability is synonomous with greater efficiency. In reality, profits increase with farm size, irrespective of efficiency, which eventually declines . . . As efficiency levels off, or even decreases slightly, total net profits continue to increase (Vogeler, 1981: 95).

> The Minnesota study indicated that the one-man dairy farm could realize little, if any, increase in efficiency by doubling farm size and hiring an additional worker, but the increase in volume would give rise to considerably higher profits (Madden, 1967: 70).

More subtle than this determination of loan usage is the creditors' selection of who is to farm. By selecting only those farmers with certain characteristics as clients, lenders are able to eliminate from agriculture those producers who wish to farm for reasons other than mere profit-maximization. Hence, while it appears that farmers themselves determine these trends in agriculture, only those who are inclined to make such decisions are allowed (by the creditors) to remain. What are these selection criteria? "The first is what Hottel calls the 'human factor'— the applicant's personal integrity and business skills. Personal integrity involves a borrower's honesty, determination to meet obligations and cooperativeness" (Mirror, 1982: 13). Nelson et al. refer to this as:

> credit character . . . those qualities of a borrower that make him want or intend to pay when a loan is due—qualities of honesty and integrity, denoting determination to fulfill his obligations irrespective of contingencies that may arise. To live up to the promise above their signatures, some borrowers are willing to sacrifice much more than others, making great sacrifices and denying themselves and their families the prime essentials of life. On the other extreme, there are those having little regard for moral obligations, who would escape payment through a legal loophole if they could find one (Nelson et al., 1973: 244–45).

While we may question the morality of paying interest to capital while denying one's family the "prime essentials of life" nevertheless we see that personality evaluation is essential to credit extension. The creditor's selection process screens out those with substantively rational goals in farming in favor of the formally rational producer (Mooney: 1983, 1985). In the long run, substantive rationality in agriculture is not reproduced and production is transformed into a formally rationalized system via the mechanism of borrower selection. Even when substantively rational borrowers are allowed credit, their rationality may be overridden by the creditors' demands. To the extent that substantively rational producers survive it is, in part, because they never enter into the credit relation, remaining immune to the filtering process and the external control of their management.

Historically, debt has been associated with most of American agriculture from the start. Bogue (1955) has shown the demand for credit in the Midwestern homesteading processes. Parker notes the heaviness of mortgage debts, their constraint on full operator ownership and that while the diversity and flexibility of the family-size farm "could absorb the shocks of instability by compressing their own incomes and standard of living. Only where fixed interest charges, debt repayments and taxes were high was a depression of income fatal" (1972: 404).

Federal policy has assured the agricultural sector a steadily expanded flow of capital with what Halcrow (1977: 4) calls "the most complete system of federally sponsored credit found in any sector of the American economy." The state's provision of credit for agriculture is especially important in light of Parker's observation that "until recent years . . . alternative objects of investment in industry, trade, and transport were abundant" (1972: 398).

Unfortunately, the inconsistency of the categories used in the Agricultural Census precludes consistent comparison across time of the percentage of farms which have fallen into indebtedness. However, we can ascertain that the WW II period allowed many farmers to pay off their debts. In 1940, 43.7 percent of U.S. farms and 60.3 percent of Wisconsin farms were mortgaged. By 1950, these figures declined to 30.0 percent and 42.4 percent, respectively. Since 1950, the percentage of mortgaged farms has steadily increased. The 1969 Census of Agriculture estimated the percentage of farms with real and/or non-real estate debt to be 74.3 percent for the U.S. and 71.1 percent for Wisconsin. The 1978 Agricultural Census estimated that 53.8 percent of U.S. farms and 62.2 percent of Wisconsin farms were mortgaged. In 1956, Wisconsin farmers paid $16.1 million in interest payments on mortgage debt. In 1982, they paid $359.8 million on mortgage debt. In 1948, interest payments accounted for about 1 percent of the production expenses incurred by farmers. By 1982, 8 percent of the cost of agricultural production went to interest payments.

There are several indicators of farm debt distress. One of the most commonly used is the ratio of farm debt to farm assets. The prevailing tendency in the post-World War II period is an ever weaker position of the farm sector with respect to the assets it brings to bear on its expanding debt. This deterioration, which was particularly strong and steady throughout the 1960s, received some relief with the boom in land prices following increased export sales and higher farm prices in the early 1970s. This period of relief is now over. Land prices in several vital agricultural states (e.g. Illinois and Iowa) have been falling since 1979. Wisconsin began to see this loss of asset value in 1981. Prices received by farmers have not been high enough to recover the debt entered into when their land was more valuable.

Thus, we can expect to witness an increase in a second indicator of farm debt distress: extended and delinquent loans. Except for a sharp increase in such distress in Wisconsin between 1962 and 1965 (precisely the period when the NFO penetrated Wisconsin) the trends in the U.S. parallel Wisconsin quite strongly. The period 1951–1955 saw a dramatic rise in extended and delinquent Federal Land Bank loans in both Wisconsin and the U.S. This 'distress' gave way to strong increases in a third indicator of distress: foreclosure, the number of which more than doubled from 1953 to 1956 in the U.S. and from 1952 to 1956 in the Lake States region (Wisconsin, Minnesota and Michigan). The past few years have seen tremendous pressure on farmers to meet the demands of creditors. Low farm prices, declining land prices and high interest rates have pushed the number of extended and delinquent loans to the point where a new wave of foreclosures has begun. This wave of foreclosures has triggered a final but perhaps most important indicator of farm debt distress: the mobilization of farmers against the creditors.[5]

Summarizing the discussion of tenancy and indebtedness, if we are interested in the elimination of exploitation (appropriation of surplus value) of cultivators by non-cultivators, we find only a transformation of the form in which that surplus value is appropriated (i.e. from rent to interest). If we are interested in the distribution of control over the allocation of resources, both human (labor power) and financial, we find only a different non-cultivator (i.e. the creditor rather than the landlord) directing the production process. In short, we find not a tranformation of mode of production but a transformation of the form of production within that mode. In both cases the mode of production in question may be characterized as semi-proletarianized production. In the first case (tenancy), capital dominates direct producers through absentee ownership. In the second case (credit), capital controls the purse strings which allow both individual land ownership and access to the means of production. It is only with the latter that such ownership of land is enabled to set the production process in motion so that a return capable of reproducing the direct producer's labor is possible.

Similarly, in the larger pattern of capitalist penetration, absentee (non-local) landlords draw surplus value not only from the individual farmer, but also from the rural community, just as the large urban banks pull the surplus value from the periphery to the geographic centers of capitalist development.[6] This point is lost more often to the economist, for whom capital is often geographically or even socially undifferentiated, than to farmers themselves, who continue to exhibit a sense of indignation at the entry of outsiders into both their household and their local economies. In this sense, the credit form of production enjoys greater legitimacy as it more readily mystifies (through correspondent relations between center and periphery banks) this penetration. Both forms of production, however, serve to further the accumulation of capital by non-producers.

Contract Production

Heffernan (1972) pioneered the sociological investigation of contract production in his study of alienation among poultry producers. Davis (1980) provides a Marxist approach to this form of capitalist penetration in agriculture. He abandons the traditional Marxist dogma that posits individual private property as a sufficient barrier to capitalist penetration but finds, in Marx, the basis for viewing the erosion of the autonomy of the possessor of means of production as a process of integrating the agricultural producer "into a system of exploitative capitalist relations" (1980: 141).

It is in Marx's analysis of piece-work that Davis finds the equivalent of contract production in agriculture (where a specified quantity of product is exchanged for a predetermined price). Marx's conclusion "that wages by the piece are 'nothing else than a converted form of wages by time'" (Davis, 1980: 140) is used to explain an appropriation of surplus value from the agricultural producer in which the product becomes the "vehicle" by which surplus value is transferred. This exploitative relation undermines the independence of the propertied producer both directly and indirectly. Explicit control over the producer's labor process, investment strategy, and use of the means of production varies from tight supervision of the entire production cycle (often taking the harvest away from the producer by utilizing processor-hired wage labor using equipment owned by the capitalist firm) to indirect control that relies on incentives implicit in the relationship to enforce a strict supervision on the quality and intensity of production with minimal risk to the processor.

Davis' concise explication of this position contributes a theorization, within a Marxist analysis, of contract production as a specifically capitalist form of exploitation. Descriptions of the producers' loss of control over the labor process, the means of production, and investment to monopsonist firms may be found in the most mainstream discussions of contract production in agriculture.

However, even the agricultural producer completely dependent upon contract production in a rigidly supervised and scheduled production process may not be considered fully proletarianized as long as he holds title to such a crucial means of production as land. Like the variability within both the tenant and debtor forms of production, the class location of contract producers at the economic level ranges between petty bourgeoisie and proletariat. They, too, fall into this contradictory class location in which Wright's term "semi-autonomous employee" is particularly accurate.

Contract production often develops where the marketing channel for a certain commodity is monopolized by one processor or buyer. The nature of the contract agreement, and thus the relationship between farmer and processor, can vary. Roy distinguishes two types of contract production, both seen as part of a vertical integration process. In what Roy calls the limited management contract the relationship permits "the farmer to make all production decisions and restricts him only in a limited manner." (1972: 5) This type often involves the extension of credit by the contractor, which reflects the developing and encompassing relationship of dependence and subordination. Under the "full management contract" the farmer is guaranteed a price for his product but "must follow the rigid schedule set up under the contract and must allow for close supervision of his activities." (Roy, 1972: 5) In this latter case, the farmer may become what seems a semi-autonomous employee of the processor. While the farm operator maintains legal ownership of the land and machinery, most of the decisions and use of variable inputs are furnished by the processor. The farmer's position becomes quite similar to the holder of a restaurant or gas station franchise. Some courts have, in fact, ruled that contract producers are employees subject to wage-and-hour guidelines (Roy, 1972: 516). We are most interested here in those circumstances which approximate this latter form.

As Roy enumerates the advantages and disadvantages of contract farming it (1972: 9–11) becomes abundantly clear that the farmer's loss is the processor's gain and vice versa. Where the farmers avoid the risks of the market, they also lose the opportunities which it may provide.

A bargaining relationship develops in this situation where the farmer's interests and the contractor's interests may be as much at odds as those of factory workers and factory owners. The farmers' incomes are set by the contract and the extent of their bargaining power in contract negotiation becomes vital. Roy notes that "the contract farmer continues to suffer from lack of bargaining power" (1972: 11). This follows from the contractor's monopolization of the local/regional market.

Unfortunately, historical comparison of contract production is difficult because of inadequate attention by the Census Bureau. It has collected data on contract production only between 1964–74, and this is not presented in comparable form.

Across Wisconsin in 1974, 7.6 percent of farmers worked under some contract, with vegetable production leading the way. Far more contracts were used in production of vegetables for processing (2,677) than in vegetables for fresh market (60). In the former category, 45.5 percent (1,219) were production contracts with, mostly, private processors (84.6 percent). Very few were with cooperatives. That the number of contracts (2,677) for vegetables exceeds the number of predominantly vegetable farms (1,883) points not only to the heavy domination of vegetable producers by contract production but also shows that hundreds of farmers concerned primarily with other commodities have found it wise or necessary to contract some land to vegetable production.

Off-Farm Work

Steeves (1972) focused on off-farm work as the primary determinant of proletarianization. When off-farm work is wage labor, it clearly constitutes proletarianization. The complexity of the problem of off-farm work for the present purposes is twofold: (1) the nature and extent of dependence on off-farm work for household reproduction, and (2) the limitation of Wright's theoretical framework to analysis of only one occupation. This discussion will assume off-farm work to be salaried or wage labor and will not differentiate off-farm work in industrial or urban employment from labor on another farm.

The engagement in off-farm work may characterize two distinct sets of farmers ("hobby farmers" are omitted because their livelihood lies elsewhere). Off-farm work may supplement the income of persons trying to establish themselves in agriculture, particularly young farmers whose parents are still actively engaged in farming. On the other hand, off-farm work may supplement the income of established farmers, particularly those suffering temporarily low returns or who are in the process of being pushed out of farming; and the off-farm work is an attempt to resist complete proletarianization. Cutting across both categories is the process of differentiation within the household.

Dependence on off-farm work may not, of course, always fall upon the male head, whom we usually designate as "the farmer." Farm women may increasingly be subject to proletarianization in that they subsidize, if not actually provide, the means for the reproduction of an otherwise simple commodity form of production. Similarly, children may fulfill this function. Clearly, family life cycle is an extremely important factor in analysis of off-farm work as an indicator of proletarianization. The possibly transitional character of off-farm work may negate the effects of this economic activity at the political and ideological levels as will the differentiation within the household where functions of the reproduction process are distributed unevenly between simple commodity and capitalist modes of production. For the purposes at hand, we are interested in off-farm work entered into as a means of (re)producing or attempting to (re)produce simple commodity production. We are particularly concerned with those situations in which such dependence becomes permanent, which proletarianizes either husband or wife for the duration of their adult life.

Wright's dependence on occupation to determine class location raises problems for the analysis of off-farm work. When a farmer takes off-farm work, he has two occupations and thus, in this scheme, two locations. Each position may be a pure class position with no inherently contradictory quality. A farmer may, for instance, be a simple commodity producer, while the off-farm work may be proletarian. If we are working toward a class model that will eventually incorporate the political and the ideological levels, then we must, at this point, change the unit of analysis and abandon the "position" in favor of the "person." In the last instance, positions do not carry consciousness, but people do.

Problems appear, of course, with a positional analysis even at the economic level. Assuming the proletarian character of off-farm work, we necessarily conclude that farmers suffer an appropriation of surplus value in the sale of their labor power and that they control neither investments, means of production, nor their own labor process in their off-farm work. On the other hand, this same off-farm work may be a means by which they are able to avoid debt, tenancy, or contractual integration. In short, the off-farm work may maintain a 'separate' sphere of agricultural production in which they surrender neither surplus value nor control over their means of agricultural production, farm investments, or farm work; but this is only at the price of selling their labor power elsewhere.

If we take the person as the unit of analysis, off-farm work must be considered to move the farmer into a contradictory class location between petty bourgeoisie and proletariat.

Following World War II there has been a fairly steady increase in off-farm employment among Wisconsin farmers, falling slightly only in 1974 during a period of high farm prices. At the end of WW II, 22 percent of Wisconsin farmers had some off-farm work. By 1978, 46 percent were employed off the farm. Full-time off-farm work (more than 200 days) increased from 7 percent in 1945 to 28 percent in 1978.

A trend toward increasing off-farm work existed across the state, with the exceptions of Milwaukee and Vilas counties. The greatest increases occurred in those counties which had low percentages of off-farm work such as the highly productive southwestern counties. In 1950, only 12 counties had more than 25 percent of their farmers employed off the farm. These 12 counties were mostly in the northern tier and near Milwaukee. By 1974, only 12 counties had less than 25 percent off-farm employment. Six of these were the southwestern counties which, though doubling or tripling their off-farm work since 1950, still had relatively low percentages of off-farm employment.

An interesting issue is the variation in off-farm work between dairy farmers and others. In 1974, for instance, 45.5 percent of Wisconsin cash grain farmers had off-farm employment while only 11.5 percent of dairy farmers had off-farm employment and vegetable farmers had 47.9 percent off farm employment. Presumably dairy farmers are at a considerable disadvantage in obtaining off-farm work. To the extent that dairy farmers are prevented, by the nature of their work, from supplementing their total family income with off-farm employment they are somewhat left behind in their standard of living unless dairy prices were to rise enough to meet the difference, an event which is very much in the hands of the federal government via milk marketing orders and prices. While one might suppose that an increase in off-farm opportunitites might tempt dairy producers to sell their herds and switch to cash grain or some other field crop, we must consider that both dairying and off-farm employment provide a steady and sure income which is a highly valued situation in the more risky, up-and-down grain markets.

Hired Labor

In much Marxian analysis, hired labor is the singular form in which capitalism is expected to penetrate agriculture, and it is limited only by the extent to which mechanization (which can be understood as dead wage labor) may displace the need for such labor.

The analytical perspective taken here examines the farmer who hires labor. This is the focus of Bell and Newby (1974) in their analysis of the place of farmers in British class structure. Unlike the four relationships discussed above, the hiring of labor constitutes a contradictory class location between petty bourgeoisie and capitalist rather than between petty bourgeoisie and proletariat. This location, too, varies with the extent of dependence on hired labor. Marx speaks of the capitalist "who operates on such a small scale that he resembles those self-employed producers" (1977:600). The critical indicator of this variation must be the ratio of involvement in the total direct production between farmers and their hired workers. Direct production must here be considered manual labor. The farmer who engages only in mental labor, which leaves the manual tasks to wage workers, represents the typical division of the capitalist labor process in control of investments, means of production, and labor process. What is distinct from modern capitalism in this case is the unity of ownership and management (control) in one person.

Wright's identification of this contradictory class location as "small employers" needs no further clarification for agriculture other than to note the often temporary or seasonal character of such employment rather than a small number of workers. At the present level of analysis, this distinction is of little consequence. The extraction of surplus value from direct producers (wage workers) in coincidence with the control of all three aspects of production by the farmer (owner) constitutes a transformation of simple commodity production to capitalist production. This transformation is here considered complete when all labor productive of surplus value is labor hired by the farmers, and none of it is performed by themselves.

One way of looking at the distinction between petty bourgeois and capitalist production is to examine the percentage of total cost of production which is paid to labor.[7] The percentage of production costs going to labor for the entire state of Wisconsin declined slightly from 6.7 percent in 1969 to 5.7 percent in 1974. The dairy farm sector was below this figure, with only 4.4 percent of total production expenses going for labor. Hired labor in fruit and nut production required the highest percentage of labor expenses (28.2 percent) with vegetable production taking 15.9 percent and "other field crops" taking 14.4 percent of production expenses. Tobacco production costs included 10.3 percent for labor while other major commodity groupings were near the state average.

Tobacco farms tended toward higher percentages of farms using hired labor across the series of censuses. This hired labor is clearly the most seasonal use of hired labor with over 100 seasonal workers for every regular worker in 1969, 1974, and 1978. In 1974, 91.1 percent of the hired labor on tobacco farms worked less than 25 days. The dependence on hired labor dropped off in both "other field crops" and "vegetable and melon" farms. The seasonality of such work also declined in relation to other farm types. These commodity groups have the lowest percentage of highly seasonal labor. Clearly, this reflects the mechanization of harvest operations, a development which not only diminished the need for hired laborers but also transferred the hiring function over to processors. The snap bean harvester, for example, reduced Wisconsin State Employment Service total placements from 92,000 in 1954 to 18,000 in 1960. Sweet corn harvest, too, came to be mechanized during the early 1950s (Wisconsin State Employment Service Farm Labor Report, 1960). With mechanization, farmers themselves no longer hired the labor but, under contract with processors, were often relieved of harvest responsibility. For most producers of such crops, machinery is far too expensive to purchase for use on one farm once a year. Processors, however, make more profitable use of such equipment by coordinating contract production on many farms.[8]

Dairy farms have tended to increase their employment of hired labor relative to other farm types. This increased dependence on hired labor is also increasingly characterized by seasonal employment (most likely in baling hay and other harvest activity). Throughout the 1950s the censuses (1950, 1954, and 1959) show slightly more use of regular hired labor than seasonal hired labor on farms employing labor. By 1969, however, there were more than twice as many seasonal laborers as regular workers on dairy farms. That characteristic appears to hold through the 1978 census. In 1974, 61.4 percent of dairy hired laborers worked less than 25 days. The intensification of production in dairy has more generally been through increased productivity per cow (capital intensification) rather than increased herd size which would require additional labor.

In coincidence with national trends the use of migrant labor has diminished considerably over the time period in question. In the post-Bracero program period, the number of migrant workers peaked at 11,700 in 1967. By 1972, only 5,650 were so employed. Beginning in the early

1970s, the declines in migrant labor were accelerated by increasing local unemployment rates. Migrant jobs, both in the field and in the processing plants were increasingly being filled by unemployed and underemployed local men and women.

The more explicit role of the state in the agricultural hired labor market consists of two functions: 1) to provide research and development for the mechanization of agricultural production and failing that; 2) to coordinate the recruitment and supply of labor to the fields and processing plants. The former function is a story unto itself better told elsewhere (e.g. Hightower, 1973) though we may note here that mechanization itself is also a manifestation of the process of formal rationalization. The dependency on migrant labor impeded precise calculability within the production/harvest process. Mechanization, even if more expensive, at least allows a constant cost to enter the calculation, rather than risking the variability characteristic of dependence on migrant labor. Labor recruitment and supply by the state also facilitates the reduction of uncertainty and thus the ability to rationalize production.

AN ECONOMIC MODEL OF
AGRICULTURAL CLASS STRUCTURE

Marxian analysis often contains, sometimes implicitly, a teleology concerning the destruction of simple commodity production and the movement of these persons toward a polarized class structure where the capitalist class faces only the proletariat. The concept 'contradictory class location' developed in Wright's class analysis constitutes a break from this tradition insofar as such locations are not merely transitional but have effects or perhaps even some degree of permanence in capitalist social formations. Having discussed the five social relations of production in isolation, the complex reality of the current conjuncture requires that we take Wright's "contradictory class location" one step further: to the contradictory combination of contradictory class locations.

There are no reasons to believe that any of the class relations described above are mutually exclusive of one another in agricultural production. This is not problematic with respect to combinations of relations that constitute proletarianization; their interaction simply indicates a greater extent of proletarianization. But the possibility also exists that one may move simultaneously toward both capitalist and proletarian locations. This is not only held to be possible but, in some historical circumstances, probable. The engagement in debt or rent, for instance, often constitutes an expansionary process. This expansion may coincide with the use of hired labor. In this case, the surplus value appropriated in the form of interest or rent is no longer an exploitation of farmers but of their hired

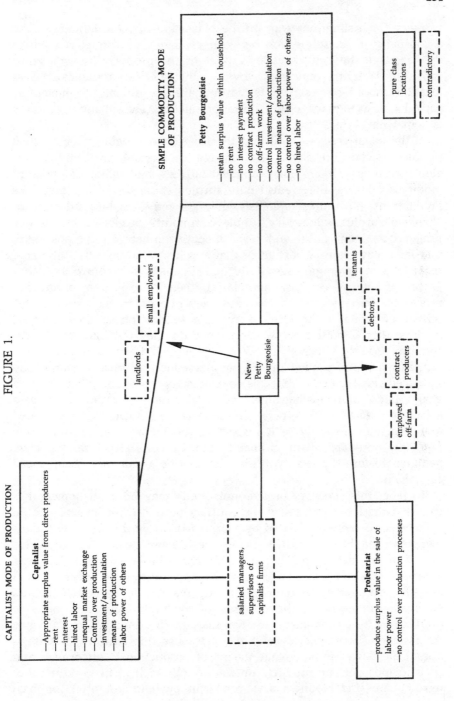

FIGURE 1.

CAPITALIST MODE OF PRODUCTION

Capitalist
—Appropriate surplus value from direct producers
—rent
—interest
—hired labor
—unequal market exchange
—Control over production
—investment/accumulation
—means of production
—labor power of others

SIMPLE COMMODITY MODE
OF PRODUCTION

Petty Bourgeoisie
—retain surplus value within household
—no rent
—no interest payment
—no contract production
—no off-farm work
—control investment/accumulation
—control means of production
—no control over labor power of others
—no hired labor

pure class
locations

contradictory

small employers

landlords

New Petty
Bourgeoisie

debtors

tenants

contract
producers

employed
off-farm

salaried managers,
supervisors of
capitalist firms

Proletariat
—produce surplus value in the sale of
labor power
—no control over production processes

workers. Such situations warrant the placement of these farmers nearer a contradictory class location between capitalist and proletariat where they manage the bank's money-capital or the property owner's land-capital. In Wright's framework, however, that specific contradictory class location should be reserved for farm managers directly employed by capitalist firms to manage agricultural production. The situation described is somewhat different.

In the usual case, we will find that the tenants, debtors, or contract producers who hire labor also engage in manual production tasks alongside their workers. Like capitalist farmers, but unlike simple commodity producers, they redistribute surplus value to the creditor. Like proletarians, but unlike capitalists, they are active in the production of alienated surplus value. Like simple commodity producers, but unlike proletarians, managerial and work incentive inhere in the possibility that they may retain a portion of that surplus value, which allow them more than the average wage. With the capitalists, they control the labor power of others. With the proletariat, their control over production processes, perhaps even the workers they hire, is immediately circumscribed by capital in the terms of credit, lease, or contract. These farmers fit none of the pure class locations, nor do they fall into any of the contradictory class locations in Wright's model. They move nearer the capitalist mode of production but simultaneously approach theoretically polarized classes. Even then, this contradictory trajectory retains a good deal of petty bourgeois baggage. This combination of contradictory class locations reflects a "new petty bourgeoisie." As such, it is considered to be an anomaly only with respect to the theory that presumes the historical necessity of an ultimately bipolar class structure. Far from being an historical anomaly, it may actually be a tendency of advanced capitalism.

To label this process "proletarianization" may be a misnomer. It is true that the labor process of the contract producer, for instance, could become completely dominated by a processor while the producer retains ownership of the land. Theoretically, he has not been deprived of his means of production, but this applies only if he is willing to fall back on mere subsistence, in which case he appears more as peasant than as petty bourgeois. Domination of the market by monopoly capital eliminates an essential characteristic of the petty bourgeois mode of production, free exchange on an open market. This domination constrains the farmer's "economic ownership," if we use this term as Poulantzos does: "the power to assign the means of production to given uses and so to dispose of the products obtained." (1974: 18) The conditions of tenancy and indebtedness also constrain or hold potential for such constraint on economic ownership while the contract may be seen as a mere formalization/legalization of the already existing subordinate relationship. We may say that such producers will never be fully proletarian; but neither will they be fully petty bourgeois. Wright's concept of contradictory class location makes apparent the contradictory nature of the producer's location while another term might obscure this important aspect of contrary roles.

If and when the petty bourgeois mode of production is destroyed, in what direction are the petty bourgeoisie pushed? Do they become capitalist farmers, proletarian or semi-proletarian farmers, or some contradictory combination of both? In the application of the theoretical scheme, using a sample of Wisconsin farmers (see Mooney, 1985), we find that there are many possible combinations of hired labor, contract production, debt, rent, and off-farm work. With these indicators we can operationalize our concept of purely (traditional) petty bourgeois producers as those who have no off-farm work, no hired labor, no contract, no debt, and no rent. We find that only 14.5 percent fall into this category.

Defining the capitalist farmer as one who hires labor but has no characteristics of what we have defined as indicators of proletarianization (no rent, no contract, no off-farm employment, and no debt) our survey found only 3.9 percent, most (17 of 20) of whom hired three or more months of labor. Lastly, our operationalization of the greatest extent of proletarianization includes those who have no hired labor, but do have debt, contracts, rents and off-farm employment. Obviously, as in the case of movement toward capitalist location, this is a matter of degree as debt, rent, off-farm work and dependency on contracts may vary considerably. We find no farmers in our survey with more than $5,000 farm debt, more than 100 days of off-farm work, full tenant status, contract production and no hired labor.

Thus, the three ideal-typical locations account for only 18.4 percent of farmers. The hypothesis that the destruction of petty bourgeoisie yields neither a capitalist nor proletarian agriculture is supported by this data. It does appear to create farmers who, as individuals, remain only semi-proletarian or who bring together contradictory tendencies of movement toward both capitalist and proletarian location.

EXTENSIONS AND LIMITATIONS OF THE MODEL

Before turning to a discussion of the limitations of the above model it is important to examine some of the advantages gained. While the model focuses on relations rather than gradations as constitutive of class categories, it also recognizes the variability of dependency within each class relation. The extent of integration into capitalist class relations should be quantifiable. Such quantification should be relatively accessible, since the Census Bureau and USDA publish data on each of these five relations, allowing analysis of historical trends. This approach leads us away from assuming the nonpenetration of capital in agriculture. We can no longer accept the assurance of the USDA that the family farm is "the mainstay of the farm economy" (Nikolitch, 1965). The focus on relations of production demystifies such appearances. Much effort has been expended discovering "obstacles" that explain capitalism's supposed inability to penetrate an agriculture which this model would suggest has already been penetrated. The model formulated here is intended to lay the basis for analysis of the "detours" that capital develops to circumvent such barriers. Following Davis' work on the exploitation of the propertied laborer (1980) and Vogeler's book *The Myth of the Family Farm* (1981) this model begins to answer Kautsky's question: in what ways is capital taking hold of agriculture . . . and establishing new forms?

A critical limitation of the model is, of course, the reduction of class to the economic level or to "class-in-itself." Only through analysis of the relation of the political and ideological to the specified class relations can we begin to approach knowledge of class formation and class struggle. The present model merely allows the formulation of the limits that the economic structure imposes on the development of "class-for-itself."

It is necessary to take the concept and analysis of class formation beyond the issue of production relations with an inquiry into the political and ideological dimensions. The prior presentation of class has carried a theoretical reductionism in its focus on the relations of production. As Thompson writes: "It is easy to suppose that class takes place, not as historical process, but inside our own heads . . . models or structures are theorized that are supposed to give us objective determinants of class: for example, as expressions of differential productive relations" (1978: 147).

Thompson also notes, however, that such static structural analysis is both valuable and essential. His fear is that it will lead toward a "determining logic" and away from historical investigation. In this sense, our preoccupation with the relations of production is an artifact of our manner of presentation. Though admittedly a focus on the relations of production was intended, we always expected to arrive at the analysis of political and ideological elements. More than that, it was an interest in the active struggles of agricultural producers (i.e. the role of agency) in reproducing/transforming their worlds that led us to this point.

Methodologically, we have been following Thompson all along: "If we return to class as a historical category, we can see that historians can employ the concept in two different senses: (a) with reference to real, empirically observable correspondent historical content; (b) as a heuristic or analytic category to organize historical evidence which has a very much less direct correspondence" (1978: 148).

In the latter sense, we have often employed the concept of class as equivalent to the relations of production (i.e. primarily as an analytic category to organize historical evidence). Through that compilation of the history and nature of the relations of production we are now in a position to move to the more complex task of assessing class as it "eventuates as men and women *live* their productive relations, and as they *experience* their determinate situations, within the *ensemble* of the social relations, with their inherited culture and expectations, and as they handle these experiences in cultural ways" (Thompson, 1978: 150).

Political and Ideological Implications

The model for most recent work on agrarian political behavior has been *The American Voter* (Campbell, et al., 1960). Their chapter on "Agrarian Political Behavior" has become a standard reference point for research.

The first characteristic of the farm vote described by Campbell, *et al.*, (1960) is its volatility: "In the national elections since 1948, the two-party vote division among farmers outside the South has fluctuated more sharply than it has within any of the other major occupation groupings." (1960: 402).

This variability in the division of the vote combines with a particularly irregular level of voter turnout to create an extremely volatile electorate. Campbell, *et al.* reject the importance of "mechanical" explanations (such as isolation from national events, poor transportation to polls or increased personal contacts with candidates) for this phenomenon. Instead, they claim that: "a large part of this peculiarity must reside in a state of mind, a total posture toward the ongoing political process that survives changes in external aspects of his life situation" (1960: 408).

This variability is, somewhat cautiously, ascribed to a peculiar economic sensitivity of farmers: "Farm people who voted counter to their normal party affiliation in the 1956 election appear to have done so as a function of their immediate economic situation . . . the economic element in the farmer's partisan choice seems reliably documented" (1960: 419).

The tendency of Campbell, *et al.* to focus on the psychology of the rural vote rather than objective conditions led them to reject arguments, such as Lipset's, that a peculiar economic sensitivity of farmers derives from their unique position in the social structure. Campbell, *et al.* write: "It seems psychologically unsound to believe that the farmer, when subjected to a given degree of economic pressure, suffers more intensely or is more motivated to act than the urban laborer. What is peculiar is not the sensitivity itself, rather, it is the manner in which *partisan meaning* is ascribed to economic pressure" (1960: 429–30).

Their contention is that farmers are "psychologically free" to vary their vote and split their ticket because they lack long-standing loyalty to political parties. This seems to beg the question. We must ask: Why do farmers lack such traditional ties to political parties? We return to Lipset's contention that this is due to farmers' occupation of a unique position in the economic structure. Lipset, however, may be right for the wrong reasons. He attributes such uniqueness to the farmers' insecurity (again, a psychologically-based explanation) in dependence on weather, state intervention in markets, etc. What is unique are the mix of the social relations of production (i.e. the mix of capitalist, manager and laborer in the petty bourgeoisie or the contradictory strains on producers in contradictory class locations). The two major parties base their ideological appeal on interests approximating (though certainly not identical with) those of the dominant classes. The farmers' interests, given this analysis of his/her economic class position, are only coincidentally on the agendas of these parties. This is what "frees" the farmer to variability in political behavior. It is also the basis for the appeal of third party solutions. As the authors of *The American Voter* write:

> It is an irony of almost epic proportions that political programs generated in the city on behalf of urban labor and tailored to its policy concerns often won warmer reception on the remote prairies in times of economic stress. The most successful attempt to build a third party for labor in the U.S., represented by the Socialist Party just after the turn of the century, appears to have attained the modest electoral pinnacle which it achieved not on the basis of urban labor support but largely from agrarian areas (Campbell, *et al.*, 1960: 422).

Not only do Campbell, *et al.* ignore the substance of such movements (i.e. do such parties appeal to the specific interests of farmers?) but they again beg the question by viewing the agrarian attraction of third parties as a consequence of their lack of integration into the two major parties. They assert that such behavior should fade as the farmer becomes better educated and a "more socialized political actor" (1960: 432).

They use similar reasoning to explain the apparently confused ideology of agrarian populations. In this case, they argue that farmers are the least likely political group in which "more than a handful" can comprehend the ideological program proposed by the elite (1960: 436).

Again, we would argue that the contradictory forces of their class relations negate acceptance of 'pure' ideologies while enhancing the development of ideology that appears, to the analyst, as logically inconsistent and incoherent. Lipset is referenced in support of their assertion of the incoherence of agrarian ideology and "the paucity of anything resembling ideological comprehension" (Campbell, *et al.*, 1960: 437): "The farmers struck out at random at the most visible economic evils that affected them. They opposed the banks, the railroads, the wheat-elevator companies and the shortage of money, but they saw each as an evil in itself, not as part of the total economic system" (1960: 438).

First, it hardly seems fair to characterize the selection of such targets as "random" since they were, in fact, the immediate manifestations of more fundamental opponents (e.g. finance capital and monopoly 'market' capital). Second, it is not clear how such lashing out is different from organized labor's preoccupation with management, inflation, wages, etc. rather than with the transformation of the total economic system. Weber observed this general tendency:

> Class antagonisms that are conditioned through the market situations are usually most bitter between those who actually and directly participate as opponents in price wars. It is not the rentier, the share-holder and the banker who suffer the ill will of the worker, but almost exclusively the manufacturer and the business executives who are the direct opponents of workers in wage conflicts. This is so in spite of the fact that it is precisely the cash boxes of the rentier, the share-holder, and the banker into which the more or less unearned gains flow, rather than into the pockets of the manufacturers or of the business executives (1978: 931).

Wisconsin has not escaped this history of a volatile farm electorate. Epstein's study (1958) of the post-war politics of Wisconsin and Adamany's (1963) follow-up study of the 1960 election provide evidence that Wisconsin farmers are ever-ready to switch their partisan vote from election to election. Epstein writes of Wisconsin farmers: "If farmers are capable, in favorable circumstances, of being more Republican than any other group in the state, they can also, as in 1954, be much less Republican than voters in all groups of cities except those over 50,000. This volatility gives the farm vote an importance in Wisconsin politics beyond that indicated by mere numbers" (1958: 72).

In four gubernatorial elections, Epstein found "great fluctuation of the Democratic percentage from year to year." The Wisconsin farm vote dropped more sharply than "any other place category in 1952" and "rose appreciably more in 1954" (1958: 71). Epstein raised the issue of economic sensitivity by arguing that while economic issues may explain the shift in 1954, the shift in 1952 appears unrelated to economic matters. Epstein's analysis suggests that much of the Republicanism often attributed to the farm population is actually an effect of Republican strength in the small cities and villages of rural Wisconsin. The farm vote was more Democratic than the small city and village vote, with the exception of the strong shift in 1952 toward the Republican candidate, which Adamany suggests was a vote against the Democrats' Korean War (1963: 153). The significance of Epstein's findings is not only that the volatility of the farm vote extends into state politics (i.e. gubernatorial elections), but that Wisconsin appears to parallel national (non-South) tendencies discussed above. As Epstein concludes: "Even the temporary deviation of farmers from Republican voting preferences represents significantly different behavior from that of small cities and villages, and, for that matter, from that of medium-sized cities as well" (1958: 72).

Adamany's (1963) replication of Epstein's study analyzed national elections (Senate, President), which we would expect to more strongly reflect the economic sensitivity of farmers, insofar as farm policy is generally federal policy. Adamany's findings corroborate Epstein's in demonstrating that "the farm vote is the most changeable bloc in Wisconsin politics" (1963: 152), though he also claims that his "purer sample" may indicate an even "greater general Democratic leaning among farm voters" (1963: 151).

Campbell, *et al.* held that as farm people become more educated and politically socialized the volatility would decline. Though we cannot duplicate Epstein's and Adamany's analysis, we can gain some approximation of the continued volatility of the farm vote by examining the vote of non-metro (non-SMSA) counties in the 1968 and 1976 presidential elections. These two elections were particularly close in Wisconsin.

In 1968, Nixon carried 48 non-metro counties while Humphrey won only 11 such counties. Nixon also won nine of 13 SMSA counties. Thus the Republicans carried 81 percent of the non-metro counties and 69 percent of the metropolitan counties. In 1976, Ford carried eight of 13 SMSA counties (only Ozaukee County went Democratic) for 62 percent of the metropolitan counties. By contrast, the Democrats (who had won in only 11 non-metro counties in 1968) won in 35 non-metro counties while the Republican candidate won in only 24 non-metro counties (one-half the number of counties won in 1968).

The weakness of this rather rough analysis is, of course, the inclusion of the non-farm population in the non-metro county vote totals. We also know, however, that it is the small town and small city population that is a source of Republican strength. In addition, between 1968 and 1976 there was considerable growth in many non-metro counties which were adjacent to SMSA counties. Elimination of such adjacent counties and focusing only on non-adjacent counties gives a better estimate of the farm vote. In this case, too we find a complete inversion of partisan voting from 1968 to 1976. Nixon won 24 of 31 (77 percent) non-adjacent counties in 1968. Carter, however, won 22 (71 percent) of those same counties in 1976. Though we cannot contend, with the same reliability of Epstein or Adamany, that the farm vote alone accounts for this volatility, we can see that rural Wisconsin counties as a whole are still far more volatile than more urbanized counties.

Adamany drew the following conclusion from his analysis of the farm vote:

> Despite the erratic nature of farm voting, its tendency to be somewhat more Democratic than the state may indicate that the Democrats will be serious contenders for statewide power on a more-or-less permanent basis. Their hard-core strength in the large cities is coupled with considerable strength in the farm areas to make Wisconsin an area of serious two party competition. At the same time, the highly changeable nature of farm voting may spell the difference between success and failure for both parties (1963: 161).

Such observations affirm our contention that, though farmers may appear as peripheral actors in the class structure, their volatile role at the political level of the class struggle may, to the same extent, be crucially important to ultimate outcomes. As Epstein writes: "The farm vote as here defined comprises less than one-fifth of the total state vote. This proportion is not what is responsible for the lavish attention which politicians of both parties give to farmers and farm issues. Rather it is the demonstrated capacity of Wisconsin farmers for wholesale switching of party allegiance" (1958: 72).

The adaptation of the notion of contradictory class location to agriculture provides a novel explanation of the volatility of the farm vote. Since nearly all Wisconsin farmers can be seen as "cut in half" with respect to class location (whether they be petty bourgeois or in contradictory class locations), we may argue that they are thus rendered relatively (as compared with non-farm voters) autonomous from allegiance to parties which reflect a representation of the immediate interests of either major class. While the extreme volatility itself is evidence for this contention, this autonomy is further evidenced by findings which indicate both the significance of debt's prediction of independence from identification with either party and the effect of off-farm works in the integration of farmers into the Democratic Party (Mooney, 1985). The final interpretation of this matter is unclear. Perhaps the petty bourgeoisie and those in contradictory class locations simply cannot find their fundamental interests to be comprehensively included in the agenda of either major party. On the other hand, it may be argued that people in such locations have no fundamental interests, as a class or even as a group. In either case, the effects may be similar: volatility and independence in voting behavior, often in coincidence with single-issue voting. This explanation makes more sociologically plausible previous psychologically-based explanations, such as peculiar economic sensitivities or insecurities with respect to weather and/or markets.

The establishment of the volatile character of the farm vote necessitated analysis of the farm vote as a unit (in comparison with other voting groups). While the economic sensitivity thesis justifies such analysis, farmers are not one homogeneous group. Some authors of the research discussed above are aware of this matter. Campbell, *et al.*, for instance, write: "The status polarization of the farm community as a function of both stable and short-term differences in economic fortune illustrates with great clarity the folly of treating the farm vote as unitary. . . . The farmer appears to respond to his own economic situation with little reference to the manner in which others in the same occupational category are faring" (1960: 419–20).

Similarly, Knoke and Henry note that "on most issues the rural and urban populations each has almost as much internal differentiation in attitudes as does the total population" (1977: 50). Thus, it is also necessary to examine political and ideological differentiation among farmers. Following the above model we focus on the part of the analysis (Mooney, 1985) which pertains to the effects of the social relations of production in determining political and ideological differentiation.

Perhaps the most striking finding in the analysis of politics and ideology is the inconsistency of effects of those relations which, at the economic level, were theorized as 'proletarianized' relations. At times, relations theorized as approaching proletarianization had the same effects as relations theorized as leading toward capitalist location. This was the case, for instance, in the positive relationship between political participation and both indebtedness and use of hired labor. In other cases, relations which shared the economic characteristics of proletarianization led to opposite effects at the level of politics and ideology. This was the case concerning both political ideology and party identification. While tenancy lent support for state intervention, both off-farm work and indebtedness were negatively related to such support. Similarly, where debt led farmers away from identification with either party toward an independent status, off-farm work led toward identification with the Democratic Party. The significance of such findings is, of course, that where the concept of proletarianization is defined only at the level of economy it is too general and abstract to assist in the interpretation of the development of class as it appears in the complex interplay of forces in the lives and struggles of concrete historical actors.

Similarly, Gillespie's (1981) adaptation of Mooney (1978) to Census Bureau data on New York agriculture contains a criticism that the above model reflects an 'additive bias' in that the indicators of differentiation are indistinct. In the analysis of the social formation at the economic level, the investigation of proletarianization must be made more concrete. While each of the relations analyzed above share the criteria for proletarianization established by Braverman (1974) and Wright (1978), it is also true that each relation remains qualitatively distinct in practice. This distinction could be made institutionally: a landlord is not a bank nor a processor. This differentiation would open analysis of the unique aspects of each relation and perhaps begin to address the issue of selection among alternative forms of exploitation. Such analysis would benefit from the examination of "market situation" to use Weber's term. This responds, I think, to the gist of Gillespie's critique: that there are, in fact, differences between these relations, which the general concept 'proletarianization' glosses over but which are revealed at a more concrete level of analysis, as we have seen in the above analysis of politics and ideology.

A more fundamental criticism concerns not only the concrete differences between the various relations but *within* them. The problem appears to begin with the assumption, which Marxism often shares with neo-classical economics, that economic behavior is based on what Weber calls "formal rationality" (i.e. that people enter into each of these relations under a calculation of the optimal financial profitability, given their situation with respect to land, labor, credit, and commodity markets). Extended interviews with Wisconsin farmers reveal quite divergent goal orientations. Where one farmer may engage in a relationship of indebtedness in the hopes of ultimately accumulating profit (a capitalist end), another farmer may enter into debt in the hopes of adapting technology that will enhance skill development as a farmer (a petty bourgeois or proletarian end). In other words, the same objective relationship may be entered into with quite diverse implications for (subjective) class location. The examination of objective behavior is inconclusive with regard to the ends toward which entry into these relationships is oriented. I have suggested elsewhere (Mooney, 1983) the significance of Weber's concepts of rationality and rationalization for this task.

Research is needed which will examine class formation not as "an effect of an ulterior structure, of which men are not the makers but the vectors" (Thompson, 1978a: 46) but as an active effort of farmers to affect that structure. Such analysis lays the balance of the examination of class formation in the lap of what Giddens defined as "agency" (1980). Agency is not, of course, a sufficient condition for consideration of a group as a fully formed class. It is, however, considered here as a necessary condition. When struggle focuses on transformation/defense of the relations of production it becomes class struggle. Further, when participants are aware that their common concern is with the relations of production and their common interest is in transforming/defending those relations we have complete class formation (class consciousness).

This theoretical orientation is consistent with Thompson:

> In my view, far too much theoretical attention (much of it plainly a-historical) has been paid to 'class,' and far too little to 'class-struggle.' Indeed, class-struggle is the prior, as well as the more universal, concept. To put it bluntly: classes do not exist as separate entities, look around, find an enemy class and then start to struggle. On the contrary, people find themselves in a society structured in determined ways (crucially, but not exclusively, in productive relations), they experience exploitation (or the need to maintain power over those whom they exploit), they identify points of antagonistic interest, they commence to struggle around these issues and in the process of struggling they discover themselves as classes, they come to know this discovery as class-consciousness. Class and class-consciousness are always the last, not the first, stage in the real historical process. . . . All this squalid mess around us (whether sociological positivism or Marxist-structuralist idealism) is the consequence of the prior error: that classes exist, independent of historical relationship and struggle, and that they struggle because they exist, rather than coming into existence out of that struggle (1978: 149).

This chapter has provided a grounding in the ways in which midwestern farm people find their society structured, especially with respect to the social relations of production. It is hoped that analysis of the dynamic interaction between structure and agency will clarify the problem of class formation as a complex historical process involving economic structure as well as political and ideological formations. Further research might examine the ways in which that social structure influences the experience of exploitation and the specific historical conjunctures in which these forces coalesce to give rise to (or impede) certain forms of organization and struggle.

CONCLUSIONS

In a class analysis of Midwestern agriculture which focuses on the expropriation of surplus value and control over the labor process, it is difficult to avoid the fact that outside capital has increasingly penetrated and circumscribed the form of agricultural production traditionally known as the "family farm." The family must increasingly reach outside itself for credit/capital, land and labor. The simple commodity producer is constrained by monopolized markets and subject to exploitation by landlords, creditors, contractors, and rural industrialization. In short, we should revise our consideration of the Midwestern farmer as a simple commodity producer.

Application of Wright's neo-Marxist class structure model to the agriculture of the Midwestern United States provides a unique picture of capitalist development. Capitalist penetration has adapted to the peculiar "efficiencies" of family farm production by finding both new and thinly disguised old means of transforming this work into labor which is productive, for capital, of surplus value. The result is an agricultural production system in which class relations are neither fully petty bourgeois nor capitalist. Wright's notion of contradictory class location captures this phenomenon with particular accuracy. The possible permanence of such a structure calls into question the Marxist assumption of the historical necessity of a complete polarization of the petty bourgeoisie into either capitalists or proletariat. This teleology is further undermined by the appearance of a process in which traditional petty bourgeoisie move simultaneously toward both capitalist and proletarian locations. We referred to this class as the new petty bourgeoisie.

While this analysis has found little evidence of any unilinear pro-letarianization process *within* post-WW II Wisconsin agriculture, it has found, at the economic level, the development of an increasingly complex class structure as simple commodity production gives way to diverse forms of capitalist penetration. Though the economic concept of pro-letarianization fails to provide a basis for delineating consequent politics and ideology, it raises questions concerning the importance of the social relations of production to political and ideological struggle. The concept of rationalization may be more effective in explaining the historical transformations observed. We may argue, in fact, that rationalization encompasses the most significant aspects of proletarianization.

For the young Marx, the essence of the proletarianization process may be understood as the alienation of human beings from their work and its products, from each other and from themselves. Such forms of alienation are negated by the substantive rationality of craftship, which I have elsewhere (Mooney, 1983) shown to be possible, in general, only under simple commodity production. The incursion of formal rationality, which comes hand-in-hand with capitalist relations of production, how-ever, embraces such alienation:

Marx compared man in bourgeois society with the commodity, as a product of simple labor. For like a commodity, man assumes a questionable 'double

FIGURE 2.

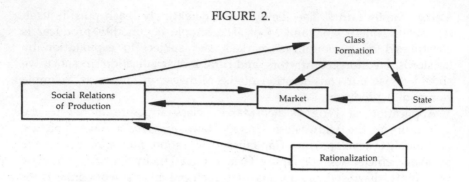

character': in economic terms a 'value form,' and a 'natural form.' As a commodity—that is, as incorporated labor—something is worth a certain sum of money, and in that context its natural characteristics are more or less irrelevant (Lowith, 1982: 73).

In the rationalization of agriculture through the development of formal rationality, the emphasis turns toward the 'value form' of one's work and away from the "natural" non-alienated forms of a labor process which is integrated internally, with respect to the division of labor (cooperation, unity of conception and execution), and externally, with respect to a 'way of life.' The formally rational farmer calculates the monetary value of his own labor, as in opportunity and/or transfer cost, and imposes on himself certain disciplines derived from the calculation of profit-maximization. Thus, the often-used phrase "being my own boss," while supposedly telling of independence subtly informs us of the self-alienation of such a prospect. The phrase itself suggests the setting up of "man against himself" in the objectification of his own labor. Marx foresaw the extent of such rationalization in capitalist society when he wrote: "Separation appears as the normal relation. . . . Separation is maintained as the relation even when one person unites the separate functions" (1969: 408–9). This commodification of one's own labor through the development of formal rationality is not, of course, an autonomous process. Its development is a dynamic, reciprocal process in which rationalization interacts with the social relations of production, the market, the state and even influences the forms which struggle takes.

Figure 2 briefly summarizes a more complete model (see Mooney, 1985). The social relations of production contribute, along with de- mographic and status factors, to the formation of class at the level of politics and ideology. That constellation of economic, political and ideological structures interfaces with both market and state structures which change with considerable, but not complete, autonomy from the agricultural structure. Class formation at the level of struggle must select forms appropriate to such conditions. These struggles may range from mere political appeals for direct assistance to political appeals for market interventions to direct economic action without recourse to political systems. Transformations of both market and state, whether they derive from autonomous development or as effects of the struggles of farmers themselves, facilitate the trend toward formally rational agriculture. This rationalization, in turn, transforms the social relations of production at which point the dynamic is begun anew. Transformations need not, of course, always follow this complex scheme. The social relations of production may be transformed, for instance, in mere interaction with the market. In large part, however, the more interesting and significant transformations will involve a complex interplay of all such forces in historical process.

The role of the state in this historical process is perhaps the most underdeveloped, yet fertile, ground for further research. Both Marx and Weber noted the fundamental importance of the State as a mechanism in the process of rationalizing agriculture. Marx wrote of the potential for the state bureaucracy to subjugate simple commodity production: "By its very nature, small holding property forms a suitable basis for an all-powerful and unnumerable bureaucracy. It creates a uniform level of relationship and persons over the whole surface of the land. Hence it also permits of uniform action from a supreme center on all points of this uniform mass" (1973: 482)

Likewise, Weber emphasized the importance of formal law, enforced by specialists trained in the service of that law, in creating the predictable environment required for capitalist development. An important question may be raised concerning the long-term role of the state in the rationalization process. Many have argued, including this very work, that the state plays a facilitating role in the development of a more rational agriculture. In the longer term, however, we may wonder if this role does not run up against the barrier imposed by democracy. Agricultural "policy," over the period in question, has not had the predictable consistency which the rationality of capitalism demands. On the contrary, it has been drastically altered, at times reversed, not only upon changes in administration, but also within administrations in response to other political developments. This barrier imposed by political democracy may be found at the most elemental levels of the state. The USDA's Hardin (1967), for example, argued for elimination of democratically elected county committees in order that the basic hierarchical principles of bureaucratic authority might be imposed. Similarly, we find the cooperatively organized Farm Credit System to be subjected to increasing constraints as it poses a potentially powerful form of economic democracy in an agriculture evermore dependent on credit-based production.

I am aware that I run against the grain of most recent work with the suggestion that the nature of the democratic state may impede, rather than facilitate, rationalization and capitalist development in agriculture. However, the present work itself is in large part a response to the literature which either assumes that: the family farm was "thriving" or the eventual destruction of simple commodity production in the agriculture of the advanced capitalist societies. Just as the present analysis has demonstrated a more complex historical development of class structure, so too, may comparative historical analysis of the role of the state in that development point to a more complex, perhaps even contradictory role.

NOTES

1. This paper was originally written in 1978 in conjunction with Professor Havens' sociology of agriculture study group. As such it circulated the rural sociological "underground" along with certain other chapters in this volume. A great deal has changed since that time, both in Midwestern agriculture and in terms of my own thinking. The emergence of the credit crisis in agriculture and my introduction to the work of Max Weber being, respectively, among the foremost changes. I have tried to update both data and analysis in the present version of that paper, while at the same time remaining true to the essence of the original. I must, however, refer the reader to my dissertation (Mooney, 1985) for elaboration of most of the material which is presented here in abridged form. Since 1978, many persons have read and commented on this model. However, I owe particular thanks to Max Pfeffer, Greg Hooks, Len Bloomquist for their comments on the most recent drafts of this paper. Finally, I must also express an intellectual debt to the work of Eric Olin Wright.

2. Traditional leftist analyses often posit farmers against workers, insofar as parity-level farm prices are alleged to increase the labor time necessary for the proletariat to buy food products (e.g. Kohl, 1982). However, as Carlson, et al. (1981) note, only 15 percent of the cost of food is attributable to the farmer. Increased wages among union employees in the tractor assembly and food processing plants impact the cost of food as severely as increased farm-level prices. In this sense, farmers, as producers of food, are no more opposed to the proletariat, in general, than workers who build houses are opposed to workers who make shoes.

3. Marxist analyses often deny that the "family farm" can survive in a capitalist world. Amin, for example, writes: "whereas the pre-capitalist formations were marked by a stable coexistence of different modes, linked together and arranged hierarchically, the capitalist mode tends to become exclusive, destroying all others" (1976: 22).

4. Why this pattern of particularly high tenancy rates in the southwestern counties of the state? Part of the explanation may be found deep in Wisconsin's past. The lead mines of the southwestern counties brought settlement to this part of the state earlier than the rest, except for the Milwaukee area. According to Nesbit (1973) with such settlement came agitation for land sales. Land could not be sold until it was surveyed and the surveying began from the southwestern corner of the state. These lands went on sale in 1834–35 during a period of intense buying by speculators in all parts of the public domain that became available for purchase. Nesbit estimates that speculators obtained 600,000 of the 878,014 acres of Wisconsin that were sold before 1836. However: "The full force of the speculative fever that consumed Michigan and Illinois land bypassed Wisconsin. In each of these states nearly 2,000,000 acres were sold in the year 1835 alone, sowing the seeds of future tenancy and land monopoly, particularly in the Illinois cornbelt" (1973: 143).

If Nesbit is right, the southwestern corner inherited a tenure pattern distinct from the rest of the state, for although the southeastern counties were surveyed in 1835, Presidents Jackson and Van Buren intervened to hold these sales off the market until 1839. The rest of the state escaped such speculation because surveyance either coincided with or followed both the Panic of 1837 (after which land sales plummeted) and the passage of an 1838 pre-emption act (which entitled squatters to claim land settled after December, 1833).

5. Ironically, while indebtedness is often pointed to as a factor in the mobilization of farm movements, it may, at the same time, place constraints on their potential for action. This is readily seen in movements stressing holding actions or strikes. If loan payments are due, one is forced to put at least some of his production on the market. The constraint of indebtedness was strong enough that many wheat farmers were led to demand nationalization of 'their' land and use-leasing by the State under the control of the political power. Lipset quotes: "Why should we worry about property rights, the farmers ask, when you suggest that they are striking at the fundamental economic structure . . . When your farm is covered with mortgages, your machinery attached by a chattel mortgage, your previous year's taxes unpaid, and your coming crop covered by a seed lien—and then you get no crop—you fail to see just what it is you may lose with the collapse of capitalism" (1950: 122).

6. This process suggests the possible relevence of dependency theory for analysis of capitalist development within the U.S. social formation. Read, for example dos Santos' (1970) account of 'Third World dependency which results from the imperialism of capitalist centers': "Trade relations are based on monopolistic control of the market, which leads to the transfer of surplus generated in the dependent countries, financial relations are, from the viewpoint of the dominant powers, based on loans and the export of capital, which permit them to receive interest and profits, thus increasing their domestic surplus and strengthening their control over the economies of the other countries. For the dependent countries these relations represent an export of profits and interest which carries off part of the surplus generated domestically and leads to a loss of control over their productive resources." If we think of these relations of

capitalist centers with the simple commodity mode of production rather than dependent nation states then we see clearly the similar dependency and exploitation of the family farm by capital. The imperialist/colonialist drive is merely turned inward toward those sectors of the capitalist social formation which are not yet fully integrated into the capitalist system.

7. The data available for historical analysis of this hired labor are, however, miserable. The Census of Agriculture is quite aware that farm labor data "are not fully comparable from one census to another primarily because of differences in the period to which they relate" (U.S. Bureau of the Census, XVIII, 1961).

The Statistical Reporting Service of the USDA also publishes data on farm labor. Its distinction of family workers and hired workers is, however, questionable. Paid family workers are counted as hired workers. For our purposes, this is problematic since kinship considerably modifies the relationship between employer and worker. The historical analysis is impeded by the possible (probable) fluctuation in the payment of family members.

8. Since a great deal of the hired labor involves those commodities produced under contract, this is a matter of no small importance in describing the nature of hired labor relations in Wisconsin agriculture. The presence or absence of a contract for the grower of a commodity requiring hired labor may not only mean access to a supply of workers but may influence the allocation of the operator's resources and his/her own control over the physical means of production. The allocation of a production unit (or a portion of it) to a specific commodity may depend upon the year-to-year renewal of a contract with the processor. The processor may exercise (and usually does) complete control over organizational decisions concerning the physical means of production.

REFERENCES

Adamany, David. "The 1960 Election in Wisconsin" unpublished Master's Thesis, Department of Political Science, University of Wisconsin-Madison 1963.

Amin, Samir. Unequal Development (New York: Monthly Review Press), 1976.

Bell, Colin and Howard Newby. "Capitalist Farmers in the British Class Structure" Sociologia Ruralis, Vol. 14, No. 1/2, 1974.

Bogue, Allan G. Money at Interest (Ithaca, New York: Cornell University Press), 1955.

Boulding, Kenneth. A Reconstruction of Economics (New York: Wiley and Sons), 1950.

Braverman, Harry. Labor and Monopoly Capital: The Degradation of Work in the Twentieth Century (New York: Monthly Review Press), 1974.

Campbell, Angus; Philip E. Converse; Warren E. Miller; and Donald E. Stokes. The American Voter (New York: John Wiley and Sons, Inc.), 1960.

Carlson, John E., Marie L. Lassey and William R. Lassey. Rural Society and Environment in America (New York: McGraw-Hill, Inc.), 1981.

Davis, John Emmeus. "Capitalist Agricultural Development and the Exploitation of the Propertied Laborer" in The Rural Sociology of the Advanced Societies, (ed.) Frederick Buttel and Howard Newby (Montclair, New Jersey: Allanheld, Osmun and Co.), 1980.

dos Santos, Theotonio. "The Structure of Dependence" in The Political Economy of Development and Underdevelopment (New York: Random House), 1973.

Dunaway, Bob and Alvin J. Morrow. Farm Lease Guide (Des Moines: Wallace-Homestead Book Co.), 1980.

Engels, Friedrich. "Revolution and Counter-Revolution in Germany," Marx and Engels: Selected Works, Vol. 1 (Moscow: Progress Publishers), 1973.

Epstein, Leon D. Politics in Wisconsin (Madison: University of Wisconsin Press), 1958.

Giddens, Anthony. New Rules of Sociological Method: A Positive Critique of Interpretive Sociologies (New York: Basic Books, Inc.), 1976.

Gillespie, Gilbert W., Jr. "Differentiation of family labor farmers in New York state: an analysis of census data," Paper presented at annual meeting of Midwest Sociological Society, Minneapolis, 1981.

Halcrow, Harold G. Food Policy for America (McGraw-Hill, Inc.), 1977.

Hardin, Charles M. "Food and Fiber in the Nation's Politics" Technical Papers Vol. 3 National Advisory Commission on Food and Fiber (Washington, D.C.: U.S. Government Printing Office), August 1967

Heffernan, William D. "Sociological Dimensions of Agricultural Structures in the U.S." Sociologia Ruralis, pp. 481–99, 1972.

Hightower, James. Hard Tomatoes, Hard Times (Cambridge, Mass.: Schenkman Publishing Company), 1973.

———. Eat Your Heart Out (New York: Vintage Books), 1976.

Kautsky, Karl. "Summary of selected parts of the agrarian question." Edited by Jarius Banaji in The Rural Sociology of the Advanced Societies. Frederick Buttel and Howard Newby (eds.), (Montclair, New Jersey: Allanheld, Osmun and Co.), 1980.

Knoke, David and Constance Henry. "Political Structure of Rural America" Annals of American Academy of Political and Social Science, Vol. 429, pp. 51–62, January 1977.

Kohl, Barbara A. "Whatever Happened to the American Agriculture Movement? Socio-Political Bases of Agrarian Neo-Populism" The Rural Sociologist, Vol. 2, No. 3, May 1982.

Lipset, Seymour Martin. Agrarian Socialism (Berkeley: University of California Press), 1971.

Lowith, Karl. Max Weber and Karl Marx. Edited by Tom Bottomore and William Outhwaite and translated by Hans Fantel (London: George Allen and Unwin), 1982.

Madden, J. Patrick. Economies of Size in Farming Agricultural Economic Report No. 107. United States Department of Agriculture Economic Research Service, 1967.

Marx, Karl. "The eighteenth brumaire of Louis Bonaparte." in Karl Marx and Frederick Engels: Selected Works, Vol. 1 pp. 394–487. Moscow: Progress Publishers, 1973.

———. Capital, Volume I (New York: International Publishers) 1977.

————. Theories of Surplus Value Parts I and III (London: Lawrence and Wishart), 1969.

Mirror. "Farm Loans: Where to Get One, How to Get One," pp.13–15, Winter, 1982.

Mooney, Patrick H. "Class Relations and Class Structure in the Midwest," unpublished manuscript, 1978.

————. "Toward a Class Analysis of Midwestern Agriculture," Rural Sociology, Vol. 48, No. 4, Winter, 1983.

————. "The Transformation of Class Relations in Wisconsin Agriculture: 1945-1982," Ph.D. Dissertation, Department of Sociology, University of Wisconsin-Madison, 1985.

Nelson, Aaron G.; Warren F. Lee and William G. Murray. Agricultural Finance, 6th edition (Ames: Iowa State University Press), 1973.

Nesbit, Robert C. Wisconsin: A History (Madison: University of Wisconsin Press), 1973.

Nikolitch, Radoje. "The adequate family farm-mainstay of the farm economy, "Washington, D.C.: USDA-ERS, Report 247, 1965.

Parker, Bill. "Agriculture" in Lance E. Davis, et al. American Economic Growth: An Economists History of the U.S. (NY: Harper and Row), NY, 1972.

Poulantzos, Nicos. Classes in Contemporary Capitalism (London: Verso Editions), 1974.

————. Political Power and Social Classes (London: Verso Editions), 1978.

Roy, Ewell Paul. Contract Farming and Economic Integration (Danville, Ill.: Interstate Printers and Publishers, Inc.), 1972.

Soltwedel, Norbert Louis. "The Managerial Participation by Landlord and Tenant Within the Framework of the Farm Lease" Master's Thesis (M.S.) University of Illinois, 1967.

Steeves, Allan D. "Proletarianization and Class Identification," Rural Sociology, Vol. 37, No. 1, pp. 5–26, March 1972.

Stinchcombe, Arthur. "Agricultural Enterprise and Rural Class Relations," American Journal of Sociology, Vol. 67, No. 2, September 1961.

Sublett, Michael D. Farmers on the Road: Interfarm Migration and the Farming of Noncontiguous Lands in Three Midwestern Townships, 1939–1969 (Chicago: University of Chicago Department of Geography Research Paper No. 168), 1975.

Sweezy, Paul M. The Theory of Capitalist Development (New York: Monthly Review Press), 1942.

Thompson, E.P. The Poverty of Theory (New York: Monthly Review Press), 1978.

————. "Eighteenth Century English Society: Class Struggle Without Class? Social History, Vol. 3, No. 2, pp. 133–165, May 1978.

United States Bureau of the Census; Census of Agriculture Wisconsin State and County Data, 1950, 1954, 1959, 1964, 1969, 1974, 1978, 1982.

Vogeler, Ingolf. The Myth of the Family Farm: Agribusisess Dominance of U.S. Agriculture (Boulder: Westview Press), 1981.

Weber, Max. Economy and Society edited by Guenther Roth and Claus Wittich (Berkeley: University of California Press), 1978.

Wisconsin State Employment Service. Farm Labor Report annual series 1959-1972 (Madison: Rural Industries Division of the Industrial Commission of Wisconsin); after 1966 (Madison: Farm Labor Service, Division of Wisconsin Department of Industry, Labor and Human Relations).

Wright, Erik Olin. Class, Crisis and the State (London: New Left Books), 1978.

8
Immigration Policy and Class Relations in California Agriculture[1]

Max J. Pfeffer

INTRODUCTION

Citizens of Mexico have been a potential source of labor for growers* in the southwestern U.S., particularly California, since the Mexican Revolution of 1910. In fact, large numbers of Mexicans have been employed in California agriculture since that time (Samora, 1971: p. 18).

The existence of a large reserve of available Mexican workers is a varied and complex issue. Mexico's economy has been one of the most rapidly expanding economies in Latin America. Rapid economic expansion since the revolution has broken the semi-feudalistic bondage of the Mexican peasantry, resulting in migration to urban industrial centers in Mexico and the U.S. border. While the existence and perpetuation of a large surplus population in Mexico is an important issue, it will not be the focus of this chapter. Rather, I will focus on the harvest work force in California fruit and vegetable production.

California is the leading agricultural state in the U.S. in terms of farm sales and is the largest employer of farm labor. Fruit and vegetable production is highly labor-intensive and employs as much as three-fourths of all seasonal farm workers in California. In 1980 California produced over 40 percent of the of fruits and vegetables produced in the entire U.S.

Agriculture in California is characterized by highly specialized crop production. In the words of Lloyd Fisher: "the dominant feature of California agriculture is the extraordinary diversity of the crops it

---

*The term grower is used throughout this study to refer to capitalist farmers. The term is useful in emphasizing that farmers are capitalists who own and control the means of production and employ workers but have special concerns arising from the nature of the production process in which they are engaged.

produces, and the specialization of individual farms within the pattern of diversity (1953: p. 1)." Harvest operations in a geographical area characterized by specialized crop production as well as by a number of crops ripening at similar times call for the employment of an extremely large work force for very short periods of time.

California growers have maintained such a harvest work force for almost a century by exploiting farm workers from a variety of national origins. These nationalities have included Chinese, Japanese, Filipino, Mexican and others (see McWilliams, 1971). Mexican workers have been an important element in California's farm work force since World War II in particular. Since that time, Mexican workers undoubtedly have been the most important foreign element of the harvest work force in California crop production. The focus of this chapter will be on the relationship between the labor process in crop production and Mexican workers employed in such production.

The characteristics of the labor process in crop production place constraints on the forms of control growers must exert over workers for profitable completion of the harvest. Controls over workers within the labor process commonly exercised by capitalists in industries other than agriculture are not suited to crop production. The inappropriateness of otherwise common forms of control over workers is due to the peculiarities of crop production. Thus, growers have sought and been offered more directly political forms of control over workers. These political forms of control have been exercised by the U.S. government. The actualization of these controls has changed over the past several decades. In this discussion I will argue that, while the particular manifestations of these political forms of control may have changed, labor requirements in crop production have remained stable. The varying manifestations of directly political forms of control over workers merely reflect different strategies on the part of the U.S. government to insure the existence of a work force having characteristics consistent with the labor requirements of crop production, given changes in the prevailing political climate.

THE LABOR PROCESS IN CROP PRODUCTION

The labor requirements of crop production are defined by a general characteristic of such production: there is a disjuncture between production time and labor time (Marx, Volume 2, 1967: p. 241). Unlike other industries, where production is continuous, bringing in returns to capital on a regular basis, the returns to investment in crop production are realized only infrequently, that is, at harvest time. Labor time is concentrated in the harvest. It is the direct production of commodities, the sale of which allows for the realization of value. Only when commodities are sold can profits be realized. This characteristic, as will be discussed below, constrains the forms of control available to growers.

Concentration of labor time in the harvest dictates that the employment of workers in crop production be of a highly *seasonal* nature. That is, their employment will coincide with the harvest. Lloyd Fisher made this point: "The major labor consuming operation on the farm is the harvest, and no other aspect of agricultural production approaches it in the quantity of labor which it employs (1953: p. 3)." Three-Fourths of all workers working less than 150 days in 1974 were employed on fruit and vegetable farms. It was expected that the employment of seasonal labor would decrease somewhat over the years with the introduction of mechanical methods of crop harvesting. In 1968, "only 2 percent of the total production of fruits and vegetables in the U.S. was harvested mechanically (Davis, 1970: p.11)." It was estimated that by 1975, 17 percent of this production would be mechanically harvested (Ibid: p. 11). However, the seasonal nature of employment in California agriculture appears to be rather persistent. There was actually a 7.9 percent increase in the employment of temporary farm workers from 1969 to 1974, which is about the same as the increase in harvested crop land between the two years (U.S. Bureau of Census, 1969, 1974). This fact emphasizes the continued importance of seasonal workers in California agriculture.

CONTROL OVER WORKERS AND THE LABOR PROCESS

The defining characteristic of crop production, that is, the disjuncture between production time and labor time, and the consequent seasonal employment of harvest workers, poses a special problem to growers in terms of control over workers. The exceptional nature of this problem can be seen by a comparison with forms of control over workers within the labor process in other industries.

The need for control over the labor process, according to Richard Edwards (1979), arises from the nature of capitalist production. Capitalists purchase the commodity, labor power, from workers. Capitalists thus own this labor power for a specified period of time (e.g. eight hours). Having purchased this commodity, they expect to produce as large a quantity of saleable commodities as possible with the quantity of labor power they have at their disposal. The quantity of labor power available for exploitation is somewhat elastic. That is, capitalists can, to some extent, stretch the amount of labor extracted from workers within a particular span of time. However, there are limits to how far the labor power of workers can be stretched.

Labor power is not a neutral commodity. Although it has been sold, it continues to reside in the body of the worker. Because of the nature of this commodity, workers can restrict the amount of labor power extracted by the capitalist. Thus, there is a tension between capitalists, on the one hand, who attempt to extract as much production as possible from the labor power purchased from workers, and workers, on the other hand, who attempt to protect their labor power from exploitation by capitalists (Edwards, 1979: p. 12). In the interest of maximizing their rate of profit capitalists institute controls over workers within the labor process.

Control, according to Edwards is "transforming purchased labor power into labor actually done (1979: p. 112)." These controls are intended to secure high productivity on the part of workers, that is, these controls stretch the production extracted from workers for the period of time their labor power has been purchased by capitalists. Edwards summarizes these efforts to control workers:

> Faced with chronic resistance to their effort to compel production, employers over the years have attempted to resolve the matter by reorganizing, indeed revolutionizing, the labor process itself. Their goal remains profits; their strategies aim at establishing structures of control at work. That is, capitalists have attempted to organize production in such a way as to minimize workers' opportunities for resistance (p. 16).

Edwards poses three forms of control that capitalists generally exercise over workers. However, the usefulness of such forms of control is limited in crop production because of the seasonal nature of such production.

Technical, Bureaucratic, and Simple Forms of Control

Technical control refers to the direction and pacing of workers within the labor process via the technological organization of production (Edwards, 1979: p. 113). In this case, control over the labor process is beyond control by any one individual (i.e., foreman or boss) and is "truly structural." The design of the machine defines both the task to be carried out and the pace at which that task is to be completed. Examples of industries utilizing this form of control are southern textiles, auto and steel plants (e.g., assembly lines), and chemical production (e.g., monitoring).

The adoption of technical forms of control over the labor process in crop production is limited by the dissociation of production time and labor time. Since labor time is concentrated in the harvest, harvesting machinery with the capacity to pace and direct workers in the labor process would be put to use only for a short period of time each year (i.e., six weeks or less, or for the duration of the harvest). However, machines are constant capital. That is to say, they are acquired by the capitalist on a permanent, or at the very least, a semi-permanent basis. Machines are the property of the grower and are not easily disposed of. Furthermore, the successful completion of the harvest is a point of perpetual uncertainty to growers. Weather conditions may limit or completely eliminate the possibility of successfully completing the harvest.

Thus, for instance, should weather conditions prevent the harvesting of the crop, the grower remains obligated to pay the cost of the machine. Furthermore, such machinery tends to be designed specifically for the harvesting of a particular crop due to varying crop characteristics. If the grower is faced with unfavorable market conditions for a particular crop, such specifically designed machinery makes shifts in the production of one crop to another difficult and limits the grower's ability to take advantage of profitable opportunities in the production of alternative crops. Also, acreage reductions in the production of a particular crop become undesirable because of economies of scale. That is, for the operation of the machine to be profitable, a certain number of acres must be harvested. Capitalization of harvest operations, thus, undermines the flexibility of the grower in dealing with the uncertainties of crop production.

The grower engaged in labor-intensive crop production, by contrast, is able to eliminate or reduce the uncertainties of crop production in two ways. First of all, he can recruit a large army of workers, pay them at a piece-rate, and harvest the crop as quickly as possible to avoid interference on the part of Mother Nature. This method of crop harvesting implies, of course, that a large number of workers have employment for only a very short period of time. However, because employment tends to be by piece-rate, the cost of hiring a large army of workers is no greater than hiring a smaller one for a longer period of time. In this fashion farm workers assume part of the risks of crop production in the form of reduced employment (Fisher, 1953: p. 6). Stable and secure employment is sacrificed to the growers' profit motivations which dictate that they keep costs of crop loss to a minimum.

Secondly, wage labor is variable capital. That is, workers can be employed or discharged at the whim of the grower. Should weather, market, or any other conditions outside the growers' realm of control make the harvesting of the crop impossible or undesirable, the growers' losses are greatly reduced by simply failing to employ harvest workers. This response is effective due to the fact that the greatest cost factor in labor-intensive harvesting operations is labor (Pfeffer, 1980: 27). Once again, the costs associated with the uncertainties of crop production are absorbed by workers in the form of reduced employment. Furthermore, by employing variable capital the grower is able to shift from the production of one commodity to another from year to year or reduce acreage with relative ease as market and other conditions and the possibilities for profit maximization change.

The contention here is not that growers will forever fail to adopt technical forms of control over harvest workers. The fact is that such forms of control have been adopted. The mechanization of California's processing tomato harvest is a relatively recent case in point (see Friedland and Barton, 1975). However, because of the nature of crop production, mechanization of harvest operations is retarded. Such mechanization is considered only as a last resort, that is, when other forms of control fail and workers become unavailable or recalcitrant. The reluctance of growers to adopt technical forms of control over workers is, in part, substantiated by the fact, already cited, that only 2 percent of the total U.S. production of fruits and vegetables was harvested mechanically in 1968. Given the proliferation of harvest mechanization technology through the 1960s and 1970s, purely technical impediments to the mechanization of harvest operations explain only a small portion of the retarded development and adoption of the machine harvesting of crops. For instance, an effective mechanical iceberg lettuce harvester had been developed by 1965 but has not been put to use in place of hand harvesting in spite of the fact that studies have shown that there is no cost difference between hand harvesting and machine harvesting of iceberg lettuce (Johnson and Zahara, 1977: p. 1).

Edwards also discusses bureaucratic control as a form of structural control over workers in the labor process. For Edwards, bureaucratic control is "embedded in the social and organizational structure of the firm and is built into job categories, work rules, promotion procedures, wage scales, definitions of responsibilities and the like. Bureaucratic control establishes the impersonal force of 'company rules' or 'company policy' as the basis for control" (p. 131). As was pointed out above, growers prefer the employment of workers as a variable investment in the harvesting of crops. Growers have this preference because the bulk of all workers are employed only during the harvest.

For this reason, bureaucratic forms of control over workers employed in crop production are not adopted. Edwards points out that, "bureaucratic control speeds up the process of converting the wage bill from a variable to a fixed cost (p. 157)." Thus, bureaucratic control would be fundamentally at odds with the seasonal nature of employment in crop production.

Historically, farm workers have been excluded from privileges granted other workers which would have established the possibility of "converting the wage bill from a variable to a fixed cost (Hayes and Mamer, 1977: p. 4)." Examples of this fact are the exclusion of farm workers from collective bargaining rights under the Wagner Act of 1935 and exclusion from unemployment insurance coverage. Only recently were these privileges extended to farm workers in California. Hayes and Mamer comment on the attitude of growers to the institution of bureaucratic checks for workers on the part of the United Farm Workers: "Management may find it less difficult and less costly to adjust to rigidity of wage rates than to reduce flexibility in recruiting workers, assigning tasks, organizing crews, and securing performance of work according to specified standards" (Ibid: p. 4)

Furthermore, even if bureaucratic controls were established to reasonably deal with the inherently seasonal nature of crop production from the point of view of the grower, it would be extremely difficult to maintain any continuity in such control from one season to the next. Workers would be outside this web of rules and procedures for the better part of the year. It would be difficult to reestablish job categories, work rules, promotion procedures, discipline, wage scales, definitions of responsibilities, etc. at the start of each harvest season.

Edwards' notion of "simple control" seems to correspond most closely to the control exercised over workers in the labor process by growers. Under such control, Edwards contends, "The personal power and authority of the capitalist (and a coterie of managers, straw bosses, and foremen) constituted the primary mechanism for control (p. 25)."

In fact, once growers secure the necessary harvest work force, control over the labor power of workers is relatively simple. Wages for agricultural workers historically have been low relative to the wages of other industries (Cargill and Rossmiller, 1969; Pfeffer, 1980: 28). Because they are often paid at low piece-rates, workers are forced to work at top speed for as long as possible to earn what they can, given those rates of pay. Because the harvest is of short duration, workers have yet another incentive to work as hard as possible. They try to maximize earnings as long as work is available. Payment of harvest workers on a piece-rate has been particularly suited to labor intensive crop harvesting. Not only is the labor power purchased by growers stretched as far as possible as long as wages are held low, but workers also work as quickly as possible, completing the harvest as rapidly as possible. A quick harvest helps growers avoid actual and potential costs of crop loss brought about by unfavorable weather conditions. As was pointed out above, because harvest workers tend to be paid by piece-rate, the cost of hiring a large army of workers is no greater than hiring a smaller one for a longer period of time. While the growers' risks are minimized the seasonal peaks of employment are accentuated as Fisher has pointed out:

If the farmer would assume certain risks with regard to weather and loss of quality, the crop might be harvested with a smaller agricultural labor force employed over a longer period of time. If, on the other hand, the risks were to be borne by the agricultural laborer in the form of shorter periods of employment, then it was true that employment for shorter periods can be found for 40,000 or 100,000 additional agricultural workers (1953: p. 6).

Because of the nature of crop production the adoption of the structural forms of control referred to by Edwards are retarded or simply never come about. Control over workers within the production process is relatively simple for growers as long as their supply of workers has been unrestricted. Thus, the successful completion of the harvest, barring unfavorable weather conditions, has been tied to the ability of growers to secure the necessary supply of workers at the appropriate time.

Control over the supply of workers is beyond the scope of simple control. For such control to be effective growers must have an unrestricted supply of labor. Securing the necessary harvest work force in accordance with the timing of the harvest has necessitated controls over workers which are largely outside the labor process and more directly concerned with the manipulation of the supply of workers. Control over workers within the labor process is dependent on control over the supply of workers as well. That is, control over the supply of workers is the primary consideration in terms of growers' control over workers in the labor process.

Elements of Control Over the Work Force in Crop Production

Because of the seasonal nature of crop production growers must maintain control over the supply of workers. Such control is necessary in order to secure the work force required for the harvest. There are four elements of control over the supply of workers.

First, workers must be willing to accept short term employment. Securing such control is most problematic in geographical areas where crop specialization is most advanced. In these areas the disparity between slack period of employment and employment at the harvest peak is most pronounced. This situation stands in contrast to geographical areas characterized by the production of a wide variety of crops. There, the harvest would be extended over a broader time frame because of the varying growth patterns of the different crops. Specialized crop production has been characteristic of California for most of its history as a major agricultural state.

Given the specialized nature of California crop production, the first element of control over the supply of workers is most likely to be achieved when the bulk of the work force is of a transient or migratory nature, since alternative sources of employment are generally not available for so many workers in rural areas. Unless substantial income supplements are available few workers can survive on the meager income generated from such short term employment and the low wages characteristic of farm work. However, income supplements are costly and lead to increases in taxation, indirectly constituting a cost to capitalists. Thus, a migratory harvest work force is preferred by growers as it is the least costly alternative. As long as the harvest work force remains migratory, growers must only pay to support workers while directly employed in the production of commodities, and, of course, profits.

In spite of its desirability, a migratory seasonal harvest work force in crop production creates considerable uncertainty amongst growers as to the availability of workers come harvest time. For example, most fruits and vegetables are of a highly perishable nature. Once these crops are ripe they must be picked in short order. A delay in the harvest because of an insufficient supply of workers can lead to considerable losses in the form of crops rotting in the fields. This characteristic of fruit and vegetable production is articulated by a lettuce grower: "The labor must be on hand to harvest this crop when the lettuce has reached its proper stage of growth and maturity. The economic importance of this is such that the farmer cannot afford . . . the cost or the incertainty in the supply of labor" (Senate Fact Finding Committee, 1961: p. 72).

Therefore, the second element in control over the harvest work force is that workers must be readily recruited at harvest time. Although the workers have sold their labor power, it continues to reside in the bodies of those workers. Thus, growers can retain control over this commodity only for limited amounts of time and as long as the workers, physically present, make that commodity available. Because of the perishable nature of many crops, especially fruits and vegetables, growers must control the availability of workers and their labor power. That is, growers must have the necessary number of workers available for the duration of the harvest. The harvest cannot be postponed for the crops will simply rot in the fields.

Control over the availability of workers through to the completion of the harvest is especially important in crops where harvesting is carried out in several successive operations. Usually the first and perhaps the second pick are most productive and enable workers to earn fairly high wages. Consequently, when employment opportunities appear in other fields with more desirable working conditions or in fields undergoing the first or second picking, workers are likely to move to those fields, leaving the grower with too few workers to complete the final picking before the crop becomes overripe. For example, the harvesting of tomatoes, grapes, pears, peaches, and nuts all take place at about the same time, providing workers with employment alternatives (Thor and Mamer, 1965).

Harvest workers, like other workers in the secondary labor market, exhibit a high degree of voluntary turnover. Their jobs are a "dead-end." That is, such employment offers virtually no job security and only very low wages (Edwards, 1979: p. 168). There is little to prevent such workers from seeking more desirable alternative employment. Heavy turnover of workers arouses considerable anxiety on the part of growers with respect to the successful completion of the harvest. Scruggs described this concern on the part of growers: "Yet, even in times of labor surplus, such as the 1930's, farmers have consistently mainfested a keen desire for more workers. . . . The growers of highly perishable crops have always been plagued with fears of labor shortage and rotting crops" (1960: p. 140). Consequently, in the absence of effective controls over the mobility of workers competitive bidding for workers by growers results, driving up wage rates (Benedict, 1953: p. 437).[2] Even wage agreements among growers designed to keep wages stable fail given the propensity of harvest workers to seek more desirable employment. The relationship between wage rates in crop production and the mobility of harvest workers between jobs is expressed by Fisher:

> Another factor limiting the effectiveness of employer wage agreements is the limited scope which characterizes them. They commonly cover a single commodity only, and there are growers of other commodities able to employ the same labor, who are governed by different and frequently inconsistent agreements. Consequently, the area of single agreement is always less than the labor market, even when that is narrowly defined. . . . In consequence, the control of competition, even when successfully managed for single crops, is only imperfectly accomplished for the labor market as a whole (1953: p. 116).

Thus, the third element of control over the harvest work force is: Workers must be available for employment for the duration of the harvest. Growers have for an extended period of time suffered the effects of the cost-price squeeze. That is, the costs of farm inputs rise at a faster rate than the prices growers receive for their commodities. For example, the cost of selected farm inputs[3] rose more than twice as much as the value of fruits and vegetables rose between 1950 and 1974 (U.S. Bureau of Census, 1950, 1974). Few growers are large enough to independently wield significant market power against the other sectors of the food industry (e.g. food processors and distributors). Therefore, they are forced to accept the rising costs of farm inputs and must accept less than optimal prices for the commodities they market.

While growers may be relatively powerless in this respect, with respect to other elements of capital, they do retain power over the workers they employ by virtue of their ownership and control of the means of production. Faced with the pressures of the cost-price squeeze, growers are forced to exercise what power they have in keeping the wages of workers low. Thus, a fourth element of control over harvest workers in the production of crops takes on importance: The wages of workers must be held relatively low.

However, the ability of growers to maintain this power over workers is dependent on other elements of control discussed above. First of all, workers must be available for employment for the duration of the harvest. As long as this condition is met growers can more readily avoid competitive bidding for workers and the driving up of wage rates. Secondly, as long as harvest workers maintain their migratory status their organization into trade unions which could effectively bargain for wage increases is difficult. This problem was recognized long ago (Morin, 1952; p. 37).

Thus, control over wages by growers is largely dependent on broader controls over the supply of workers. At this point the question to be answered is: How are these elements of control over the work force in crop production actualized?

POLITICAL SOLUTIONS TO CONTROL THE HARVEST WORK FORCE

Few, if any, growers are large enough to wield significant control over the harvest work force as outlined above. Therefore, growers have sought and been offered more directly political forms of control, established and administered by the state.

Such controls have prevailed in California agriculture since the late nineteenth century. The state has been involved in importing and subsequently regulating the flow of Chinese, Japanese, Hindustani, Filipino, Mexican, and other workers employed in California's fields (McWilliams, 1971). Since 1942, state regulation of the flow of immigrant workers in California has been geared primarily to Mexican workers. Because an important part of California agriculture's most important resource—workers—is located in Mexico across a national boundary, state intervention is necessitated.

Many Mexican workers cross the border without documentation. Mexican workers are the predominant element of the California farm work force (Hayes and Mamer, 1977: p. 9).[4] This fact is a reflection of the policies of the U.S. government, which have been geared towards satisfying the elements of control over the harvest work force demanded by growers in the southwestern U.S. in general and California growers in particular. This point has been made by Julian Samora:

.The evolution of . . . immigration policy . . . may best be understood as an extensive farm labor program—an efficient policy representing a consistent desire for Mexicans as laborers rather than as settlers. This policy stands out as a legitimized and profitable means of acquiring needed labor without incurring the price that characterized the immigration, utilization, and the eventual settlement of European and Oriental immigrants (1971: p. 57).

But why would the state be persuaded and even willingly offer to establish and administer political forms of control over the harvest work force?

State controls over the harvest work force contribute to the maintenance of a stable and cheap supply of food. The importance of such controls is underscored by the fact that California alone produces more than 40% of all fruits and vegetables in the U.S.[5] Furthermore, a very high proportion of California's seasonal farm work force has primarily been engaged in the production of fruits and vegetables (Pfeffer, 1980: 30). Securing a work force with characteristics attuned to the requirements of the labor process in fruit and vegetable production is important in assuring the entire nation a stable and cheap supply of fruits and vegetables.

Since 1942 the state has intervened in satisfying the elements of control over the harvest work force outlined above in basically two ways: 1) through an administrative system of control; and 2) through the manipulation of the size of the reserve army of labor. Although the particular form of these interventions has changed, the role of the state in securing a work force satisfying the elements of control demanded by the crop harvest has remained stable.

The Braceros: A Semi-Captive Work Force

The work force employed by growers in Cafifornia and other parts of the U.S. after 1951 was in part made up of a large number of Mexican workers brought to the U.S. under contract with growers or the representatives of growers. These workers were commonly referred to as *braceros*. The contracting of Mexican workers actually began in 1942, in response to fears of labor shortages in U.S. agriculture because of the manpower drain brought about by World War II. This contracting was not institutionalized until 1951, as Public Law 78 and was at that time defended as a response to fears of manpower shortages resulting

Table 1.   Braceros as Percent of All Seasonal Workers, California, 1951-1962

Year	Percent
1951	15.1
1952	18.3
1953	18.6
1954	20.1
1955	26.5
1956	33.2
1957	34.2
1958	32.0
1959	31.5
1960	29.3
1961	24.4
1962	23.6

Source: Senate Fact Finding Committee, 1961.

Table 2.   Braceros as Percent of All Seasonal Labor Used in Selected Activity,
           California, 1962

Crop	Percent
Lemon, Harvest	81.6
Tomatoes, Harvest	79.9
Lettuce, All Activities	71.4
Asparagus, Harvest	54.4

Source: Senate Fact Finding Committee, 1961.

from the Korean War. In the period 1942 to 1951, braceros represented only a small proportion of the Mexicans employed in U.S. agriculture. Undocumented workers were an important part of the farm work force at that time in the southwestern U.S. in general and in California in particular (Samora, 1971: p. 44). However, in the 1950s growers became aware of the fact that braceros represented a practically ideal work force. By 1956 California growers were the largest employers of braceros in the U.S. (Galarza, 1964: p. 79).

Braceros made up a significant proportion of the seasonal workers employed in agriculture during the 1950s and 1960s as Table 1 shows. An indication of how well suited braceros were to the labor requirements of fruit and vegetable production is the extent of their employment in the harvesting of those crops: 93 percent of the crops employing braceros in 1959 were fruit and vegetable crops (Galarza, 1964: p. 88). Table 2 shows that braceros made up the majority of the seasonal work force in several important fruit and vegetable crops in California. Why were braceros such desirable workers in the harvesting of fruits and vegetables?

The entire program was designed and managed so as to meet the grower's needs for harvest workers.

The bracero program was jointly administered by the United States and Mexican governements. Under the terms of the Migrant Labor Agreement of 1951, the Mexican government assumed responsibility for assembling and screening prospective workers. These activities were conducted at "migratory stations" in Mexico (Senate Fact Finding Committee, 1961: p. 85).

Public Law 78, which was signed into effect July 12, 1951, established the administrative framework within which Mexican workers were employed in U.S. agriculture. This program was administered by the federal government through the Department of Labor, which coordinated the various agencies of government participating in the administration of the bracero program.

The administrative channels through which the program functioned were as follows:

> The Secretary (of Labor) implements the program at the federal level through the U.S. Employment Service, Bureau of Employment Security, U.S. Department of Labor, and assigns authority and responsibilities for state and local operations . . . to the California State Department of Employment by agreement . . . (Senate Fact Finding Committee, 1961: p. 85).

The activities of the Department of Labor under P.L. 78 are summarized by Galarza:

> It [P.L. 78] authorized the Secretary of Labor to recruit such workers, establish and operate reception centers, provide transportation, finance subsistence and medical care in transit, assist workers and employers in negotiating contracts and guarantee the performance by employers of such contracts (1964: p. 72).

Furthermore, Galarza outlines the functions of the Department of Labor:

> the determination of shortages of labor; the certification of need; the establishment of housing standards; advising employers as to their responsibilities under the agreement; investigating grievances and resolving complaints; collecting fees; making wage surveys; assisting growers to keep the program in good repute with the public; returning braceros to the border; collecting unpaid wages; negotiating amendments to the agreements and the contracts . . . (p. 84).

Workers were transported from the "migratory stations" in Mexico to the "reception centers" in the U.S.[6] under the supervision of the

Department of Labor. There they received additional health and security screening.[7] But most importantly, they were assembled at these centers for contracting growers.

The number of workers necessary for contracting by growers was assured by procedures under which workers were authorized for migration. First of all, growers or their representatives submitted a statement of expected need for braceros to the California State Department of Employment. It was on the basis of such statements that the California State Department of Employment was able to detail "the county or counties of crop activity, total labor demand, expected domestic supply, and estimated shortage for which foreign labor may later [have been] requested" (Senate Fact Finding Committee, 1961: p. 86). Subsequently, the California State Department of Employment submitted to the U.S. Bureau of Employment Security (BES) a preseason farm labor market report for peak seasons of activity in fields throughout the state. The report included information covering expected acreages and production, past employment, and estimated future labor demands, supplies, and shortages. With this information the BES established upper limits to the hiring of braceros. These reports were in turn referred to the Secretary of Labor who finally authorized the contracting of the specified number of braceros (Senate Fact Finding Committee, 1961: p. 85).

Workers remained in the U.S. for the duration of their contract. At the completion of the contract period, workers were returned home along the same channels as they had come. They could be contracted either directly by growers or by their representatives. Although individual growers could directly contract braceros, most contracting was conducted by the growers' associations which contracted braceros and later distributed them among grower-members. In 1960, there were 54 such associations representing approximately 12,000 growers-members in California. In contrast there were only 27 individual growers contracting in 1959 (Senate Fact Finding Committee, 1961: p. 86).

The normal contract period was from six weeks to six months. Two extensions of fifteen days each were automatically granted as part of the contractual arrangement. Further extensions were relatively easy to obtain, provided the worker did not remain in the U.S. for more than eighteen consecutive months (Senate Fact Finding Committee, 1961: p. 88). Under the terms of the contract, growers were to provide workers with food at cost and transportation to and from work free of charge. The contracts also included provisions concerning wage rates and types of work braceros were permitted to perform, although they were quite flexible in this respect. Finally, workers could be contracted in this fashion year after year provided they were not blacklisted for inappropriate behavior. The bracero program established an administrative framework which was the underpinning of a system of "managed migration." This system was especially well suited to the requirements of the labor process in fruit and vegetable production.

Because of the high degree of temporal and geographical concentration of the production of fruits and vegetables in California, a migratory work force whose movement was planned and managed was practically ideal. This dual concentration of the harvest necessitated a work force that was migratory. A very large work force, too large to be recruited locally, was required because the work force was employed only for the duration of the harvest, so many workers would find it difficult, if not impossible, to secure employment in the off-season. Furthermore, uncontrolled migration left a great deal of uncertainty with growers: they had no assurance that harvest workers would migrate in a timely fashion or to their area at all.

Many critics of the bracero program have described this work force as "captive" (e.g., Galarza, 1964 and Anderson, 1963). As will be shown below, the captive nature of this work force was essential to satisfy the elements of control over the harvest work force needed by growers. However, simply to label this a captive work force is to overstate the case. The harvest work force was ideally migratory and only semi-captive. That is, a captive work force was of use to growers only for the duration of the harvest.

Braceros were males who migrated to the U.S. without their families. Yet this work force continued to be reproduced in Mexico.[8] The social costs of supporting the families of seasonally unemployed non-migratory farm workers would have been enormous. The bracero arrangement permitted these costs to be borne in rural Mexico.[9] Michael Burawoy discusses this aspect of migrant labor: "The significance of migrant labor lies in the separation of the processes of maintainance and renewal (reproduction), so that renewal takes place where living standards are low and maintenance takes place within easy access of employment (1977: p. 1082). The maintenance of braceros was of relatively little concern to growers for the duration of the contract. Since surveys of the expected number of braceros needed were conducted in advance, growers could with little difficulty contract and transport workers to the fields in such a way as to coincide with the start of the harvest. The fact that braceros provided an assurance that the crop would be harvested in the most efficient manner made the costs of such items as housing and transportation of little significance to growers. Thus, this system of managed migration was ideal both for the fact that workers could be supplied to growers on location at a specified time and for the fact that those workers would be returned to Mexico in an orderly fashion.

A highly controlled harvest work force was especially important given the uncertainties faced by growers in relation to the perishable nature of the fruit and vegetable crops. A delay in the harvesting of the crop could result in crippling losses to the grower. The uncertainties of a successful harvest could be effectively reduced only if the work force were available in a timely fashion according to the ripening of the crop and if work stoppages and slowdowns on the part of workers could be avoided.

An acceptable supply of workers at the crucial stage of plant maturity was assured by the very administrative arrangements of the bracero program. The surveys were conducted by the California Department of Employment prior to the harvest provided for the adjustment of the supply of workers to suit the needs of growers. Furthermore, the delivery of workers from Mexico was relatively prompt, and with careful planning growers could assure the availability of the necessary number of workers at the crucial point in the harvest. In fact, workers could be contracted within two weeks after the notification of the Mexican government of the desired number of workers. Once contracted, workers could be obtained in as few as forty-eight hours. According to Galarza, "It may well have been that the abundance of Mexican contract labor accounted for crop conservation. No crops were lost due to manpower shortages in the state between 1942 and 1960 (1962: p. 240)."

Once the harvest was in progress, holding worker resistance to a minimum was essential. Unnecessary delays in the harvest would only result in overripe and unmarketable commodities. Braceros were well suited to the harvesting of fruits and vegetables in this respect; resistance to exploitation on their part was unlikely. These workers were "strangers in a strange land." Galarza characterizes the work life of braceros: "In the life of the barracks and the field gang he was an individual, detachable unit. The circle of trust and confidence was small. Only with some luck he might (have found) himself in camp with a fellow worker from his rancheria, municipio, or ejido" (1964: p. 226).

Because braceros were employed by the associations of growers, they could be manipulated as individuals in the interests of growers. The bracero might have worked for several growers in a broad geographical area in the course of his contract period. Galarza illustrates the effect of this arrangement on worker solidarity amongst braceros: "The organization of braceros as union members in any case would have been difficult. Their camps were isolated. . . . Gangs were dispersed overnight and men transferred to other camps continually. Leadership was completely absent; its infrequent manifestations only led to prompt reprisal" (1964: p. 224). Braceros were eager to maximize their earnings before returning to the poverty of rural Mexico. Attempts to lead worker resistance could undermine the bracero's ability to secure future employment in the U.S. The potential gains of resistance against exploitation had to be weighed against the costs of reprisals by employers, reprisals which would jeopardize both the present and future employment of the bracero. In any case the cards were stacked against worker resistance amongst braceros. In fact, "in the two decades of managed migration there was no record of a single strike [by braceros] . . ." (Galarza, 1964: p. 224). Thus, the bracero program provided a captive supply of workers specifically attuned to the needs of growers for the duration of the harvest. Galarza captures this point with an analogy: "Like the sprinkling systems of mechanized irrigation braceros could be tuned on and off (1978: p. 265)."

Another threat to the stability of the harvest work force in fruit and vegetable production arose from the characteristics of particular crop harvests and their relationships to harvests in other crops. The onset of each stage of the harvest operations was determined to a large extent by weather conditions as they affected the rate at which the crops ripened. Yet, once the crops had reached the proper stage of maturity they had to be picked in short order to prevent overripening. Growers needed a work force that would be available at the onset and for the duration of the harvest.

Taking into account the relationship between various crops with respect to the timing of the harvest is important. As was pointed out above, the harvesting of several fruit and vegetable crops took place simultaneously. Work in some crop harvests (e.g., pears, peaches, grapes) was generally considered more desirable than the work of harvesting others (e.g., tomatoes, asparagus, strawberries). This relationship between the various harvests had important consequences for the maintenance of the work force in crops with less desirable working conditions. It was problematic for growers to maintain a work force for the duration of the harvest.

Once again the bracero program answered the needs of growers. Growers could employ healthy male workers with relative precision in terms of the initiation of harvest operations. Braceros, already contracted by the growers' associations, could be summoned to the fields on short notice and in sufficient numbers. This substantially reduced uncertainties related to the recruitment of workers and eased fears as to the rotting of crops in the fields because of a lack of workers. Because braceros were contracted on the behalf of growers by the growers' associations, they were essentially bound by contract to remain in the fields for the duration of the harvest. Should the braceros decide to "skip" or leave the employer prior to the expiration of the contract, they would lose his legal status, and face the possibility of no future contracts. Contracts could be broken only by mutual agreement between the bracero and his employer, or by either party unilaterally upon complaint and subsequent joint determination by the Mexican Consul and the Secretary of Labor's representative (Senate Fact Finding Committee, 1961: p. 88). In effect, braceros were captive workers for the duration of the harvest. Furthermore, should weather conditions (e.g., rain) delay the harvest, growers faced little anxiety about losing workers. Braceros could be transferred to the fields of other grower-members of the associations which were unaffected by those same weather conditions. Once workers could get back into the fields they were returned to work. Braceros, too, were happy with such arrangements since they avoided "downtime" and continued to earn money during the delay in harvest operations.

The captive nature of the bracero work force was an important factor in the efforts of growers to maintain their rate of profit in the face of the cost-price squeeze. As was pointed out above, with respect to both the costs of production and the prices received for their products, growers were in a relatively powerless position.

However, an important exception to this powerlessness existed. Growers maintained unilateral control over the wage rates of braceros. Workers and growers did not bargain for wages. Wages were predetermined and written into the bracero contract. Galarza describes this practice: "Raisin, fruit, and tomato growers in the Central Valley continued their familiar practice of meeting and deciding upon what all were expected to pay. The rate set by the Tomato Growers Association in July 1957 for the fall harvest was 11 cents a box" (1964: p. 127). He goes on: "These wages (had) been determined by unilateral farmer action to be those prevailing in the given areas, and although they (could) be modified by the government after a survey they rarely [were]" (p. 139). These practices considerably stabilized wage rates since the individual growers no longer bargained with workers over wages and no competitive bidding for workers between growers took place because the supply of workers was administered.

The bracero program, through its administrative structure, satisfied the four elements of control over the harvest work force demanded by fruit and vegetable growers, given the seasonal nature of such production.

The essence of the desirability of bracero workers on the part of growers is best summed up by the following quotation: "The main advantages of Mexican [bracero] labor, from the point of view of employers, is that it is easier to recruit, simpler to control, and noticeably less subject to labor turnover" (U.S. Department of Labor, 1969: p. 175).

The Drive for Unionization and
Termination of the Bracero Program

As we have seen, the bracero program was practically an ideal in terms of satisfying the elements of control over the work force demanded by fruit and vegetable production. While the bracero program served the needs of growers so well, it had detrimental effects on the interests of domestic farm workers. Efforts at union organization of farm workers were virtually halted in the course of the 1950s. The formal institution of P.L. 78 and the subsequent growth in the employment of braceros in California agriculture put an end to the effective organization of farm workers by such organizations as the National Farm Labor Union (NFLU), which had made such attempts in the early 1950s. Galarza points out, "The history of domestic harvesters in California from 1952 to 1959 was not one of union organization but of relocation under the sustained pressure of the bracero system (1978: p. 242)." Braceros by virtue of the terms of their contracts and the general terms of P.L. 78, were next to impossible to organize. It became apparent to union organizers and sympathizers that an attack on the bracero program was a necessary first step in revitalizing the effort to organize farm workers in California.[10] This became the focus, for instance, of NFLU activities in the course of the 1950s. However, while the NFLU did make progress in bringing into question the legitimacy of the bracero program, it was unsuccessful in causing its termination. This was largely due to a lack of funds.[11]

Lack of resources in the drive to organize farm workers and the struggle for termination of the bracero program was significantly altered in 1959 when the AFL-CIO established the Agricultural Workers Organizing Committee (AWOC).[12] The creation of AWOC made for the channeling of significant funding into the organization of California's farm workers. In addition, the entry of the AFL-CIO into the California farm labor scene aroused nationwide interest in the plight of farm workers and the relationship of the bracero program to this issue. Ed Hayes (1961), a member of the California Tomato Growers Association, lamented this development:

> The unions have announced that they're going to kill the bracero program and they are influencing the Department of Labor, Department of Employment, and the social welfare and religious groups in the matter. The National Council of Churches in convention in San Francisco last month again passed resolutions endorsing the efforts to organize farm workers into the union and for minimum wage laws for agriculture. The unions have given tribute to the recent TV show *Harvest of Shame* and letters are beginning to appear in the daily press from people taken in by that kind of propaganda.

AWOC was aggressive in its drive to organize California's farm workers. In the period 1960 to 1962 there were 148 agricultural strikes in California, 95 percent of which were centered on the harvest (Senate Fact Finding Committee, 1963: p. 64). Wage increases for agricultural workers during this period were largely attributed to AWOC's organizing efforts, but virtually all strikes ended in AWOC's failure to secure union recognition (Senate Fact Finding Committee, 1963: p. 65). This was in part attributable to misguided strategy on the part of the AWOC leadership (London and Anderson, 1970: p. 49). However, the continued importation of braceros was an obstacle to the successful organization of California's farm workers into a union.

It comes as no surprise that AWOC's aim was to secure the termination of the bracero program. In a condensed version of an AWOC strategy the need to eliminate bracero workers from employment in California agriculture is articulated from the union point of view: "The Mexican National Program, under P.L. 78, constitutes a barrier, a deterrent, and a threat to AWOC's organizing effort. The mobile army created under the law depresses domestic farm wages, damages the economy, and erodes the small business community. Besides being a wage breaking force the bracero army is a strike breaking force" (Pickett, 1960: p. 211).

However, the government-administered bracero program embodied a fundamental contradition of government in capitalist society. On the one hand, in assuring the smooth functioning of society, government must formulate and administer policies which permit capitalists to operate their enterprises at a profit. On the other hand, government must present itself as acting in the interests of all members of society, regardless of class distinctions. Government, in fulfilling its function, depends on the loyalty and support of all members of society. That is, it must maintain its legitimacy in conjunction with its function of providing a favorable climate for profit making on the part of the capitalists. However, these functions are often contradictory (O'Connor, 1973: p. 6).

While P.L. 78 served the interests of growers both in spirit and practice, the text of the law did provide certain safeguards or checks for domestic farm workers. The institution of the bracero program, first as an informal executive agreement between the governments of Mexico and the U.S. in 1942, and later, in 1951, as the Migrant Labor Agreement and P.L. 78 was undoubtedly a response to the interests of growers (Galarza, 1964: p. 72). However, in order to maintain legitimacy in the eyes of their entire populaces, the respective governments had to include certain provisions in the agreements protecting their workers. Whether such provision were enforced was another matter. In drafting the agreements the Mexican government was the party most interested in insuring the rights of workers. This concern on the part of the Mexican government arose from unfavorable accounts of the treatment of Mexican migrants in the U.S. and "the vivid recollections of Mexico of the return of over 50,000 immigrants following the Great Depression, which many regarded as a mass expulsion" (Galarza, 1964: p. 46). Protections in P.L. 78 for domestic workers were largely a response to opposition on the part of organized labor in the U.S. (Hawley, 1966: p. 158). What lent legitimacy to and gained support for the bracero program on both sides of the border in 1951 "was the assurance, reiterated by its proponents, that braceros would be contracted only in the event of a scarcity of domestic workers and only for the duration of the need. The public credit of the system could only be maintained so long as there was no evidence that braceros were driving out domestics" (Galarza, 1964: p. 218). Ostensibly the contracting of bracero workers under the provisions of P.L. 78 was to be allowed only when certain conditions were met. These were: 1) that the U.S. Secretary of Labor had certified that a sufficient number of domestic workers were not available; 2) that the wages and working conditions of domestic workers would not be adversely affected by bracero workers; 3) that employers had made reasonable efforts to attract domestic laborers for employment (Galarza, 1964: p. 72). These provisions, in addition to other provisions to be discussed below, proved to be crucial in the effectiveness of the drive for the termination of the bracero program.

Under pressure from a liberal-labor coalition of interests centered around the National Advisory Committee on Farm Labor[13] in 1958, then Secretary of Labor, James Mitchell, ordered strict enforcement of the "domestic preference" provisions of P.L. 78 which, as had become increasingly apparent, had been side-stepped by growers and the government agencies involved in the administration of the bracero program (Jenkins, 1975: p. 252). Whether such enforcement did take place at that time is doubtful. Nevertheless, it did represent a major shift in policy, to a position more favorable to the interests of workers, on the part of the U.S. Department of Labor. With sustained pressure from farm labor organizers and sympathizers, Mitchell appointed a panel of consultants from outside the Department of Labor to review the bracero program. This panel went on to substantiate the claims of farm labor support groups that domestic workers suffered adverse affects from the employment of bracero workers. The panel recommended the establishment of a minimum wage for agricultural workers and a requirement that domestic workers be offered the same conditions and benefits of employment as were offered braceros (Jenkins, 1975: p. 253).

By 1962 the Department of Labor, now operating under a relatively sympathetic Kennedy administration, acted in partial response to demands from farm labor advocates by introducing more stringent guidelines regarding the "undue hardship" clause of P.L. 78. This clause provided that growers were to provide "substantially the same conditions of employment" to domestic workers as they provide for braceros before growers were considered to be suffering from "undue hardship" due to a lack of available workers and requests for the importation of braceros would be considered. Under the more stringent guidelines set forth by the Department of Labor growers were expected to offer the following conditions of employment to domestic farm workers: 1) within certain limits, free transportation and subsistence while en route to the job, 2) return transportation upon satisfactory completion of the job, 3) free daily transportation between residence and work, 4) free housing and occupational insurance, 5) where there were central food service facilities, meals at cost, but not to exceed $1.75 per day, and 6) guarantee of employment for at least three-fourths of the work days of the total period for which the worker was hired (*The California Citrograph*, 1962: p. 9). These guidelines had the effect not only of raising the costs and complicating the process of securing the harvest work force, but also of undermining the strategy of substituting the semi-captive bracero workers for "undependable" and uncontrollable domestic workers. Domestic workers were not bound to work under the guidelines of an administrative framework as were braceros. This made the application of standards within P.L. 78 to domestic workers extremely undesirable to growers. They were expected to provide domestic workers with the same benefits as braceros without themselves being granted any of the assurances associated with the employment of a semi-captive work force.

There was also a provision in P.L. 78 which, if enforced, would directly affect worker insurgency in the fields. Article 22 of P.L. 78 provided that no bracero could fill a job which the Secretary of Labor found to be vacant because the worker was out on a strike or locked out in the course of a labor dispute. It also provided that in the event of a strike or a lockout which seriously affected the operations in which the braceros were employed the Secretary of Labor must remove the braceros (Perluss, 1960: p. 8).

Intital strike actions by AWOC revealed that Article 22 had little meaning in practice. For instance, in 1960 AWOC organized a strike in the tomato fields near Tracy. This action was defused through the use of braceros as strike breakers (Jenkins, 1975: p. 196).

To bring about the enforcement of Article 22 "the union forwarded notes to the Mexican government and union officials and to Secretary [of Labor] Goldberg, warning that the dangers of continued bracero hiring were very great, that in the present explosive situation there was considerable danger to the health and safety of the Mexican workers" (Jenkins, 1975: p. 202). In response to such pressure the Department of Labor issued two administrative rulings related to Article 22. Previously, when the Department of Labor had been prodded to act at all in a strike situation it had removed braceros on a field by field basis. Thus, a grower affected by a strike action could continue operations employing braceros as long as workers from those *same* fields were not engaged in the strike action. In 1961 the Department of Labor ruled that any grower whose workers were part of a certified strike was subject to the loss of *all* his braceros, rather than simply on a field by field basis. This gave the union considerably more leverage in dealing with growers since growers were deprived of an effective strike breaking force. In a second important decision the Department of Labor ruled that only 50 percent of the *domestic* workers employed by a grower who also employed braceros had to go on strike for a strike to be certified which then required that the Secretary of Labor suspend authorization for the employment of braceros by that grower (Jenkins, 1975: p. 207). Because of the small population of domestic workers making up the harvest work force of various fruit and vegetable crops (see Table 2), a small number of these workers could initiate a strike and cripple the growers' operations provided the braceros were removed by the Secretary of Labor. If nothing else, this presented a threat and introduced an element of uncertainty into the once stable and secure bracero work force. A writer for the *California Tomato Grower* (January 1962) both articulates and laments this threat: "A relatively small percentage of domestic workers could create a pseudo-strike situation causing loss to the grower of all his supplemental labor and the resultant loss of his crop. This interpretation placed the employer of Mexican contract workers at the mercy of organized labor."

The ruling reinforced a tactic already being used by AWOC. Since no crop harvest in California relied entirely on braceros, a portion of the domestic work force was recruited by some growers at early morning "shape-ups." Prospective farm workers would gather at a certain location in cities such as Stockton and Sacramento to be picked up by growers for a day's work. AWOC organizers were able to infiltrate the ranks of the harvest work force by taking advantage of this method of domestic farm worker recruitment. In 1960, AWOC organizers spread throughout the Central Valley to cover local shape-ups. Once hired they quickly organized strikes, which if certified by the Department of Labor would allow braceros to be removed from the fields and further referrals of braceros to be cut off (Jenkins, 1975: p. 193).

During the early 1960s the work force continued to be readily recruited at harvest time, migratory and willing to accept short-term employment. However, with interpretation and enforcement of Article 22 of P.L. 78 in a light more favorable to the interests of farm workers, the conditions that workers remain employed for the duration of the harvest became problematic. With the new treatment of Article 22, growers became vulnerable to a strike action on the part of just a few domestic workers. Such a strike action would result in the removal of braceros from the growers' employment, and in some crops, the loss of virtually the entire harvest work force. Furthermore, with the enforcement of Article 15, growers were forced to continue to actively recruit domestic workers which simply added to the possibility of a strike.

Continued agitation on the part of farm labor organizations and sympathizers progressively undermined the condition that the rates of pay be under unilateral control of growers. It was the contention of farm labor sympathizers that the recruitment of domestic workers was impossible as long as wage rates in agriculture remained depressed. Pressure for the recognition of Article 15 of P.L. 78, which provided that the wage and working conditions of domestic workers should not be adversely affected by bracero workers, led to enforced increases in wage rates in some crops by the California Department of Employment acting under the authority of the U.S. Department of Labor. As a result, farm workers could no longer be the sole bearers of the pressure of the cost-price squeeze.

Finally, in 1964, Congress under pressure from farm labor organizers and sympathizers failed to renew authorization for the contracting of braceros and the bracero program came to an end.

The AFL-CIO had been an ardent anti-communist ally of the U.S. government. The anti-communist stance of the AFL-CIO was embodied in the persons of George Meany and Walter Reuther, both important actors in the formation of the union's foreign policy (Gershman, 1975). Reuther, as president of the United Auto Workers, was foremost amongst the leaders of organized labor as a supporter of struggles to organize farm workers. With the intensification of the Cold War experienced in the early 1960s (e.g., the Cuban missile crisis, the arms race), officials of both Congress and the Executive were leery of antagonizing labor leaders and creating the possibility of domestic dissent. This possibility was real as tension over high rates of unemployment already existed between the federal government and organized labor (Jenkins and Perrow, 1977: pp. 261–262). Termination of the bracero program served to appease organized labor at relatively little cost to the growers affected, given the alternatives provided by the state.

With termination of the bracero program, growers were forced to seek alternatives to the employment of large numbers of braceros. Portes points out the response of capitalists in such situations: "the defense of the rate of profit against labor scarcity and higher labor costs takes two historical forms: 1) increasing the productivity per worker; and 2) finding new sources of low cost labor" (1978: p. 473).Thus, one alternative open to growers was to substantially reduce the size of the work force through the mechanization of harvest operations.

Some crops could readily be mechanized (e.g., tomatoes) and research in harvest mechanization was promoted by both the USDA and the state of California. Development of a mechanical lettuce harvester is an example of such an effort carried out by both USDA and the University of California (See Friedland, Barton and Thomas, 1981).

But as was postulated above, as long as growers are able to maintain a work force suited to the requirements of the labor intensive crop harvest they will maintain labor intensive harvest operations. The other alternative was to find a suitable alternative work force to replace the braceros.

Undocumented Workers: A Reserve Army of Labor

Termination of the bracero program aroused considerable controversy around the issue of a labor shortage for the crop harvest. However, the fear of a substantial shortage of labor seemed justified only when considered in terms of the pressure on growers by the U.S. Department of Labor for the replacement of Mexican workers solely with domestic workers. There is little doubt that any serious attempt at this would have been difficult.

However, indications are that there was no such effort in any significant sense and that no serious labor shortage for California agriculture as a whole occurred after termination of the bracero program.[14] According to then Secretary of Labor, Willard Wirtz, "In 1965, U.S. farmers were on the whole able to maintain adequate labor supplies" (1966: p. 35). Also, "Those labor shortages that did develop were less severe than growers had predicted" (p. 19).[15] Termination of the bracero program did not significantly affect the availability of Mexican workers for employment by growers. Jenkins contends: "Termination of the bracero program in 1964 had virtually no effect on the alien portion of the labor force. When bracero traffic dropped off, the illegal and "green card" traffic quickly replaced it" (1975: 78).

The increased migration of undocumented workers has been more than a coincidence with the termination of the bracero program.[16] It reflects a new strategy on the part of the state to satisfy the elements of control over the harvest work force so crucial to fruit and vegetable production in particular. This strategy has been to flood the labor market with available workers and to allow these elements of control to be satisfied by the coercive function of an over-supply of workers. As Edwards has pointed out: "It is the lack of job security and the ever-present possibility of immediate replacement by others from the reserve army that marks a secondary job" (1979: p. 169).

The U.S. Government has endeavored to ensure the continued stability of Southwestern agriculture in general and California agriculture in particular by permitting a large flow of undocumented Mexican workers to enter the U.S. However, this flow has not been unregulated. This migration is a reflection of a conscious policy on the part of the U.S. government.

Historically, the flow of Mexican workers to the U.S. has been regulated by the state. Simply in terms of logistics, the U.S. border could be closed to the migration of undocumented Mexican workers. Samora contends: "Without a doubt the border can be controlled effectively, as was illustrated by Project Intercept (1970). The real question is whether the U.S. is willing to take that action" (1971: p. 60). In the past, operations to prevent such migration have been linked with considerations of labor supply in the U.S. "Anti-Mexican alien" campaigns have historically coincided with high rates of unemployment in the U.S. (Bustamante, 1977: p. 150). This fact was apparent in "Operation Deportation" which took place in the 1930s (Samora and Bustamante, 1970: p. 4788) and "Operation Wetback" which took place from 1953 to 1956 and resulted in the expulsion of approximately 4 million Mexicans from the U.S. (Portes, 1974: p. 40). In the latter case, the apprehension and deportation of Mexican workers coincided with the consolidation of the bracero program, and with a severe drought in the 1950's which disrupted the demand for agricultural labor (Frisbie, 1975).

However, since 1964 the policies of the U.S. government have encouraged the migration of undocumented Mexican workers to the U.S. First of all, efforts to enforce immigration laws and halt the flow of undocumented workers have been perfunctory. The Immigration and Naturalization Service (INS), which is charged with enforcing those laws, has not been alotted the resources to effectively secure the border. According to Jenkins, "The Border Patrol budget and staffing have been overwhelmingly inadequate to the scale of the task" (1978: p. 527).

Secondly, laws have facilitated the employment of undocumented workers. Under the terms of the "Texas Proviso" (Public Law 283, 1952) it is a felony to import and harbor undocumented workers, but it is not a felony to employ undocumented workers (Samora, 1971: p. 54–55). Consistent with this law, efforts to apprehend documented workers have been centered along the border and not at the place of employment (Jenkins, 1978: p. 527). Undocumented migration of Mexican workers to the U.S. continues unchecked as a conscious policy of the U.S. government to insure the availability of the necessary supply of workers for U.S. employers. Portes points out: "The impunity with which employers have made use of this source of labor continues to be a major 'pull' factor stimulating illegal migration" (1974: p. 46).

Like the bracero program, the administration of which secured workers specifically for employment in agriculture, current border enforcement policies have been instrumental in satisfying the elements of control over the work force required by crop production. Although undocumented Mexican workers are increasingly employed in competitive industries outside of agriculture (Jenkins, 1978: p. 518), historically the primary concern of U.S. immigration policy regarding Mexicans has been with satisfying the labor requirements of Southwestern agriculture of which California is such an important part. Jenkins comments on this point: "Southwestern agriculture comes in for detailed treatment because it is the sector of the U.S. economy in which immigrant workers entering from Mexico have historically had the most persistent and thorough involvement" (1978: p. 525).

Employment opportunities for Mexican workers are centered in both the agricultural and small-scale manufacturing sectors (Bach, 1978: p. 536). However, the perpetuation of a substantial flow of undocumented workers across the U.S.-Mexican border effectively satisfies the labor requirements of the agricultural sector in particular since most Mexican immigrants secure initial employment in agriculture (Jenkins, 1977: pp. 179–180). Because California's farm labor force is dominated by Mexicans (Hayes and Mamer, 1977: p. 9), that current Mexican migration to the U.S. satisfies the labor requirements of California agriculture seems to be a reasonable conclusion. But how does manipulation of the reserve army of labor satisfy the elements of control over the work force demanded by growers in the harvesting of crops?

Estimates at the end of the 1970s of the number of undocumented Mexican workers in the U.S. ranged from 1 to 5 million (Portes, 1978: p. 480 and Jenkins, 1978: p. 520). One estimate went so far as to claim that nearly "twenty percent of the total increase in the U.S. labor force between 1963 and 1973" was comprised of undocumented workers (Jenkins, 1978: p. 520). Given the magnitude of undocumented Mexican workers entering the U.S. and the limited employment opportunities open to these workers (Bach, 1978: p. 536), the condition that workers be willing to accept short-term employment is readily satisfied. Mexicans accept risks in migrating to the U.S. in order to find work and when faced with limited employment opportunities are willing to accept even the most temporary of employment as in harvest operations. Because of the nature of agricultural production, harvest operations are inherently short-term. Because alternative employment opportunities are not widely available in rural areas, workers must be migratory unless income supplements are provided, and indications are that undocumented Mexican workers employed in harvest operations are migratory. One study found that: "Fewer than 4 percent of the (undocumented Mexican) immigrants had children in the U.S. schools and only one half of one percent had received welfare benefits" (Bustamante, 1977: p. 151). Portes has commented on the migratory nature of these workers, "As available studies indicate, illegal Mexican workers respond to long-term unemployment by simply returning home" (1978: p. 475).

Furthermore, the illegal status of these Mexican workers makes their staying in one place and seeking income supplements undesirable, for in the long run they run the risk of being apprehended and deported. They either migrate back to Mexico or to other areas in the U.S. in search of employment. Thus, the costs of reproducing the work force are not borne by those who employ Mexican workers on a seasonal basis.

The recruitment of workers at the onset of the harvest is relatively simple because of the sheer magnitude of the migration of Mexican workers to the U.S. and the limited employment opportunities open to those workers once in the U.S. An abundance of workers is likely to eagerly be awaiting employment at the start of the harvest. Furthermore, many of these migrants are involved in agriculture prior to migration and, as was pointed out above, the majority initially secure employment in agriculture in the U.S. (Jenkins, 1977: pp. 179–180). These characteristics of the Mexican migrants together with the maintenance of an oversupply of workers substantially reduces uncertainties surrrounding the recruitment of the necessary supply of workers at harvest time.

An over-supply of workers, even in the face of a high rate of employee turnover, satisfies the condition that workers be available for employment for the duration of the harvest. Replacements for unskilled workers leaving employment prior to completion of the harvest are easily found among the ranks of the unemployed. In addition, it is reasonable to assume that workers will remain on the job until the completion of the harvest when faced with the discipline of the reserve of army of labor, that is, the inability to secure alternative employment. This discipline of the reserve army of labor is reinforced by the precarious status of the undocumented Mexican workers. Samora described the predicament of these workers: "The individual alien has the strange experience of leaving his family, friends, community, and country for an extended period of time. He lives outside the law, on the fringes of society, in constant fear of being apprehended. Invariably he leads a life of hardship, and he is at the mercy of those who would exploit him" (1971: p. 4).

Thus, by employing undocumented Mexican workers the grower reduces the risks of crop loss resulting from an unsufficient supply of workers. In addition, the chance of harvest delays resulting from workers resistance are effectively reduced. Jenkins contends, "the recruitment of illegal workers has played a decisive role in undercutting the strikes of the United Farm Workers" (1978: p. 530).

Given the fact that growers are under pressure from the cost-price squeeze it seems unlikely that they will voluntarily increase wages and further undermine their margin of profit. Although farm wages have risen more rapidly than selected farm inputs between 1964 and 1974, it appears that the employment of undocumented workers on the part of growers has put a brake on increasing wage rates. Immigrant workers have historically been an instrument used by capitalists to hold wages down and defend the rate of profit (Portes, 1978: p. 473).

First of all, the employment of undocumented workers has served as a weapon for growers in combating unionization efforts which, if successful, would provide farm workers with the power to demand higher wages and other employment benefits. In a strike by the United Farm Workers against lettuce growers in California which began on January 19, 1979, undocumented workers played a major role as strike breakers (*Madison Press Connection*, April, 1979).

Second, undocumented workers, because of their illegal status, are vulnerable to growers and must accept the most unreasonable terms of employment. A number of studies have found that not only are undocumented workers confined to low paying unskilled jobs but "relative to unskilled domestic workers performing the same jobs at the same time illegals [receive] lower wages" (Jenkins, 1978: p. 529). Because of their illegal status, these Mexican workers are forced to accept such conditions of employment. Portes states:

> The status of violator of legal codes prevents open challenge to work conditions and creates serious barriers in efforts to involve the immigrant in organizations of the domestic working class. This juridical weakness is "appropriated" by employers in the form of a higher rate of profit. The rate of exploitation of these workers is thus in direct relationship to their status as a legally defenseless group (1978: p. 474).

Thus, manipulation of the size of the reserve army of labor through the regulation of the flow of undocumented workers from Mexico on the part of the U.S. government has played an important role in satisfying the elements of control over the harvest work force demanded by growers.

CONCLUSION

Considerable controversy has centered on the issue of undocumented Mexican workers in the U.S. Faced with high rates of unemployment, domestic workers, especially those with low skill levels, view undocumented Mexican migrants with hostility. These Mexicans are seen as stealing limited employment opportunities. Organized labor has sided with domestic workers on this issue. Samora states: "In the U.S., organized labor views the aliens as both a threat and obstacle: a threat in the sense that they will work for whatever wage is offered and will even be strikebreakers, and an obstacle in that the aliens hinder unionization and collective bargaining efforts" (1971: p. 5).

Furthermore, there is concern that undocumented workers are taxing social services in the U.S. However, Jorge Bustamante (1977: p. 151) reported that one study found that 77 percent of undocumented Mexican immigrants paid Social Security, and 73 percent have paid federal income tax. Furthermore, less than 4 percent of the immigrants had children in the U.S. schools and only one-half of 1 percent received welfare benefits. Thus, this study suggests that undocumented Mexican workers have been made scapegoats for the "fiscal crisis of the state," and do not in fact tax social services in the U.S. to any significant extent.

Controversies situated around the issue of undocumented workers in the U.S. have placed the onus for such problems as high unemployment and rising taxes on those workers. These workers are branded "illegal" for crossing the U.S.-Mexican border in search of employment. Proposals for dealing with the issue of undocumented Mexican migration to the U.S. have centered on the treatment of these workers once in the U.S. and available for employment. Recent efforts to forge new immigration legislation have included proposals for the reinstitution of a system of "administered migration" similar to the bracero program. Agricultural interests are likely to favor the latter alternative, because any legislation completely restricting the employment of foreign workers would be disastrous to agribusiness.

In any case, the focus has been on Mexican workers in the U.S. "illegally" and not on their role in the U.S. economy. The issue of undocumented workers in the U.S. is seen in a considerably different light when considered in terms of the foregoing discussion. These workers are not simply intruders in the U.S. On the contrary, their migration had been encouraged and facilitated by the U.S. government in response to the labor requirements of U.S. industry, particularly agriculture. Mexican workers are especially important in Southwestern agriculture. Although undocumented Mexican workers are increasingly found in a variety of jobs outside of agriculture, the labor needs of the agricultural sector have predominated in the formation of U.S. government policy. The bracero program was designed specifically to provide a harvest work force for agriculture. Immigration policies since 1964 and the termination of the bracero program have provided growers with the necessary supply of harvest workers and the discipline to make them work. Therefore, the wrath of many groups opposing the migration of undocumented workers to the U.S. has been misdirected. These workers are merely seeking work and have been encouraged to do so by the U.S. government, whether directly or indirectly.

NOTES

1. Another version of this paper appeared in the *Insurgent Sociologist,* Vol. X, No. 2, Fall, 1980, pp. 25–44.

2. This was the case at the outbreak of World War II when growers were faced with a short supply of labor.

3. Selected farm inputs include: gasoline, petroleum, fuel oil for farm business, machine hire, custom and contract work, seeds, bulbs, plants, trees, fertilizer and fertilizing materials.

4. The term undocumented worker will be used throughout this discussion rather than such commonly used terms as "wetback" and "illegal alien." It is the opinion of this writer than no individual should be branded a criminal for attempting to resist poverty and earn a living.

5. California is used as an example in this study because it is the leading agricultural state in the U.S. and is the largest single employer of farm labor. This is not to suggest that California alone sways state policy or is the sole beneficiary of those policies.

6. There was one reception center serving California at El Centro.

7. It should be noted that workers were screened for medical and security purposes at each stage of the migration process, allowing only the workers most desirable for employment by growers to reach the U.S. for work.

8. Reproduction of the work force refers to the education and raising of prospective workers.

9. "Oscar Lewis, writing of the bracero movement, "also indicates the central region [of Mexico] as the chief source of this kind of immigration where 'traditional village agricultural practices prevail and government efforts at irrigation, mechanization, and the distribution of the land to the landless have been at a minimum" (Padfield and Martin, 1965: p. 185).

10. This realization was made by virtually every group concerned with the plight of farm workers in the U.S., including the National Agricultural Workers Union, the National Farm Labor Union, the Agricultural Workers Organizing Committee, Cesar Chavez's Community Service Organization, the United Packinghouse Workers of America, and an array of other sympathetic groups. (For more detail see Jenkins, 1975: especially pp. 129, 274.)

11. The NFLU was unable throughout the 1950s to obtain sustained and substantial financial support from its most logical ally, organized labor. As Jenkins points out, the NFLU's efforts to obtain financial support were characterized by "prevailing problems of labor politics (1975: p. 136)." What support the NFLU did realize "was limited to begin with and deteriorated instead of grew" (p. 137).

12. The decision on the part of the AFL-CIO to make a substantial commitment to the organization of farm workers may come as a shock in view of the dismal history on the part of organized labor in the area. Jenkins contends that the AFL-CIO's decision was influenced by several pressures, including pressure from several liberal political groups concerned with the plight of farm workers, the declining proportion of the work force under union membership in the 1950s, internal political struggles centered on leadership of the union, and pressures from other unions such as the International Longshoreman's and Warehouseman's Union to organize farm workers (1975: pp. 187–188).

13. This effort was organized around efforts on the part of the National Advisory Committee on Farm Labor to organize lobbying in the interests of farm workers. The NACFL, founded in 1958, served to rally support from left labor circles and elements of the early civil rights movement as well as groups such as the Migrant Ministry and Catholic Rural Life conference (Jenkins, 1975: p. 251–252).

14. Yet even domestic workers may have been in abundant supply in 1965 as the following account suggests: "the California State Director of agriculture announced that growers have been deluged with domestic workers, many from out of state and had to turn large numbers away" (Turner, 1965: p. 26).

15. Apparent labor shortages in the 1965 strawberry and asparagus harvests did occur. However, it appears that crop losses were in part due to a lack of cooperation on the part of growers in utilizing available workers (Calfornia Department of Employment, 1966) and unfavorable weather conditions which turned away many workers (Wirtz, 1966: p. 23).

16. In addition to undocumented workers resident alien Mexican workers (i.e. "green carders") are employed in California agriculture. Their employment in U.S. agriculture is yet another example of the role of the state in satisfying the elements of control over the harvest work force. Because of time and space limitations the characteristics of these workers will not be discussed here.

REFERENCES

Anderson, Henry. 1963. Fields of Bondage: The Mexican Contract Labor System in Industrialized Agriculture. Unpublished Manuscript.

Bach, Robert L. 1978. "Mexican Immigration and the American State." International Migration Review. Winter.

Benedict, Murray R. 1953. Farm Policies of the United States, 1790–1950. New York: Twentieth Century Fund.

Brandt, Jon A., B.C. French, and E.V. Jesse. 1978. Economic Performance of the Processing Tomato Industry. California. University Division of Agricultural Sciences. Bulletin 1888.

Burawoy, Michael. 1977. "The Functions of Reproduction of Migrant Labor: Comparative Material From Southern Africa and the United States." American Journal of Sociology. Vol. 31. No. 5.

Bustamante, Jorge A. 1977. "Undocumented Immigration From Mexico: Research Report." International Migration Review. Summer.

California Citrograph. 1962. "Stricter Rules for Use of Mexican Nationals." No. 48. December.

California Tomato Grower. 1962. "Current Labor Situation." January.

Cargill, B.F. and G. E. Rosmiller, eds. 1969. Fruit and Vegetable Harvest Mechanization, Technological Implications. East Lansing, Michigan: Rural Manpower Center.

Davis, Velmar W. 1970. Farm Labor Developments. Washington, D.C.: U.S. Department of Labor

Edwards, Richard. 1979. Contested Terrain, Transformation of the Work Place in the Twentieth Century. New York: Basic Books, Inc.

Fisher, Lloyd. 1953. The Harvest Labor Market in California. Cambridge: Harvard University Press.

Friedland, William H. and Amy Barton. 1975. Destalking the Wily Tomato: A Case Study in Social Consequences in California Agricultural Research. Davis: California. University. Department of Applied Behavioral Sciences. Research Monograph No. 15.

Friedland, William H., Amy Barton, and Robert J. Thomas. 1981. Manufacturing Green Gold. New York: Cambridge University Press.

Frisbie, Parker. 1975. "Illegal Immigration From Mexico to the U.S." International Migration Review. Spring.

Galarza, Ernesto. 1964. Merchants of Labor: The Mexican Bracero Story. Charlotte, N.C.: McMally and Loftin.

_____. 1978. Farm Workers and Agribusiness in California, 1947–1960. Notre Dame: University of Notre Dame Press.

Gershman, Carl. 1975. "The Foreign Policy of American Labor," Washington Papers. Beverly Hills: Sage Publications.

Hawley, Ellis W. 1966. "The Politics of the Mexican Labor Issue." Agricultural History. Vol. XL. No. 3. July.

Hayes, Ed. 1961. "Excerpts From Talk Given at Board of Directors Seminar, Monterey." California Tomato Grower. January.

Hayes, Sue and John Mamer. 1977. Pressures on Agriculture. California University. Division of Agricultural Sciences. April.

Jenkins, J. Craig. 1975. Farm Workers and the Powers: Insurgency and Political Conflict (1946–1972). Stony Brook: State University of New York. Ph.D. Dissertation.

_____. 1977. "Push/Pull in Mexican Migration to the U.S." International Migration Review.

_____. 1978. "The Demand for Immigrant Workers: Labor Scarcity or Social Control? International Migration Review. Winter.

Jenkins, J. Craig and Charles Perrow. 1977. "Insurgency of the Powerless: Farm Workers' Movements (1946–1972)." American Sociological Review. Vol. 42. April.

Johnson, Stanley S. and Mike Zahara. 1977. Mechanical Harvesting of Iceberg Lettuce. Washington, D.C.: U.S. Department of Agriculture. Economic Research Service. Agricultural Report No. 357.

London, Joan and Henry Anderson. 1970. So Shall Reap. New York: Thomas Y. Crowell and Company.

Madison Press Connection. 1978. "Chavez Claims U.S. Helping Break Strike." April.

Marx, Karl. 1967. Capital, Volume 2. New York: International Publishers.

––––––. Capital, Volume 3. New York: International Publishers.

McWilliams, Carey. 1971. Factories in the Fields. Santa Barbara: Peregrine Publishers.

Morin, Alexander. 1952. The Organizability of Farm Labor in the United States. Cambridge: Harvard University Press.

O'Connor, James. 1973. The Fiscal Crisis of the State. New York: St. Martin's Press.

Padfield, Harlan and William C. Martin. 1965. Farmers, Workers, and Machines. Tucson: University of Arizona Press.

Perluss, Irving H. 1960. "Trade Disputes in Agriculture." California Tomato Grower. August.

Pfeffer, Max J. 1980. "The Labor Process and Corporate Agriculture; Mexican Workers in California," The Insurgent Sociologist, Vol. X, No. 2, Fall, 1980, pp. 25–44.

Pickett, Jack T. 1960. "Blue Print for Unionization." California Farmer. September 17.

Portes, Aljendro. 1974. "Return of the Wetback." Society. March/April.

––––––. 1978. "Toward a Structural Analysis of Illegal (Undocumented) Immigration." International Migration Review. Winter.

Samora, Julian. 1971. Los Mojados: The Wetback Story. Notre Dame: University of Notre Dame Press.

Scruggs, Otey M. 1960. "Evolution of the Mexican Farm Labor Agreement of 1942." Agricultural History. July.

Senate Fact Finding Committee on Labor and Welfare. 1961. California Farm Labor Problems, Part I. Senate of the State of California.

––––––. 1963. California Farm Labor Problems, Part II. Senate of the State of California.

Turner, Don. 1965. "No Dice for Braceros." Ramparts. September.

Thor, Eric and John Mamer. 1965. "California Cannery Tomatoes—1965 Labor Situation." California. University. Mimeograph.

U.S. Bureau of Census. 1940–1974. U.S. Census of Agriculture. Volume I. California.

U.S. Department of Labor. 1969. Farm Labor Fact Book. New York: Greenwood Press.

Wirtz, Willard. 1966. Farm Labor Developments. March.

9
Agriculture and the State:
An Analytical Approach

**A. Eugene Havens
and Howard Newby**

The purpose of this chapter is to develop an heuristic model for the comparative study of state intervention in agriculture in advanced capitalist societies. As recently as a decade ago it is doubtful that any paper emanating from rural sociology in North America would have been written with this objective in mind. The emergence of a more holistic (and critical) rural sociology over the intervening period has created a new research agenda in which the present analysis is not considered exceptional. This signifies the extent to which rural sociology is slowly emerging from the endemic difficulties of the 1970's (see Newby, 1980) by emphasizing somewhat different issues from those which occupied its practitioners during previous decades. As this book suggests, the principal research foci of rural sociology are slowly changing to an analysis of the structure of agriculture, state agricultural policy, agricultural labor, regional inequality and agricultural ecology (Newby and Buttel, 1980, p. 15). While this book has dealt with the issue of state and agriculture in the United States and has identified three levels of analysis that must be considered in order to conduct such research, it has not really dealt with the state *per se*. It provides a backdrop for the specification of what steps must be taken to deal more empirically with the level of mode of production where the capitalist state is defined. This book notwithstanding, there are numerous gaps in our knowledge of crucial causes *and* consequences. This chapter outlines an approach to analysing the form of the state and the nature and types of state intervention and how they vary within the general confines of capitalism.

AGRICULTURAL POLICY
AND POLITICAL ECONOMY

Until quite recently one of the common themes of North American and European rural sociology concerned the fact that the economic activity of the countryside was largely ignored. Sociologists typically devoted a great deal of effort to charting patterns of rural sociability, kinship, customs, traditions and community change, but paid little attention to the *raison d'etre* of most rural communities, namely work. For example, the system of agricultural production has conventionally been taken to be an exogenous factor, which occasionally impinged upon the values, culture and folkways of the rural population, but which was not examined too closely. Consequently, rural sociologists have tended to demonstrate a remarkable ignorance of the factors which shape modern agricultural production, not merely the technical aspects of plant and animal husbandry, but even the broader structural features of the contemporary farming system. As Rodefeld has pointed out in a discussion of trends in the United States, rural sociologists now find themselves hindered in the task of developing a sociology of agriculture by not only the lack of previous research in this area, but also by the lack of quite basic descriptive statistics in a form suitable for sociological analysis (Rodefeld, 1978, p. 176).

The reason for this lack of concern with economic activity lies partly in the division of labor between rural sociologists and agricultural economists, a division institutionalized within the land grant colleges which comprise the major institutional setting for rural sociology in the United States. To understand the underlying trends in agricultural production, rural sociologists have traditionally looked to agricultural economists to provide them with an understanding of those economic factors which will affect the organization of rural society. Thus, with only a few exceptions, rural sociologists have shown little interest in, or understanding of, the economic factors which have changed the face of agricultural production and rural society in all advanced capitalist societies since the Second World War, nor have they bothered to inquire into the admittedly intricate agricultural price support policies now adopted by virtually all governments and which have induced far-reaching changes in the structure of agriculture. Indeed, one of the most apparent gaps in the sociological literature is the absence of systematic studies of the social consequences of state intervention in agricultural production, both in terms of the *direction* of such intervention (for example, the extent to which it encourages or discourages increases in the scale and concentration of production) and the mechanisms employed (not only various forms of price supports and market intervention, but policies relating to landownership, capital taxation, inheritance, etc.). Such studies would not only go a considerable way towards developing a holistic sociology of agriculture, but would also provide a means of monitoring current policies and re-formulating future forms of intervention.

While rural sociologists have been culpable in paying little attention to such matters, agricultural economists have also been slow to provide the kind of macro-economic, institutional analysis—or broadly-based political economy—which would be most compatible with the requirements of sociologists. The tendency within agricultural economics has generally been to reduce the discussion of such issues to narrowly technocratic predictive models based upon multiple regression equations. Somewhere in the middle of this process the issues which interest sociologists get operationalized out, leaving behind a sanitized, one-dimensional view of the problem. Predictive models then emerge which, to sociologists at least, appear to be based upon unreal assumptions. Important dimensions of the problem are often put aside, since to consider them would involve "political" (i.e. evaluative) considerations—something which seems to be regarded almost as unprofessional. Nevertheless there remains a tradition of policy analysis among agricultural economists which is very relevant to the interests of sociologists. "Policy," in this case, is often a euphemism for "politics," and it thus allows questions of social and political values to be introduced in an idiomatic form. It is in this context that agricultural economists have been forced to confront macro-theories of social and historical change as part of the background from which particular farm policies have evolved.

We shall interpret the phrase "agricultural policy" to mean that set of measures taken by the governments of nation-states to influence, directly or indirectly, agricultural factor and product markets. As Josling (1974) has pointed out, it is at this point that theoretical and meta-theoretical disputes among agricultural econmists tend to come to the fore. In other words (and it is by no means coincidental) that the kinds of disputes which have been endemic to sociology have become part of the discourse within a subdiscipline which consists of "substantive" economists *par excellence*. Thus current policy analysis, developed primarily in the United States, but taken as representative of the position in any industrial or semi-industrial society, ranges

> from a predominantly institutional view of society in which policy is formed by the interaction of different groups within a political and legal system, at one extreme, and a non-institutional, apolitical view at the other, in which the role of government is to correct any structural defects which might mar an otherwise 'perfect' market system" (*ibid.*, p. 235).

The orthodoxy (as presented in most textbooks, for example) is undoubtedly the latter. However, this basically involves a neo-classical appraisal of agriculture as an atomistic industry in which, due to the multiplicity of enterprises, near-perfect competition prevails. It then proceeds to emphasize the conditions of the product market where a combination of supply instability, rapid technological change, increases in food production, low-income and elasticity of demand for food cause chronic overproduction and/or violent fluctuations in both production and price (see, for example, Metcalf, 1969; Capstick, 1970; Johnson, 1973). All governments in advanced industrial societies have therefore felt it necessary to intervene to iron out these 'imperfections.' Tinkering with the precise ways in which intervention has taken place has also furthered other desired policy objectives: increasing scale of production; specialization; capitalization; etc. This approach therefore emphasized the *facilitating* role of the state, "an aberration which would be absent in an ideal society" (Josling, 1974, p. 235). This is an approach which therefore begins from an analysis of the conditions necessary for market equilibrium rather than any particular social or political context.

The alternative, "institutional" approach to policy analysis adopts a completely different emphasis. The perfect market model is abandoned except, perhaps, as a myth which allows some understanding of the rationality of individual farmers. The exigencies of the market are regarded as the outcome of a complex system of bargaining between various agencies of the state, farmers' organizations and the oligopolistic market power of those corporatons which control the supply of farm inputs and the marketing, distribution and processing of farm outputs. Policies are therefore formulated via an overtly political bargaining process which takes account of such factors as the urban demand for cheap food, the political mobilization of farmers, the division of earnings between farmers and others in the food-production chain, the reliability of foreign sources of supply and the use of food stocks as strategic reserves and weapons (see Friedmann, 1978, 1981; George, 1978, 1980). Although some agricultural economists have favored such an approach (for example, Hathaway, 1963; McCrone, 1962; and, with reservations, Josling, 1974), the initiative for such studies has lain much more with political scientists (for example, Self and Storing, 1962; Wilson, 1977).

Our concern with the origins and consequences of agricultural policies brings us into the terrain of political scientists. At the present stage of our research, we are concentrating more on the origins of policies and their social consequences. As such, we are not concerned with the specifics of implementation at present nor in the vast 'public administration' literature. After we have addressed our primary concerns we will return to other important issues. Some examples of political science analyses of agricultural policy formation include: Ross Talbot and Don Hadwiger, *The Policy Process in American Agriculture.* (San Francisco: Chandler Publishing Co., 1968); William Peterson, *The Great Farm Problem,* (Chicago: Henry Regnery Co., 1959); Grant McConnell, *The*

Decline of Agrarian Democracy. (New York: Atheneum, 1969); Willard Cochrane, *American Farm Policy, 1948–1973.* (Minneapolis: University of Minnesota Press, 1976).

As in our study of agricultural production and society more generally, we will be concerned with the structural origins of and constraints upon agricultural policies. We will, therefore, rely more heavily upon the 'institutionalist' than the behaviorist or pluralist view of the policy process (Katzenstein 1978; Krasner 1978; Shonfield 1965; Solo 1982). The institutionalists have given great attention not only to identifying the content of policy and the important actors in its drafting, but also to elucidating the institutional and structural dynamics of policy. This literature provides us with insights into the varying forms and capacities of the nation states and may even suggest how agriculture fits into the broader political-economy. However, political scientists of recent years have evinced a greater concern with the 'hot' issues of the day—inflation, unemployment, the energy crisis, etc.—and have not given primary attention to agriculture. As a result, the examination of state policy in agriculture and its social consequences can complement political science literature.

Thus, although a considerable literature exists on agricultural policy in the major advanced capitalist societies, the sociological dimension of policy formulation and implementation is almost entirely overlooked. Moreover, little of this research is comparative, or even cumulative. As Josling has noted: "policy research in Europe and North America looks somewhat slender. A new set of social values, beliefs and objectives have become relevant, but this has scarcely been incorporated into the economic analysis of such policies" (1974, pp. 236–7). Furthermore the analysis of agricultural policy has failed to attract the attention of sociologists whose interests lie in constructing a comparative theory of the state. This seems a strange omission, for we can recognize in the intervention of the state in agriculture one of the most extensive and sociologically significant forms of intervention of the modern state. As Hopkins and Puchala have agreed:

> Securing adequate food is one of the oldest problems confronting political institutions. Historically this intimate connection between food and politics has emerged in diverse forms. From the "minimal government" of nomadic herdsmen and hunting-gathering peoples and the complex despotisms found in societies relying on irrigation to the elaborate regulations for food-growing and marketing in most contemporary states, the processing of food has been a central factor in shaping political patterns and, in most cases, encouraging substantial government intervention (1978, pp. 3–4).

Moreover, as Moore (1966) has reminded us, the class composition of precapitalist agriculture has had a considerable impact upon the form and political character of the capitalist state. It is this historic relationship between the growth of the state and means of organizing the production of food for its citizens which is reflected in the long-standing and extremely comprehensive nature of state intervention in agriculture in all advanced capitalist societies today. The state has taken on the role of one of the principal agencies of change in the agricultural sector (and, by extension, much of rual society) so that the significance of state intervention is difficult to overestimate.

SOCIOLOGICAL THEORIES OF THE STATE

Surprisingly, rural sociologists have not included an analysis of the state as an integral part of their research on changing agrarian structure. Thus, research on changing structure has remained largely descriptive. Part of the explanation for this lack of analysis of the state can be attributed to pluralist conceptions of power and the assumption that state policy is merely an output of the conflict management process. Thus, typically, pluralists define society as an aggregate of dissimilar but equally influential special interest groups with diverse and conflicting interests (Bentley, 1967; Truman, 1951; Dahl, 1961; Rose, 1967; Easton, 1971). The groups that make up society can range from corporations to sporting clubs. Nevertheless, these supposed relatively equal power blocks attempt to influence governmental policy which is seen as the product of the countervailing pressure of all these groups with no single groups or alliance of groups being dominant. The balance between the conflicting demands on the state is represented by state policy. The various interest groups negotiate and bargain to reach a mutual enhancement of effort. In the political process, this tends to maximize the interests and concerns of all participants.

There are two principal problems with the pluralist view of power. First, the assumption that society is composed of a wide diversity of equally powerful groups organized around conflicting interests is not empirically defensible (Mills, 1956). For example, only about half the U.S. population belongs to any voluntary association. It is precisely for this reason that membership in organizations is frequently measured as a dimension of a person's relative status. Moreover, it is clear that the 15 million members of the AFL-CIO do not have as much effect on state policy as do the 1,300 members of the Council on Foreign Relations. Finally, most voluntary associations make decisions without consulting members (Szymanski, 1978).

Second, the assumption that output of the state is an accurate and direct result of the relative strength of the various interest groups implies that any state policy is a real possibility. That is, that the determination of state "output" is a function of the "input" of the various pressure groups. In reality, the state can follow only a limited number of effective policies without causing general socio-economic disruption. Although various interest groups may want a given policy, it may not be feasible vis-à-vis the very structure that the state is charged with preserving.

These underlying assumptions—pluralism, volunteerism, and conflict regulation governed by mutual restraint—have guided research on the structure of agriculture away from the *political* component of political economy. It has been assumed that any category of farmers (family farms, commodity groups, farm workers) have rather equal capacities to protect its interests. However, the state is a major component of the concentration of power which allows for the perpetuation of unequal access to resources: we cannot, therefore, conceptualize the state as merely a "black box" which transforms a given set of inputs into a given set of outputs in a purely technocratic, utility-maximizing or other politically-neutral way.

In recent years there has been a renewed concern with the conceptualization of what constitutes the state and what is the role of the state in directing the process of change and development in advanced industrial societies. The reasons for this are not difficult to discern. The prolonged economic stagnation in the West during the 1970's has led to increasing state intervention in "civil society" at all levels. Thus, on empirical grounds it has become impossible to continue an analysis of advanced industrial society without taking into account the burgeoning role of the state. However, the recent interest in the role of the state has been stimulated by more than mere empirical observations, for behind this there has lain more deeply-rooted theoretical concerns which have ensured a prolonged, and as yet unresolved, debate on the nature of the modern state.

These theoretical concerns may be summarized by relating them to two distinct paradigmatic ends. On the one hand there are those within the liberal tradition whose analytical perspective focuses on pluralism, voluntarism and conflict management; on the other hand Marxist analysis has tended to focus on class struggle, capitalist crisis due to inherent contradictions in capitalist social relations and the goal of socialist transformation. Given the different assumptions that underlie the analysis of the state, it is not surprising that the debate has often been of a highly partisan character (see for example, Parkin, 1978), but it has also been conducted at a highly abstract, and often speculative, theoretical level. The main pre-occupation of recent writing on the state has been

to devise theoretically "adequate" and politically "correct" conceptu-
alizations *a priori*, with only a tenuous, uneven and unsystematic
examination of concrete empirical reality.

The liberal tradition of analysis has lent itself to a rather greater
concern with empirical research, but it has been of a somewhat partial
kind. Because its theoretical origin stems largely from the work of Weber
(1968) and a concern with bureaucratization, this liberal tradition has
the advantage of a coherent theoretical starting-point and a clear political
stance—the threat to liberal democracy posed by the rise of a bureaucratic
state apparatus. Weber's writings on stratification also begin from an
analysis of the state and the struggle of different groups (which may
or may not be economic classes depending upon contingent economic
circumstances) for control of the state and the "monopoly of the use
of physical force" which it embodies. In the Weberian view, the state
is an organization that has somewhat unlimited ends toward which its
actions may be oriented. The selection of ends depends upon the degree
of autonomy of the state and how plural groups in society can organize
to place demands upon it. The prime concern of empirical work in this
tradition has therefore been with the interconnected problems of state
rationality and legitimacy. More specifically research effort (especially
in Europe) has concentrated on historical studies of fascism, the role of
the state in economic crisis-management and the conjoining of these
two themes in the study of "corporatism" (for a summary, see Winkler,
1976). The routinized involvement of the state in determining the life-
chances of its citizens has—with the important exception of studies of
the "welfare state"—been underemphasized.

Most of the recent writings on the state have, however, been produced
from a Marxist perspective. A capitalist crisis has once more (in the
1970's as in the 1930's) failed to produce a noticeable shift towards
socialism in the proletariat of the advanced capitalist societies, and
attention has therefore focused on the state for confounding Marxist
expectations. Marx himself had little to say about the state, so that
Marxist analysis tends to begin from the work of Lenin (1969). Ironically,
Lenin's analysis of the state coincides in certain respects with that of
Weber: they both view the state as a political organization that is ruled
ultimately by the use of force and regard it as an instrument to be
captured and used to achieve specified goals by a politically mobilized
grouping. However, Lenin departs from Weber's analysis by relating the
state explicitly to the suppression of class struggle and the maintenance
of a ruling class. For Lenin the state is conceived more as a structure
that reflects class interests, than as an organization controlled by an
elite. Thus what is important to Lenin is not primarily the individuals
who formulate the policies of the state, but rather the class whose rule

is guaranteed by the structures within which these policies are formulated (see Wright, 1978).

It is at this point that recent Marxist analysis of the state has become fraught with difficulty. Is the state merely the instrument of a ruling class? Or does the state have an autonomous interest in directing economic and political change? In the early 1970's these issues were at the center of so-called "instrumentalist" versus "structuralist" conceptions of the state, fought out in the celebrated debate between Miliband (1965) and Poulantzas (1973). Recently this debate has become somewhat superseded (see, for example, Therborn, 1978; Wright, 1978; Mouffe, 1979). There has been an acknowledgement by the "instrumentalists" that the state cannot entertain an unlimited range of policy options without changing its own structure and with it the overall social organization of society. However, those who began from a "structuralist" perspective have conceded that the state cannot be understood (except tautologically) in terms of the fulfillment of functions dictated solely by the class structure of capitalism or as the ideal expression of those relations. Rather the state must be analyzed in terms of the historically specific ways in which certain "conditions of existence" of capitalist production relations have been secured. The securing of these conditions of existence, it is argued, can never be taken for granted and is never guaranteed by the simple fact of capitalist class relations. The phrase "relative autonomy" is the concept employed to avoid the possible Weberian implications of this argument. (See the theoretical trajectory from Hindess and Hirst, 1975, to Cutler et al., 1977.) The matter is further confused by the re-emergence of the influence of the Frankfurt school's writing on the state, influenced strongly by Weberian notions of rationality and legitimacy, and yet accorded serious attention by recent Marxist analysis (see Offe, 1974; Offe and Ronge, 1975; Habermas, 1975; Connerton, 1976; Therborn, 1978; and Wolfe, 1974).

Although these perspectives suggest fruitful areas for empirical research, one of the more remarkable aspects of the recent upsurge of interest in the state is, in fact, the lack of empirical substantiation. Moreover, as the literature on the state has proliferated, this has not necessarily been accompanied by conceptual clarification. It is our contention that to achieve further conceptual clarity concerning the state and modern society, research must proceed by: 1) carefully documenting a specific set of policy formulations; 2) determining how these policies came about; and 3) assessing the consequences of these policies in terms of their impact on the social structure of the societies under consideration. The following section will specify what aspects of state policy should be analyzed and why the selection of government intervention in agriculture is appropriate for clarifying the broader theoretical debate which has been addressed.

THE ROLE OF THE STATE IN THE CHANGING STRUCTURE OF AGRICULTURE

A tentative and oversimplified heuristic model which illustrates how sociologists might approach the investigation of the role of the state in the changing structure of agriculture in advanced capitalist societies is shown in Figure 1. This is a dynamic model which both begins and ends with transformations in the social structure of agriculture. We use the term "social structure" in order not to pre-empt the complex theoretical debates which are currently engaging rural sociologists over how this social structure is most usefully conceptualized. For example, there has been a recent revival of interest in the issue of how best to devise a set of class categories that can be meaningfully applied to the agricultural population. In part, this has emanated from various Marxist analyses of pre-capitalist social formations in agriculture and how far the peasantry can be regarded as a class (see, for example, Shanin, 1968 for an early statement of this problem and the important discussion by Ennew *et al.*, 1976 which summarizes much of the debate). However, it is also part of a much older debate concerning the "agrarian question" in socialist politics (Banaji, 1976) and the "boundary problem" (Parkin, 1978) in Marxist class theory. In recent rural sociology the debate has moved on from the early statement by Stinchcombe (1961) to Goss *et al.* (1980), but there remains little discussion which directly relates the class structure to the state (but see Mann and Dickinson, 1980; Sinclair, 1980). Nevertheless very few attempts to document changes in the relations of production in agriculture can be encountered in the socio-logical and economic literature. Consequently, there is virtually no agreed upon basis for determining class structure and class relations in agri-culture. Little information exists on how agricultural producers have been simultaneously tranformed into an industrial proletariat, and an agricultural proletariat: owners of land and equipment who have lost control over what to produce and how to produce it, tenants, contract farmers, and a class of surplus appropriators both in and out of agriculture. In brief, class analysis has not been part of the historical record of agricultural social scientists in North America and elsewhere.

Our model recognizes that the causes of structural change in con-temporary agriculture essentially turn around the nature of the market economy *and* the role of the state in attempting to develop a definition of how agricultural production (its organization and output) relates to changing notions of public interest. The concept of "public interest" is

FIGURE 1. The Role of the State in Agricultural Structures

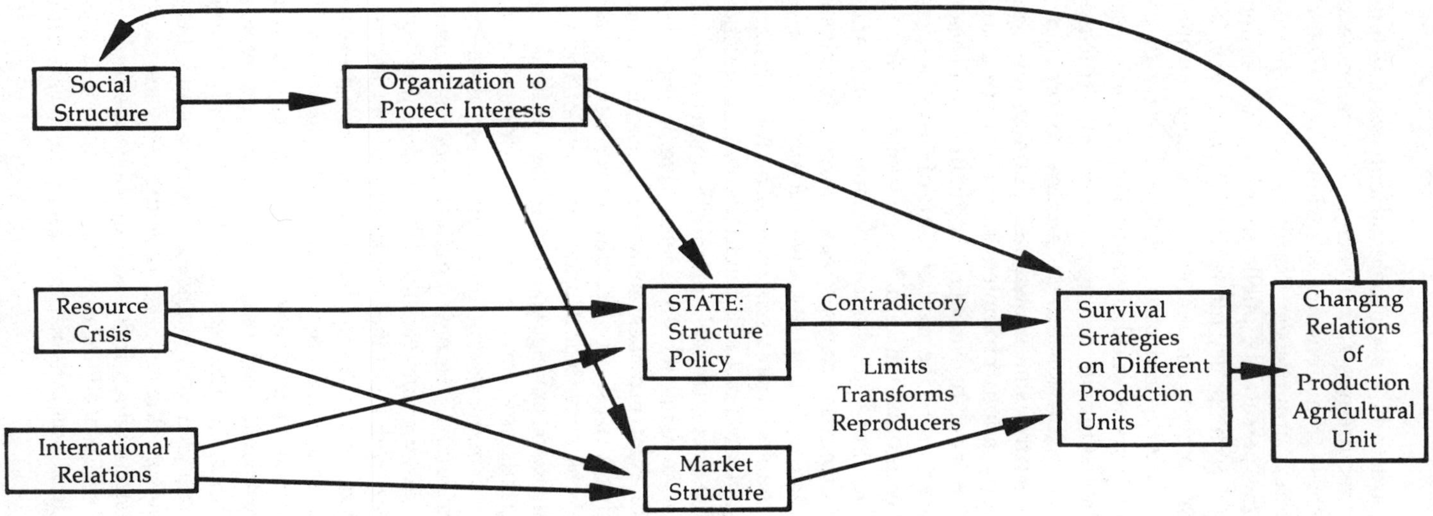

itself to be regarded as a socio-political construct determined not only by the general requirements of a society to guarantee its food supply, but by how these requirements are defined by various, and often conflicting, interest groups (see Paarlberg, 1980). In seeking to define and promote the perceived "public interest," governments are drawn into negotiations with "policy influentials" (Hathaway, 1963). These take place within a context defined by: 1) general economic conditions (inflation, growth, etc.) and attempts by the state to control them; 2) international relations with other nation states, particularly with respect to trade; 3) the nature of the agrarian social structure as expressed through the ability of constituent groups to organize and mobilize politically; and 4) the state's own definition of the "public interest." These policy formulations promote a particular structure of agricultural production, both directly through "structure" policies and indirectly through manipulation of the market. Out of these policies, then, emerge the conditions of production of different groups of food producers. The state enhances the survival chances of some groups and disadvantages others. This, in turn, has "down-stream" effects on the structure of rural society, while also providing the renewed stimulus for a further round of changes in the social and economic structure of agriculture.

While a model of this kind would depart in several respects from conventional (i.e. neo-classical, pluralist) approaches, it must be emphasized that it remains wholly speculative: a model which prompts questions rather than provides answers. There is a considerable need for a comparative analysis of state intervention in agriculture. It should take account of the sociological underpinnings of the varying forms of political mobilization among significant agricultural groups (farmers, landowners, agribusiness corporations, farm workers, food retailers, etc.) and their success in hindering or accelerating observed trends in the structure of agriculture. As new political processes unfold, the state is forced to play an ever-increasing role in directing, or attempting to direct, the nature of changes in the relations of production in agriculture. We must analyze how these political processes present rural families with changing conditions for survival and how families attempt to respond by presenting the state with contradictory demands for subsidies, cheap credit, restricted land use, new markets, more water, new technology or, at times, for the state to adopt a nonintervention policy.

The major research foci outlined above should be set within an analytical framework that will capture the relevant national and international dimensions which influence rural change and produce changes in class structures and alliances.

These considerations produce the first set of basic research questions, which are:

1. What changing socio-economic conditions have affected the organization of agricultural production?
2. How have the different sectors of agricultural producers organized to protect their interests vis-à-vis these changing conditions?
3. What types of alliances have occurred between sectors of agricultural producers and other classes in rural society in their attempts to determine how agricultural production should be organized and what should be produced.
4. How have the conflicts of interest between and within these sectors been reflected in the construction of government agricultural policy.
5. How does the structure and policy of the capitalist state affecting agriculture vary between different advanced capitalist societies?

Answering this set of questions is necessary for analyzing the changing survival strategies of different agricultural production units. These strategies in turn explain the changing relations of production on different agricultural production units. The concern with survival strategies arises from the analytical link between causes of changing structures, the nature of state intervention in organizing agricultural production, and the changing class structure of the rural sector. This concern produces the second set of basic research questions.

1. What are the different labor processes encountered in the food production chain?
2. How have the direct producers involved in these distinct labor processes attempted to reproduce themselves?
3. How has state intervention affected this reproduction process?
4. What are the current structural limitations on these different survival strategies?
5. How do these structural limitations affect the potential for establishing and/or reproducing different forms of agricultural production?

This research program assumes that the state is not only a reflection of power but a source of power that reproduces the various forms of domination that exist in a society. It also assumes that the changing structure of rural society is best studied by mapping the relations of production which determine people's capacities to affect governmental policy which impinges on their everyday life.

CONCLUSIONS

Our intent in this chapter has been to stimulate debate regarding the conceptualization of the state and its relationship to changing agrarian structure. At this point we will state some broad propositions that seem to be warrantable and that may contribute to this debate. First, we suggest a conceptualization of the state that moves away from the narrow instrumentalist view. The state is a set of social relationships that turn around the issue of domination and subordination and is charged with reproducing extant social structure. However, the state is not a mere executive committee of dominant classes but reflects the full range of class relations and class struggle. Thus its interventions to reproduce extant structure is contradictory. These interventions simultaneously reproduce class relations but also undermine their future reproduction. Our second major proposition is that different classes and fractions of classes have varying capacities to affect the form and content of state intervention. Since these capacities are historically unique in a single social formation, it is necessary to compare the advanced capitalist social formations to analyze the full range of interventions that the capitalist state has developed to organize agrarian space.

In both physical and social terms, the spatial structure of agrarian production is grounded in the historically specific capacities of dominant and dominated classes to express their class interests in the social relations of control over land, the labor process and labor power. The relationship between economic, political and ideological dimensions of these class relationships cannot simply be deduced by stating that the capitalist mode of production is dominant. However, where it is dominant, social relations of production, their reproduction and their relationship to the process of capital accumulation, will be the determinant factor in the organization of agrarian space. Political and ideological struggles within an historically specific situation can, therefore, best be understood in terms of their relationship to the contradictions of capital accumulation within the particular historical development of a given society. Despite the many conceptual difficulties to which we alluded earlier in this chapter, the focus on the class structure of agriculture leads to a means of studying the organizational and structural capacities of agrarian classes in terms of how the inherent contradictions of capitalist agriculture shape the process of social and economic development.

Clearly, different forms of agricultural production have varying needs for the organization of agrarian space and for the domination of social relations of control between classes. For example, industrial agriculture (large scale agricultural commodity production for distant markets), requires a well developed transportation infrastructure, stable and relatively invariant or predictable weather, water and soil conditions and a readily available supply of labor. In addition, the question of the "turn-around time" in the rotation of capital becomes important as investment in agriculture is compared with the relative profitability of other areas of investment. At different stages in the process of capital accumulation, the dominance of different sectors of capital within the dominant class, has left its imprint on the spatial and social organization of agricultural production. Yet a changing political economy requires new transformations in the agrarian sector. Thus "the agrarian problem" (transformative class struggles within agriculture) becomes a central conduit for studies aimed at understanding the process of capital accumulation. The dual question of reproduction and transformation of class relations within the ongoing process of capital accumulation provides empirical analysis with a key to understanding the recurrent crisis of agriculture. As class interests and capacities at the level of the social formation is transformed, the terrain of class struggle is manifested in the reshaping of the spatial and social organization of agarian production.

The specific historical forms of determination through which different sectors of agrarian production are integrated with the overall process of capital accumulation are expressed most directly in the social relations of production and appropriation. Extending accumulation means that capital must confront both historically-given social relations that contradict that extension and physical/ecological factors that act as barriers to accumulation. Within agriculture it is essential that one specify the structural determinations that limit agrarian capital's capacity to extend accumulation and which lead to the selection of specific sectors of production as the object of a strategy of accumulation, i.e., of transformative class struggles. This does not imply that all transformative class struggles are initiated by capital. Nor is it the case that all are successful or that capital seeks to transform social relations of production in the direction of increased commoditization. The forms of the transformation are diverse, arise from both dominant and dominated classes, expressing struggles that always have both a defensive and a progressive dimensions for all classes. Of course, in the stage of monopoly capital the satisfaction of the wage/food basket is no longer remote from the international integration of agricultural production. But the provision of agricultural commodities, whether on the world market or in the reproduction of non-capitalist social relations of production within particular nation states, has led to the increasing necessity of the state to intervene and resolve the failure of capital to satisfy collective consumption needs. The heuristic model presented in this paper suggests one way to develop a clearer understanding of the nature of these interventions in agriculture in advanced capitalist societies.

REFERENCES

Banaji, J. 1976. "Summary of Selected Parts of Kautsky's Agrarian Question," Economy and Society, Vol. 5, No. 1, pp. 2–49.

Bentley, Arthur. 1967. The Process of Government. Cambridge, Massachusetts: Bethnap Press.

Buttel, Frederick and Howard Newby (editors). 1980. The Rural Sociology of Advanced Societies. Montclair, New Jersey: Allanheld, Osmun, and Co.

Capstick, M. 1970. The Economics of Agriculture. London: Allen and Unwin.

Coles, Robert. 1977. Children of Crisis. Boston, Massachusetts: Little, Brown, and Co.

Connerton, Paul. 1976. Critical Sociology. London: Penguin.

Cutler, Anthony et al. 1977. Marx's Capital and Capitalism Today, Vol. 1. London: Routledge and Kegan Paul.

Dahl, Robert. 1961. Who Governs? New Haven, Connecticut: Yale University Press.

Easton, David. 1971. The Political System. New York, New York: Alfred A. Knopf, Inc.

Ennew, Judith, Paul Hirst and Keith Tribe. 1976. "Peasantry as an Economic Category," Journal of Peasant Studies, Vol. 4, No. 3, pp. 295–322.

Friedmann, Harriet. 1978. "World Market, State and Family Farm: Social Bases of Household Production in the Era of Wage Labor," Comparative Studies in Society and History, Vol. 20, No. 4, pp. 545–586.

———. 1981. "The Political Economy of Food: Class Politics and International Politics in the World Wheat Economy," American Journal of Sociology. Forthcoming.

George, Susan. 1978. How the Other Half Dies. Hamondsworth: Penguin Books.

———. 1980. Feeding the Few: Corporate Control of Food. Washington, D.C.: Institute for Policy Studies.

Habermas, Jurgen. 1975. Legitimation Crisis. Boston: Beacon Press.

Hathaway, D. E. 1963. Government and Agriculture. London: Macmillan.

Hindress, Barry and Paul Q. Hirst. 1975. Pre-Capitalist Modes of Production. London: Routledge and Kegan Paul.

Hopkins, Raymond F. and Dorcus J. Puchala (eds.). 1978. The Global Political Economy of Food. Madison, WI: University of Wisconsin.

Johnson, D. G. 1973. World Agriculture in Disarray. London: Fontana.

Josling, T. E. 1974. "Agricultural Policies in Developed Countries: A Review," Journal of Agricultural Economics, Vol. 25, No. 2, pp. 229–263.

Katzenstein, Peter. 1978. Between Power and Plenty. Madison: University of Wisconsin Press.

Lenin, V. I. 1969. The State and Revolution. Moscow: Foreign Publishers Press.

Mann, Susan A. and James A. Dickinson. 1980. "State and Agriculture in Two Eras of American Capitalism" in F. Buttel and H. Newby (eds.) (1980) pp. 283–326.

McCrone, G. 1962. The Economics of Subsidiary Agriculture. London: Allen and Unwin.

Metcalf, D. 1969. The Economics of Agriculture. Hamondswcrth: Penguin Books.

Miliband, Ralph. 1965. The State in Capitalist Society. London: Merlin.

Mills, C. Wright. 1956. The Power Elite. New York: Oxford University Press.

Moore, Barrington. 1966. The Social Origins of Dictatorship and Democracy. London: Allen.

Mouffe, Ghantal. 1979. Francisco and Marxist Theory. London: Routledge and Kegan Paul.

Newby, Howard. 1980. "Rural Sociology—A Trend Report" Current Sociology, Vol. 28, No. 1, pp. 1–141.

Newby, Howard and Frederick H. Buttel. 1980. "Towards a Critical Rural Sociology" in Buttel and Newby (eds.) (1980).

Offe, Claus. 1974. "Structural Problems of the Capitalist State: Class Rule and the Political System. On the Selectiveness of Political Institutions." in Von Blyme (ed.) German Political Studies. New York: Sage Publications.

Offe, Claus and Ronge Volker. 1975. "Theses on the Theory of the State." New German Critique, No. 6, Fall.

Paarlberg, D. 1980. Farm and Food Policy: Issues of the 1980's. Lincoln, Nebraska: University Press.

Parkin, Frank. 1978. Marxism and the Class Structure: A Bourgeois Critique. London: Tavistock.

Poulantzas, Nicos. 1973. Political Power and Social Classes. London: New Left Books.

Rodefeld, Richard D. 1978. "Trends in U.S. Farm Organizational Structure and Type" in R. Rodefeld *et al.* (eds.) *Change in Rural America: Causes, Consequences and Alternatives.* St. Louis: C. V. Mosby.

Rose, Arnold. 1967. The Power Structure. New York, NY: Oxford University Press.

Self, P. and H. Storing. 1962. The State and the Farmer. London: Allen and Unwin.

Shanin, T. 1968. The Awkward Class. Oxford: Oxford University Press.

Shonfield, Andrew. 1965. Modern Capitalism. London: Oxford University Press.

Sinclair, Peter R. 1980. "Agricultural Policy and the Decline of Commercial Family Farming: A Comparative Analysis of the U.S., Sweden and the Netherlands" in F. Buttel and H. Newby (eds.) (1980) pp. 327–352.

Solo, Robert. 1982. The Positive State. Cincinnati: Southwestern Publishing Co.

Stinchcombe, A. 1961. "Agricultural Enterprise and Rural Class Relatives." American Journal of Sociology, Vol. 67, No. 2, pp. 169–176.

Szymanski, Albert. 1978. The Capitalist State and the Politics of Class. Cambridge, Massachusetts: Winthrop Publishers.

Therborn, Gordan. 1978. What Does the Ruling Class Do When It Rules? London: New Left Books.

Truman, David. 1951. The Government Process. New York, NY: Alfred A. Knopf, Inc.

Weber, Max. 1968. Economy and Society. New York: Bedminster Press.

Wilson, F. S. 1977. Special Interests and Policy-Making. London: Wiley.

Winkler, J. T. 1976. "Corporatism." European Journal of Sociology, Vol. 17, No. 1.

Wolfe, Alan. 1974. "New Directions in Marxist Theory of Politics." Politics and Society, Vol. 4:2.

Wright, E. O. 1978. Class, Crisis and the State. London: New Left Books.

Index

AAA. *See* Agricultural Adjustment Act;
  Agricultural Adjustment
  Administration
Accumulation of capital. *See* Capital,
  accumulation
AFBF. *See* American Farm Bureau
  Federation
AFL-CIO. *See* American Federation of
  Labor and Congress of Industrial
  Organizations
Africa, 48
Agrarian populism. *See* Populist
  movement, agrarian
Agrarian revolt. *See* Farmers' movements
Agricultural Adjustment Act (AAA)
  (1933), 2, 35, 51, 139, 161–166, 168,
  171, 190
Agricultural Adjustment Administration
  (AAA), 4
  and farmer committee systems, 151–
  152, 157, 160–172
  See also Agricultural Adjustment Act;
  Agricultural Stabilization and
  Conservation Service
Agricultural colleges. *See under* Land
  grant system
Agricultural economics. *See* Agricultural
  economists; Class structure,
  economic model; Commodities,
  prices; Cost-price squeeze; Credit;
  Crop liens; Export/imports;
  Markets; Monopoly; Oklahoma,
  economic structure; Production
  systems; State intervention; Surplus
Agricultural economists, 4, 5(table), 208,
  288–290
"Agricultural Enterprise and Rural Class
  Relations" (Stinchcombe), 214
Agricultural labor. *See* Braceros and the
  bracero program; Farmers; Labor
  and laboring class; Migrant workers

Agricultural Stabilization and
  Conservation Service (ASCS), 151,
  157, 171
Agricultural structure, 288, 297(table)
  current forms, 39–42, 43(table), 44–47
  transformation process, 105–108, 114–
  115, 152–155, 179–204, 245, 296,
  297(table)
  See also Class structure; Farmers'
  movements
Agricultural Workers Organizing
  Committee (AWOC), 271–272, 274–
  275, 283(n10)
Agriculture
  in California, 252–286
  and capitalist development, 26–52,
  53–54(table), 106–108, 129, 211
  and critical sociology, 1–22, 288
  economics. *See* Agricultural economics
  ideology, 32, 37, 236–237, 240–242
  in the Midwest, 27, 104–147, 206–
  245, 246(n1)
  in Oklahoma, 179–204
  policy, 288–291
  in the South, 60–100, 150–175
  See also Agricultural structure; Class
  relations; Class structure; Farms;
  Farmers; Production systems; State
  intervention; State, the
Agriculture, Department of (USDA)
  county agents, 132–133
  and crop reduction programs, 170–
  171, 190
  and displaced farmers, 171
  educational programs, 125
  established, 113
  and farm mechanization, 277
  and the Grange, 116
  New Deal reform agency, 3–4, 7, 8–
  12
  and rural sociologists, 1